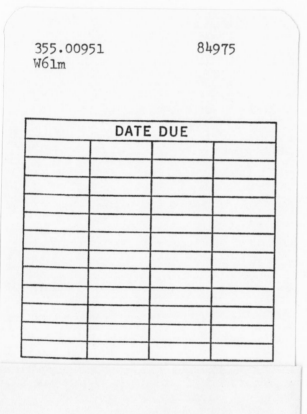

DATE DUE

The Military and
Political Power in
China in the 1970s

edited by
William W. Whitson

The Praeger Special Studies program—utilizing the most modern and efficient book production techniques and a selective worldwide distribution network—makes available to the academic, government, and business communities significant, timely research in U.S. and international economic, social, and political development.

The Military and Political Power in China in the 1970s

PRAEGER SPECIAL STUDIES IN INTERNATIONAL POLITICS AND PUBLIC AFFAIRS

Praeger Publishers New York Washington London

PRAEGER PUBLISHERS
111 Fourth Avenue, New York, N.Y. 10003, U.S.A.
5, Cromwell Place, London S.W.7, England

Published in the United States of America in 1972
by Praeger Publishers, Inc.

Second printing, 1973

Library of Congress Catalog Card Number: 78-189842

Printed in the United States of America

CONTENTS

PART III: THE ORGANIZATION OF
MILITARY POWER IN
CHINA

LIST OF TABLES

LIST OF FIGURES

LIST OF ABBREVIATIONS

CC	Central Committee
CCP	Chinese Communist Party
CPPCC	Chinese People's Political Consultative Conference
CPSU	Communist Party of the Soviet Union
CPV	Chinese People's Volunteer Forces
CRG	Central Cultural Revolutionary Group
DRV	Democratic Republic of Vietnam
GPD	General Political Department
GRSD	General Rear Services Department
ICBM	Intercontinental ballistic missile
IRBM	Intermediate-range ballistic missile
KGB	Committee for State Security (USSR)
KMT	Kuomintang
MAC	Military Affairs Committee
MRBM	Medium-range ballistic missile
PLA	People's Liberation Army
PRC	People's Republic of China
RC	Revolutionary committee
SEATO	Southeast Asia Treaty Organization

Abbreviations Used in the Notes

CB   Current Background

CNA   China News Analysis

FBIS   Foreign Broadcast Information Service

HC   Hung Ch'i (Red Flag)

JAS   Journal of Asian Studies

JMJP   Jen-min Jih-pao (People's Daily)

JPRS   Joint Publications Research Service

LAD   Liberation Army Daily

NCNA   New China News Agency

PR   Peking Review

SCMM   Selections from China Mainland Magazines

SCMP   Survey of China Mainland Press

In the summer of 1970, the editor sought nongovernmental financial support for a conference on the role of the military in China. With some encouragement from several sources of funds, he asked various experts in particular fields to contribute papers. When the declining fortunes of the American economy and the field of China studies dictated the decision to postpone the projected conference, he was gratified to discover that Praeger Publishers wished to publish the collected papers anyway. Needless to say, that decision was timely, given the increasing power of the military in China, President Nixon's spring, 1971, decision to travel to Peking, China's admission to the United Nations, and the late 1971 intramilitary struggle that exploded in Peking.

It is not the purpose of this book to explain the causes for all of those events. Nor does this collection of papers promise predictions from which Chinese political-military factions will not deviate. Instead, contributors were asked to draw on their profound knowledge of the recent past, perceived as a continuity of China's sweeping history, to hazard some general judgements about trends in what the editor has called the basic questions of "military ethic and style" that is, contributors have been asked to examine alternative Chinese answers to the following six questions: (1) the role of the military in society; (2) the execution of that role, and the degree to which professional commanders should have authority over both material and human resources; (3) criteria for the selection of future generations of generals; (4) the actual organization of military power; (5) appropriate strategies; and (6) appropriate tactics.[1]

In order to provide focus for both analysts and readers, the editor specified a five-year time frame for prediction. Thus, readers will seek in vain for carefully constructed explanations for the events of September, 1971, including a cutback in the Chinese air force; the crash of a VIP aircraft in Mongolia; the disappearances of Defense Minister Lin Piao, Chief of General Staff Huang Yung-sheng, Commander of the Air Force Wu Fa-hsien, and Commissar of the Navy Li Tso-p'eng, all members of the Politburo; and the cancellation of the National Day celebrations in Peking. Indeed, most of these chapters were written before these events took place; those that were submitted approximately one month after the deadline for submission were no more successful in clarifying those events than the earlier chapters.

The chapters were not originally intended to be so precise as to present the reader with a ready explanation for the minutiae of personnel purges, promotions, and deaths. To draw on another crisis arena more familiar to most readers, experts in the securities business are rarely successful or very persuasive in explaining precisely why stocks fluctuate daily; their standard phrase is "market psychology." Similarly, medical experts use "virus" as an explanation when they do not know the precise answer to an unexpected deviation from a "normal" illness.

The concern is thus with trends over the past five years and over the next five years. Each part of the book contains several chapters covering the main concern of that section. Part I seeks to identify the continuities from premodern Chinese practice and the most recent aspects of the role of the military in Chinese society, the fundamental issue in contention. Part II examines the issue of command and control, present and future. Part III then discusses major organizational ingredients of military power in China. Some of the material in these chapters has never been presented with quite the authority and expertise that has been assembled here. Finally, Part IV completes the discussion with an assessment of Chinese alternative strategies—their preferred means for projecting their military power within and beyond their borders.

While many authors in this book use the term "the Chinese" for purposes of simplicity and brevity, it should be clear that none believe in the existence of "the Chinese" as a unitary actor. Indeed, the chapters are dedicated to an investigation of organizational and individual differences in attitude and behavioral style. Of particular interest are the organizational forms, both formal and informal, through which Chinese military leaders have learned to seek power and, once attained, to employ for their collective and personal ends. In an earlier work, the editor accented the evolution of a set of informal relationships that must remain of great significance in determining individual and collective choices among conflicting loyalties, personal and institutional.[2]

While this book is not meant to deny the importance of those informal relationships, this volume seeks to examine more carefully those formal career organizations through which older loyalties are being channeled as the Chinese empire responds slowly to the efforts of its leaders to create a sense of nationhood among hundreds of millions of people whose entire lives have rarely taken them more than one hundred miles from their home villages. Yet, the focus of this book on judgments about the future demands that the probability of service-oriented loyalties replacing old field-army and military-region loyalties be seriously considered as a younger generation begins moving into key positions during the late 1970s. It is in anticipation of that shift that Part III has been structured along formal organizational lines, emphasizing the ground forces, local forces, General Political Department (GPD), General Rear Services Department (GRSD), the navy, and the air force as six separate career lines, each increasingly jealous of its own collective values, organizational routines, and organizational equity in distinctive weapons systems, budgets, political-military roles, promotion systems, and perceptions of threat priorities.

THE ROLE OF THE MILITARY IN SOCIETY

All contributors have given some consideration to the question of the People's Liberation Army (PLA) leadership's perception of the military role in society. In brief, should military power be directed against internal or external threats? Because the issue has been argued and misunderstood so long and so frequently by various students of the subject, the editor would draw the reader's attention to the fact that the great majority of the authors emphasize the military equivalent of the "Middle Kingdom syndrome"; namely, internal threats, defined in the broadest possible terms, have been and are likely to remain far more important to the current generation of military leaders than external threats.

The implications of this focus for all questions of military ethic and style may only be hinted at in this introduction. But students of Chinese military politics, organization, and strategy must understand those implications for the allocation of Chinese energies, their probable future allocation of resources to conventional versus advanced weapons, their perceptions of external threats as levers for influencing the course of internal events, and their probable reluctance to squander limited resources on the costly escalator of the nuclear game. Their concern with China's domestic political dialogue must also be understood by the policy planners of China's friends and adversaries. The art of political signaling must begin with the premise that Chinese receptivity of a foreign initiative has been, is, and will remain primarily a function of the utility that such an initiative has for the major factions contending for domestic distribution of power and status.

To put this point in another perspective, arguments among American military leaders about the relative priority of foreign threats have frequently been too clearly related to interservice competition for internal status, reflected in budgets, roles, and missions. One may imagine how much more bitter those debates might have been if service leaders simultaneously had held political posts, the retention of which depended in part on support from national, regional, and local military colleagues.

In Chapter 1, Edward Dreyer points out that Chinese emperors have traditionally attempted to employ military power not to fight an external enemy, but to establish and maintain order in China's sprawling empire while thwarting a strong propensity toward warlordism and local disloyalty to the throne. In Chapter 2, James Jordan emphasizes Mao's traditional interest in the army's internal role as a mobilizing and educating elite.

Ting Wang, in Chapter 6, is perhaps most authoritative in his use of statistics to show how far the proliferation and penetration of military roles had proceeded by the summer of 1971. Nothing some similarities with conditions in 1949, he points up the distinctive qualitative difference in 1971: The concentration of military, Party, and governmental power in one military man's hands at the Provincial Party Committee levels all over China. Underlining the penetration of a military bureaucracy from the lowest administrative to the highest Politburo levels of the Party and the government, Ting suggests that the proliferation of internal military roles reflects a priority concern with the rationalization of resource allocation and decision-making within China, a consolidation and continuation of the internal social and political revolution rather than its expansion abroad. The editor's views on these questions have rarely deviated far from those of Ting and remain essentially the same as the analysis contained in Chapter 6.

The analysis of military role shifts from a general discussion of civil-military perceptions of the internal-external role dichotomy to ingredients and implications of burgeoning interservice rivalry in Part III. In Chapters 7 through 11, the contributors provide consistent evidence in support of institutional affiliation with an internal role for each of the four services (ground forces, local forces, GPD, and those elements of the GRSD concerned with conventional weapons development and deployment). This is not to say that these four institutions agree on roles, missions, weapons systems, and budget allocations. While Joseph Heinlein (Chapter 8) and Harvey Nelsen (Chapter 7) agree that both the regular ground forces and the paramilitary militia focus on their internal roles, responding even more dramatically to the internal crises during the Cultural Revolution than they have to external Soviet threats since 1968, it is clear that professional ground-force commanders have been most reluctant to divert vital resources to the succor of an untrained militia but have wished to retain control over those forces for the purpose of ensuring internal stability if only through maintaining an inventory over small arms. In their wish to minimize diversion of resources to the militia, ground-force commanders have frequently been supported by civil officials who wished to employ peasant resources for production, not defense; at the same time, they have often been opposed by military commissars who wished to retain a capability to mobilize those peasants in the event of a "People's War" of defense against an invader.

In Chapter 9, Glenn Dick points out that the GPD historically has been most dependent on strong sponsorship from key central leaders for its survival. He questions its future viability without more support, a judgment of special significance for future perceptions of military role since the commissar system has been a fundamental Maoist device for thwarting the emergence of a "bourgeois military mentality" and its many professional premises, values, and goals. Indeed, the commissars' obsession with the Maoist notion of the PLA's internal roles probably qualified them in Mao's eyes to lead many aspects of the Cultural Revolution until opposition from ground-force commanders first brought their downfall at the top (the removal of the entire senior staff of the GPD in August, 1967), then the public and private criticism of them by Chou En-lai and Lin Piao, and finally their rehabilitation in 1969, under the direction of a veteran commander rather than a commissar (Li Teh-sheng, a close associate of Hsü Shih-yu and Su Yu, senior long-term members of the Third Field Army elite with its power base in Nanking). One may recall that the same procedure has prevailed on Taiwan for some years. No professional commissar has commanded the General Political Warfare Department since at least 1950. Given the fact that the GPD derived nothing but organizational grief from China's major foreign war in Korea, it may be assumed that the GPD will continue to foster the primacy of internal threats and internal roles for the sake of its own organizational survival.

In their discussion of Chinese military economy, Richard Gillespie and John Sims (Chapter 10) and James Blaker (Chapter 11) bring new insights to the investigation of the military role. Underscoring the historical debt of GRSD leaders to commissar perceptions of role, essentially devoted to the mobilization of villagers to support regular units in civil war, Gillespie and Sims emphasize GRSD concern for the viability of local county and provincial economies. They describe a system of local storage facilities, local procurement from the civilian economy, and, therefore, local loyalties. Blaker reinforces those themes with an analysis of major conventional weapons production centers in an attempt to discern the rationale for their distribution. He concludes that arsenals have been so distributed as to reflect a primary concern at the center for internal threats, rather than an external enemy. The distribution of heavy-equipment production centers seems to have denied any single military-region commander the degree of self-sufficiency that would encourage warlordism. While all military-region commanders have had some capability to produce small arms, suitable for securing national-defense installations and political elites against local rebellion and criminals, they were mutually dependent for the production and final assembly of tanks, artillery, mortars, aircraft, and missiles. In effect, central authority retained final control over the production of those weapons, barring a conspiracy among the three most wealthy military-region commanders in Peking, Shenyang, and Nanking.

In this analytical context, with which the editor is in complete agreement, it is fascinating to speculate about the internal political implications of the rumored reassignment of Hsü Shih-yu to Peking in June or July, 1971, possibly to replace both Lin Piao and Huang Yung-sheng. Such a shift would have placed in Hsü's hands the re-sources of both the Peking and Nanking military regions at the same time the Shenyang Military Region was under the control of one of Hsü's oldest friends, Ch'en Hsi-lien. This would lead to the question of whether Huang Yung-sheng's appointment to (or seizure of) the post of Chief of General Staff in early 1968 was merely the first step in a game of musical chairs in which regional military leaders, uncon-sciously or consciously emulating the behavior of warlord claimants to central authority in the 1920s, once again had embarked on an in-ternal struggle to "unify" the Chinese empire.

In contrast with the ground-forces, GPD, and GRSD perceptions of role, Franz Mogdis (Chapter 13) underscores the essential concerns of the airforce for external threats. It seems probable that the functional imperative of the Air Force and the Navy toward external defense qualified both of them to be the most responsive tools of central authority during the Cultural Revolution when ground-force, local-force, GRSD, and GPD local leaders frequently supported the local Party instead of the Central Cultural Revolutionary Group. A careful reading of Mogdis' study provides evidence of incipient inter-service revalry for budgets and power, the rewards for making the right organizational choices among the basic issues of military ethic and style, and the basic dichotomies of central versus regional authority, conventional versus advanced weapons modernization, and so on.

In Part IV, contributors focus on some of the operational implica-tions of the basic questions of Chinese military ethic and style. Paul Elmquist specifically discusses the role and capability of the PLA in handling internal threats. Of particular significance is his point that the PLA has adequate resources for suppressing rebellion in isolation while being almost totally incapable of stopping revolution. Indeed, in conversations about his work, Elmquist has pointed out that precisely because the PLA is a "People's Army," the ground forces in particular would most likely move to the forefront of revolution just as regular forces in south China provided the leadership for the 1911 revolution.

Richard Wich (Chapter 16) reviews the entire post-World War II period to demonstrate the proposition that central authority must adopt a flexible and ambiguous foreign policy when internal affairs are most demanding. Manifestations of such foreign policy include Peking's encouragement of self-reliance (i.e., no material help from Peking) to China's clients abroad, sponsorship of an image of Chinese conservatism and weakness, and shifts in the identity of adversaries, the invitation to President Nixon being the latest example of flexible Chinese foreign-policy initiatives in a period of serious internal political controversy.

In one sense, John Coon notes the reverse corollary of Wich's thesis; namely, that the PLA has demonstrated its power to project effective military power for a limited distance beyond China's borders when central and regional military authority can agree on threat priorities. Indeed, the reader is recommended to Coon's chapter for its splendid representation of a school of thought that argues that the PLA's normal focus on internal affairs reflects its responsiveness to Maoist philosophy and its faith in People's War. Whether or not the reader agrees with this interpretation of values and goals underlying PLA behavior, Coon's chapter provides a balance to any assertion that Chinese military leaders have neither an interest nor a capability in the Asian regional or global security dialogue. He outlines a host of techniques that have emerged from China's fundamental military poverty. Furthermore, he argues that the PLA was essentially responsive to the central authority throughout the Cultural Revolution and is likely to remain the primary institution through which that central authority may continue to impose its will on China's population.

In the final chapter, Harry Harding indicates that the question of military role is not simply one of civil-military relations or Party-military conflict, the favorite dichotomy of the uninitiated and the lazy in "explaining" China's internal squabbles. In particular, Harding underscores the importance of the time factor as a distinguishing element in contending elite perspectives. His emphasis on the advocates of the "quick-fix" military posture, principally focused on immediate external threats and largely unconcerned with budget constraints and domestic military threats or economic opportunity costs paid for accenting advanced weapons, reminds one of air-force and navy perspectives. Although Harding does not identify these as airforce views, the editor would be so inclined. Conversely, Chou Enlai and his state-planners would be assigned to the category of "long-term modernizers," men determined to give priority to a balance between internal political stability and economic growth, thus emphasizing the bond between internal socioeconomic change and conventional weapons modernization in opposition to external initiative with costly and provocative advanced weapons development and deployment.

If these priorities and the personalities associated with them are approximately accurate, one is forced to reexamine the relationship between Chou En-lai and his closest General Staff and regional ground-force military colleagues, on the one hand, and Mao, Lin, and Lin's air-force and navy general staff and regional colleagues, on the other. It must be concluded that interservice as well as interregional and central-regional conflict over military role priorities has been a main issue in Peking's most recent political drama and is likely to remain so in the contention among future military and civil factions.

THE POWER AND FUTURE OF PROFESSIONAL COMMANDERS

As has already been suggested above, the resolution of the issue of inter-service rivalry for power and budgets over any given time period must be a function of the relative power relationship between representatives of civil authority and commanders of military power. The power of a commander, the extent to which that power is actually constrained and directed by nonmilitary values, and the actual criteria employed for promoting younger military men to positions of power are questions that must reflect shifting compromises on the more fundamental issue of military role in society. Many contributors have commented on these questions beyond the themes already discussed above.

The fear of "the man on horseback"—a dominant military figure emerging from obscurity to assume the "dragon throne" is evinced in Dreyer's description in Chapter 1 of the historic Chinese tradition of civil control even at the expense of military effectiveness. Emperors have employed such devices as the shifting of generals from the provinces to the capital soon after the beginning of a new dynasty, awarding them with honorific titles, moving them about frequently, while leaving local civil officials relatively stable and distinguishing the civil from the military class by the criterion of literacy. Furthermore, at the center of authority, a military professional rarely was commander-in-chief of the field forces.

The perceptive student of twentieth-century China will note that Yuan Shih-k'ai, Chiang Kai-shek, and Mao Tse-tung have all shared the same problem, but have seemed incapable of accepting or applying the lessons of history. Indeed, Dreyer notes, with an ominous portent for the People's Republic, that warlordism traditionally has emerged in China whenever two factors finally become insistent and pervasive elements of the political system: the evolution of a large standing army, whether for reasons of internal or external strife, and the removal of the layer of civil officials that normally provided an administrative bridge between central authority and local military power.

In Chapter 2, Jordan describes Maoist theories for ensuring Party civil dominance of "the gun." Mao's fear of a large standing army has reflected his close reading of Chinese history and has been expressed in a host of policies and actions ranging from his removal of the great ground-force modernizer, P'eng Teh-huai, to his emphasis on the local, ill-trained militia, to his probable sponsorship of advanced weapons for a highly modern air force, essentially useless on the internal political stage but immensely important for image-building on the Asian regional and global strategic stages. Mao has thus preferred a widely dispersed and decentralized regular ground force—the GPD commissars—dedicated principally to nonmilitary internal functions under the constant vigilance of a separate chain of command, a kind of institutional conscience, whose mission it has been to thwart the emergence of a "bourgeois professional" military class. It is in that context that one may recall the 1964 removal of ranks throughout the PLA, a futile effort to arrest the trend of the military toward a separate professional status.

In Chapter 3, Parris Chang shows precisely how that device and Maoist theories generally either backfired or failed to stop a secular trend toward military erosion of civil authority at the local, regional, and finally national levels as the Maoist "dynasty" moved toward its close. As if to confirm the theses postulated in Chapter 1, Chang points out Mao's early effort at Kut'ien in 1929 to define the subordination of the military to the Party, a relationship that has so rarely characterized the actual status of the one institution to the other that it must be considered a fiction, an ideal that Mao himself has honored in the breach whenever it suited him to employ the army to challenge the Party for his own personal purposes. Thus, he challenged the

Party Central Committee, Li Li-san, and Chou En-lai in 1929-31 until Chou, with the help of Yeh Chien-ying, removed Mao from military, then political power, while regularizing the ground forces and redefining more clearly the division of labor between professional soldiers and professional Party cadres, the military commissar receiving an unenviable middle status reflecting Chou's essential disdain for those "Party soldiers." Once again, Mao attempted the same exploitation of the military during the Cultural Revolution. It seems an irony that Chou En-lai and Yeh Chien-ying, forty years after the first Maoist challenge to Central Committee authority over the regional military, should once again combine their talents to attempt to return China's internal civil-military power balance to an ideal from which it has so clearly deviated dangerously.

Tracing the history of specialization of function that characterized civil-military relations immediately after 1950, Chang argues persuasively that that process contributed to a growing sense of mutual suspicion throughout the Chinese bureaucracy as professional civil cadres sought to isolate their professional military colleagues. When Mao, dissatisfied with the increasing regidity of the Party bureaucracy, encouraged first the military commissars (in the 1964 "learn from the PLA" campaign) and then certain allegedly loyal units (after January, 1967, in the Cultural Revolution) to "support the left" in purging the Party, Mao committed the dynastic sin of removing the crucial middle layer of civil officials in favor of an ideologically unsophisticated military bureaucracy. Chang's statistics and those of other contributors show how far the military takeover proceeded by the summer of 1971, when professional military authority dominated all twenty-nine newly elected Provincial Party Committees.

Thomas Robinson (Chapter 4), John Simmonds (Chapter 5), and John Coon (Chapter 18) generally disagree with other authors, especially Ting, regarding the loyalty of the military bureaucracy to Mao personally and to central authority generally. Robinson has concluded that Lin Piao, who tends to symbolize an entire generation of military leaders now passing from the scene, was deeply loyal personally to Mao's ideals and methods. The reader may draw his own conclusion about both Lin's and the PLA's loyalties (about which this editor's skepticism is a matter of record since 1968) from other chapters. Simmonds argues that the PLA has been a "reserve bureaucracy" that Mao threw into gear when the civil bureaucracy was no longer satisfactory. Indeed, he traces what he believes was a deliberate strategy of personnel assignments after 1960 to prepare the PLA for its substitute role in 1967, a role presumably to be performed in complete loyalty to Mao and the central authority. Yet,

Simmonds also accents the notion that there is not one but at least twenty-nine Chinas—a perception that deserves special attention in the search for the subordinate institutional actors on the Chinese stage.

Of particular interest in Simmond's analysis is the notion that Mao's fear of a military takeover prompted a sequence of military reassignments beginning in 1963 aimed initially at greater security for civil officials in Peking. Whether or not Maoist fear of opposition civil-military factions dictated those personnel changes, Mao (according to Nelsen's analysis) tried to disperse the standing army in 1960. Also, it is known that Lin's writings during those years reflected an obsession with coup politics. During the Cultural Revolution, the world was shaken by accusations by Maoist "loyalists" against Marshal Ho Lung and his associates for allegedly conspiring to overthrow Mao. Simmonds then proceeds to show how personnel shifts gradually spread from military to civil spheres, where "promotions" of regionally entrenched civil leaders in 1964-65 were a prelude to the more devastating purge of the Party in 1966-67. As suggested earlier, that process ultimately contributed to the most dangerous internal political situation confronting China since its military unification under Communist generals in 1949: the dominance of administrative organs by professional military men and a resurgence of regionalism, only partially constrained and directed by Chou En-lai and his oldest military friend and colleague, Yeh Chien-ying.

In Chapter 6, Ting Wang provides a host of fresh statistics to demonstrate both professional military dominance and over regional cleavage from the small central group of "royalists." Turning to the question of the generation of leaders likely to rule China over the next five years, Ting warns that they contrast with Mao's generation in their limited formal educational background. Indeed, the reader will recall that the majority of these members of the "second military generation" entered the PLA from central China between May, 1928, and November, 1931, and were drawn almost entirely from poor peasant families. One village group (Huangan-Mach'eng) in Hupei had provided more than a hundred generals from this generation to the PLA by 1965. Simmonds estimates that their rise to power in the Politburo meant a 70 percent drop in the Western-educated members of the top leadership. This decline in the number of cosmopolitan leaders at central and regional levels could be reversed dramatically over the next five years if the third military generation succeeds in assuming power without revolution. That generation (which entered the PLA between November, 1931, and December, 1936) and the fourth (which entered between December, 1936, and December, 1940) includes many well-educated high school and college graduates who flocked to the Communist standard to fight an external invader, the Japanese, rather than an internal threat, the Nationalists. But as long as the second generation retains its power, and the odds are that they will attempt to do so to the bitter end, their self-confidence in their ability to mobilize China's peasantry and to orchestrate China's resources through a traditional internal balance of power process is likely to sustain the twentieth-century record of tragic civil and military strife. The ultimate shift of power to the younger generation must be further complicated by the fact that the fourth generation is almost entirely drawn from North China, the consequence of the Communist movement's long residence in the north after the Long March.

Thus, Ting Wang's prediction of an emerging military class bears further research and careful analysis by foreign military and civil planners, for the odds suggests a repetition of the events of the early 1920s when a young generation of extremely well-educated military graduates of Paoting Military Academy (about 9,000 men) spread across China to guide a poorly educated generation of warlords in the higher values and goals of Bismarckian national unification. Indeed, their faith in the political obligation as well as the political importance of the gun would have stood the test of any loyal Maoist committed to the same theme. Yet, China's millions, its geographic immensity, and a long tradition of localism soon frustrated the vision of most of these men, of whom only a few found their way to Whampoa to support Sun Yat-sen. Must China endure once again a repetition of the same cycle? Generational and educational ingredients seem to favor such a repetition. What is to be learned from Communist Chinese military style? Specifically, has Communist organization of military power promised rational decision-making, national unity, and China's emergence on the world stage as a great power in fact as well as in image?

ORGANIZATION OF CHINESE MILITARY POWER

Before one attempts to answer the preceding questions, he must take into account Chinese tradition. Dreyer cites the repetitive decay of military power in China that resulted from its dispersion (out of fear of misuse by local and regional aspirants to the throne), from its application to civil endeavors, and finally from its ultimate inability to defend even local civil authority against younger, technologically more competent militants or domestic military-political factions that managed to retain relatively greater military effectiveness, frequently because of their priority defense role on China's borders. He thus identifies several conflicting orientations for Chinese organization of military power: dispersion versus concentration, civil pursuits versus combat training and readiness, and traditional technology versus advanced professional technology. He particularly underscores the ironic possibility that forces deployed and trained for maximum combat readiness against external enemies may ultimately become most threatening internally when regular and local forces charged with internal roles refuse or fail to resolve internal conflicts.

Jordan likewise notes the conflicting Maoist theses of military modernization for external defense versus PLA self-sufficiency for internal defense and minimized burdens on local economies. Simmonds describes what he calls the two PLAs: one, a regularized conventional force subordinate to professionals in a professional chain of command, marginally influenced by Party committees at each level of the PLA; and the second, a sprawling system of paramilitary forces, allegedly subordinate historically to civil Party committees at provincial and administrative district levels.

Nelsen provides even more details about the latter. The poorly equipped local forces and militia constant spawn or threaten to spawn disaffection, corruption, and banditry because their officers find themselves in a career "dead end." Their members receive little or no pay, depending upon local custom; their military effectiveness reflects the marginal value of a limited supply of small arms; and the future, like that for the GPD, is dependent upon central agreement on limited budget allocations. Potentially effective as a conscription pool for the regular forces, a role that became of less significance after the beginning of annual conscription in 1955, these paramilitary forces are estimated to have received more than 3 million small arms by mid-1971, providing approximately 30 to 40 percent of the strength of the PLA ground forces. Despite their alleged subordination to regular forces, especially since the Cultural Revolution, Nelsen offers no assurance that these forces could not or would not provide the manpower and weapons for a revived system of personal and local armies should central military authority fail to resolve the two fundamental issues already discussed—namely, the role of the military in society and the proper authority of civil versus military leaders.

Heinlein provides charts to describe the formal structure of the ground forces. While portraying an illusion of central control, these charts fail to clarify the reasons for the relative inter-military-Region immobility of ground-force units over the past fifteen years.

Other authors' comments would suggest that that immobility has reflected the highly localized nature of ground-force loyalties and,
therefore, the dominant role played by informal rather than formal
chains of command and influence.

Thus, there is at least a question about the status of the ground
forces as a truly national army, organization charts notwithstanding.
That question acquires increasing relevance to other issues of military ethic and style when one recalls the nearly total destruction of
the civil Party system during the Cultural Revolution. If, as the
editor believes, the army is not a highly politicized force devoutly
loyal and responsive to Mao, but is instead a congeries of conflicting
loyalties and uneven skills, responsive principally to eleven military-
region commanders, then central authority in China over the next five
years must rest on the fortuitous whim of regional commanders' collective compromises plus the loyalties of the military Party system,
the GRSD, and the air- and naval-force elites.

The fate of the military Party system during the Cultural Revolution has already been outlined. Dick, while failing to identify the
essential disagreement over many issues between commanders and
commissars, describes the trend toward increasing central—Military
Affairs Committee (MAC)—control over the commissar system after
MAC purged Hsiao Hua and senior officers of the GPD in August, 1967.
Reflecting the displeasure of many senior professional commanders,
a viewpoint that Dick describes in detail, the purge was the climax to
a post-Korean War secular trend of professional opposition to commissar interference in military training. Temporarily interrupted
between 1960 and 1967, when Lin Piao breathed new life into the GPD
the trend has now resumed and points toward a diminished role for
GPD professionals, a role that would support rather than guide the
values and goals of professional combat commanders.

Yet, Dick recalls the earlier discussion of military role in his
stimulating analysis of alternative futures for the GPD. He notes
how an increased internal threat to established authority might demand
increased GPD propaganda activity in support of local and central
military leaders. On the other hand, a foreign war would once again
probably remove the GPD from the domestic stage to a generally
hostile environment where its role would be even more seriously constrained by the priorities of combat.

The odds are great that internal disagreements may continue
to take priority over external threats and wars, unless the USSR
should fail to perceive the essentially favorable direction of internal

Chinese trends (favorable from the Soviet viewpoint). A Soviet invasion of north China might barely save China from another round of internecine civil and even military conflict, just as the Japanese invasion of 1937 temporarily buried domestic Chinese political differences and sponsored the second united front. Barring such a foreign attack, the GPD may very well provide the military intellectuals from whom the mutually contending second military generation of commanders must derive the rationale for their future ruling style, whether it be termed Maoist, Liuist, Chouist, or Chang Kuo-t'aoist.

An essential ingredient of that style and the tools of its administration must be the GRSD. As in the broader PLA, the GRSD has two major informal components: namely, the localized corps of conventional logistics units and services in support of the regular maneuver forces (ground forces and the air forces, each evidently claiming its own GRSD) and the more advanced research, development, and manufacturing facilities in support of the Second Artillery, the missile force still under slow development.

In Chapter 10, Gillespie and Sims describe both systems, noting that the conventional system first began to modernize only in 1954, after the Korean War demonstrated its inadequacies for sustaining the operations of a modern army. At that time, a full-time corps of specialists in logistics began to build a career field. Nevertheless, these specialists and their principal clients, the combat commanders, had learned their trade in a context of military poverty in which even the length of a battle, not to mention the decision to fight at all, was often determined by the limited availability of ammunition and the throughput capacity of coolie-labor battalions since neither vehicles on roads nor boats on waterways were usually adequate for support of a major campaign. Thus, the commissar founders of the GRSD usually relied heavily on their ability to mobilize the peasant masses in support of field operations. As late as 1948, Communist arsenals could provide only about 50 percent of required weapons and ammunition, the remainder coming from equipment captured in battle.

By 1971, according to Blaker's excellent analysis of conventional-weapons production in China, about 75 percent of all conventional weapons were being produced in four military regions, the traditional industrial regions of Shenyang, Peking, Nanking, and Wuhan. Construction and control of railroads, roads, and waterways were largely under PLA-GRSD supervision. Machine-building ministries were clearly dominated by professional military leaders. But the loyalty of the nationwide system of GRSD officers, men, and production workers was still hostage to local equities and a tradition of local service.

In Chapter 12, Charles Horner describes some of the implications of Chinese choices of alternative nuclear-weapons production techniques. Also under GRSD influence, scientists and workers associated with the advanced-weapons program were members of "the other GRSD," a system of military and civilian technocrats largely isolated from the conventional weapons producers and users. Although Horner suggests that those scientists suffered minimal interference during the Cultural Revolution, delays in projected schedules of nuclear-weapons production have been explained on a variety of grounds, of which problems of strategic doctrine seem to receive least attention. This will be discussed further below.

It seems clear that the viability and utility of China's military organizations in the future must remain a function of the GRSD's improved professionalism. Chapters 10, 11, and 12 do not encourage a belief that agreements about the meaning of professionalism or even the balance between military and civilian production have yet been reached. In late 1971, reports of controversy between those advocating an emphasis on heavy industry versus those advocating more resources for advanced-electronics production symbolized the continuing dispute over weapons-systems utilities. In effect, the two broad components of the GRSD were being split apart on the issues of military style, of which alternative strategies were the second significant dimension.

ALTERNATIVE CHINESE STRATEGIES

Because Chinese deployment of military power has been influenced by its own history, especially relevant is Dreyer's emphasis on several continuities, although he explicitly denies the debt of the Communists to imperial tradition in strategy. Chinese xenophobia, their preference for the defense, their penchant for fixed defenses around key cities as focal administrative centers, and their disinterest in war for the purpose of territorial expansion have all found expression in public statements or military deployments in China throughout the history of the Communist Party.

Of special importance to an understanding of Chinese strategy is Dreyer's point that military power has traditionally been employed as a means for creating both psychological images and corresponding political postures. But the emphasis on adversary and allied states of mind has origins in the earliest records of Chinese dynastic history. Indeed, one of the most significant targets for military maneuvers abroad has been the state of mind of <u>domestic</u> clients and adversaries. Thus, Simmonds argues that one of the motives of the Sino-Indian border conflict of 1962 was to demonstrate the reliability and effectiveness of PLA power to the Chinese people.

In this sphere, Scott Boorman's Chapter 17 on deception provides the reader with important analytical concepts for comparing American and Chinese perceptions of power and its uses. He notes that strategem has little to do with political sophistication. Instead, its levels of effort must be defined in terms of target and purposes. Its least imaginative forms, best known to western practitioners, seek to react to enemy capabilities. The possibility of outwitting the enemy motivates the deception plan. In contrast, a higher level of deception, fully comprehended by the Chinese because it is so deeply rooted in their strategic angle of vision, aims at altering an adversary's intentions and priorities by manipulating his perceptions of reality. Thus, Sun Tzu urges the successful strategist to deliberately anger his opponent in order to encourage the irrationality of arrogance.

In the realm of strategic communication and political signaling, Boorman's analysis is a reminder that most if not all Chinese maneuvers aim at altering adversary perception both of their own capabilities and their own intentions. The problem for the future Sino-American dialogue on strategic subjects will therefore be one of finding a common glossary of terms. The American sophistication in weapons hardware as an expression of power is not shared by the Chinese, whose notion of power is more deeply influenced and defined by the apparent state of mind of all players on the strategic stage. Boorman cites C.W.C. Oman's remark that war has always been an art in the East and merely a matter of hard fighting in the West.

Military technology and relative military wealth have also played a role in defining Sino-American contrasts in strategic style. Deception warfare is an inevitable consequence of military poverty, which demands that the planner define power in terms of what he can make his adversary believe it to be. Americans have almost lost the capacity to so define or measure power, principally because their energies must be poured into the management of enormous quantities of things, a complex of logistical facilities and bases ultimately in support of a few fighting units but so difficult to conceal as to divert most American military planners from any confidence in their own ability to deceive or to manipulate an enemy high command.

In Chapter 16, Wich reviews the Chinese handling of their post-1950 security-policy problem of identifying the main versus the secondary enemy, a starting point for Chinese strategic analysis. In contrast with Boorman, Wich underlines what he believes is a Chinese propensity to increase high-risk initiatives, including the employment of military power, to destablize an unsatisfactory status quo, especially along China's borders. Thus, Chinese strategy is unlikely to commit direct Chinese military power unless a direct threat has been posed to China's borders. And even then, other forms of power may be expected before the leadership will hazard the internal controversy that might attend the requisite shifts of reserve forces to offensive positions.

Yet, Wich's point deserves special attention from foreign military planners who have been lulled into believing that a Maoist defensive-offensive People's War is likely to be the norm. Indeed, if one examines Chinese military behavior through the post-liberation years, it seems clear that the preemptive attack is a favorite form of military defensive strategy among China's professionals. Their behavior in Korea in 1950, in India in 1962, in Vietnam in 1966, and along the Ussuri River in 1969 suggests that this generation of military leaders will not "stand idly by" to wait for an external attack should it appear to be imminent.

Whether or not Chinese military power in its various forms may be used under circumstances less than critical is the subject of Coon's analysis in Chapter 18. While he may disagree with various contributors regarding the loyalty of the PLA to central authority, he underlines the flexibility of the high command in employing various low-cost, low-risk military instruments to harass, pressure, and otherwise seek to alter foreign perceptions of reality. On the one hand, agreeing that prospects are dim for future People's Republic of China (PRC) commitment of major forces abroad in the Korean War mode, Coon still warns the reader against complacency about the small units of military power being carefully deployed abroad. From individual advisers, to military aid, to actual invasion by two- to six-division forces, Chinese military power, Coon as well as Boorman would argue, has a multiplier effect precisely because Chinese military leaders deliberately seek to create such an effect through public and private statements and political maneuver. Coon reminds us that 25 percent of China's military aid has gone to countries south of the Sahara. He sees them laying the foundations for a race war or an ICBM range. But above all, he credits their planners with the skill to match a foreign-security situation with appropriate but never excessive amounts of military power.

Assuming that such credits are deserved, the prospects for internal conflict in China are such that continued emphasis on defense seems to be a clear preference for military leaders over the next five years. That preference is likely to inhibit the rapid deployment of large numbers of offensive nuclear weapons, even if technological and productive capacities provide the requisite mobilization base. Chinese external projections of power in the 1970s are likely to rely heavily and routinely on diplomatic and psychological maneuvering in search of Asian regional and global security from interference in China's internal political and economic development by the superpowers and Japan.

In order for Chinese planners to sustain the credibility of muted or strident threats to employ nuclear weapons after the mid-1970s, they must achieve at least two crucial psychological goals in the minds of adversaries and neutrals, especially those in the Asian region. First, they must convince observers that they are capable of the assured destruction of at least one or two major American and Russian cities, even after a disarming strike by either adversary. To achieve that capability, the Chinese need only deploy two or three SLBMs in the late 1970s. Those submarines (even if armed only with IRBMS) would provide Chinese military leaders with a flexibility that they have lacked on the global stage to date. Second, they would need to create the impression that "damage limitation" is not a Chinese problem since (they have argued) China's vast and dispersed population could not be seriously damaged by even a thousand nuclear weapons. This psychological goal has clearly dominated Chinese thinking for the past two decades and, in some measure, has confused Western military thinkers.

The objective of both these psychological images would be an alteration of American and Russian utility perceptions to the effect that the marginal political and economic cost to them of a small Chinese nuclear attack would far outweigh the marginal costs to the Chinese of a massive Russian or American attack. Even if the Chinese could not clearly demonstrate their success in so altering the utility perceptions of adversaries, they would have gone far toward persuading third-world leaders that such a condition of comparative marginal utilities did apparently prevail. So persuaded, third-world leaders must behave as if American deterrence were no longer credible. The limited number of nuclear weapons then available to Chinese strategic planners would thus significantly enhance their still-preferred techniques of diplomacy, psychological pressure, and low-intensity conflict, backed by a modernizing conventional force that could no longer be discounted by third-world leaders in light of an apparent American impotence. It would not matter that the Chinese had not come close to closing the qualitative and quantitative gap between their own and adversary nuclear capabilities. Quantitative superiority would be classified in the paper-tiger category, marginal utilities receiving major emphasis in the assertion that the imperialist, revisionist nuclear monopoly had been broken.

But such psychological objectives are not likely to be of focal importance for Chinese central and regional strategists during the next five years. Instead, resource allocations are likely to shift from advanced weapons to conventional-weapons development for the purpose of satisfying the pressing demands of ground-force leaders and state planners for lower-cost symbols of internal authority. In short, the chapters of this book suggest that the dominant authority of military leaders in China is not likely to diminish significantly in the near future. Instead, it may still generate intramural conflict before the current generation of leaders has ended their collective search for a new internal balance of power, both intramilitary and civil-military.

NOTES

1. For a detailed discussion of the sources and implications of Chinese military ethic and style, see the introduction of William W. Whitson, The Chinese Communist High Command, 1928-1970: A History of Military Politics (New York: Praeger Publishers, 1972).

2. Ibid., Ch. 9 and 11.

THE ROLE OF THE MILITARY IN CHINESE SOCIETY: AN HISTORICAL OVERVIEW

1

MILITARY CONTINUITIES:
THE PLA
AND IMPERIAL CHINA

Edward L. Dreyer

When the Western powers came to China in the nineteenth century, they met with a civilization that had been developing independently
for four thousand years. The long tradition of autonomous development
ensured that China's response to the West would involve the synthesis
of Chinese and Western institutions, rather than the total displacement
of the Chinese past. Even the Communist government in power since
1949, though rhetorically committed to the complete revolutionization
of Chinese society, has in practice been forced to come to terms with
attitudes inherited from Chinese imperial history. Chinese Communist
military institutions and practices similarly contain important continuities with the imperial past. An attempt to establish this shall
be made by considering the role of military institutions in imperial
China and the possible congruences between military operations in
imperial and modern times and will conclude by analyzing the implications of the Chinese past for the future development of the People's
Liberation Army (PLA).

THE MILITARY IN IMPERIAL CHINA

Chinese dynasties came into being as a result of successful
military action, and their founders were always successful generals.
This would lead one to expect that armies with the professional
tradition and prestige of, for example, the Roman legions would be
among the principal institutions of each dynasty. In fact, the establishment of each of the four major dynasties of Chinese origin (Han,
T'ang, Sung, and Ming) was soon followed by a shift in the basis of
support on which the dynasty rested. In the Han and Ming dynasties,
the founding emperors brutally purged and executed their original
military supporters. During the T'ang reign of Empress Wu (684-705),

3

the social status of the common soldier was systematically degraded. The founder of the Sung dynasty from the beginning of his reign followed the policy of concentrating his armies in the vicinity of the capital and raising his generals in honorific rank while at the same time depriving them of the command of their troops; the weakening of the army that followed was considered preferable to a revival of the warlordism that had characterized the immediately preceding Five-Dynasties period.

In all four cases, the beneficiary of the fall in political influence and social status of the military was the Confucian literati class from which the civil service was recruited. This class tended to monopolize both literacy and prestige in imperial China, and the elite civil service was chosen from it on the basis of extremely difficult competitive examinations that stressed knowledge of the Confucian classics. As the authoritative interpreter of the ideology to which Chinese society adhered and as the sole master of the administrative techniques needed to make the government function, the dominant position of the civil service in the Chinese state structure was unshakeable. In periods of stable dynastic authority, then, the organization and command of the armed forces and the role and status of their officers and men all had to be adapted to the practices and prejudices of civil-service rule.

Organization and Command

The Chinese in imperial times always maintained a distinction between the administration of the armed forces and the command of armies in the field. The former required the regular writing and filing of papers and reports and therefore could only be performed by literate officials; as such, it became one of the recognized functions of the civil service. Military command, on the other hand, was exercised by military officers who were often illiterate.

The department primarily responsible for military administration from the end of the sixth century to the beginning of the twentieth century was the Board of War (ping-pu), the fourth of the six boards that constituted the core of the central government. Subordinate to the Board of War were four bureaus, of which the first dealt with the appointments, promotions, and transfers of military officers; the second, with maps of the various regions of the empire and charts of city walls and other fortifications; the third, with a variety of subjects including supervision of arsenals and shipyards, provision of horses and weapons, and the control of the postal system; and the fourth, with the control of granaries and stores depots for military use. In the normal Chinese view, which corresponded with reality during long periods in the Han, T'ang, and Ming dynasties, the armed forces were to be self-supporting in peacetime, but in the event that additional funds were needed from nonmilitary revenues, these would be appropriated by the Board of Revenue. The only other important civil-service department concerned with military administration was the Court of the Imperial Stud, charged with operating the government pastures from which the army's horses were drawn.

In contrast to the long continuity of the offices dealing with military administration, the arrangements for the actual command of the armed forces were far less regular. The emperor, of course, held the supreme military, as well as civil, authority and in exceptional cases might take the field in person, but the Chinese office of emperor, unlike the Western office of king, did not develop out of a tribal war-chieftainship. Chinese military literature posits as the normal situation that the ruler will remain in the capital while a professional general leads the army in the field. Furthermore, in peacetime most of the army would be demobilized and regular commanders would be needed only for guards in the capital and small frontier garrisons. These factors militated against the existence of regular institutions of supreme military command, yet such institutions did exist at various times. During the Han, the Grand Commandant was one of the three highest ministers of state and exercised supreme command of the armies; however, this position was filled only when the armies were mobilized. More important was the shu-mi-yüan (usually translated Bureau of Military Affairs) set up in the latter part of the T'ang. During the succeeding Five-Dynasties period, the head of the shu-mi-yüan was the principal military deputy of the emperor, and, when military command was centralized in the Sung, after 960, it was exercised by that office. With one change of name, the shu-mi-yüan survived until the beginning of the Ming dynasty. In 1380, however, as part of the general process of destroying any authority that might rival his own, Chu Yüan-chang (emperor in 1368-98) divided the office into five headquarters of equal rank, all located in the capital, but each responsible for the command of all the troops in its arbitrarily designated geographical region. The five headquarters were discontinued by the Ch'ing dynasty, which remained without a regular organ of supreme military command during its entire period of power.

Despite the long history of the shu-mi-yüan and its successors, these offices only occasionally exercised the function of military

command prescribed by their official descriptions. Typically, the
problem of military command only arose when a specific campaign
was being planned, at which time a high military officer, usually one
already holding a high rank in the shu-mi-yüan or equivalent, would
receive a special commission entrusting him with military command
for the duration. His immediate subordinates would be chosen from
the military officers holding lower ranks in the shu-mi-yüan or equivalent, so that these agencies thereby came to be transformed into
dummy organizations whose sole function was to confer permanent
rank on military officers who were potentially eligible for selection
to the command of armies. The Ch'ing did not consider this function
important enough to warrant the continuation of the central agencies
of military command.

Under the Ch'ing, regular agencies of military command did
exist at the provincial level, in the form of the Tartar-Generals, who
controlled the provincial detachments of the Manchu Banner forces
that had originally conquered China, and the provincial commanders-
in-chief of the Green Standard armies, recruited after 1644 from
among the Chinese population. Also, the Manchu system included
civil governors and governors-general whose offices, inherited from
the Ming, also had certain military functions. The Manchu system
was the end result of a long struggle to find a stable system of provincial government and local military command, a struggle whose opposing
themes were warlordism and the usurpation of the military-command
function by civil officials. Warlordism was the major problem from
the mid-eighth-century rebellion of An Lu-shan down to the founding
of the Sung, and it had its origin in the promotion practices adopted
before the An Lu-shan rebellion, which guaranteed that the regional
military commands would go to professional soldiers who had spent
their lives in their specific regions and had built up networks of
personal loyalties there that were not balanced by any sense of obligation toward the dynasty. The armies of this period were militarily
effective, but their independence had to be curtailed for the sake of
dynastic stability. This was done after 960, and warlordism from
then until 1911 was not a problem, except during a few short and
unusual interludes; rather, the later dynasties were confronted in
mid-course by a catastrophic decay in the effectiveness of their military forces. The function of raising and commanding new military
forces extemporized to meet recurrent specific crises then devolved
upon civil officials. The names of Li Hung-chang, Tseng Kuo-fan,
Tso Tsung-t'ang, and others, who organized and led the militia armies
that suppressed the mid-nineteenth-century T'ai-p'ing rebellion, are
paralled by a number of great Ming civil officials after 1449. The
civil officials did not develop into warlords, but, since they treated

their military duties merely as interludes in basically civil careers, they also generally failed to develop permanent military institutions.

The higher organization of the Chinese armed forces in imperial times was thus characterized by civil administration, military command improvised for the occasion, and regionalism. The improvised nature of military-command institutions derives partly from the persistent Chinese belief that war is an abnormal state of affairs, which led dynastic founders to disband their armies after conquering the empire, in the hope that the condition of peace that they had achieved could be maintained permanently by good administration and moral example, rather than by force. Even rulers of non-Chinese origin, who were seldom subject to this delusion, however, dealt with military command in the same way, and this implies that the twin phenomena of regionalism and the failure of central-command institutions to develop stems from the sheer impossibility, in a pretelegraphic technology, of controlling operations from a capital that might be hundreds of miles distant (even allowing for the well-known efficiency of the Chinese military postal relay system). Chinese military literature and tradition explicitly recognized the desirability of leaving control of the actual operations to the general on the spot, and Chinese military practice usually corresponded.

The Military-Officer Class

The civil administration of the military establishment and the civil usurpation of regional military command as described above were not the accidental consequences of any one dynasty's administrative arrangements. Rather, they follow from the whole pattern of selection and training of the military officer, his view of his role and, in particular, the relationship of the military-officer class to the more important civil-official class. This relationship is the key to understanding the position of the military in imperial China, and it precedes and goes much deeper than the contempt for the soldier that has sometimes, but by no means always, been part of the Chinese value structure.

The official arrangements of the various Chinese dynasties always distinguished formally between civil posts (wen-kuan) and military posts (wu-kuan) and the two kinds of officials were always distinguished by differences in official dress and other visible marks. There were also two distinct series of titular offices, one civil and the other military. Also, civil and military were distinguished by certain styles of life: the civil official, for example, would let his fingernails grow to indicate his freedom from manual labor and usually rode a sedan chair, while the military officer had to trim his fingernails in order to handle weapons and usually rode a horse.

It is important to define civil and military in terms of these formal marks of differentiation because the boundary between the two professions was drawn differently than in the West. The civil official's duties included everything that presupposed literacy. This meant that in a normal situation—one in which peace had prevailed for a long time—most of the administrative work of maintaining the military establishment (in particular the appointment and promotion of officers) would have been taken over by civil officials, and the most important policy decisions taken in peacetime (the strength of the standing forces, etc.) would be made by the all-civilian Board of War. Military commands at lower levels also had civil officials attached to them to handle their administrative work.

The professional role of the military officer was thus confined to the actual leadership of his troops on the battlefield, and the qualities of the ideal military commander were all related to this role. In biographies of military commanders, the following points are usually stressed: imposing physical presence and courage, horsemanship and personal acquaintance with weapons, good judgment in an actual battlefield situation, and, most important of all, firm maintenance of military discipline. A theme that recurs constantly in the histories is that a general who can capture a city without sacking it is more valuable than a perhaps more capable general who does not maintain discipline. Thus, with military officers as with their civil counterparts, moral qualities were stressed and technical abilities deemphasized. In the modern West, military professionalism generally means that the technical expertise of the military officer is recognized and valued and that the officers have the degree of institutional autonomy necessary for the exercise of this expertise, so that, once the decision to go to war or to allocate certain resources to defense has been made, the execution of the decision will be left to the military professionals. In imperial China, the development of such a concept of professionalism was not possible, partly because of the low esteem in which all kinds of technical expertise were held and partly because of the extent to which military functions remained within the province of civil officials. As long as military administration was merely part of the general administration and military policy merely an aspect of the general political goals of the state, it remained impossible for the military-officer class to gain the control over the military establishment necessary for the development of professionalism.

This generalization is subject to challenge on at least three grounds: imperial China was frequently at war for periods of several generations at a time, and thus required large standing armies whose generals were major ministers of state despite the limits of the military officer's role; career patterns were not always fixed, so that it was possible at times to have a career that included both field commands and high positions within the Board of War; and the existence of a large body of technical military literature refutes the contention that military professionalism did not develop. The answers to these three objections are to some degree interrelated and revolve around the education and selection processes characteristic of civil officials. The second can be dealt with first. During the Sui and the first half of the T'ang, political powers rested in the hands of an aristocracy whose status rested on birth rather than on education, and members of this aristocracy might hold civil and military positions indifferently in the course of their government careers. After the An Lu-shan rebellion, this aristocracy lost its political importance and the civil-service class, recruited by examination and embodying the ideology of Confucianism, took its place as the leading class in the state. Subsequent examples of mixed careers are actually spurious. Generals were on some occasions given high civil-service positions without being regarded as real civil officials by their colleagues, who had come up through the examinations, whereas civil officials delegated to raise armies and suppress rebellions never lost awareness of the fact that they were civil officials and were always careful to maintain the visible insignia of this distinction.

After the rise of the examinations, then, the body of Chinese officialdom is sharply divided into civil and military classes and the world-view of the former is wholly dominated by the educational curriculum required to pass the examinations. The civil officials have a common upbringing and a strong sense of being the guardians of the moral tradition that is the basis of all civilized society, and this gives them a strong feeling of corporate unity. Despite the Confucian preference for moral qualities over technical expertise, the civil officials provided imperial China's nearest equivalent to a professional body, and, despite their frequent financial corruption, their loyalty to Confucianism and to the reigning dynasty was always dependable. Military officers, on the other hand, did not have a selection process that endowed them with a common outlook and common values, and their loyalties in consequence tended to be particularistic, directed to the official or commander who had furthered their careers, rather than to the state as a whole. At various times, military examinations were offered on the analogy of the civil ones, the subjects of which were the military classics combined with tests of strength, horsemanship, archery, and so on. These did not succeed in providing the required number of officers, as any one possessed of the literary skill needed to master the military literature would naturally devote himself instead to studying for the civil-service examinations.

The result was that the position of military officer tended to be either explicitly hereditary, as during the Yüan and Ming dynasties, or based on local patronage and tending to become hereditary in fact, as during the T'ang and Sung dynasties. The Ch'ing military establishment combined both features. Military officers in consequence were often illiterate, and in any event their general level of education was much lower than that of their civil counterparts. This fact was generally recognized and meant that military officers had much lower prestige than civil officials of corresponding ranks.

As long as the state was at war, however, the power and importance of the leading generals maintained the prestige of the officer class, and constant battlefield practice maintained their military technique. While civilians continued to have a perhaps excessive say in administration and strategic planning, the generals participated in the conferences as well. On the other hand, large standing armies increased the need for officers, which added to the patronage powers of military commanders and made even more particularistic the structure of loyalties among the officers. The result of a long period of war, therefore, was never military professionalism in the modern sense of the term, but led instead the great danger of a breakdown into warlordism; this danger led emperors and civil officials alike to view the control of standing armies as an even more important problem than making them militarily efficient enough to deal with the dangers that had caused them to be raised. It should be stressed that this problem of the personal nature of military loyalties is felt even at the time of the founding of a dynasty, when one would expect imperial power to be at its strongest; however, it is the fact that his generals will not necessarily be loyal to his son that leads the dynastic founder to eliminate them. The problem of finding an institutional device to integrate the military officers as a class and focus their loyalties on emperor and state—performed in Western countries by military academies—was never solved in imperial China, and the most natural-seeming device, a system of military examinations, failed because of the degree to which the civil examinations attracted the talent of the empire.

Continuous war did not develop military professionalism, but continuous peace was absolutely fatal to the existence of the

military-officer class. This followed immediately from the limitations
of the military officer's role. With the armies demobilized and military installations under the administration of civil officials, the military officer was left with nothing to do. If this state of affairs lasted
for a generation or more, the officer class naturally degenerated
into a herd of sinecurists of no value in war. This happened repeatedly
in Chinese imperial history, always to the great surprise of the civil
officials. Their response was to create new armies, improvised to
deal with a particular crisis and with both officers and men selected
from the regular officer class and the registered military population,
respectively, but under the command of a civil official acting concurrently as provincial governor, aided by numerous other civil officials.
This pattern is characteristic of both the late Ming and late Ch'ing
dynasties. In both, the armies so created were successful in dealing
with the immediate threat, but were no solution to the over-all problem
of the decay of the dynasty's military institutions. The new armies
were usually confined to a province rather than part of an empire-wide
system, and their officers were tied to the throne only through loyalty
to the civil officials who had appointed them. Removal of these intermediate civil officials led instantly to regionally based warlordism.

Finally, Chinese military literature has been largely shaped
by the needs and interests of civil officials. In addition to the major
part that the chronicle of wars plays in the official histories of the
various dynasties, the Chinese have produced a large amount of
specialized military literature. The earliest and most famous example
of this is the work translated by Samuel Griffith as Sun-Tzu: The Art
of War, which continued to be widely read throughout imperial times.
Much of the instruction given by this work stresses the relationship
of war to over-all political ends. Thus, the ruler is exhorted not to
go to war until all other possibilities have been exhausted and to know
the relationship of his military strength to geographical and economic
factors. For the general, the ideal held up by the work is to destroy
the enemy's strength without fighting, and most of the specific advice
relating to operations deals with ways by which the general may
attack the morale and cohesion of the enemy while preserving the
discipline and will to fight of his own troops. Literature of this sort
is rather vague on the actual details of military affairs; at later
periods—particularly in the sixteenth century—a number of comprehensive military manuals were produced, which gave descriptions and
illustrations of weapons, walls, ships, tactical formations, and the
like, along with instructions on how to organize and lead an army,
all explained with the help of more recent historical examples.
These manuals were read by civil officials, who were likely to be
charged with organizing the defense of areas under their administration.

The flourishing of this literature thus coincides with and is directly related to the decline of the Ming military-officer class.

Some of the Chinese novels, in particularly the thirteenth-century Romance of the Three Kingdoms (set in the third century A.D.), contain a lot of military activity, and, because of the popularity of these novels, it has often been assumed that Chinese who concerned themselves with military affairs were greatly influenced by them. Of course, much of the material in the novels is concerned with magic or is otherwise fantastic, and most of the rest deals with the heroism and other stereotyped attributes of the protagonists. The novels, however, share with actual military history the themes of deception and treachery. Techniques of deception include, for example, the lighting of vast numbers of cooking fires (at night) or the raising of clouds of dust (in the daytime) to simulate the presence of larger forces, putting suits of armor stuffed with straw on the walls of a besieged city for the same purpose, and having spies spread false rumors in the enemy camp. When it comes to actual fighting, a well-executed ambush is considered the height of tactical skill in both the novels and the histories, and one of the most common techniques for arranging an ambush is to have a subordinate commander pretend to defect, thereby luring the enemy army to a specific place at a prearranged time. A Chinese military man might pick up useful ideas for ruses of this sort either from novels or from actual historical examples. When dealing with armies held together chiefly by personal loyalties in periods of civil war, a promise to betray one's superior was always credible, and this provides a final comment on the weak institutional basis of the Chinese military-officer class.

The Ordinary Soldier

The barbarian dynasties of conquest viewed their tribes as nations in arms, which after the period of conquest settled down to the role of an hereditary military elite ruling over a subject Chinese population. The native Chinese dynasties, on the other hand, tended to view military service merely as one aspect of the labor service due from the peasant population in general, and their military institutions were based on the assumption that the soldier would be a farmer most of the year, being called up for military service for perhaps one month of the year or whenever a crisis supervened. Systems of this sort supplied the soldiers of the Han, T'ang, and Ming dynasties, but the latter two were heavily influenced by preceding dynasties of conquest, with the result that under both the T'ang fu-ping system and the Ming wei-so system the military obligation was restricted

to a minority of the population. Under the fu-ping system, about 600
military-administrative units called fu were distributed about the
empire; under each of these were about 1,000 troops, who generally
came from the more well-to-do strata of the peasantry and were
called up by rotation to serve as guards at the capital or to garrison
the frontiers. The Ming system was based on units of about 5,000
men called wei, each divided into five so of about 1,000 men. Each
unit was assigned state-owned land that the soldiers were supposed
to farm when not actually engaged in military service. In the early
fifteenth century, there were 329 wei and 65 independent so, together
comprising nearly two million troops engaged in farming about one
tenth of the arable land of the empire. Here again, the military obligation was hereditary, with families of soldiers being placed on a special
"military register" and so distinguished from the ordinary civilian
population. The armies were originally constituted from three classes
of persons: the original followers of Chu Yüan-chang, troops of
Chu Yüan-chang's rivals who had surrendered to him, and criminals
consigned to the army as a punishment.

The military system in both the T'ang and the Ming dynasties
maintained its vitality during the phase of military consolidation
with which both dynasties began. The decline of the army began with
the coming of more or less permanent peace (ca. 650 in the T'ang
and ca. 1430 in the Ming), after which the soldiers deteriorated into
an especially disadvantaged sector of the ordinary peasant population.
In both dynasties, this was partly due to the fact that the soldiers in
peacetime were made to perform their military obligation by serving
as common laborers. In the T'ang, this caused the richer strata of
the peasantry to avoid enrollment in the fu-ping system, the burden
of which then fell on the poorer peasants, with the result that the
system lost its effectiveness completely by the early decades of the
eighth century. In the Ming, this factor was also present, but more
important was the hereditary nature of the officer class. As the
dynasty wore on, the officers strove, on the whole successfully, to
turn the lands set aside for the support of the army into hereditary
personal estates, with the military population as their tenants. By
1450, this process had gone very far, and, while subsequent Ming
armies were usually recruited from the registered military population,
this was simply a legal anomaly, for the troops so obtained were now
simply raw conscripts.

The system of making military service the hereditary obligation
of a minority of the population thus broke down when the governing
class failed to maintain the specifically military features of the institution of conscription, and China's sporadic approaches to universal

military service fared no better. The other alternative, a paid standing
army relieved of all other obligations and available for military duties
all year round, was associated in imperial China with times of dynastic
breakdown and permanent military crisis and was expensive; for both
reasons, it was unattractive to the officials who designed China's
military institutions. When standing armies nevertheless had to be
maintained, their administration was hampered by the lack of a national
system of currency or of weights and measures, which made it inevitable that the troops would be paid by their immediate commanders
or by local authorities, from which stemmed countless opportunities
for the financial corruption that victimized the soldier. The situation
of the common soldier in a standing army was thus even more precarious than that of an ordinary peasant, and a common soldier could
not hope to maintain a family on his pay. This meant that the soldiers
had to be recruited from among landless laborers and other drifting
elements too poor to marry and fit into one of the recognized respectable categories of Chinese society, and from this fact—rather than
from any pacifist feeling, as is occasionally alleged—comes the famous
Chinese disdain for the soldier.

The over-all record of military institutions in imperial China
does not compare favorably with that of other civilizations at comparable technological levels. It is characterized by the usurpation of
military functions by civil officials, the failure of the officer class
to develop military professionalism, and the tendency of the common
soldier to sink to the bottom level of society. These characteristics
resulted in the failure of imperial China to develop armies capable
of maintaining their morale, organization, and military technique for
any long period of time, and the want of such forces exacerbated the
troubles caused by foreign invasion and domestic rebellion.

MILITARY OPERATIONS IN IMPERIAL CHINA

Despite its rather drab record on the institutional side, the
history of imperial China contains a long series of impressive military
campaigns, including wars of foreign conquest as well as wars fought
to obtain the supreme imperial power in China itself. Whenever
unified to any reasonable extent, China was the paramount power in
the Far East and was usually able to make its unequal view of foreign
relations prevail on the smaller states in the region. This relative
military success stems from different factors in different periods.
China has produced its fair share of military geniuses, the greatest
of whom have founded the major dynasties while others have managed
the conquest of the south or west or have led armies against the

"barbarians" of Central Asia. The latter in turn have occasionally
conquered China or parts of it, founding regimes that married their
own native military skills to Chinese administrative efficiency and
agricultural wealth. Under native Chinese dynasties, military power
stemmed, and was seen as stemming, from administrative control
over agricultural regions, whose people could be mobilized either
as soldiers or as laborers and whose resources in grain could be
gathered and used to free expeditionary armies from logistical dependence on the next areas to be invaded. Administrative control of
large territories made it possible for Chinese governments to field
large armies whose size usually (but not always) overbalanced their
deficiencies in morale and technique; this control was the great
achievement of the civil service, which compensated to some extent
for the negative impact that this same civil service had on the development of military institutions.

Regions were administered from walled cities that were centers
of government and communications for districts (hsien) and higher
levels of government, as well as the places in which large reserves
of grain were stored. Administrative control of the land was the pre-
condition for further conquest, yet such control could be gained only
by capturing the walled cities. The latter thus became the principal
military objectives in wars fought within China, and the historical
accounts of such wars often consist merely of a series of short
notices of sieges. Pitched battles in the field were relatively less
common, usually occurring as the result of an attempt to break up a
siege. The fall of a city, whether to treachery, simple assault, or protracted blockade, would be followed swiftly the acknowledgment by the
region administratively dependent on the city of the authority of the
conqueror, who would then have at his disposal for further operations
the resources of the region; conversely, an army operating in a region
but failing to capture its cities would most likely be driven from the
region in the end. The capture of a city and the continuation of the
administration associated with it also brought the local civil officials
into relationship with the conqueror, which helped to establish the
political legitimacy of the latter. The foregoing implies that the culminating stage of the military consolidation of dynastic power is a
period in which the walled cities of the empire are conquered or
otherwise brought to acknowledge the authority of the founding emperor.
The authority of the government over the peasantry is then extended
downward from the walled cities. This generalization applies equally
to the dynasties (Han and Ming) founded by peasant leaders with the
help of armies manned and officered by peasants.

The predominance of the walled city in the military landscape

of pre-twentieth-century China is the result of both social and technological factors. Socially, the Confucian state was well equipped to
conscript its population for massive public-works projects. The
irrigation and flood-control aspects of these have traditionally been
given the greatest stress, but the military works were probably of
greater importance. The Great Wall precedes the Grand Canal by
over 800 years, and the basically military nature of cities is indicated
by the fact that the words for city and wall (ch'eng) are identical. No
foreigner, comparing Chinese cities to Western ones, ever failed to
be awestruck by their walls, and it should be stressed that the sheer
size of their earthen fortifications made them relatively less vulnerable
to the arts of siegecraft, even though these were as well developed in
China as in the West. Similarly, earthen walls, if they are very thick,
are less vulnerable to solid shot from primitive cannon than stone
walls, a fact that enabled the Chinese walled city to retain its military
importance until the introduction of truly modern artillery.

Once dynastic authority had been assured by the capture of the
cities, the next military objective was the defense of the border. Here,
the problem of the northern border, where Chinese civilization faced
a succession of nomadic barbarian nations, overshadowed the other
frontiers. Dynasties of barbarian origin themselves ruled over some
of the peoples north of the border and used troops drawn there from
in wars with the other tribes. This was the Manchu solution to the
problem of border defense, and it proved so successful that the northern
borderlands came to be incorporated into the empire itself. Dynasties
of purely Chinese origin could not, however, so incorporate border
tribes through the device of personal union and so were forced back
on other methods. One such method was to recruit and train an army
of Chinese horse-archers to go out and chastise the barbarians on
their own ground; this was a notable feature of the reigns of the Han
Emperor Wu (140-87 B.C.) and the Ming Emperor Yung-lo (1402-24).
Despite the successes of Chinese arms on both occasions, the institutional failures of Chinese military organization cited above came
into play, and, after the deaths of the emperors and generals responsible for their creation, the armies of Chinese horse-archers disappeared.

If the Chinese could not maintain efficient armies over long
periods, they nevertheless could maintain walls, and so during the
Han, T'ang, and Ming dynasties the defense of the border was based
on the Great Wall. Under the Han, the system whereby the wall was
garrisoned by conscript soldiers stationed in the watchtowers found
at intervals throughout its length was developed. Naturally, the entire
wall could not be garrisoned in strength, but even ungarrisoned it

was a great obstacle to horses; even if a raiding party got through, the Chinese counterattack would force them to fight with their backs to the wall on their retreat. Under the Han, the border defense based on the wall was successful; degree of such success may be gauged by the fact that the Han were able to ward off the attacks of the Hsiung-nu empire and ultimately to destroy it, while the Chin (a dynasty of non-Chinese origin that did not garrison the wall) fell before the attacks of the Mongols, who were no stronger than the Hsiung-nu at their prime. Under the T'ang, while the line of frontier defense was originally in the region of the Great Wall, the armies formed to defend it included large numbers of barbarian auxiliaries. These armies caused the civil wars that ultimately destroyed the dynasty, and in the following Five-Dynasties period most of the Great Wall fell under the control of two non-Chinese dynasties (Hsi-hsia and Liao), with the result that the wall was no longer available as the northern defense line when the Sung dynasty was founded in 960.

When the Ming dynasty (1368-1644) emerged after a long barbarian interlude, it once again made the Great Wall the basis of its border defense. During the civil wars leading to the establishment of the Ming dynasty, cannon had come into widespread use in Chinese armies, and by the beginning of the fifteenth century muskets also existed, with a special agency in Peking charged with training in their use. The result was to give the Chinese army on the northern frontier an unprecedented technological superiority over the nomadic horse-archers, with the result that the Ming military frontier was successfully maintained (with two dramatic exceptions that were without long-range effects) until the end of the dynasty, despite the collapse of the Ming regime from within.

Logistical support of the armies, meaning primarily the transport of grain, was a major factor in military operations. If an important campaign was undertaken, a civil official would be given charge of this under the general direction of the commander-in-chief. Wherever possible, grain was moved by water. In the interconnected river and canal systems of central and south China, this was the normal pattern of communications. Extended to north China, the military grain-transport system evolved into a regular institution of government, headed by a civil official but actually operated by military officers and men, using the Grand Canal to transport the grain needed by the population of the capital and the armies on the northern frontier.

In central and south China, in addition to transporting military supplies, ships were used both to transport the troops themselves and to aid in the assault of cities situated on the banks of rivers.

During periods of protracted warfare, assemblies of such ships metamorphosed into true fighting fleets. This was the case during the Three-Kingdoms period (220-65), during the Southern Sung, and particularly during the civil wars leading up to the founding of the Ming. The latter instance was followed by the famous voyages of Cheng Ho, during which Chinese armadas of very large sailing ships ranged the South China Sea and the Indian Ocean, exacting tribute from native rulers and extending Chinese authority further south than it had ever gone before. The ships used in these voyages were built in a special navy yard in Nanking, and the whole operation was carried out under the supervision of eunuchs in the confidence of Emperor Yung-lo. After the latter's death, the civil officials reasserted their customary influence, and their hostility to both eunuchs and foreign adventures ended the voyages for all time, another instance of the failure of individual military successes to result in the creation of permanent military institutions. When the Ming were confronted with the threat of Japanese piracy in the sixteenth century, they responded by proliferating coastal garrisons, but this approach did not succeed in controlling the piracy, which ceased only with the unification of Japan in the 1590s. The Ch'ing dynasty followed the late Ming practice and did not maintain a navy as such; instead, individual squadrons were scattered along the coast under the control of the provincial Green Standard armies.

The theory that military operations should be undertaken only in response to clearly articulated political goals is a basic element in Chinese military thinking. The ultimate goal of military operations was to compel the enemy to acknowledge imperial authority. This meant that the concepts of "total war" and "unconditional surrender" had no application in imperial China. A rebel who surrendered after nominal resistance might legitimately expect to be left in possession of his troops and titles, and a foreign tribe or nation that went to war with China could usually escape the consequences of defeat by formally recognizing the overlordship of the Chinese emperor. These political considerations entered into the conduct of operations at all levels, so that Chinese soldiers were constrained to fight in such a manner as to leave open at all times the possibility of negotiated surrender. Militarism and territorial expansion by military means, on the other hand, has not been an important feature of Chinese history, although strong dynasties have attempted to maintain control over important peripheral regions, such as Sinkiang.

The conduct of war in imperial China was thus limited to the objectives imposed by prior political considerations and was characterized operationally by the tactical predominance of walled cities

and the Great Wall and the means employed in attacking and defending
them, while logistically it was characterized by the inland water transport of grain. Within this framework, China has an impressive military
history of the establishment and maintenance of dynasties, and the
military science developed therefrom was an adequate guide to the
civil officials charged with recreating Chinese military power after
periods of decay. The assumptions of this military science, however,
rested on a technological basis whose changes prior to 1800 had tended
to reinforce traditional Chinese military practices. The kaleidoscopic
changes in military technology during the nineteenth century made a
military science of siege operations and river transport obsolete, and
the growing complexity of weapons and tactics also made obsolete
an institutional pattern wherein armies were improvised for the
occasion by civil officials who were military amateurs. These twin
challenges—the need for both modern technology and military professionalism—are the main underlying factors in China's recent military
history.

THE COMMUNIST RECEPTION OF THE IMPERIAL
MILITARY TRADITION

The Chinese Communist movement avows its intention of completely changing the structure of Chinese society, and since coming
to power in 1949 the regime has in fact worked major transformations
in many areas of Chinese life. Nevertheless, from the perspective
of two decades, it is clear that the major significance of 1949 is to
mark the end of the era of encroachment on China by the Western
maritime powers. During that era, China's traditional institutions
were in decay, and as the era wore on it seemed that the most vital
sectors of Chinese society—from a westernized intelligentsia to
modernized armies—were those created in imitation of Western
models and based economically and socially on the society of the
treaty ports. In 1949, all of this changed. China passed under the
control of a regime that had succeeded in establishing its authority
over the rural hinterland before taking over the treaty ports, whose
military power was generated in precisely those areas that had been
least subject to Western influence, and whose policies after 1949
showed real hostility both generally to the Western powers and specifically to the treaty ports that had been the spearheads of Western
penetration. During the 1950s, it was arguable that Western influence
had merely been replaced by Russian influence, as the Chinese Communists created their new institutions in deliberate imitation of
Russian models. The subsequent break with the USSR, accompanied
by claims to doctrinal creativity, symbolized the view of the Chinese

leadership that all foreign cultural influences must be rejected; China would henceforth attempt to modernize itself, but without relying on foreign models. The more recent Chinese policy of isolation from the rest of the world resembles previous periods of xenophobia, notably during the Ming and Ch'ing dynasties, and both of those dynasties also had the distinction of reestablishing order after a period in which China's weakness had been exploited by foreign invaders.

Communist ideology plays a role in the current Chinese regime analogous to that played by Confucianism under the imperial dynasties. The ideology is the source of all values, and the position of the elite is secured by the fact that only they can authoritatively interpret the ideology. The fact that today's cadres have taken on the appearance of yesterday's mandarins was belatedly recognized by Mao Tse-tung and his entourage, and the Cultural Revolution was their desperate and unsuccessful attempt to reverse a trend that will in the end deprive Chinese Communism of its revolutionary features. The military institutions and practices of imperial China that linger on in the PLA similarly do so by wearing revolutionary masks and rationalizing themselves in terms of Communist ideology.

These continuities are to be found in the realm of military insti-tutions rather than in the realm of operations. The type of operations characteristic of imperial China has been rendered obsolete by the developments in military technology that have rendered the walled city a military absurdity. The Communist conquest of China after World War II was based on the recognition of this fact. The Commu-nist armies avoided defended cities initially and instead consolidated their control over the countryside, in the process extending communist organizations among the peasant population. Once isolated, the indivi-dual cities could not defend themselves against an enemy even modestly supplied with artillery, and so fell one by one. Most observers of the Communist takeover assumed that their pattern of conquest had antecedents in Chinese imperial history, but in fact it did not. Previous civil wars in China had indeed furnished many examples of peasant rebels looting undefended cities, but the process of dynastic foundation always involved first the conquest of the walled cities and only then the extension of governmental authority downward to the peasantry. This was the Kuomintang (KMT) strategy during the civil war, a strategy that had succeeded in suppressing the T'ai-p'ing rebellion and all of the previous peasant movements in Chinese history. Its failure in 1945-49 symbolized the passing-away forever of the walled city and the military arts associated with it. Since then, city walls have been pulled down throughout China, while the PLA has based its operational doctrine on the experiences of the Chinese civil war. As refurbished and given a theoretically universal application under the title "People's War," this doctrine indeed shows signs of becoming a shibboleth that will impede the PLA's ability to respond creatively to new military situations, but it is not by itself a survival of China's imperial military tradition.

Institutional continuities between Communist China and the imperial past are found today in three general areas: (1) the close relationship of military objectives to Communist ideology and the use of the PLA for various nonmilitary functions, which parallels the imperial failure to separate army and state and the influence of Confucian ideology in imperial times; (2) the rejection of the Western ideal of the professional military officer, symbolized by the abolition of rank titles and insignia of rank; and (3) the militia system and the assignment of farms to PLA units to cultivate, which revive the old imperial ideal of a part-time conscript army that is self-supporting in peacetime. In all three respects, these developments are in accordance with general Marxist-Leninist military theory, which is characterized by distrust for professional officers and standing armies; however, whereas in the USSR the armed forces have largely succeeded in their efforts to free themselves from the incubus of Marxist-Leninist military thought, in China the successful application of an allegedly Marxist-Leninist revolutionary theory has had the effect of reinforcing these traditional aspects of Chinese military institutions.

Chinese Communist military organization from the earliest times imitated the then contemporary Soviet practice of attaching political commissars to commanders at all higher levels. In the Soviet armies, this was necessary because the commanders were usually former Tsarist officers whose loyalty to the new regime was doubtful; the role of the commissar was to ensure that loyalty. In the early Communist armies of China, however, the officers were persons associated with the movement from the beginning whose loyalties were not particularly suspect, and the commissar thus developed into a political specialist whose main role was the indoctrination of the soldiers. For long periods in the Chinese civil war, the PLA was an army without a country, compelled to operate in territories whose defense it could not guarantee. Under these circumstances, the success of the PLA depended largely on its relationship with the peasant population in these territories. The PLA was therefore thoroughly indoctrinated with the need for discipline and ordered not to harm the people, to pay for everything requisitioned, and so on. When prisoners were taken, they were to be treated favorably and encouraged to defect. Finally, the PLA was the instrument through which Communist organizations were extended throughout the peasantry, and it was the force in reserve when social policies that aroused wide opposition (such as land reform) were to be carried out. Since 1949, various nonmilitary roles of the PLA (such as disaster relief) have been highlighted, and at the peak of the Cultural Revolution the PLA was said to be leading the nation in the assuredly nonmilitary task of studying the quotations of Chairman Mao. At the same time, PLA units were running schools and factories and in general taking over the duties of civil institutions that had been temporarily destroyed.

The importance of strict enforcement of discipline is paralleled in previous civil wars by the repeated injunctions (not always followed, of course) not to plunder the civil population, and, similarly, favorable treatment of prisoners in order to encourage further defections is a favorite strategy of imperial times. Underlying these elements is the belief, common to Communism and Confucianism, that wars are fought primarily in order to establish or maintain a desired social order, and that the degree of legitimacy of the various contenders for political power will be made manifest by the means employed to prosecute the war. Both ideologies therefore give the greatest weight to political objectives, and both view all wars as essentially civil wars, in which the enemy's will to resist is particularly subject to political attack, so that the political objectives of the war must constantly be kept in mind by all military personnel down to the lowest-ranking soldier. This is very different from the Western view of civil-military relations, in which political considerations establish the ends for which military means are to be used, but the means themselves are applied by military officers who are conceived to be technical (and, ideally, apolitical) experts in their use and therefore not subject to political interference as long as they remain within the proper bounds of their profession. In Chinese Communist thinking, political ends and technical means are so inextricably intermingled that the concept of the technician's aloofness from politics is not permitted; politics takes command, and not only in the military sphere.

The 1965 decision to abolish rank titles and distinctive insignia of rank in fact symbolized a fundamental change in the definition of the officer's role. The democratization of the PLA entailed by this change has been exaggerated; a division commander, for example, remains a division commander in name as well as in fact, and it is doubtful that his actual authority suffers from occasionally drilling with his men. What was abolished in 1965 was the specifically Western feature of rank as a personal attribute of the individual officer, while the traditional Chinese aspect of rank, in which the offices themselves are arranged in a definite order, remains. The abolition of rank was one of the opening guns of the Cultural Revolution, and it is difficult to distinguish its consequences from the other results of that upheaval.

Presumably, military positions will continue to be filled by internal promotion, though in principle they could be filled by any cadre. The abolition of rank and insignia, however, eliminates the distinction between the officer's corps and the general body of cadres and correspondingly weakens the claim of the officers to a monopoly of technical expertise. The specific military ranks had been introduced as part of P'eng Teh-huai's policy of modernizing the PLA on the Russian model; their abolition is a feature of Lin Piao's policy of developing the PLA along the lines of the experience of the Chinese civil war. The fact that P'eng favored and Lin opposed greater professionalization is well known, and the abolition of rank constitutes, as one would expect, a retrograde step from that viewpoint.

The revival of local forces stems directly from the emphasis placed on preparing the nation for People's War, which has been characteristic of Lin Piao's tenure in the Ministry of National Defense. The militia are organized and administered by the people's communes, on whose lands they live and work. They correspond to the militia forces of previous dynasties in that they are organized and led by local civil authorities with only loose supervision by higher military agencies. Militia systems in the past have been associated with dynastic breakdown, but this is not so of the system of assigning plots for army units to cultivate, currently in practice, which corresponds to the way in which the regular army was organized at the height of the Ming dynasty; then, as now, the practice was motivated by a desire to curtail the expenses of the standing army in peacetime. What suffers, of course, is the standard of military training. The local forces, which are not integrated into higher-level organizational or logistical patterns, rely on their communes for sustenance and would probably be useless in combat away from their native regions. The situation in the PLA proper is more serious. Most of their conscripts are peasants to begin with and will never become soldiers if a large period of their military service is devoted to farming. On the basis of the experience of previous dynasties, one would predict the deterioration of the PLA into a depressed sector of the peasantry if this system (and with it peace) endures.

The foregoing survey has led to the conclusion that the principal legacy of the imperial past to contemporary Chinese military practice is an institutional syndrome characterized by failure to separate political ends and military means, dominance of a generalist ideology and consequent failure to develop military professionalism, and the assignment of soldiers to farming and other nonmilitary duties in peacetime. This legacy is, of course, not the only doctrinal force operating within the Chinese military establishment, but it has been most compatibly wedded to the doctrine of People's War and both have grown in influence during the decade of the 1960s. During the same period, the power of the PLA in relation to the other institutions of Chinese society has increased dramatically, so that at the moment of writing Lin Piao is Mao Tse-tung's heir-apparent, and the PLA has at least temporarily replaced the Chinese Communist Party as the principal hierarchy of rule. As the PLA grows in power within the Chinese state, however, its specifically military character becomes progressively diluted, and increasing reliance is placed on the dogma of People's War and on those elements that constitute the imperial legacy. While the latter elements may also be traced to early Marxist military thinking, the Soviet Union and most other Communist countries have largely abandoned them in favor of a military system that provides for a great deal of professional autonomy. The survival of this institutional syndrome in contemporary China, therefore, indicates the strength of the Chinese historical tradition, which reinforces the Communist prejudice against a professional military. Strong traditions, however, are not necessarily good ones, and in fact the functioning of Chinese military institutions was always somewhat of a tour de force even under the technologically less-developed circumstances that prevailed before the Western impact. Contemporary technology requires an expert, professional, and institutionally autonomous military establishment to provide effective defense. China's defense forces will continue to deteriorate in over-all effectiveness until this need is met by a leadership with enough sense of purpose to scuttle both the theory of People's War and the traditions inherited from China's imperial past.

2

THE MAOIST
VS.
THE PROFESSIONAL VISION
OF A PEOPLE'S ARMY

James D. Jordan

A fundamental factor that has influenced the orientation of the PLA since its 1927 origins has been Mao Tse-tung's interpretation of sinified Marxist-Leninist ideology as it applies to military ethic and style. Basically, that interpretation has visualized a primarily domestic role/or the PLA in applying two general principles: the employment of the "mass line" in all enterprises, and the struggle to eliminate class differences in Chinese Communist society.

Depending upon whether or not the views and style of Chinese generals accurately reflected the Maoist vision, they have been labeled either "proletarian" or "bourgeois".[1] Ideally, a proletarian army is an army of the people in which the people identify themselves as part of the military system, and soldiers regard themselves as members of the masses. A proletarian army is one that is politically active and attempts to be responsive to the party of the proletariat. A bourgeois army is, by contrast, a force divorced from the people. It is an instrument of the state and is described by Samuel Huntington as a "professional" army.[2] Ideally, a professional army, according to Huntington, is politically sterile.

Although the terms "proletarian army" and "bourgeois army" are not entirely synonymous with "revolutionary army" and "professional army," historically the Chinese PLA has certainly been proletarian in the sense of being of the masses and relying on the masses for support. As early as the 1946-50 civil war, however, and especially after the ending of the Korean War in 1953, the PLA has tended to adopt the values and goals of a professional army.* By the nature

---

*Nearly every contributor to this book has commented on the implications of this "Red vs. expert" Theme for his subject.—Ed.

of its requirements for sophisticated tactics, techniques, and equipment, the PLA has had a tendency to become increasingly differentiated and isolated from the civilian masses.

THE MAOIST VISION

The fundamentals of Marxism-Leninism from which the Chinese Communists have developed their ideology have been strongly influenced in China by Chinese thought and culture. In recognition of the need for sinification of Marxism, Mao Tse-tung wrote in 1938:

> Hence to apply Marxism concretely in China so that its
> every manifestation has an indubitably Chinese character,
> i.e., to apply Marxism in the light of Chinese specific
> characteristics, becomes a problem which it is urgent
> for the whole party to understand and solve.[3]

One Marxist-Leninist military principle adopted by the Chinese Communists has been an emphasis on the concept of "mass" and an "army of the people."[4] In Chinese Communist ideology, the "mass line" is a basic principle not only in military doctrine, but in all other activities as well. The mass line is characterized by Ralph Powell as a "mystical belief in the capabilities of the mobilized and indoctrinated masses."[5] A firm belief in the "mass line" by China's leadership should foster certain fundamental military policy premises: the superiority of men over weapons, protracted war, and, most important, "politics should take command."

A second fundamental ideological principle is that of the single class. Communist belief holds that all social ills (including war) are the result of class struggle, and the way to end the problem of constant class struggle is to eliminate class distinctions. Society may eliminate these distinctions by establishing a dictatorship of the proletariat. The military implication of this principle would be the creation of a proletarian-class army.[6] Such an army could not have class differences within itself, nor could it form a class separate from the rest of society. In a truly single-class society, as envisioned by Peking's leaders, all people are to be simultaneously producers and fighters.[7]

Before 1946, the role of the military in Mao's China seemed to conform to the principles outlined above. The pre-civil war revolutionary army had been basically a decentralized semi-professional army in which maneuver elements were relatively small, weapons and equipment unsophisticated, and all supported by a rather

rudimentary logistical system. Despite its semi-professional characteristics, however, its essential focus on domestic roles imparted
and reflected qualities that Mao considered essential even in a modern
military force. It was an army of the people, an army controlled by
the Party, and an army deeply involved in the creation of a new China.
According to Chairman Mao, the army was responsible for the creation
of Party organizations, of cadres, of schools, of culture, and of the
mass movements so essential to Chinese Communism. Thus, the
army was indispensable to the creation and survival of the Communist
system in China. Indeed, after 1936 and the end of the Long March,
it had been responsible for Communist success in Shensi: "Everything
in Yenan has been created by having guns," Mao explains.

With the formation of the new Communist state in 1949, Mao
continued to perceive the army not only as the primary work force,
but also as the principal instrument of power to ensure Party control.
In Mao's words: "Every Communist must grasp the truth. Political
power grows from the barrel of a gun. Our principle is that the Party
controls the gun, and the gun must never be allowed to command the
Party."[8]

THE PROFESSIONAL VISION

Planning for the modernized army commenced simultaneously
with the establishment of the People's Republic of China (PRC). The
Common Program adopted by the Chinese People's Political Consultive
Conference (CPPCC) in September, 1949, stated the intention to build
a "unified army" with a "unified system, unified organization, and
unified discipline."[9] It further provided for modernization of the
land force and the establishment of an air force and navy. The Korean
War was probably instrumental in speeding up the modernization of
the Chinese army, but modernization was not undertaken in anticipation
of Chinese involvement in Korea.

There seems little doubt, however, that Mao was aware of
North Korea's intention to invade the south. Mao was in Moscow at
the same time as was Kim Il Sung of North Korea—the winter of
1949-50. Edgar Snow writes that "it would be naive to suppose that
the North Korean Government began the war without China's knowledge."[10] The evidence does seem to indicate, however, that China
participated in the Korean War with reluctance and that the necessity
for such action had not been foreseen.[11] Almost immediately upon
Chinese entry into the war, the Soviet Union commenced a military-aid
program to replace the hodge-podge of Chinese, American, and

Japanese weapons in the arsenal of the PLA.[12] Accompanying the equipment was a large number of Soviet military advisers who assisted the PLA as it set about to remold itself formally on the Soviet model.[13]

Clear evidence of the Chinese adoption of the Soviet model was the publishing of the "Regulations on the Service of Officers of the Chinese People's Liberation Army" in February, 1955.[14] This document classified and assigned officers in fields of specialization and provided for distinctive uniforms and rank insignia. A regular pay scale replaced the previous system, which relied primarily on allowances. A conscription law based on that of the Soviet Union was introduced, replacing the traditional volunteer system of the Communist army and specifying periods of service in the various armed services of the PLA.[15]

Almost at once, with the inception of modernization, a professional vision began to emerge in opposition to both the principles of the mass line and class struggle. Modernization along the lines of the Soviet model and professionalization of the Chinese officer corps challenged the continued relevance of Mao Tse-tung's principle of the army as a work force as well as a fighting force. The continued employment of the army as a work force evoked professional officers' opposition to such a diversion of military resources and time on non-military tasks, a diversion that might adversely affect the efficiency of a modern military establishment. In addition, the creation of a professional officer corps brought a new sense of military eliteness, a sense of class consciousness and an estrangement between officers and men.

One of the early casualties resulting from burgeoning professionalism in the PLA was the People's Militia.* Article 23 of the Common Program states:

> The Chinese People's Republic shall enforce the system
> of people's militia to maintain local order, lay the founda-
> tion for national mobilization and prepare for the enforce-
> ment of an obligatory military service system at the appro-
> priate moment.[16]

———————————

*The role of the militia and "local forces" as an indicator of the relative influence of the professional vs. the Maoist vision is discussed by Harvey Nelsen in Chapter 7.—Ed.

According to James Garvey, the Chinese military system had tended
to be unique in its affection for the generalized militia concept as
part of the mass line—"The people armed and militant."[17]

Early in Mao's revolutionary experience, during the 1927 Autumn
Harvest Uprisings, he formulated his theory of the role of the peasant
militia. Here, Mao developed his principle that "without the poor
peasants there can be no revolution. To reject them is to reject the
revolution."[18] The Autumn Harvest Uprisings, which sought to arouse
the peasants, were a failure because the masses were not sufficiently
organized and indoctrinated to take part in the insurrection. Mao was
criticized by the Party, which asserted that armed insurrection meant
insurrection by the workers and peasants themselves, who should have
been secretely trained and armed. They should, the Party claimed,
suddenly rise up to overthrow the government and sieze power.[19] In
the vanguard of the peasant army would march a highly disciplined
and politically concious Red Army, but the "people" should make up
the main force. Failure to maintain a militia meant failure to use
the mass line.

Since 1949, sporadic attempts to revive the militia have met
with limited success. Even the massive "Everyone a Soldier" campaign
of 1958 (which claimed an enrollment of 200 million people in the
militia) fell far short of its objective. Published militia figures,
like many of the statistics of the Great Leap Forward period, must
be regarded with caution. Powell states, "The hastily enlarged
militia suffered from a 'degree of formalism'—a Marxian euphemism
for a paper organization."[20] In referring to militia problems, the
official army journal wrote in 1958:

> For a certain time after our country was liberated, the
> glorious tradition of unity of labor and army was neglec-
> ted by people and lost. Some comrades mistakenly be-
> lieved that in the modernized war against imperialism
> the usefulness of the militia was no longer very great.
> Therefore, in practical work, they allowed their leader-
> ship of the militia to lapse, with the result that the work
> of the peoples armed forces was weakened and the mili-
> tia's organization became dissipated.[21]

Three years later, however, military units were still being told that
"the militia must be put in the hands of reliable people" and "the
militia activities this year must take hold at the primary level."[22]

The development of professional officers in place of the

traditional guerrilla-type officers created the greatest change in the relationship between military commanders and the political officers of units of the PLA. This change reinforced a dichotomy within the army that hampered its ability to act as a unified force.* During and prior to the Korean War, there was minimal friction resulting from the dual political and military leadership of army units. The majority of both military and political officers had had considerable battle experience. Military commanders were capable in the political field, and most political officers were experienced combat soldiers. In theory, they were co-leaders, and neither had superiority over the other. Since the political officer was also secretary of the "Party" element of the military unit, however, the dictum that the "Party will always command the gun" threw the balance of authority to the political officer.

With the growth of professionalism in the army, however, young political officers had little experience other than the political training they had received; junior military commanders were technically qualified but not sufficiently politically educated. The younger, school-trained officers were no doubt strongly influenced by their Soviet advisers and leaned toward the Soviet model, in which the political arm played a less dominant day-by-day role. By 1961, the deterioration of the influence of the political officer had become especially significant in the lower echelons of the PLA, where it was reported that 7,000 companies, or roughly one third of the PLA, had failed to establish Party branch committees.[23] Some of the remaining companies, having established committees, failed to allow the committees to carry out their functions of recruiting Party members.

The second major ideological principle to be violated through professionalization was that of a "single-classed" society. Modernization was creating a gulf between officers and men and difficulties in army/civilian relationships. A salaried officer corps provided the means by which officers could bring their families to remote stations and live on a much higher scale than did the enlisted men and the peasants in the locality. The availability of salary allowed some officers to dabble in the black market and other bourgeois activities. The creation of rank in the army brought complaints of "big bossism,"

---

*The extent to which the professional commanders finally dominated commissars imbued with the Maoist vision is discussed in Chapter 3 by Parris Chang. Also see Chapter 9 by Glenn Dick for a detailed treatment of the GPD.

of harsh disciplinary measures, and of arrogations of privilege by officers.[24] Furthermore, some officers were found to be avoiding physical labor and exhibiting a superior attitude toward those who labored.[25] In particular, the newly emerged professional officer was accused of adopting an overbearing attitude toward subordinates and of failing to appreciate the primacy of politics over all phases of the Communist system. Finally, he was blamed for being indifferent to the well-being of the local civilian population.[26]

The Maoists were thus threatened by the emergence of a military class that was becoming alienated from the civilians. Some military leaders were accused of adopting an arrogant attitude and committing highhanded actions in commandeering school buildings, restricting scenic spots, and seducing village girls and women. In the construction of camps, barracks, and drill fields, a great deal of arable land was usurped and the peasants evicted. Probably many of the PLA members felt that, since the revolutionary war was over and the conscription system provided a regular input into the army, good relations with the people were no longer important. Therefore, conformance to the traditional Communist three main rules of discipline and eight major points of attention, which regulated soldier behavior with civilians, was no longer necessary.[27]

THE CRISIS OF 1959

The deterioration of political influence in the PLA was obviously inimical to the stated doctrine of Mao Tse-tung on military affairs and to the traditions of the PLA. To Mao, political awareness was as necessary an ingredient of the military system as it was among the masses. Expertise should be gained through modernization, but not at the expense of a lapse in political ideology. Political motivation was credited with providing the one resource in which the Chinese army had an acknowledged superiority—esprit.[28] One had to be "Red and expert," and, if a contradiction developed, then "redness" was more important than "expertness." Redness emphasized the ideological factor of the mass line.

By 1959, the Maoists believed that they had discovered a solution to the emergence of class distinctions within the PLA. In an attempt to instill appreciation for the democratic values of the old Red Army officer-enlistee camaraderie, they initiated the Officers to the Ranks (hsia-lien tang-ping) movement. This movement was the result of a September 28, 1958, directive by the GPD of the PLA. It required every officer to spend thirty days each year performing the duties of an ordinary soldier.[29] By February, 1959, over 150,000 officers, including 160 generals, had "returned to the ranks" and had performed such menial tasks as mess duty, cleaning spittoons, and sweeping out barracks. Eventually, the extreme measures of the movement were abandoned, but the practice and encouragement of officers to return to the ranks continued at least until 1966.

Despite these preliminary countermeasures against adverse manifestations of professionalism in the PLA, a polarization developed between professional military leaders and Maoist ideologues. It is difficult to isolate the purely ideological factors in the reaction that began in 1958. Contributing factors certainly included the Chinese disillusionment with the USSR and certain failures in the Great Leap Forward programs.[30] Maoist perspectives and military policies were reflected in at least six visible spheres: (1) the "men versus weapons" theme; (2) the rejection of the Soviet military model; (3) the democratization of the army with the Officers to the Ranks movement; (4) the massive Everyone a Soldier militia campaign; (5) the struggle for ideological control within the army; and (6) the diversion of military resouces of men and material into the Great Leap Forward programs.

The question of a professional army as opposed to a revolutionary army became a basic one. Representing professionalism was Marshal P'eng Teh-huai, Minister of Defense, a soldier with a long and distinguished military record. Directly opposed to P'eng was Mao Tse-tung, an ideologue who believed in the military superiority of the politically indoctrinated masses over a professional army. Probably the main factor in P'eng's complaint was the diversion of PLA resources into nonmilitary production. In 1959, P'eng's GPD wrote:

> There is a definite conflict between participation in national construction and training in their respective demands for time . . . Needless to say, as the army is an armed combat organization, it must carry out its task as a "work force" in such a way that its task as a "combat force" is not affected . . . It is obviously wrong to think that, as no war is going on at present, the army should exert itself mainly in the direction of production construction, or set too high requirements concerning the army's participation in construction and labor production. Anything that may weaken war preparations and training tasks is impermissible.[31]

Since the Common Program (see above) provided that the PLA was to be a "work force" when not training or operating as a "combat force," the disagreement was one of degree, with considerable support for both sides. The debate reached a climax at the meeting of the Eighth Plenum of the Central Committee at Lushan (August 2-16, 1959) with Mao's attempt to take control of the army from P'eng Teh-huai. According to David A. Charles:

> At one stage there was an emotional scene when Mao, in reply to a suggestion that the disgrace of P'eng might be a signal for a revolt by the armed forces due to his popularity with them in the country, declared with tears in his eyes that, if this happened, he would go back to the villages and recruit another army.[32]

Mao eventually prevailed at the conference and P'eng was shortly dismissed from his position as Minister of Defense. The primary cause, as given by the Chinese, was P'eng's espousal of a "bourgeois military line" against the Party's "proletarian military line."[33]

The showdown at the Lushan conference brought a close-fought victory to Mao Tse-tung in the ousting of P'eng Teh-huai and some advocates of a professional army, but at the expense of Mao's resignation from the post of Chairman of the People's Republic. Surrender of the government post was probably also influenced by the failures of the majority of the programs of the Great Leap Forward. In any case, it allowed Mao to avoid the responsibility for the three difficult years that were to follow.

One may conjecture that a compromise was reached that allowed Mao to retain his position as Chairman of the Party and of the Politburo, while relinquishing control of the government bureaucracy. It is too simplistic to state merely that Mao was "forced to resign." He retained his positions in the Party and controlled the army through the appointment of his trusted marshal, Lin Piao, who was named Minister of Defense and head of the powerful Military Affairs Committee (MAC). As to Mao himself, some analysts believe that Mao's power and influence actually increased after his retirement from the post of Chairman of the People's Republic.[34]

IDEOLOGICAL RESTRUCTURING OF THE PLA

Almost immediately after Lin Piao became Minister of Defense and, more important, de facto chief of MAC, he launched the rebuilding of the army according to the thought of Mao Tse-tung. Under Mao's guidance, Lin Piao commenced to restore Party leadership in the army. Within a year, a detailed program for political and ideological work in the army was clearly spelled out in a resolution at the October, 1960, meeting of MAC.

The endorsement by the central authorities states that the resolution "pointed out the direction of ideological work in the army in the new historical period that has begun. . . ."[35] It is apparent that reemphasis on political and ideological work in the army was a first step toward renewed political and ideological conciousness among professional military leaders. The endorsement stated further that the program should be distributed to the local committee level and above for use in "Party organizations, government organs, schools, and enterprises at various levels . . ." It is also clear that the central authorities on December 21, 1960, when they ratified the resolution, were themselves aware that Mao's thought was being sanctified. The first page of the resolution contains the statement that "Mao Tse-tung's Thought, whether in the past, at present or in the future, serves always as the guide for building up of our army . . . "[36]

The immediate effect of emphasis on politics in the PLA was the restoration of political leadership at the company level and below. Political officers and platoon representatives were assigned to lower-level military units, and recruiting for Party membership was stepped up. It has been reported that 78,000 cadres were transferred from other duties to the company level, and 229,000 new Party members were recruited by the PLA during 1960. All companies that had lacked Party committees (or in which Party committees had been inactive) now established them. Eighty percent of the platoons of the PLA organized Party cells, and 50 percent of the squads had at least one Party member.[37] Of all the elements that make up Chinese society, the soldiers of the PLA became probably the most politically motivated, if not politically conscious.* Military commissars sought to imbue them with the utopian aspects of Mao's vision of Communist China and the mass line.

By 1964, central leaders evidently felt that the army had been remolded sufficiently to serve as an example for the rest of society.

---

*Whether or not this "political consciousness" proved useful to Mao during and after the Cultural Revolution is debatable. Chapters 3 and 6, for example, suggest that the most important ingredient of that new consciousness is loyalty to local leaders, not national or central leaders. —Ed.

Mao undertook to revive the army's mass-line domestic role. A massive campaign called for the whole country to "learn from the PLA."[38] The campaign stressed the unity of the army and the people and the need to apply the principle of "putting politics in command." The People's Daily editorial asserted:

> In learning from the PLA, comrades on each front should raise even higher the Red Banner of Mao Tse-tung's thinking, and resolutely use it as a guiding principle to constantly examine their own ideology, work and behavior and to study and sum up their own work experience.[39]

The use of the PLA example to instill ideological rebirth and political control in industry and agriculture was summed up by Chou En-lai at the Third National People's Congress in December, 1964. Chou said: "All our Party and government organs and the broad mass of our cadres should learn from the thoroughly revolutionary spirit and style of work of the Liberation Army . . . and advance along the road of revolution."[40]

The emergence of class distinctions was another matter and still had to be dealt with. Theoretically, in a revolutionary army, no particular deference should be paid to rank; officers and men should live together, eat the same food, dress alike, and be financially and socially equal.[41] In the modernized army, however, troops had become differentiated according to rank and branch of service, and officers, by virtue of the graduated pay system, lived better than enlisted men.[42] The new system of discipline in the professional army had encouraged officers to adopt perquisites and demand privileges according to their rank. A new class had thus been created within the hitherto single-class army and even the Officers to the Ranks movement had been insufficient to regain unity.

In 1965, the Standing Committee of the National People's Congress announced the abolition of the system of rank in the PLA. While the order was signed by Liu Shao-ch'i, as Chairman of the PRC, it is apparent from the wording of the order that the decision was initiated by Mao Tse-tung, as Chairman of the Party, and that the army was an instrument of the Party rather than the state.

> The state adopted the following decision . . . so that the revolutionary spirit and glorious tradition of the PLA — a great army led by the great CCP and guided by the great Mao Tse-tung's thinking—should have full expression and so there should be identity between the three services and between officers and men . . .[43]

The order went on to say that the cap insignia, epaulettes and collar insignia, and the insignia denoting various services, arms, and branches should be abolished. The Liberation Army Daily editorial on the democratization measure stated:

> Our army had no system of military rank during the pro-
> tracted revolutionary wars in the past. This system [rank,
> different uniforms, and so on] came into effect in 1955,
> after victory throughout the country. Ten years of practice
> has proved that it is not in conformity with our army's
> glorious tradition with the close relation between officers
> and men, between the higher and lower levels, and between
> the army and the people . . .[44]

While stating that in general the system of rank was not in conformity with the army's glorious traditions, the editorial went on to specify benefits to be derived from abolition of rank differentiations

> The abolition of the open expression of gradations in mili-
> tary rank will help eliminate certain objective factors con-
> tributing to breeding rank conciousness and ideas to gain
> fame and wealth; it will also help us more conciously to
> place ourselves in the position of ordinary soldiers and
> ordinary workers, remold ourselves ideologically, and
> go further in establishing the idea of whole hearted ser-
> vice to the people.[45]

The editorial concluded that the effect of the order would promote the revolutionization of the army, and, under the leadership of Mao Tse-tung, make it "an extremely proletarian and militant army."

THE ATTEMPTED USE OF THE ARMY IN
THE CULTURAL REVOLUTION

Politization and democratization of the army had apparently brought it more into line with Mao Tse-tung's ideology. The influence of political officers and Party representatives had increased greatly in the PLA, and now Mao was prepared to use the army* in the ideolo-gical indoctrination and reformation of the masses. As early as 1964, Chou En-lai foretold the coming storm of the Cultural Revolution.

---

*Specifically, the GPD. —Ed.

As he summed up the campaign to "learn from the PLA" at the Third
National People's Congress, he warned that constant vigilance was
necessary to attain and retain a uni-class society. He stated:

> New bourgeois elements, new bourgeois intellectuals and
> other new exploiters will be ceaselessly generated in
> society, in Party and government organs, in economic
> organizations, and in cultural and education departments.
> These new bourgeois elements and other exploiters will
> invariably try to find their protectors and agents in the
> higher leading organizations.[46]

Chou went on to warn that a great debate was taking place on a series
of questions of principle, involving philosophy, political economy,
history, education, culture, and art. He specified, "In the Cultural
Revolution building of the new comes only after, or side by side with
the destruction of the old."[47]

The Cultural Revolution finally exploded in August, 1966, and
heralded two turbulent years of struggle to reform the Chinese people
as the PLA had been reformed. On August 8, the Central Committee
of the Chinese Communist Party issued its sixteen-point decision
aimed at crushing "those persons in authority taking the capitalist
road." It was apparent that Mao felt that the ideological indoctrination
of the PLA needed little additional guidance. In the twelve columns
of type in which the decision was printed, only six lines were devoted
to the PLA. These read:

> In the armed forces, the Cultural Revolution and the social-
> ist education movement should be carried out in accordance
> with the instructions of the Military Commission of the Cen-
> tral Committee and the General Political Department of
> the People's Liberation Army.[48]

The decision to use the army to take sides and support the "side of
the left," was probably not anticipated, but the use of the army to
indoctrinate the masses was certainly planned.[49] As early as 1966,
it was reported that members of the PLA were transferred to teaching
positions in schools while remaining full-time members of the army.[50]

Ideologically reliable and politically indoctrinated teams of
soldiers were formed to propagated the "thought of Mao Tse-tung"
throughout the countryside. CNA reports in June, 1968:

> Some troops in North China organized 100,000 persons

for the propaganda of the Thoughts; the troops in Lanchow
sent 15,000 military Party members in 500 Mao Thought
Propaganda Teams to the villages of 110 counties.
Mukden and Tsinan troops each sent 100,000 of their men
to the villages; the troops stationed on Hainan Island went
to the hamlets of the national minorities of Li and Miao
tribes.[51]

Fifteen thousand troops organized into 500 teams would mean teams
of 30 soldiers each. If the same organization were used by the North
China troops, this would amount to 3,300 teams of 30 soldiers each
in that part of North China alone. There are only slightly more than
2,000 counties (hsien) in the whole of China. If the function of propaganda teams was carried out in all military regions on the same
scale, it seems a reasonable calculation that a majority of the people
were reached by the PLA Mao-Thought teams.

Not only was the PLA used in ideological indoctrination, but it
was also instrumental in the formation of Revolutionary Committees
through which China has been governed since the Cultural Revolution.
(Party Committees on the provincial, hsien, and municipal level are
still being formed and will presumably take over some of the responsibilities of the Revolutionary Committees. The PLA is also substantially represented on these).*

Since the Cultural Revolution, the army has been lauded as "a
pillar of proletarian dictatorship,"[52] and a great deal of care has
been taken to ensure that the soldier and civilian population do not
become alienated from each other—that the army and the people are
one and the same. It is through identification of the people with the
army that the leaders of Communist China retain control over the
military.

There still remains, however, the issue of civil (Party) control
over the army to ensure that the gun does not control the Party. As
the aim of objective control of a professional army is to render it
"politically sterile," subjective control over military forces is attained
by "denial of an independent military sphere, and maximum participation by the military in politics."[53] Mao Tse-tung and Minister of
Defense Lin Piao have repeatedly attempted to avoid identification
of the army as distinct from the people. To accomplish this, numerous

---

*For statistics, see Chapter 6 by Ting Wang.—Ed.

campaigns have been organized to "serve the People" and "learn from the PLA," culminating in the movement to Support the Armed Forces and Love the People. This latter movement was originated in 1956, but received a great deal of attention as a result of army involvement in the Cultural Revolution.[54] Lin Piao clearly stated the position of the PLA in his report to the Ninth Party Congress:

> The People's Liberation Army is the mighty pillar of the dictatorship of the proletariat. Chairman Mao has pointed out many times. [sic] From the Marxist point of view the main component of the state is the army. The Chinese People's Liberation Army personally founded and led by Chairman Mao is an army of the workers and peasants, an army of the proletariat . . . We must carry forward the glorious tradition of "supporting the government and cherishing the people," strengthen the unity between the army and the people, strengthen the building of the militia and of national defense and do a still better job in all our work.[55]

Thus, the dual ideological principles of the mass line and class conciousness continue to govern the orientation and style of the PLA. The PLA depends on the active support of the politically indoctrinated and aroused people. The PLA itself is a politically active and highly indoctrinated element of Chinese society. Second, the revolutionary army is identified synonymously with the "people" and hence does not represent a military class distinct from the people. Its role, however, must remain that of a servant of the people and never the master. In this respect, the People's Daily states: "An army above class is non-existent in this world and an army without the leadership of the 'Party' is non-existent . . ."[56]

If in the 1970s the PLA continues to adhere to the principles of the mass line and a single class in practice, it will be unique among the armies of the world. Certainly, its strength will lie in the active support of the masses and in its identification as an army of the Party of the proletariat. While organizationally the PLA may remain an element of the state government, in practice it will probably be the army of the new Chinese Communist Party.

NOTES

1. See "Basic Differences Between the Proletarian and Bourgeois Military Lines," PR, No. 48, November 24, 1967, pp. 11-16; reprinted in SCMP, no. 4028, September, 1967.

2. Samuel P. Huntington, The Soldier and the State (New York: Vintage Books, 1957).

3. Mao Tse-tung, Selected Works of Mao Tse-tung, 4 vols., II (Peking: Foreign Languages Press, 1965), 209.

4. See James Emmett Garvey, Marxist-Leninist China: Military and Social Doctrine (New York: Exposition Press, 1960), pp. 105-45.

5. Ralph L. Powell, Communist China's Military Doctrines, RAC-TP-269 (McLean, Va.: Research Analysis Corporation, November, 1967), p. 10.

6. See Garvey, Marxist-Leninist China, pp. 106-11. See also Mao Tse-tung, "On Contradiction," Selected Works, I, 311-46, in which Mao discusses the antagonisms of class and clearly implies that the elimination of the bourgeois class will resolve these antagonisms.

7. Garvey, Marxist-Leninist China, p. 208.

8. Mao Tse-tung, Selected Works, II, 224.

9. See NCNA, "Common Program of the CPPCC," September 29, 1949.

10. Edgar Snow, The Other Side of the River: Red China Today (New York: Random House, 1961), p. 714. See also Samuel B. Griffith II, The Chinese People's Liberation Army (New York, McGraw-Hill, 1967), p. 106; and Allen S. Whiting, China Crosses the Yalu (New York: The Macmillan Company, 1960), passim.

11. See Whiting, China Crosses the Yalu, pp. 80, 90, 126, 159-60. Chow Ching-wen, Ten Years of Storm (New York: Holt, Rinehart and Winston, 1960), pp. 116-17, states that heated debate took place regarding the advisability of entry into the Korean War. Those against such entry included not only civilians, but some army generals as well. Mao Tse-tung is said to have paced the floor for three days and nights before he reached a decision to intervene.

12. Griffith, The Chinese People's Liberation Army, p. 103, states that captured weapons and supplies in the Chinese Communist arsenal included a reported 54,400 artillery pieces (this figure may include mortars), 319 machine guns, 1,000 tanks and armored cars, 20,000 motor vehicles, and great quantities of other arms and

equipment. In regard to Soviet aid, between 1950 and 1957 the Soviets provided China with approximately $2 billion in aid; not until 1965 was the debt thus incurred repaid in full. See Raymond L. Garthoff, "Sino-Soviet Military Relations, 1945-66," in Raymond L. Garthoff, ed. Sino-Soviet Military Relations (New York: Frederick A. Praeger, 1966), p. 85.

13. See John Gittings, The Role of the Chinese Army (New York: Oxford University Press, 1967), pp. 144-48.

14. NCNA, "Regulations on the Service of Officers of the Chinese People's Liberation Army," February 9, 1955; CB (American Consulate General, Hong Kong), No. 312, February, 1955.

15. See Ellis Joffe, "The Conflict Between the Old and the New," in Roderick MacFanquhar, ed., China Under Mao (Cambridge, Mass.: The M.I.T. Press, 1966).

16. NCNA, "Common Program," February 9, 1955. The CPPCC, which adopted this Common Program, presumably met in September, 1954, at the time of the convening of the First National People's Congress. See also Franz Schurmann, Ideology and Organization in Communist China (Berkeley and Los Angeles: University of California Press, 1968), pp. 178-79; and Handbook on People's China (Peking: Foreign Languages Press, 1957), pp. 204-5.

17. Garvey, Marxist-Leninist China, p. 208.

18. Griffith, The Chinese People's Liberation Army, p. 22. See also Ralph L. Powell, "Everyone a Soldier," Foreign Affairs, xxxix, 1 (October, 1960). For background in formation, see Stuart R. Schram, "Mao's Military Deviation," Problems of Communism, XIII, 1 (January-February, 1964), pp. 49-56; and W. T. de Bary, "Chinese Despotism and the Confucian Ideal," in John K. Fairbank, ed., Chinese Thought and Institutions (Chicago: University of Chicago Press, 1957), pp. 192-93.

19. Schram, "Mao's Military Deviation."

20. Powell, "Everyone a Soldier", pp. 100-111.

21. "Develop the Glorious Tradition of the Unity of Arms and Labour," LAD, June 26, 1958.

22. See "We Must Do Substantial Work in Building Up the

Militia," in J. Chester Cheng, ed., PLA Kung-tso Tung-hsun: The Politics of the Chinese Red Army (Stanford, Cal.: The Hoover Institution on War, Revolution, and Peace, 1966), pp. 559-65.

23. See "Summing-up Report of the General Political Department on the Adjustment of Party Branches," in Cheng, Kung-tso, p. 595. See also Gittings, The Role of the Chinese Army, pp. 246-47.

24. Ellis Joffe, Party and Army: Professionalism and Political Control in the Chinese Officer Corps, 1949-1964 (Cambridge, Mass.: Harvard University Press, 1967), pp. 70-80; also Gittings, The Role of the Chinese Army, p. 158.

25. Joffe, "The Conflict Between the Old and the New," p. 43.

26. "Strengthen Party Committee Leadership Over Battle Training," editorial, LAD March 24, 1965.

27. These regulations may be found in Mao Tse-tung, Selected Works, III, 224, and IV, 155-56; and in Mao Tse-tung, Selected Military Writings (Peking: Foreign Language Press, 1963) pp. 341-42. They were originally set down in 1928 by Mao Tse-tung when the Workers' and Peasants' Army was in the Kingkang Mountains of Kiangsi. In 1947, they were reissued in the following form:

Three Main Rules of Discipline:
  1. Obey orders in all your actions
  2. Don't take a single needle or piece of thread from
     the masses
  3. Turn in everything captured

Eight Points of Attention:
  1. Speak politely
  2. Pay fairly for what you buy
  3. Return everything you borrow
  4. Pay for anything you damage
  5. Don't hit or swear at people
  6. Don't damage crops
  7. Don't take liberties with women
  8. Don't ill-treat captives

28. Richard D. Baum, "Red and Expert: The Political-Ideological Foundations of China's Great Leap Forward," Asian Survey, IV, 9 (September, 1964), p. 1049.

29. For additional reading on the Officers to the Ranks movement, see Griffith, The Chinese People's Liberation Army, p. 227; Joffe, "The Conflict Between the Old and the New," p. 136; Joffe, Party and Army, pp. 133-37; and Gittings, The Role of the Chinese Army, pp. 192-95.

30. Analysis of the Sino-Soviet differences at the time can be found in The Origin and Development of the Differences Between the Leadership of the CSPU and Ourselves (Peking: Foreign Languages Press, 1963); Harold P. Ford, "The Eruption of Sino-Soviet Politico-Military Problems 1957-1960," in Garthoff, Sino-Soviet Military Relations; John R. Thomas, "The Limits of Alliance," ibid.; Alice L. Hsieh, Communist China's Strategy in the Nuclear Era (Englewood Cliffs, N.J.: Prentice-Hall, 1962); and Harold C. Hinton, Communist China in World Politics (Boston: Houghton Mifflin Company, 1966).

The Great Leap Forward initially referred only to programs of China's economic development under the Three Red Banners (San Mien Hung Ch'i). Subsequently, the entire program has come to be known as the Great Leap Forward. See Asia Research Centre, The Great Cultural Revolution in China (Hong Kong: The Green Pagoda Press, 1967).

31. Hsiao Hua, "Participation in National Construction is a Glorious Task of the PLA," HC, August 1, 1959; SCMM (American Consulate General, Hong Kong), No. 182, September, 1959.

32. David A. Charles, "The Dismissal of Marshal P'eng Teh-huai," in Roderick MacFarquhar, ed., China Under Mao (Boston: MIT Press, 1966)

33. "Basic Differences Between the Proletarian and the Bourgeois Military Lines," pp. 11-16.

34. Hinton, Communist China in World Politics, p. 65. Cf. James T. Meyers, "The Fall of Chairman Mao," Current Scene (American Consulate General, Hong Kong), VI, 10 (June 15, 1968), p. 6.

35. A full translation of the endorsement and the resolution appears in Cheng, Kung-tso, pp. 65-74. Emphasis added.

36. Ibid., p. 66ff.

37. See Alexander George, The Chinese Communist Army in Action (New York: Columbia University Press, 1967), p. 205.

38. "The Whole Country Must Learn from the PLA," JMJP, editorial, February 1, 1964; FBIS, No. 24, February 4, 1964. See also John Gittings "The 'Learn from the PLA' Campaign," China Quarterly, No. 18, March-June, 1964; Ralph L. Powell, "Commissars in the Economy, 'Learn from the PLA' Movement in China," Asian Survey, V, 3 (March, 1965), 125-38; and CNA No. 506, February 28, 1964.

39. Ibid.

40. NCNA, "Summary of Chou En-lai's Report at Third NCP," December 30, 1964; FBIS, No. 254, December 31, 1964, p. ccc15.

41. Griffith, The Chinese People's Liberation Army, p. 28.

42. See "Regulations on the Service of Officers."

43. NCNA, May 25, 1965. Also published in FBIS, No. 110, May 25, 1965, p. ccc1.

44. FBIS, No. 110, May 25, 1965, p. ccc2.

45. Ibid. Emphasis added.

46. Ibid., No. 254, December 31, 1964, p. ccc9.

47. Ibid., p. ccc11.

48. "Decision of the CCP Central Committee Concerning the Great Proletarian Cultural Revolution," PR, No. 33, August 12, 1966.

49. "Decision of the CCP Central Committee, the State Council, the Military Commission of the Central Committee, and the Cultural Revolution Group Under the Central Committee on Resolute Support for the Revolutionary Masses of the Left," CB, No. 852, January 23, 1967, p. 49.

50. See CNA, No. 715, June 5, 1968.

51. CNA No. 711, June 14, 1968. For other phases of military control, see CNA, Nos. 707, 708, 710, 712, 715.

52. See "Order Issued by the CCP Central Committee, the State Council, Central Military Affairs Committee and Central Cultural Revolution Group Forbidding the Seizure of Army Equipment, and Other Military Supplies from the PLA," SCMP, No. 4026, September 22, 1967.

53. Huntington, Soldier and the State, Ch. 4, pp. 80-97.

54. See PR, No. 37, September 8, 1967, p. 8.

55. Lin Piao, "Report to the Ninth Congress of the Chinese Communist Party," PR, No. 18, April 30, 1960, p. 25.

56. JMJP, December 11, 1968; and SCMP, No. 4326, December, 1968, p. 2.

CHANGING PATTERNS
OF MILITARY ROLES
IN CHINESE POLITICS

Parris H. Chang

As a result of the Cultural Revolution since 1966, the PLA has risen to unprecedented political ascendency in Communist China, and many important, far-reaching changes have taken place in the Chinese political system. This essay proposes to analyze the changes in military-party interactions and in the role of the PLA in Chinese politics.

THE HISTORICAL LEGACY

Since the middle of nineteenth century, due to recurrent domestic rebellions and foreign invasion, the political influence of military leaders had been in ascendency. This trend continued in Republican China after 1911 and climaxed in the warlord period of the 1920s. Although Chiang Kai-shek defeated some warlords by force and established a semblance of national unity after 1928, national unification was little more than the elimination of northern warlord forces by a coalition of southern warlord forces. That coalition then provided the backbone of the leadership of the Kuomintang and the Nationalist government during 1928-49.

In the history of the Chinese Communist movement, the military and the Party could hardly be distinguished, as most Communist leaders concurrently held leadership positions in the military and Party hierarchies. Nonetheless, a policy of civilian (Party) supremacy and control over the military was put forth in the Kut'ien Resolution in 1929. This policy, epitomized in the expression that the Party should command the gun and the gun should not be allowed to direct the Party, gradually evolved into a cardinal principle of the Chinese Communist Party (CCP) and was often invoked to settle the differences between the military and Party leaders and to justify Party control of the military.

Prior to 1949, because of the wartime situation and because the Party and military leaders were virtually identical, conflicts between the Party and the military were minimized; yet, it is also undeniable that the principle of civilian supremacy had already gained wide acceptance among the Chinese Communists, including the PLA leaders. This was further demonstrated in an orderly transition of power after the early 1950s. It will be recalled that at the time of the Communist takeover and consolidation during 1949-52 military leaders had directly ruled China through the Military Control Committee and the Military and Administrative Committee, the highest organs of authority in China's provinces and six major regions. As Communist power was consolidated, however, the military governors of the provinces rapidly "returned to the barracks" and handed political power over to civilian Party/government officials. In some cases, they themselves took up civilian posts in the provinces and gave up their military status. By 1954, the vestiges of the earlier military rule had largely disappeared. Civilian governing structures, headed by civilians (with the few exceptions of border regions like Sinkiang and Yunnan) replaced the previous military bodies in the provinces, and the Peking regime proclaimed its Constitution. From then until the early 1960s, there was more or less a separation of civilian and military functions. Party/government cadres and PLA officials became highly specialized in their respective spheres of work

Due to this division of labor and the specialization of functions between civilian Party officials and military officials, conflicts inevitably arose between the Party and PLA leadership. It is true that the top PLA officials were represented in the Party's important decision-making bodies, such as the Politburo and the Central Committee (CC). Still, the interlocking Party-military leadership could mitigate but could not eliminate conflicts of interests between the Party and the military. The military, by the nature of its special functions, had its own particular interests. Even though military leaders were also leaders of the Party, they found themselves compelled by the logic of their special responsibilities and the special concerns of their own constituency to fight for military priorities and to resist the demands of other Party leaders. There were numerous issues of contention between the Party and military leaders in 1949-66. Chief among these were the entry into the Korean War, the degree of professionalization of the PLA and politicization of the PLA, the degree of participation in economic tasks, the build-up of the militia, the Quemoy-Matsu crisis, Sino-Soviet relations, and the Chinese response to the escalation of the war in Vietnam.[1]

Without exception, each of these and other issues of contention was settled in favor of civilian Party leaders' policy priorities. One major reason for the Party's ability to impose its priorities on the PLA was the general acceptance by the polity of the principle of civilian supremacy and party control over the military. The PLA leaders, despite their control of the instrument of violence, could only lobby the Party leadership through prescribed channels. Not unlike representatives of an interest group, the PLA leaders participated in the decision-making process as claimants and advisers to the Party leadership; they advocated certain courses of action in domestic and foreign policy, demanded a greater allocation of resources, and tried to protect as well as advance their corporate interests. When the PLA could only resort to lobbying and politicking in its political conflict with the civilian Party leadership and when the arena of such conflict was in the Politburo or the CC, where the civilians had greater control, the military leaders were easily outvoted.

The best illustration of civilian supremacy was provided by the Lushan Affair in the summer of 1959. When the Party held an enlarged Politburo meeting at Lushan in July, 1959, Marshal P'eng Teh-huai, a Politburo member and Minister of Defense, submitted a memorandum attacking Mao Tse-tung's Great Leap Forward and commune policies. Although a large number of PLA officials signed the memorandum in support of P'eng's action, his challenge to the Party leadership, although short of a threat or actual use of naked force (of which P'eng was obviously capable, inasmuch as he himself and his close collaborator, General Huang Ko-cheng, the PLA's Chief of Staff, had the power to deploy troops), was eventually defeated in a CC plenum that followed the enlarged Politburo session. Marshal P'eng and General Huang were replaced by Marshal Lin Piao and General Lo Jui Ch'ing as Minister of Defense and PLA Chief of Staff, respectively.

THE RISE OF PLA POLITICAL INFLUENCE
IN THE EARLY 1960s

On assuming the leadership of the PLA in the fall of 1959, Marshal Lin Piao moved quickly and vigorously to indoctrinate the PLA in the thought of Mao Tse-tung, to raise the political-ideological standards of the PLA, to rebuild the Party control mechanism within the army, and to reverse his predecessor's alleged emphasis on professionalism. Lin Piao, in his first public statement as head of the military establishment, pledged the "unconditional loyalty of the People's Liberation Army to the Party and to Comrade Mao";[2] from 1960 onward he carried out an intensive campaign of political indoctrination in the PLA, centering on the study and application of the thought of Mao.[3]

Mao evidently adjudged the army's campaign much more effective than those that had been carried out in the nonmilitary sectors of society in the first half of the 1960s, such as the socialist-education campaign and the ideological-rectification campaign in arts and literature. Accordingly, the PLA was held up before the nation as the paradigm of the correct "Communist work style," and individual soldiers said to have distinguished themselves by their selflessness and ideological dedication, such as Lei Feng and Wang Chieh, were made models for emulation campaigns.

Further evidence that Lin Piao and the PLA were now the repositories of Mao's highest confidence was provided by the latter's call in December, 1963, for the whole country to "learn from the PLA." All political, economic, and social organizations were directed to study and emulate the army's methods of organization, operation, and ideological training. That this call was an indirect rebuke to the Party for not having done its job properly is unmistakable in retrospect. Even more important, from 1964 on steps were taken to establish a network of "political work departments"—clearly modeled after the PLA's political commissar system—in party and government organizations. These departments were staffed primarily by political cadres transferred from the PLA. PLA veterans also took over many other positions in the government, Party, and industry normally held by civilians, while civilian cadres in the economy were sent to PLA schools for training.

It is paradoxical that, on the one hand, there were extensive efforts before 1963 to bring the PLA under tight Party control and to rectify its professionalism, but, on the other hand, after 1963 the PLA increasingly became competitive with the Party and made inroads into those functions previously in the domain of the Party. The main explanation of this paradox lies in the division of the Party leadership. In the wake of the collapse of the Great Leap Forward programs, many top CCP leaders, such as Liu Shao-ch'i, Teng Hsiao-p'ing, and others, had begun seriously to doubt the infallability of Mao's leadership and questioned Mao's methods for modernizing and revolutionizing China. Opposed and obstructed by his colleagues who controlled the Party organization, Mao was compelled to find a new power base outside the Party organization to project his will, and he subsequently turned to the PLA,* which had, in his eyes, evolved into the foremost revolutionary organization in China.

It is tempting to view the political prominence of the PLA during and after the Cultural Revolution as the end result of the developments just discussed. Yet to do so would be to ignore the special and largely unforseen circumstances that came into being with the unfolding of the Cultural Revolution. To put it another way, the PLA did not seize political power through a military coup as the military has done in many other political systems. Rather, power devolved into the hands of the PLA largely by default, and the PLA's assumption of various political functions in the Chinese political system came only gradually, more as a result of outside circumstances than of its own initiative.

There is no evidence, moreover, to substantiate the thesis that Mao or Lin Piao originally planned to use the PLA to assail and re-place the Party.** Mao did use the PLA for political purposes, but initially these purposes and the political role of the PLA were limited. The emulation of individual model soldiers, such as the hero Lei Feng and the entire PLA, can in retrospect be viewed as a tactic by Mao to press the Party to reinvigorate itself with revolutionary élan.[4] In time, Mao intensified the pressure by broadening the role of the PLA, such as the establishment of a network of "political work de-partments" in Party, governmental, and economic organizations that as pointed out before, were modeled after the PLA's political organi-zation and staffed largely by its officers. Despite these efforts, Mao did not seem to have succeeded in reforming the Party and in pushing it to carry out the policies he favored. Only then did Mao apparently decide to use the PLA as a power base to attack and remove the centers of opposition within the Party.***

---

*And, particularly, the GPD.—Ed.

**The reader should note how this judgement differs from that of James D. Jordan in Chapter 2. The two authors represent two distinctive schools of thought about the relative power and influence of Mao in directing the Cultural Revolution and awarding power to the PLA.—Ed.

***Although Professor Chang has not made the distinction between professional commanders and political commissars that Jordan notes

The first such sign came on November 29, 1965, when the organ
of the PLA, the Liberation Army Daily, reproduced an article by Yao
Wen-yuan that criticized a historical play by Wu Han, vice-mayor of
Peking, and accompanied it with an "Editor's Note" that denounced the
play as a "big poisonous weed." The significance of this PLA move
should be briefly explained here. It is now well known that Mao had
harbored resentment against Wu Han, who authored the historical
play "The Dismissal of Hai Jui," allegedly to defend Marshal P'eng
Teh-huai's criticism of Mao at the Lushan Meeting. Mao had called
for the Party to publicly repudiate Wu. Mao's demand was resisted
by other Party leaders, particularly Wu's superior, P'eng Chen. Mao
then instructed Yao Wen-yuan to write an article, published on November 10, 1965, in the Shanghai Wen-hui Pao, to attack Wu Han and, by
extension, P'eng Chen and others who supported P'eng. Due to his
political skill, however, P'eng succeeded temporarily in circumventing
the publicity and minimizing the political repercussions of Yao's article by ordering newspapers and journals outside of Shanghai not to
reproduce it. The reproduction of the article in the Liberation Army
Daily, however, gave it not only the badly needed publicity but also
signaled the PLA endorsement of its attack. Moreover, the severe
indictment made by the PLA's organ had the effect of redefining the
nature of the offenses by Wu Han and his protectors.[5]

From that time on, the PLA steadily broadened its role in the
political arena as Mao used certain elements of the PLA as his instrument of power to struggle with other Party leaders who were
entrenched in the Party organizations.* On February 2, 1966, Lin
Piao entrusted Chiang Ch'ing (Madame Mao) to convene a Forum on
the Literary and Art Work in the Armed Forces in Shanghai, attended
exclusively by GPD representatives.[6] At the conclusion of the eighteen-
day forum, a summary report was prepared under Chiang Ch'ing's
guidance and revised three times by Mao personally before its release.[7]

The forum summary did not confine itself to literary matters
in the armed forces. It also spelled out the Maoist position, policy,

---

in Chapter 2, it is important to underscore the point that Mao's faith
was probably placed primarily in the GPD—not the PLA as a whole.
Note that the Liberation Army Daily is managed and produced by
the GPD. It is illusory to call it "The organ of the PLA."—Ed.

*Of these elements, the GPD was of crucial importance.—Ed.

and intention on the Cultural Revolution in the nation. It pointed out that the literary and art circles had basically failed to carry out Mao's instructions and that the cultural front was dominated by an anti-Party and antisocialist "black line." Moreover, it called for a "great socialist revolution on the cultural front" and the complete elimination of this black line and stated that the PLA "must play an important role in the socialist cultural revolution."[8] The Maoists later claimed that the summary was "in direct opposition to the counter-revolutionary 'February [1965] Outline Report,' and launched a vigorous attack on the counter-revolutionary revisionist line."[9] Clearly, Mao had secured the full backing of Lin Piao and hoped to use the most politically competent element of the PLA as a power base, but only to fight P'eng Chen and his allies in the central Party apparatus, not necessarily to replace the Party system throughout China.

In the spring of 1966, the organ of the PLA took the lead and set the pace in the attacks on Mao's intellectual critics and their supporters within the Party hierarchy. For instance, the editorial of the Liberation Army Daily on April 18, which was based on and paraphrased the PLA Forum's summary, declared war on the anti-Party, antisocialist "black line" in the nation's cultural front. Furthermore, the PLA's organ now openly challenged the Party's authority by attacking and ridiculing the editorials of the Party's organ, the People's Daily.[10] In May, Lin Piao was apparently a key figure at the enlarged Politburo session that sealed the fate of P'eng Chen and other top leaders such as Lo Tai-ch'ing and Lu Ting-yi. In a speech there, Lin expressed his wholehearted supported for Mao, warned of the danger of capitalist restoration in China, and strongly hinted that the danger was most acute at the upper levels of the Party leadership.[11]

In the summer of 1966, at least limited professional command (Lin Piao-affiliated) as well as GPD support was crucial to Mao's defeat of Liu and Teng. There were reports that troops loyal to Lin Piao were moved into Peking in June, 1966; in fact, the veteran commander Fu Ts'ung-pi, a long-time aide of another professional, Yang Cheng-wu, the newly appointed Acting Chief of Staff, took over the command of the Peking garrison at this juncture. The organ of the Party (and P'eng Chen's propaganda apparatus), the People's Daily, was reorganized on June 1 and placed under the control of the PLA. It is not known whether troops were used to intimidate Mao's opponents during the Eleventh Central Committee Plenum, held in August, 1966. Nevertheless, it is quite obvious that certain PLA leaders played a very vital role in the initial victory of Mao and the defeat of his opponents in the plenum; this can be seen from the fact that

Lin Piao was chosen as Mao's deputy and heir-apparent, and three marshals of the PLA, Yeh Chien-ying, Hsü Hsiang-ch'ien, and Nieh Jung-chen, were rewarded with membership in the Politburo.

PLA INVOLVEMENT IN THE POLITICS OF
THE CULTURAL REVOLUTION

Although a few leaders and political units of the PLA played a substantial role in helping Mao to defeat such powerful Party figures as Liu Shao-ch'i and Teng Hsiao-p'ing in the Eleventh Central Committee Plenum in August, 1966, and were also instrumental in organizing and providing transport and logistical support for the hordes of Red Guards who journeyed to Peking in the summer and fall of 1966, a more extensive PLA intervention in the Cultural Revolution was evidently not planned from the outset. In fact, it appears that many of the PLA's professional commanders were opposed to army involvement in what they considered to be an intra-Party dispute and initially adopted a hands-off policy.

Indeed, in the course of the assaults on provincial Party structures by Red Guards and "revolutionary rebels" following the Eleventh Plenum, many local PLA commanders and commissars appeared to give their sympathy to provincial authorities. Such a political posture is understandable since local PLA units had had the responsibility of assisting in the maintainence of law and order and were thus part of the establishment. Many local military leaders probably viewed those attacking the establishment with suspicion and resentment and were more inclined to align themselves with the provincial Party leaders.

Personal and organizational ties between PLA and Party leaders were also close. In many provinces, children of the local PLA leaders and local Party leaders had worked together to organize the initial Red Guard groups, an action possibly initiated by the parents and in any case quite likely to affect parental attitudes. Moreover, since senior regional-provincial Party secretaries often served concurrently as first political commissars of military regions or districts and the PLA commanders also served in the Party's regional bureaus or provincial committees, close official ties tended to be forged between civilian Party leaders and PLA officials.* The reported "confession"

---

*An additional source of local Party-military bonds was their shared experiences in the same field army that had conquered the area that the local leaders now managed.—Ed.

of Ch'en Tsai-tao, the Commander of the Wuhan Military Region until July, 1967, shed some light on the nature of the civilian-military alliance and deserves to be quoted in length:

> After recuperating for over a year, I returned to Wuhan
> in September last year [1966]. As a Standing Committee
> Member of the Hupeh Provincial Party Committee, I at-
> tended sessions of the Standing Committee after my re-
> turn to Wuhan; I listened to the opinions of Chang T'i-
> hsueh [acting first secretary] and sided with him. . . .
> I followed Chang T'i-hsueh and promptly answered his
> call whenever he wanted me. He asked me to preside
> over four general meetings convened by the conservatives
> . . . In all of the rallies that I had attended I sided with
> the provincial Party committee and the conservatives,
> supporting the conservatives and suppressing the rebels,
> embellishing the provincial Party Committee and advanc-
> ing the cause of Chang T'i-hsueh. . . . In shielding Chang
> T'i-hsueh, I accommodated him in a rented house and pro-
> vided his staff with office premises. I was even prepared
> to provide them with an office building. What for? I did
> so to hide, and provide cover for, the members of this
> black provincial Party committee and to support their
> reactionary line.[12]

In many provinces, the Party leaders deposited in the PLA headquarters the "black materials" that they had collected to prevent them from falling into the hands of the Red Guards; or they persuaded the local PLA leaders to deploy troops to guard the premises of the Party against a possible "rebel" invasion. Some civilian Party leaders allegedly also put on PLA uniforms, rode in cars carrying military license plates, and worked in the office of the local PLA headquarters, using those quarters as their "shelter."[13]

Thus, even though the PLA was originally to stay on the side-lines, the unfolding of unanticipated events and local PLA leaders' personal, political, and organizational ties rendered the PLA neutrality in the Cultural Revolution increasingly difficult. Those ties actually sustained Mao's later argument for more deliberate PLA intervention on his side. He was quoted as having said:

> The so-called "non-involvement" is false, for the army
> was already involved long ago. The question, therefore,
> is not one of involvement or non-involvement. It is one of
> whose side we should stand on and whether we should

support the revolutionaries or the conservatives or even
the rightists. The PLA should actively support the revolutionary leftists.[14]

On January 23, 1967, a central directive finally ordered the PLA
to "support the left," to intervene on the side of Maoists.[15] Although
the Maoists' leadership had thus succeeded in pushing the PLA into
support of the "revolutionary left," it was well aware that at least
some PLA leaders, both in Peking and in the provinces, were opposed
to using the PLA to crush opposition from within the Party.[16] Therefore, the Maoists reactivated the aged and semi-retired Marshal Hsü
Hsiang-ch'ien to head the All-PLA Cultural Revolution Group and
promoted Hsü and Marshal Ch'en Yi to the posts of vice-chairmen of
the Party's MAC in an apparent maneuver to commit them to Mao's
cause so that they would use their influence to win over their followers
and former associates in the PLA to Mao's side.

Any hopes that the PLA intervention would facilitate the seizure
of power were soon dispelled, however. Although some PLA units
in five provinces did help the Maoists to seize power during the first
quarter of 1967, in the rest of China the response of the PLA to the
order to support the left was rather equivocal. In many other provinces,
the PLA actually intervened against the Maoist rebels. This is understandable. The PLA has been part of the establishment; not surprisingly, it would have acted to preserve the establishment rather
than support the Maoists who sought to destroy the establishment.

Angered by the PLA's stand, the Maoists now pointed their
"spearhead of struggle" at the PLA; they invaded and stormed local
PLA headquarters and seized arms from the soldiers. In retaliation,
the PLA suppressed these groups as "reactionary" or "counterrevolutionary," and arrested their leaders and disbanded their organizations.[17] These unfavorable developments in the provinces were subsequently labeled by the Maoists as the "February [1967] adverse
current." In Peking, too, this "adverse current" found expression
in a conservative backlash in which T'an Chen-lin, a Politburo member and vice-premier in charge of the regime's over-all rural policy,
and other moderate elements in the leadership plucked up courage
to assert themselves, attacked the leadership of the Central Cultural
Revolutionary Group (CRG) headed by Ch'en Po-ta and Chiang Ch'ing,
and sought to curb the excesses of the "rebels," particularly their
indiscriminate attacks on veteran Party officials.[18]

The "February adverse current" sparked a crucial debate in
the Party's Central Work Conference at the end of March, 1967, on

the future course of the Cultural Revolution. CRG leaders who wanted to cut PLA powers apparently prevailed in the conference, for on April 1 and 6 both the CC and MAC issued orders forbidding the PLA units from arresting and persecuting "revolutionary masses," from labeling mass organizations "reactionary," and from suppressing them.[19] Instead, these orders advised the PLA to use persuasion, education, and political work.

Meanwhile, the power among provincial Party authorities was gradually devolving into the hands of local PLA leaders. On the one hand, the Red Guards' assaults on provincial authorities in what was called "seizure of power from below" (an emulation of the 1871 Paris Commune experience) had paralyzed the provincial Party and government machinery; on the other hand, the incompetence, intrigues, and infighting of different Red Guard and "revolutionary rebel" factions had resulted in the collapse of the Maoist strategy to establish a new political order. The PLA had to move into the power vacuum to maintain order. In those provinces where a Revolutionary Committee (RC), the new organ of power, had been formed (after February, 1967), military representatives constituted the backbone of the new leadership. In others where an RC had not been set up, local PLA leaders directly ruled these provinces through a Military Control Committee, virtually a military government. With the PLA becoming the new establishment, yet with its powers undercut by the early April central directives, the "revolutionary masses" now launched a new offensive against the military in various provinces. Factional struggle and infighting between opposing rebel groups continued unabated, and the incidence of "struggle by force," murders, riots, and disorderly demonstration increased throughout the country from April, 1967, onward.

As the power of the PLA had been cut, local PLA commanders apparently found it necessary to rely on some mass organizations and play them off against others; they chose to support one rebel faction over the other often on the basis of practical considerations. The groups PLA professional commanders favored and supported were usually less radical and were regarded by the CRG as "conservative." On the other hand, those groups the PLA opposed were usually more radical and vehemently antiestablishmentarian; although the PLA tended to see these unruly groups as troublemakers and react to their activities with hostility, the CRG tended to support these "revolutionary" groups. Under these circumstances, PLA leaders in quite a number of provinces were dismissed for having "committed errors in supporting the left."[20] The dismissal of local PLA leaders and the CRG's inclination to support those rebel groups that challenged the PLA authorities could not but alienate many other local PLA leaders who faced the same predicament.

Thus, when two Peking emissaries—Hsieh Fu-chih, a member of the Politburo and the MAC Standing Committee, and Wang Li, a member of the CRG and Acting Director of the Party's Propaganda Department—arrived at Wuhan on July 18 and admonished local PLA leaders for having supported the conservative faction and having suppressed the "revolutionary" faction, many senior military leaders were enraged, and an extreme reaction soon ensued. On July 20, 1967, Hsieh and Wang were kidnapped and physically abused by members of the Million Heroes, a group they had denounced, but they were supported by Ch'en Tsai-tao and Chung Han-hau, Commander and Political Commissar of the Wuhan Military Region, respectively.[21] According to Japanese reporters in Peking, PLA paratroops were dropped in Wuhan and ten warships were sent to Wuhan from the East China Sea to fight against Ch'en Tsai-tao's troops and supporters.[22] A civil war was avoided at the last minute when Ch'en capitulated and Hsieh and Wang were released on July 22. The Wuhan incident was an overt protest by local PLA commanders to the Peking leaders for not having sufficiently appreciated their plight and for allowing too much license to rebels.

Immediately after the Wuhan mutiny, the CRG officials openly called for the attack and overthrow of the "handful of capitalist power-holders in the Army, and incited rebels to drag out the "Ch'en Tsai-tao type" persons in the provinces.[23] Those rebel groups that were not supported or were hitherto suppressed by the local PLA began to take an offensive against local military authorities. Encouraged by a widely publicized statement by Chiang Ch'ing in July that "words should be used for attack and arms for defence" (wen kung wu wei), they raided the military headquarters and seized weapons from the soldiers and from the military warehouses; riots, fires, and armed clashes between the rebels and troops were widespread throughout China. In late July and August, public order in many Chinese provinces was in shambles.

THE CONSERVATIVE MILITARY BACKLASH:
THE SUBJUGATION OF RADICALS

Under these circumstances, in late July or early August, Mao apparently yielded to pressure from provincial PLA leaders, who compelled him to change the tack of the Cultural Revolution. The first sign of change came after a meeting of PLA leaders in Peking in August. On August 9, Lin Piao denounced the GPD and dismissed all of its senior members in Peking. At the end of August, Peking launched a "support the army and love the people" campaign. The obvious purpose of the campaign was to pacify the PLA and restore its prestige and authority. For instance, the editorial in the People's Daily, August 28, 1967, stated: "Without the PLA, there would be no proletarian dictatorship; and without the proletarian dictatorship, there would be no Great Proletarian Cultural Revolution. We must forever trust the PLA, support the PLA, and learn from the PLA."

In a secret speech on September 5, Chiang Ch'ing tacitly admitted the error of having advanced the slogan to attack and overthrow the "handful of capitalist power-holders in the Army," which had generated grave consequences and antagonized the military. She also enjoined the rebels not to raid the military headquarters or seize arms from the PLA. On the same day, an important directive was disseminated; this so-called September 5 Directive forbade rebels to invade the military complex or seize arms and authorized the PLA to use force to quell disobedience. In the first part of September, Mao toured six provinces in north, central, south, and east China, where serious disturbances had occurred, to confer with local military leaders.

With the balance of power in the leadership shifted against the radicals, those who had played an active role in directing the assault of the revolutionary masses on the old power structure and on the PLA met their downfall. In the fall and winter of 1967-68, Mu Hsin, Lin Chieh, Wang Li, Kuan Feng, and Ch'i Pen-yu, all members of the CRG and of the editorial staff of Red Flag, were purged. They were accused of backing and stagemanaging the ultra-left May 16 Corps, which had fiercely attacked Chou En-lai and his top aides in the State Council, particularly Ch'en Yi, Li Hsien-nien, and Li Fu-ch'un. For their own political survival, Ch'en Po-ta and Chiang Ch'ing found themselves forced to attack not only the May 16 Corps, which had probably acted under their guidance, but also their subordinates in the CRG.[24]

Moreover, as a result of the purge of the polemicists from its editorial staff and, undoubtedly, as a punitive action against its instigation of the rebels to attack the PLA, the Red Flag, the trumpet of the CRG, was suspended from publication from November, 1967, to July, 1968. Ch'en Po-ta, the head of the CRG, was reported to have made a self-criticism admitting that he had "committed serious mistakes."[25] Chiang Ch'ing also went into seclusion for seven weeks in November, 1967; according to Premier Chou, she was taking a "rest."

The political trend against extreme-left tendencies and the effect of the September 5 Directive were to make the PLA the controlling political force in China. For instance, the PLA held the dominant position in all eleven provinces where RCs were established during November, 1967, and March, 1968. The establishment of the new organ of power in these provinces, which politically symbolized the completion of "seizure of power" from the former provincial Party authorities, undermined the cause of the rebels and restricted further their scope of activities. In the same period, local military authorities, with their power enhanced and position vindicated, made great efforts to impose tight control over unruly and protesting groups. They sent the Red Guards and rebels back to schools and factories, enforced strict discipline against troublemakers, and forced various groups to disband or join the "great alliance" with rival factions in order to break up the organizational base of the rebels.

Despite occasional struggles by force among rival Red Guard and rebel groups that continued here and there, by March, 1968, the forces of the left at the top had apparently been checked and local PLA and RC authorities seemed to have the over-all situation in the provinces under control. Radical elements in the Chinese leadership, however, did regain the initiative briefly in March, 1968, resulting in the abrupt dismissal of acting PLA Chief of Staff Yang Cheng-wu, and two other military figures and in an intensive drive against rightist "opportunism," rightist "splitism," and rightist "reversal of verdict." The rebels, fired with new zeal, also intensified their attack on the RC authorities, and physical violence flared up again on a national scale. The radical upsurge, which was led by Ch'en Po-ta and Chiang Ch'ing, was short-lived, however. This was partly because the PLA and the new RC authorities had already broken up or had substantially weakened the organizational base of the CRG radicals and had severely restricted the scope of the activities of their followers in the provinces and partly because of disunity and increasing factional feuding among the leftist groups.

Even Mao himself reportedly became disillusioned with his vaunted revolutionary "vanguard." According to a story from Peking, he broke down and wept at a meeting with five top Red Guard leaders on July 28, 1968, bitterly condemning them for their failure to unite and their persistent squabbling. "You have let me down," Mao was quoted as saying, "and what is more, you have disappointed the workers, peasants, and army men of China."[26] Three days after this interview, Army Day (August 1) was celebrated with strong demonstrations of support for the PLA, and the joint editorial of the People's Daily, Red Flag, and the Liberation Army Daily hailed the PLA as "the staunch pillar of the dictatorship of the proletariat." Since August, 1968, the Red Guards have been consistently downgraded in Peking's official statements. An authoritative article published on August 25, 1968, in Red Flag (which had resumed publication in July) and reprinted prominently in the People's Daily the following day laid down the new line.27 Denouncing both the Red Guards and China's old intellectuals as vacillating and unreliable, it hailed the workers and peasants, acting in collaboration with the "commanders and fighters" of the PLA, as the staunchest and most dependable agents for carrying the Cultural Revolution through to complete victory.

Following this devaluation of their role, the Red Guards were subjected to more concrete disciplinary measures. After August, 1968, worker-peasant-soldier "teams for propagating the thought of Mao Tse-tung" physically moved into colleges, schools, and other cultural establishments to sort out recalcitrant students and intellectuals and carry out "struggle-criticism-transformation." Fresh attempts were again made to disband "illegal" mass organizations and to send students and unemployed youths to work in the countryside or in border regions.

By the early part of September, 1968, more or less stable RC's had been established in all of China's twenty-nine province-level administrative units. The completion of the new power structure, which was hailed, somewhat ironically, by the official press as a "great event" in achieving the "all-round victory" of the Cultural Revolution actually symbolized the end of the Maoist-sponsored mass movement seeking to seize power from below and to remake China's political life in an emulation of the Paris Commune. It also marked the beginning of a new era of reconstruction in which the Red Guards and rebel activists, once the vanguard of Mao's crusade, were to be kept under firm control and the power of established authority further consolidated and strengthened.

CHANGES IN THE POLITICAL ROLE OF THE PLA

As the preceding pages have shown, the pattern of military participation and the PLA's political role in the Chinese political system have changed drastically since the early 1960s, and particularly since the launching of the Cultural Revolution in 1966, with far-reaching consequences. Whereas in the 1950s PLA professional commanders acted more or less like a minority pressure group to lobby the Party civil leadership to protect and enhance corporate military interests, the PLA-Party relationship underwent a subtle but significant qualitative change in the first half of the 1960s. The GPD of the PLA, under Lin Piao's stewardship, became the Party's first competitive institution, becaming the object of national emulation after 1963 and rivaling the Party in prestige and political/ideological correctness. It also became Mao's instrument of power, used first to apply pressure on and then to attack the Party bureaucracy. In the spring and summer of 1966, the PLA GPD was virtually a veto group. It directly and closely participated in the resolution of political conflicts at the highest level, and its support for the Maoist faction resulted in the defeat and displacement of anti-Maoist Party leaders.

The open and extensive intervention in the Cultural Revolution by troop units and professional commanders of the PLA after early 1967, however, led to the substitution of PLA leaders for civilian Party/government authorities in most provinces and brought a military takeover of various political and economic functions previously performed by Party, government, and economic organizations. From the spring of 1967 onward, and for more than a year, local PLA leaders enforced a direct military rule in most of China's provinces through the mechanism of the Military Control Committee. Military predominance has continued ever since a semblance of order returned to the provinces. Thus, the PLA leaders have not only dominated the RC—the new structure of administration that replaced the previous government organization—in China's twenty-nine provincial-level units, but have also attained the highest leadership positions (first secretary) in twenty-one out of the twenty-nine reconstituted Provincial Party Committees,* previously the domain of the civilian Party officials.

In the new CC elected at the Ninth Party Congress, representatives of military-provincial forces overshadowed those of other political groups. For example, out of the 279 members (170 full members and 109 alternates), 127 (76 full members and 51 alternates), or 46 percent, are from PLA ranks. In terms of the CC members' locale of work, 127 of the 279 are working in the provinces, and 71 of

---

*Out of the 29 provincial-level Party Committees, 21 are headed by military men as first secretaries; among the 158 first secretaries, second secretaries, secretaries, and deputy secretaries, 95 (60 percent) are PLA men, 53 (33 percent) are former Party and government officials, and 10 (7 percent) are representatives of mass organizations. Moreover, 20 of the 29 Party first secretaries are also chairmen of the corresponding RCs.

these 127 are PLA men concurrently holding military and civilian posts. In the 25-man Politburo (21 full members and 4 alternates), 13 men actually wear the PLA uniform and provincial officials are represented by 3 full members and 3 alternates.

Furthermore, the provincial authorities have in recent years exercised considerable de facto control over economic activities, as was the case during the Great Leap Forward in the late 1950s, even though no decentralization measures have been formally decreed as was done in 1957-58. Many provinces have made great efforts to build up their own respective independent industrial system and are playing an important planning and production role in the drive to expand local industries. Whether such provincial efforts are undertaken in defiance of unified central planning, as has been hinted at obliquely,[28] or merely reflect a deliberate central policy, attributed to Mao himself, to disperse China's productive capacity and to make the provinces self-sufficient in preparation for a possible war cannot be easily determined. In any case, the provincial authorities have clearly enhanced their economic and political autonomy and strengthened their position vis-à-vis the central leadership.

If decentralization of power since the Cultural Revolution resembles in many aspects that of the late 1950s, it is also different in at least one important way. Whereas the provincial authorities in the late 1950s were led by civilian Party officials (except in outlying regions like Sinkiang and Tibet), local PLA commanders or professional political commisars now head the Party and government organization in most provinces, and the PLA leaders actually provide the backbone of the leadership in virtually every province. Whereas in the 1950s and prior to the Cultural Revolution in 1966, senior provincial or regional Party bureau secretaries served concurrently as first political commissars in the provincial military districts or military regions and thus provided Party control over the local PLA, today in most provinces this practice has been discontinued. Instead, local PLA commanders or professional political commissars are concurrently top provincial Party secretaries. The interlocking Party, government, and military leadership positions and the concentration of political, military, and financial power in the same hands have generated new power equations in Chinese politics. It seems very likely that the new provincial forces may ultimately prove more intractable and difficult to control by the central leadership, whoever they may be.

By mid-1968, Peking's leaders were already alarmed by signs of excessive local power and political fragmentation, as indicated by their criticism of manifestations of polycentrism. In a front-page editorial, the People's Daily emphatically stated:

> the proletarian headquarters headed by Chairman Mao . . .
> is the one and only leading centre for the whole Party,
> army, nation and all the revolutionary masses. They can
> have only such a centre and no other . . . The so-called
> theory of "many centres" is a reactionary theory of the
> bourgeois "mountain-stronghold" mentality and individ-
> ualism. It disintegrates the unity of the revolutionary
> ranks based on Mao Tse-tung's thought and hinders im-
> plementation of the proletarian revolutionary line. If
> every department and unit wanted to "make itself a
> centre" and there were many "centres" in the country,
> then there would be no centre at all.[29]

Apparently mindful of those provincial leaders who were more inclined to look after their own particular concerns in disregard of
central guidance, usually by citing special conditions in their own
areas, the same editorial called for Party officials to criticize and
repudiate the erroneous idea of "making oneself a center," strengthen
the proletarian concept of "viewing the situation as a whole," enhance
the "revolutionary sense of organization and discipline," and resolutely
carry out "all instructions" from the proletarian headquarters.

Despite these admonitions, the problems of polycentrism and
of officials acting independently of central-Party policy appear to
have persisted. This is indicated by a People's Daily editorial of
August 27, 1971, marking the completion of the reestablishment of
the twenty-nine Provincial Party Committees, that again called for
all Party members and all departments to place themselves "under
the absolute leadership of the Party and reject the reactionary theory
of many centers, that is, the theory of no center." In light of the
fact that the process of rebuilding the twenty-nine Provincial Party
Committees has taken two years and four months, since the Ninth
Party Congress of April, 1969, first laid down a new policy for Party
reconstruction, it seems reasonable to conclude that the Maoist
leadership at the center has not been able to impose its policy on
provincial authorities and may not have had the final say in the selection of officials of Provincial Party Committees.*

---

*It seems not an accident that a number of officials who had
come out to support the Maoist seizure of power in the early stages

CONCLUSIONS

The intervention of the PLA has resulted in its unpredecented rise to political predominance in the present Chinese polity. This outcome, so contrary to Mao's own dictum that the Party must direct the gun, did not seem to have been anticipated nor is it likely to be desired by him today. Now, with the mechanisms of social and political control seriously impaired and the image of the Party and its leadership badly tarnished in the course of the political turmoil of the Cultural Revolution, the ability of the regime to elicit compliance through persuasion has diminished considerably. Consequently, China's rulers have relied on, and will have to continue to rely on, coercive means of control; those wielders of the instrument of coercision—PLA commanders—will perforce remain the dominant political force in China. As long as Mao stays in the political scene, he may, by the sheer force of his personality and personal authority, keep the military leaders in check and hold the pieces together. But he is already seventy-seven and cannot live forever, and there have already been many signs that his prestige and influence are on the wane.* When he finally passes from the scene, "polycentric" tendencies may become all the more compelling.

By way of conclusion, it is appropriate to note that the equilibrium among the five field-army systems has changed drastically since the Cultural Revolution.[30] Since 1967, elite and unit distribution has undergone many important changes. The central leadership may even have adopted a policy of rotation by relocating military

---

of the Cultural Revolution and had become the top officials of the RCs were dropped from the leadership of the new provincial Party Committees. These include P'an Fu-sheng (Chairman of the Heilungkiang RC), Wang Hsiao-yü (Chairman of the Shantung RC), Liu K'o-p'ing (Chairman of the Shansi RC), Liu Chieh-t'ing and Chang Chien-t'ing (Vice-Chairmen of the Szechuan RC), Li Ts'ai-han (Chairman of the Kweichow RC), and Li Yuan (Chairman of the Hunan RC).

*The most recent and forceful example is Mao's inability to save the downfall of Ch'en Po-ta, a member of the five-man Politburo Standing Committee and Mao's long-time brain truster and right-hand man. Ch'en's political demise was probably engineered by the PLA and moderate elements in the leadership who had suffered from Ch'en's stewardship of the Red Guard attacks.

units and/or transferring their leaders. Such a policy would clearly be designed to break up the power bases of certain field-army systems and to prevent regular military units and their leaders from developing independent local sources of support.

As a result of the rise or fall of their top leaders during the Cultural Revolution, members of the different systems have accordingly suffered or benefited politically, and a new distribution of power has emerged among the five field-army systems. Due to the purge of Marshal Ho Lung and the political eclipse of Wang En-mao, the First Field Army has lost most of its political influence. The Fifth (North China) Field Army, due to the downfall of Yang Cheng-wu and the political eclipse of Marshal Nieh Jung-chen, has also suffered a considerable setback (although not as serious as the First Field Army. One of its main force units, the 69th Army, which had been in Hopei and provided the garrison forces in the Peking area since 1949, has been transferred to Shansi and Inner Mongolia.

The Fourth Field Army, to which Lin Piao and Huang Yung-sheng belong,* has emerged as the greatest beneficiary in the new equilibrium. Not only has Lin become the Party's sole vice-chairman and Mao's successor and Huang the PLA Chief of Staff, but also many members of the Fourth Field Army have replaced the members of other field-army systems in the leadership positions of major headquarters at various levels. It has made considerable inroads into the power bases of others.**

---

*It is worth noting that Huang is too quickly identified as a "Fourth Field-Army man." It should be remembered that Huang enjoyed his earliest success under Nieh Jung-chen, with whom Huang served for at least fifteen consecutive years (in Kiangsi, on the Long March, and in the Chin-Ch'a-Chi border region). I am inclined to assign Huang an independent status in the new hierarchy. His proteges—not Lin Piao's—are rapidly assuming key positions.—Ed.

**For examples, members of the Fourth Field Army System have, during the Cultural Revolution, become the commanders of the Wuhan Military Region (Tseng Szu-yu), Chengtu Military Region (Liang Hsing-ch'u), Sinkiang Military Region (Lung Shu-chin), and Canton Military Region (Ting Sheng, who succeeded Huang Yung-sheng). The former commanders of the Wuhan and Chengtu military regions are members of the Second Field Army System, while the former Commander of the Sinkiang Military Region belongs to the First Field Army System.

The Second Field Army, which has its power base in Manchuria and Southwest China, and the Third Field Army, which is strongly entrenched in East China, remain the forces to be reckoned with. They are represented, respectively, by Ch'en Hsi-lien (Commander of the Mukden Military Region and First Party Secretary of Liaoning) and Hsü shih-yu (Commander of the Nanking Military Region and First Party Secretary of Kiangsu) in the Politburo. Members of these two field armies still occupy top positions of leadership in several military regions. In a succession struggle upon Mao's death, even if Ch'en and Hsü may not become contenders for national leadership, they are likely to be kingmakers and to wield the balance of power to throw their weight on the candidate whom they favor.

Politics in any social system usually reflects the conflicts among the groups that wield power. Prior to the Cultural Revolution, Chinese politics to a large extent centered around the groups within the Party, as it was then the locus of power. Since the Cultural Revolution, the locus of power has shifted to the military, and national politics will most likely come to involve conflicts between central headquarters and regional commands, interservice rivalries, and disputes among the field-army systems.

NOTES

1. Various writers have treated some of these issues with great detail. See, for example, John Gittings, The Role of the Chinese Army (London: Oxford University Press, 1967); Ellis Joffe, Party and Army: Professionalism and Political Control in the Chinese Officer Corps, 1949-1964 (Cambridge, Mass.: Harvard University Press, 1967); Alice L. Hsieh, Communist China's Strategy in the Nuclear Era (Englewood Cliffs, N.J.: Prentice Hall, 1962); and Harry Harding and Melvin Gurtov, The Purge of Lo Jui-Ch'ing: The Politics of Chinese Strategic Planning (Santa Monica, Cal.: RAND, 1971).

2. Lin Piao, "March Ahead under the Red Flag of the Party's General Line and Mao Tse-tung's Military Thought," JMJP, September 31, 1959.

3. See "The Resolution of the Enlarged Session of the Military Affairs Committee Concerning the Strengthening of Indoctrination Work in Troop Units" (October 20, 1960), in J. Chester Cheng, ed., PLA Kung-tso Tung-hsun: The Politics of the Chinese Red Army (Stanford, Cal.: The Hoover Institution on War, Revolution, and Peace, 1966), p. 64.

4. Ellis Joffe, "The Chinese Army in the Cultural Revolution: The Politics of Intervention," Current Scene, VIII, 18 (December 7, 1970), p. 3.

5. Bowing to the pressure that the Liberation Army Daily obviously exerted, the People's Daily reproduced Yao's article the following day (November 30), but added its own "Editor's Note," said to have been authored by P'eng Chen, which mentioned nothing of the political offenses of Wu Han's play and described the issues involved as "academic."

6. NCNA, May 28, 1967; and SCMP, No. 3951, June 2, 1967, p. 10.

7. Editorial, LAD, May 29, 1967; in SCMP, No. 3951, June 2, 1967, p. 21.

8. NCNA, "Summary of the Forum on Literature and Art in the Armed Forces," May 28, 1967; in SCMP, No. 3951, June 2, 1967.

9. Editorial, JMJP, May 29, 1967; also "Two Diametrically Opposed Documents," editorial, HC, No. 9, 1967. The "February Outline Report" was put out by P'eng Chen to channel the Cultural Revolution into less-harmful academic debates.

10. See LAD, April 17 and May 20, 1966.

11. Pei-ching P'ing-lun [Peking: Propaganda Department of the Capital "December 26" Commune], No. 4, February 28, 1967.

12. "Ch'en Tsai-tao's Examination" (transcribed and edited from a recording on December 1, 1967), Na-han Chan-pao [Outcry Combat News] (Canton: Suburban Cultural-Educational Revolutionary Rebel H.Q. of Red H.Q. of Municipal Organs), No. 4, April, 1968; also translated in SCMP, No. 4167, April 30, 1968, pp. 3-4. The quoted passages are based on the SCMP translation with minor corrections in English.

13. Ta P'i-p'an T'ung-hsun [Mass Criticism and Repudiation Report] (Canton: Canton News Service of Shanghai T'ung-chi University Tung-fang Hung Corps), October 5, 1967.

14. See "Decision of the CCP Central Committee, the State Council, the Military Affiairs Commission and the Cultural Revolution Group on Resolute Support for the Revolutionary Masses of the Left" (January 23, 1967), CB, No. 852, May 6, 1958, pp. 49-50.

15. Ibid.

16. See "The PLA Resolutely Supports the Proletarian Revolutionary Faction," editorial, LAD, January 25, 1967. In late December, 1966, and early January, 1967, preceding the formal involvement of the PLA in the Cultural Revolution, several top PLA figures were purged, including Ho Lung (Vice-Chairman of MAC), Yang Yung and Liao Han-sheng (Commander and Political Commissar of the Peking Military Region, respectively), Wang Shang-jung and Lei Ying-fu (Director and Deputy Director of the PLA General Staff Department of Operations respectively), and Liang Pi-yeh (Deputy Director of the PLA GPD). They may have been the high-level examples of "capitalist power-holders in the Army" who opposed the Cultural Revolution and who were denounced in the editorials of LAD. See ibid, January 12 and 14, 1967.

17. See "Document of the CCP Central Committee," CB, No. 852, May 6, 1968, p. 111.

18. See speeches by Chiang Ch'ing and other central leaders as reported by Chu-ying Tung-fang-hung [Pearl (River) Film Studio East-Is-Red, a Canton Red Guard newspaper], April, 1968; translated in SCMP, No. 4166, April, 1968, p. 608. T'an Chen-lin was reported by another source to have attacked the CRG in a Party meeting on February 19, 1967 and declared: "I firmly disagree with the striking down of so many veteran cadres, even if it cause my head to be chopped off and my expulsion from the Party!"

19. The text of these two directives is in CB, No. 852, May 8, 1968, pp. 111-12 and 115-16.

20. By July, 1967, the military leadership of Honan, Anhwei, Inner Mongolia, Chekiang, and Tsinghai military districts and of the Cheng-tu and Kunming Military Regions and possibly other units had already been reshuffled.

21. "The Appalling July Meeting," Wuhan Kang-erh-szu, No. 38, August 22, 1967; in SCMP, No. 4073, December, 1967, pp. 1-18.

22. Mainichi Shimbun, July 24, 1967.

23. See editorials, LAD, July 26-29, 1967; "The Proletariat Must Tightly Hold the Gun" and "Fiercely Open Fire at the Major Enemies of the People," editorials, HC, No. 12, August 1, 1967, pp. 43-49; and editorial, JMJP, July 31, 1967.

24. SCMP, No. 4166, April, 1968, pp. 1-4.

25. Ch'en's self-criticism was publicized in a big-character poster and reported by Agence France-Presse, April 30, 1968.

26. John Gittings, "Stifling the Students," Far Eastern Economic Review (Hong Kong), No. 35, August 29, 1968, pp. 377-78; also, New York Times, September 1, 1968, pp. 1, 10.

27. Yao Wen-yuan, "The Working Class Must Exercise Leadership in Everything," HC, No. 2, August 25, 1968.

28. See "Achieve Greater, Faster, Better and More Economic Results in Developing Local Industries," HC, No. 6, 1970.

29. JMJP, August 5, 1968; in PR, No. 32, August 9, 1968, p. 8. See also the New Year's Day editorial, JMJP, January 1, 1969.

30. For the theory of the five field-army systems and its elaboration, see William Whitson, "The Field Army in Chinese Communist Military Politics," China Quarterly, No. 37, January-March, 1969.

COMMAND AND CONTROL:
THE SELECTION
AND POTENTIAL
OF A CHANGING
MILITARY ELITE

4

LIN PIAO:
A CHINESE
MILITARY
POLITICIAN
Thomas W. Robinson

The critical Eleventh Plenum of the CCP's Eighth Central Committee, meeting in August, 1966, designated Lin Piao as Mao Tse-tung's "closest comrade in arms," and the Party's Ninth Congress in April, 1969, officially named Lin as Mao's "successor." Until September, 1971 Lin was Mainland China's most powerful soldier and second most powerful politician. To some Western analysts, Lin had qualities that could have turned him into China's Stalin; to others, he was doomed at best to be China's Malenkov. But even though his tenure as Mao's named successor was brief, and even though he was forced, in the period before his removal, to share power with others in a collective leadership, his time in office was exceedingly important to China's domestic future and to its relations with foreign countries. Despite the fact that Lin will apparently not succeed Mao, the study of a man whose career is nearly identical with that of the CCP itself can bring important benefits to student and policy-maker alike.

The purpose of this chapter, then, is to explicate and analyze Lin's career, both for its own sake and as an illustration of the long and difficult path the Chinese Party has trod since its formation in the 1920s. Space does not permit any more than an outline of Lin's life and his role in modern Chinese military and political history.

For a more complete biography, see the writer's Lin Piao: A Political Biography, forthcoming, 1972. This chapter is a summary of parts of that work, in which will be found complete source citations. The work contains, in addition to a biography of Lin, and analysis of his writings, a section on his personality and health, and translations of all his works from 1932 to 1970.

Nonetheless, even a summary can provide important insights into Lin's personality, his operating style, his policies, and the probable future direction of CCP policy.

Born in Hupeh Province in 1907 of lower-middle-class parents, Lin Piao was involved in the Communist movement from late childhood. Educated first in local village schools and later in the middle schools of Wuhan, Lin early came under radical influence from his teachers and even members of his immediate family. By his teens, this influence, together with the antiforeign intellectual climate of the times and the modernizing atmosphere of the Wuhan region, had radicalized Lin to the extent that he wrote in left-wing journals and joined radical student groups. By 1925, Lin's leftward drift had reached the extreme end of the spectrum, and he read Communist and socialist publications, organized student strikes, and attended an antiforeign national student conference.

Because the CCP and the Kuomintang (KMT) were temporarily allied, Lin was able to gain entrance to the KMT's Whampoa Military Academy in 1925. He graduated in mid-1926, in time to participate in the Northern Expedition. Thus began Lin's military career. By 1927 a full-fledged Communist, Lin followed a career during the next few years that paralleled the fortunes of the CCP. In 1927, he participated in the Nanch'ang Uprising (organized by Mao Tse-tung), fled south after its failure with Yeh T'ing's troops under Chu Teh, and rejoined Mao's bedraggled forces at Chingkangshan in early 1928. Making a name for himself in the battles accompanying this hegira and in the period thereafter, Lin rose from second lieutenant to regiment commander. His political position in the Communist hierarchy was enhanced accordingly.

In the Kiangsi Period (1929-34), Lin's position once again reflected the fortunes of the Chinese Communists. He was, for instance, prominent in all the major military events; indeed, his military prowess was instrumental in turning back the first four Nationalist offensives against the Communists. By mid-1929, these military accomplishments earned for him, at age 23, the title of army commander, which he maintained throughout this period. Lin proved adept at mastering the art and techniques of military strategy and tactics. He learned to combine guerrilla warfare with conventional warfare, how to integrate mobility with striking power, when to seize and when to avoid occupying cities, and techniques to cope with much larger invading forces. During this learning process, he was drawn increasingly into Mao's circle, and by 1930 he was considered one of Mao's followers.

This is not to say that Lin was a slave to the Maoist viewpoint. He often participated in military maneuvers against the Nationalists planned by Mao's competitors within the Party. But he managed to avoid being trapped in the often bitter political debates between Maoists and anti-Maoists. By sticking to and excelling in his military tasks, Lin successfully exempted himself from aligning with either side while maintaining the confidence of both. His military influence was thus preserved and he was respected politically by most of his associates. In 1934, he held membership in most of the important political bodies of the Kiangsi Soviet.

Lin's military preeminence fitted him to lead the central column in the Long March, which the Nationalists' fifth offensive forced upon the Communists in 1934. Lin contributed to that undertaking notably in breaking through the Nationalist lines at the beginning of the march, in investing and then defending Tsunyi while the Communists conducted an important conference there, in skillfully conducting river-crossing operations that saved the marchers from disaster several times, in leading the difficult crossing of the Grasslands, and in defeating the Nationalist forces at Ninghsia, which opened the way for rejoining local Communist forces in Shensi. Near the end of the Long March he was promoted to deputy commander of the entire Red Army.

Lin's heretofore successful career received a temporary set-back because of disagreements with Mao Tse-tung. Lin may have thought that he had not risen fast enough politically and may have been irked that his rival, P'eng Teh-huai, was still ahead of him in the military hierarchy. Perhaps in protest, Lin refused to attend an important political conference until Chou En-lai, serving as inter-mediary, convinced him to come. More important, Lin apparently had developed a "proprietary interest" in the welfare of his own forces. When Mao ordered Lin's forces to conduct operations that Lin considered them unprepared for and when, after their defeat, Mao wanted to break up the units under Lin's command, Lin balked. Mao then relieved him of his command, and in mid-1936, instead of a principal field command and commensurate political authority, Lin had to rest content with an appointment to head the Resistance University in Yenan.

The "exile" was short-lived, however, and Lin's good behavior and the threat posed by the onset of the Sino-Japanese war in 1937 led Mao to place him in command of the newly constituted 115th Division of the 8th Route Army. Lin directed this force in the decisive battle at P'inghsingkuan, which inflicted severe losses on the Japanese in autumn, 1937. This earned him a national reputation. Lin's military style, displayed at P'inghsingkuan, was by then characteristic: a realistic, detailed plan of action; good intelligence; thorough military training and political indoctrination; confidence in subordinates; and attack in strength against a single enemy weak spot, followed by rapid withdrawal. Similar tactics were, of course, used by most Chinese Communist forces and accorded with Maoist military doctrine. In fact, comparison of Lin's and Mao's written works of this period shows striking similarities. Both stressed the advantages of protracted war and China's advantage in such a conflict. Both rejected passive defense. And both emphasized guerrilla warfare, a united front strategy, and a politically reliable, highly motivated army.

Lin did not participate in the further implementation of these principles until 1943, for in 1938 he was wounded and was sent to the Soviet Union for medical treatment. Little is known of Lin's activities in the Soviet Union, but after recuperating, he probably studied Soviet military strategy, and also served as Chinese representative to the Comintern. Lin returned to Yenan in 1942, just in time to take part in the Cheng-feng Movement, in which he declared himself for Mao and against the "International Clique." Following this, Lin apparently resumed superintending military training, readying troops for the postwar revival of warfare with the Nationalists. He also served as deputy head of the Central Party School. Finally, Lin served as one of the Communist negotiators in the unsuccessful talks with Chiang Kai-shek at Chungking and Sian. Evidently, his work was acceptable, for at the Seventh Party Congress in 1945 Lin was elected to the CC (although not to its Politburo).

Mao demonstrated his confidence in Lin by choosing him to lead the first sizable Communist force into Manchuria after the Japanese surrender in September, 1945. During the civil war that ensued, Lin held supreme military power and much of the political power in the Northeast. His job was to occupy the Northeast and then to build an army with sufficient military and political power to seize the rest of China.

Lin played a central role in the victory that the Communists achieved in 1949 after four years of almost continuous fighting. After having contained the Nationalist offensives in 1945-46, Lin gradually wrested control of the northeast from the KMT and expanded his forces. He moved on to seize North China, using widely different strategies in the key battles at Tientsin and Peking, and then raced south in pursuit of the defeated Nationalist armies in 1949 and 1950. The result was Communist conquest of all of China and international prominence for Lin as an architect of the winning strategy. The victory was not without cost, for Lin had suffered his first battlefield defeat at

Szup'ing in 1947. His writings show that he was acutely conscious of his errors there—making up his mind too fast; underestimating the capability of the opponent and committing too many of his forces against weaker enemy groups; tactical overcautiousness; misuse of artillery; waste of resources pursuing peripheral objectives; and going into battle with insufficient political support from the populace.

By the time of the formation of the PRC in October, 1949, Lin was at the peak of power. His status was accurately reflected in the wide range of central and provincial positions he occupied. Aside from membership in most of the highest policy-making bodies at the national level, Lin was supremely powerful in the central-south region, an area comprising six provinces and 175 million people. While he devoted part of his time to military matters (mopping-up operations in South China and the Hainan Island operation in the spring of 1950), most of his time was spent on regional administrative matters. Speeches and reports of his made at the time indicate a broad range of concerns, including industrial, agricultural, financial, political, and administrative questions.

This situation would undoubtedly have continued were it not for the intervention of two factors. One was the Korean War, which began in June, 1950. While the extent of Lin's participation in the war (and even whether he took part at all) has been the subject of much speculation, and while no primary Chinese source available to the author mentions Lin's role, the weight of evidence seems to indicate that Lin did actually command the Chinese forces in Korea for part of the period before the truce in 1953. First, the intervening Chinese force was composed of units of the Fourth Field Army, long under his command. Second, Lin was the most experienced of the Chinese field commanders in modern warfare and in organizing and fielding a modern military machine. Third, his movements after early May 1950, when he disappeared from view in the central-south region, and throughout the late summer and early fall, when he was reported to be in Peking and Shenyang (in Manchuria), indicate that he was no longer actively involved in regional administrative duties. Fourth, interviews with Chinese prisoners verify that Lin was the over-all commander of the army that met UN forces at the Yalu. Fifth, tactics employed against American forces in late October and November were those associated with Lin's military proclivities (the "one point-two front" ambush tactic and the "four quick, one slow" assault tactic). Up to 1950, tactics practiced by one field army had not been transferred in any major way to another. Sixth, the Chinese did not wish to admit officially that organized units led by well-known military leaders were in Korea, lest the United States declare war, at which point the recently signed alliance with the Soviet Union might be invoked and a new world war begin.

The other factor was the onset of a lengthy period of illness, possibly as early as mid-1950 (probably due either to a stomach ulcer or tuberculosis) or Korean War wounds in early 1951. In any case, whereas the Korean War took him out of the central-south adminis- trative region, illness evidently forced him to retire from active partici- pation in political and military life altogether until early 1954 and, periodically, until 1957. Several reports speak of him being removed to the Soviet Union for treatment or of him under care in tuberculosis sanitariums in China. Despite this, however, Lin remained periodi- cally active, attending major national political congresses and meetings in 1954, 1955, 1956, and 1958, being elected to important positions at each, and accompanying Mao and other leaders on state occasions. Thus, even in the nadir of illness, Lin was not so constantly and se- verely sick as to be unable to perform useful work.

The beginning of Lin's political comeback can actually be traced to the results of the purge of Kao Kang and Jao Shu-shih in early 1954. There is some evidence that Lin, along with Kao and Jao, was accused by Liu Shao-ch'i of setting up an "independent kingdom" in his region since 1949. Lin, after having been defended by Mao himself, then cleared himself by joining in the attack against Kao. Although Lin was now shorn of his regional administrative titles, with the abolition of the five administrative regions, he had still been able to consolidate his power. A decade and a half later, his regional basis of authority is still recognizable in terms of the location of the Fourth Field Army (in Manchuria and South China) and his ability to keep his followers in top Party, army, and government posts there.

Lin's political star continued to rise, albeit slowly, following the Kao-Jao purge. While he received no ministry portfolio and was indeed entirely frozen out of the Ministry of Defense by P'eng Teh- huai, he was elected a vice-premier of the State Council and vice- chairman of the National Defense Council at the National People's Congress in 1954, elevated to the Politburo in April, 1955 (confirmed at the Eighth Party Congress in 1956); and became a marshal (ranking third among ten such men) in 1955. He then appears to have dropped out of circulation until late 1957, undoubtedly for health reasons, and may even have gone back to the Soviet Union for treatment. Illness had the effect of preventing him from taking part in the debates over the various policies of the Great Leap Forward, a fact that may well have actually aided his rise, since he could not thus be accused of being a firm member of any faction (except that of Mao himself).

Confirmation of his enhanced status came in 1958 when, for the first time, he was elected to the Standing Committee of the Politburo and, concurrently, a vice-chairman of the CC. It would seem, more-over, that Lin's illness was by then at least arrested, since in mid-1958 he came into increasing public view, appearing often at official functions. It is from this time forward, perhaps, that it becomes increasingly difficult to separate Lin's own career from that of the history of the PPC as a whole. And, in fact, it is only natural to sub-merge Lin in that history, a tendency compounded by Lin's own pro-pensity to act through others and to subordinate himself rigorously to Mao.

The years 1959-65 constitute a political era, both for Lin and for China as a whole, a period dominated by three questions: the Lushan Plenum in 1959, resulting in P'eng Teh-huai's dismissal and replace-ment as Minister of Defense by Lin himself; the reemergence of the PLA under Lin as an important political force in the country; and the intramural debates of 1964-66 purge of Lo Jui-ch'ing and leading up to the Cultural Revolution itself.

Although there were many military issues of concern to him, Lin apparently did not take part in the debates preceding the Lushan Plenum in September, 1959, nor is there any evidence that he made his view-points openly known at the Plenum itself. Lin probably reasoned that with his health restored, his reputation intact, continually in favor with Mao, disposed of considerable administrative experience, and having both few political enemies (except for P'eng Teh-huai himself) and a strong "electorate" in the Fourth Field Army, he would be Mao's natural choice to succeed P'eng.

Lin's open concern about P'eng thus postdates the Plenum—that is, after P'eng was presumably safely out of the way. Moving to attack the former Minister of Defense only when he had taken the latter's job, Lin first spoke against him openly at the MAC meetings after Lushan and attacked him indirectly in internal military journals and in publicly disseminated articles. For the most part, however, Lin was circumspect in his views of P'eng. He never attacked the latter by name and seemed instead more interested in assuring continuity of military policy and in improving military efficiency and Party con-trols within the PLA. Only in the summer of 1967, during the Cultural Revolution, did Lin publicly attack P'eng directly and by name, and this seemed to be for Cultural Revolution reasons alone. Thus, Lin evidenced a tendency to minimize concern with personality matters, once it was clear that his opponent was politically impotent. This seemed a general tendency with Lin; while quite sensitive to actual competition from his associates, Lin was concerned more to assure administrative and military efficiency than striking a man when down.

Once a contender was eliminated from the running, he usually had
nothing further to fear from Lin.

Lin's efforts to reformulate military administration and strategy
in his own image in the years 1959-65 are well known. He put a stop
within the army to declining morale spreading as a result of the Great
Leap Forward disasters. He underlined the importance of Party control in the army, especially at the county (hsien) level. He increased
the percentage of Party members among military cadres, reinvigorated
the GPD, increased the authority of local Party committees and political
commisars, and stressed indoctrination in Mao's thought. He also
stressed military proficiency, combat training, and the development
of a Chinese nuclear capability and modern weapon systems. The
balance that ensued between officers and men, between various officer
corps factions, between Party and army, and between ideological
orientations, gradually alleviated the problems that were the legacy
of P'eng Teh-huai's tenure as Minister of Defense.

These successes caused Mao to increase his already high level
of confidence in Lin and the PLA to the point where the methods and
goals pioneered in the army were gradually applied to Chinese society
as a whole. What was originally a series of intramilitary political
campaigns were now generalized to every sphere of life. Such terms
as "four firsts," "the three-eight" working style, the "five-good"
soldier, and the "four-good" company came to be known by every
citizen. Lin's idea of creating political work departments at every
institutional level was now applied to all governmental and economic
departments. Military cadres were sent as instructors to other spheres
of administrations and production. These developments gave the PLA
and Lin a degree of nationwide influence that they had not possessed
since the early 1950s.

These activities obviously brought Lin to the forefront of national
political activity. It is characteristic of his operating style, however,
that his publicly known personal movements do not reflect this prominence. Part of the reason for Lin's absence from public view may
also have been due to the renewal of the range of illnesses that had
plagued him for the last decade and a half. He was thus absent from
public view for long stretches of time from 1960 to 1965, emerging
only late that year.

It seems clear in retrospect that the intra-Party debates during
the summer of 1965 were actually the opening shots in the leadership
struggles comprising the Cultural Revolution. It also seems apparent
that there were a whole series of personal and policy differences

between Lin and Lo Jui-ch'ing that, while under normal circumstances could have been resolved, in the tense domestic and international situation of the time came to hold more than ordinary importance. In general, Lo's program for enhanced defense posture against the United States would have meant the abandonment of the entire program that Lin had just put into practice. What was originally a set of differences over issues soon became personal opposition between the two men, as Lo called (to his face) for Lin's resignation and as the lines drew firm between pro- and anti-Mao factions within the Party. The inevitable confrontation between the two competing military strategies took place at a series of high Party meetings in the fall and winter of 1965-66. The essence of the charges against Lo was that he carried out the "bourgeois military line," that he was revisionist in outlook, that he opposed the Party center, that he opposed Mao and Lin personally, and that he was a careerist. He was thus ousted from his posts. This effectively served notice that Liu Shao-ch'i, P'eng Chen, and Teng Hsiao-p'ing were themselves open to attack. It also placed Lin in a position of preeminence in the Party as well as the PLA. Now, for the first time he began to pronounce authoritatively on matters of concern to the entire society. Thus, even before the important Eleventh Plenum in August 1966, Lin was playing a leading role in central politics and nonmilitary affairs.

As the struggle between the Liuist and Maoist forces drew to a head in the late spring and early summer of 1966, Lin managed to assure control of the Peking military garrison and to disarm or neutralize units of the public security force in the city. This set the stage for the series of Politburo meetings, first in Hangchow in April and May and then in Peking itself. At the most critical of these, in mid-May, Lin delivered what is probably his most significant political and philosophical pronouncement to date. In it, Lin saw ideological attitudes as the central variable in deciding what direction Chinese society would develop. More important, he placed great emphasis on politics as equivalent to coups and countercoups and hence on politics as the process of competitive purges. To him, coups from below could happen at any time, and the political task of the ruler was to stage coups preemptorily from above; the alternative was literally to risk having one's head roll. Hence, to Lin, the Cultural Revolution was not only to be a positive and universal espousal of Mao's thought, but, more negatively, the prevention of counterrevolutionary subversion and seizure of power by those who would, through revisionism, restore capitalism and eliminate Mao and his followers.

At the Eleventh Plenum, August 1-11, 1966, Lin replaced Liu Shao-ch'i as Mao's successor-designate. Lin was one of the central figures at the Plenum, delivering an important acceptance speech and, probably, arranging to carry out the Cultural Revolution in the PLA without interference from the Red Guards. Although Lin kept his distance from the Red Guards personally, there seems no doubt that the army, under his direction, did play a central role in organizing, directing, advising, billiting, and transporting the student revolutionaries. With the close of the Plenum and the announcement of Lin's new title, his style changed dramatically. He became a public figure, appearing often (for him) over the next four years, promulgating directives and making speeches, and involving himself in the sturm und drang of the sometimes near-anarchous events.

Although Lin appeared at all eight of the Red Guard mass rallies in Peking in the fall of 1966, he apparently fell ill sometime in late November and did not return to the public scene until March, 1967. He was not forced to withdraw from circulation altogether, however. For instance, he delivered an important speech setting forth his views on ideology and participated in Politburo and MAC meetings. Moreover, beginning in January, 1967, the role of the PLA in the Cultural Revolution began to increase steadily until, by 1969, the military was in physical control of institutions at nearly every administrative level and geographic location in the country. Lin was more or less constantly involved in this process, and the extent of his involvement can be measured by the degree of military involvement as a whole in Cultural Revolution politics.

One of the problems that increasingly to demanded Lin's attention was the emerging contradiction between his personal loyalty to Mao and his policies, on the one hand, and the apparently numerous officer-colleagues who began to hold strong reservations about those policies and about the utilization of the army to carry them out, on the other. One result of Lin's inability to resolve this contradiction was the increasing influence of the CRG. This led to intramilitary strife within the Army. Another consequence was de facto independence of many regional and local military commanders. This often led to their support of the "wrong" (i.e., not entirely pro-Maoist) faction among the Red Guards and revolutionary rebels and, as a result, to an ever-increasing incidence of violence. The most obvious manifestation was the Wuhan Incident of July, 1967. A third result was the attempt of some high army officers to involve themselves in the central politics of the Cultural Revolution, ending sometimes in their own demise. The best example of this was Yang Cheng-wu's attempt to assist in the purge of dissident members of the CRG as a means of protecting his own position, an attempt that led to his own removal by Lin in March 1968.

Lin was, of course, continuously wrestling with these problems, which he recognized in a number of speeches. One of these was delivered on March 30, 1967. In it, Lin admitted that the PLA had made mistakes in deciding what local revolutionary faction to support, although his recommended solutions unfortunately did not provide the means for breaking local deadlocks while simultaneously furthering Mao's revolutionary cause. Lin said that the army should "shoot as little as possible, beat up people as little as possible, and arrest as few people as possible"; should "be very cautious and modest"; and should "rely on the Left" and "use scientific Marxism-Leninism" in deciding who to support. These generalities obviously did not assist local army commanders in deciding which of several violently competing groups, each claiming true fidelity to Mao's line, was the Chairman's true local representative.

The PLA, and Lin, were thus caught in the middle between leftist revolutionaries, bent upon seizing power, and local Party and government administrators, determined not to leave office without a fight. The army was in fact specifically forbidden to use force to carry out its duties and was further weakened by the insistence of the CRG that the Red Guards must be even further encouraged in their violent activities if revolutionary momentum was to be maintained. These were some of the reasons why the Wuhan Incident, a direct military challenge by Ch'en Tsai-tao, a regional military commander, against the Party in Peking, occurred in late July, 1967, and why Lin had to admit that "there simply was no way to get at" Ch'en's insubordination before it was too late. Lin in fact may have initially felt that the situation in Wuhan was in good hands, since Ch'en had been part of Lin's entourage in the Central-South region since 1954.

The Wuhan events in fact are a perfect illustration of Lin's dilemma. He depended for his very position and influence on Mao's explicit and total trust. He also depended on a similar relationship of trust with his subordinate commanders, many of whom, such as Ch'en Tsai-tao, may well have felt they could continue during the Cultural Revolution to deal with local situations on an autonomous basis. Fortunately for Lin, it was Ch'en's insubordination that extricated him from the unpalatable implications of this dilemma. Once that occurred, Lin moved with characteristic speed and decisiveness, moving units into position, putting trusted subordinates in charge of suppressing the rebellion, and even directing certain phases of the operation himself from near Wuhan.

Wuhan was probably a net loss for Lin, however, for a number of changes in high-level army administration seemed to follow directly upon those events. Thus, the entire GPD of the PLA, headed by Lin's confidant and long-time associate, Hsiao Hua, was purged in August, 1967. Hsiao had evidently made mistakes during the Wuhan events, had sought to advance himself unduly (but not at Lin's expense), and was a victim of the crossfire between the CRG and Lin and Chou En-lai. Hsiao's dismissal differs markedly from that of Lo Jui-ch'ing; unlike Lo, Hsiao did not try to oust Lin, while Lin did his utmost to arrange Hsiao's removal as quietly as possible.

The resolution of the Wuhan crisis and the subsequent measured defeat in September, 1967, of the extreme leftists in the Maoist leadership allowed Lin to restore his authority within the army and in the Politburo and also provided for a continual increase in military authority at every level. While the PLA did not have all it wanted in terms of authority to deal with the Red Guards, since the army still did not have authority to use force, the revolutionaries were now forbidden to seize arms from the military, were ordered to return weapons already in their possession, and the army was authorized to "hit back in self-defense." On the other hand, the PLA was specifically forbidden to inject itself into factional disputes among the leftists and, in the positive sense, could only carry out political education among the revolutionaries. Lin's hand could be seen in the new political direction, for not only did the educational theme loom large, but there was a careful balancing between order and revolution and a continual emphasis upon rectifying ideological shortcomings within the army. Lin's, and the army's, influence is also seen in the stepped up formulation of provincial RCI after September. Whereas only six of twenty-nine such committees had been formed before the Wuhan Incident, now the pace was stepped up considerably so that, by September, 1968, all provinces were being governed by these new organs of power.

In March, 1968, Lin felt it necessary to purge Chief of Staff Yang Cheng-wu, himself reading out a list of nine of Yang's "crimes." While details are still lacking, a composite explanation of Yang's removal would stress the following elements. On the one hand, Yang desired to consolidate his power within the military so as to remove the probationary nature of his appointment (he was still "acting" Chief of Staff). For that reason, he tried to replace contemporary military regional commanders with his friends in the former Shensi-Jehol-Hopei Military Region. This could only ensure the ire of the former and cause discomfort to Lin. On the other hand, Yang, like Hsiao Hua, seemed to have been caught in the power struggle between Chiang Ch'ing and her supporters, who often wished to attack the PLA itself, and her opponents, who wished to pursue such less extreme policies as using the army to work out compromises between revolutionary factions and promoting the RCs. Yang, in the center of the fighting, had to balance the various sides and factions as well as secure his own position. One solution was to form his own group, to move against too-leftist elements within the army, and to cooperate with those who seemed willing to counter the moves of the CRG. Therefore, he teamed up with Yü Li-chin and Fu Ch'ung-pi to move against Hsieh Fu-chih and, possibly, Wang Li and Ch'i Pen-yu. By early 1968, Cultural Revolution politics were disorganized enough that Yang (like Ch'en Tsai-tao in Wuhan) assumed that he had Lin's backing (because of their long association) while Lin, on his part, had to withdraw his support in the face of pressures from the left. When Fu, at Yang's behest, failed (because of Chiang Ch'ing's opposition) to arrest Wang and Ch'i at the Cultural Revolution building in early March, 1968, and when Yang allegedly bugged Mao's and Lin's own houses, Lin had little choice but to remove him. The fact that it was Lin himself who announced Yang's removal, together with his own and Chou En-lai's pandering of Chiang Ch'ing in their speeches, demonstrates the leadership's attempt to maintain a precarious unity despite obvious policy disagreements and personal animosity.

Developments after Yang's purge confirmed that Lin and his followers emerged in a much stronger position in the PLA and in the country as a whole. Formation of RCs continued to accelerate. More important, the expected attacks against the army did not materialize, nor did there then appear to be any new widespread purge of army leaders. Significantly, Lin was able to consolidate his power within the military; with the appointment of Huang Yung-sheng as the new Chief of Staff, and the rise to prominence of other Lin associates such as Wu Fa-hsien, Ch'iu Hui-tso, and Li Tso-p'eng, no more was heard (at least for the while) of factionalism at the highest levels of the army. On the basis of this strength, Lin and his group were not only able to assert iron rule over the military regions but also to increase their political power at the Twelfth Plenum in October, 1968, and the Ninth Congress in April, 1969. On both of these occasions, they constituted the largest and most influential group.

The story of the Ninth Congress is, in fact, the history of the central role played by the PLA, of Lin's enhanced importance as leader of the military, and of the ratification of his status as a national political leader and Mao's legal successor. Through his seemingly loyal military associates, he managed to place the army in control of nearly every aspect of life in China. In the provincial RCs, 43 percent of the "leading cadres" were military figures; on the new CC, 45 percent were career soldiers; in MAC, 11 of the 22 known members had historic ties with Lin, while at the military-region level, the careers

of nine of the fourteen regional commanders were closely linked to
Lin's; finally, on the new Provincial Party Committees, which began
to appear after the Congress, more than half of the identifiable leadership was military. At the Congress itself, Lin was the featured speaker,
delivering an important report (24,000 words, his most sustained
forensic effort), and receiving official confirmation of his status in the
newly adopted constitution. In a clause unusual for any constitution,
Lin was mentioned by name:

> Comrade Lin Piao was consistently held high the great
> red flag of Mao Tse-tung's thought and has most loyally
> and most resolutely implemented and defended Comrade
> Mao Tse-tung's proletarian revolutionary line. Comrade
> Lin Piao is Comrade Mao Tse-tung's close comrade-in-
> arms and successor.

Lin was busy with intramilitary matters during the post-Congress
period. The purge of over 300 senior military figures, at central,
military-region, and provincial levels gave Lin the opportunity to
make the army over in his own image. The GPD reemerged in late
1969, headed by Li Teh-sheng, a man, it should be noted, not historically
associated with Lin. But the MAC structure was also filled in, and
this important institution was indeed dominated by Lin and his followers.

Huang Yung-sheng rose rapidly in power. As Lin's new Chief
of Staff, he was the most powerful soldier in the army, aside from
Lin who, given his health and his high political status, could not spend
full time on military matters. When he came to Peking in 1968, Huang
brought with him officers of the Canton Military Region. He evidently
had a hand in the appointment of at least four other Canton colleagues
to important provincial posts. He rapidly assumed an important place
in Peking's attempt to restore its pre-Cultural Revolution position in
foreign affairs, often making important policy pronouncements, receiving visiting foreign dignitaries, and even leading a Chinese delegation abroad. Although on important state occasions his name was
usually listed as occupying the number ten or eleven slot in order
of priority. On several occasions when a group of Politburo members
were mentioned in the press his name was taken out of order and placed
at the head of the list. In all, Huang presented a striking personal
contrast to Lin: a good speaker and an experienced administrator
despite his almost total lack of formal education, he presented himself as a picture of vital, healthy activism.

It is not necessarily the case, however, that Huang was Lin's
rival or that he openly coveted Lin's position. He was Lin's trusted

associate for many years. He played the part of a loyal supporter who
realized that Lin had the power to dismiss him if Lin wished and, given
Lo Jui-ch'ing's and Yang Cheng-wu's fate, knew that the position of
the Chief of the General Staff was a difficult one to fill. It may be
closer to the truth to assert that he seemed to act as Lin's front man.
It was he who pronounces the speeches that Lin did not wish to read
personally. It was he who executed Lin's orders within the army.
And it was he who substituted for Lin on those state and Party occasions
when the latter either could not or chose not to appear. There was no
direct evidence of rivalry between the two.

Chou En-lai, the Premier of the State Council, also rose in
prominence, especially as concerns foreign policy. Beginning with
the Ninth Congress, China had begun a long process of restoring its
pre-1965 position in world affairs. This had several facets. On the
one hand, China attempted to dissuade the Soviet Union from taking
any more drastic action than she had during 1969 along the Sino-Soviet
border. Hence, Peking decided to enter into border talks with Moscow
as a device to buy time until her military strength was restored, her
nuclear weaponry more advanced, and some sort of alliance system
against the Soviets constructed. It was Chou En-lai who was the
architect of this plan and the man who carried it out in detail. On the
other hand, China decided to look closer at Washington's offer for
improvement in relations. The rationale here probably was that it
was better to negotiate the United States out of Asia and out of the
Southeast Asian military conflict than to continue to act as an obstacle
to the obvious American desire to restrict the range and kind of its
commitments in Asia, just as it was wise to use the United States as
a counterweight in the effort to oppose Moscow. It was Chou, not Lin,
who met with Henry Kissinger in Peking to carry out detailed discussions of Sino-American relations and to arrange for the visit of
President Nixon to Peking. Beyond August, 1971, it was Chou En-lai
who continued at the center of the execution of this policy. In Southeast Asia, it was Chou who put together the conference of "revolutionary
peoples" following the overthrow of Norodom Sihanouk in Cambodia
and the American-South Vietnamese invasion of that country. Finally,
it was Chou who personally took over the Foreign Ministry from Ch'en
Yi in 1967 and who was in charge of retraining and reassigning China's
ambassadors called home during the Cultural Revolution.

In all this, Lin was rarely to be seen. Just as in the case of Huang
Yung-sheng, until September 1971 no one had reason to presume that
Lin has been eclipsed by Chou's more obviously public role. Mao Tse-
tung himself has been even less prominent than Lin in the publicly-know-
able features of Chinese foreign policy since early 1969. Given Lin's

personal reticence and what is known of his working style and of his
position and his power, it seemed inconceivable that he had not played
an important part in setting Chinese foreign and domestic policy. Moreover, while Chou was accorded almost all the publicity in the foreign
press, because he is the visible and personal element of that policy,
the same was not true at home. In Peking, Chou assumed his natural
place as number three behind Mao and Lin. Finally, throughout their
respective careers there is not one recorded instance known to the
author in which Lin and Chou have been known to disagree. If anything,
they had learned to work together well and had agreed on how to divide
the labor between them.

    Given the increasingly strong position of the army in post-
Cultural Revolution politics and Mao's seemingly continuous support
of Lin personally, and given the relatively placid nature of the domestic political situation during the first nine months of 1971, the news
came with a shock that "something had happened" in China during
September and that Lin's status was more and more open to question.
As 1971 drew to a close, however, factual evidence accumulated that
Lin had indeed been removed, that the coterie of his followers (including Huang Yung-sheng) had fallen with him, and that Lin was
accused of plotting against Mao even to the extent of making attempts
on the Chairman's life. Some possibility even existed that Lin may
have been on the Chinese airliner that crashed so mysteriously in
Mongolia. How is one to explain so startling a train of developments?
What does it mean for the nature of Chinese domestic politics, especially with regard to the future role of the military? And what implications do these revelations carry for Lin's historic relationship
with Mao?

    Though this chapter cannot provide a definitive and detailed
anlaysis of Lin's demise (for one thing, we must wait for more solid
information from Peking), it does appear possible to attempt preliminary answers to these questions. The related questions What
happened? and Why? are, of course, the most difficult to answer.
Any explanation must contain elements stemming both from Chinese
domestic politics and from China's foreign relations, and must include
unfortunately a large dose of hypothetical reasoning until a wider
range of generally accepted facts is at hand. Four explanations come
to mind. There is, first, the possibility that Lin was not what he had
appeared to be, that he was, in fact, biding his time until it seemed
to him that Mao was weak enough and that he, Lin, was strong enough
for Mao to be overcome. This is the official (to the extent that there

is one) Chinese explanation of Lin's demise—that Lin actually plotted against Mao, even to the extent of plotting to kill him, and that, found out at the last moment, he tried unsuccessfully to flee to the Soviet Union. Though it is certainly possible that this is what really happened, analysis of the relations between Lin and Mao, and of Lin's political behavior over the years, leads the author to believe that Lin would not have acted in this way and could have done so only under conditions of extreme adversity, which would have been apparent to the outside world.

The possibility remains that Mao decided that, having used Lin for political purposes during and immediately after the Cultural Revolution, the time had come to put the PLA back into a subordinate role and that Lin, together with such subordinates as Huang Yung-sheng, Li Tso-p'eng, Wu Fa-hsien, and Ch'iu Hui-tso, should therefore be removed as a dramatic symbol of the change in PLA-CCP relationships. It is true that, in 1971 and afterward, the PLA was required to take on a somewhat less all-powerful role as the CCP was more and more restored to its pre-Cultural Revolution position. But it was Mao himself who suffered greatly as a result of Lin's political demise. Not only had Mao invested heavily, and in the face of great opposition, in Lin as his personal choice for successor, but Lin's removal (if it was that) left Mao with no successor at a very late date. Moreover, many in China may well have asked why Mao would have done this sort of thing after having fought the Cultural Revolution itself on the very question of political succession. Mao lost much more than he may have gained in Lin's removal. Accordingly, this explanation, taken alone, does not suffice.

Nor does the thesis satisfy that Lin and his faction within the PLA and the CCP, fought, and eventually lost, the contest for the Maoist succession with the forces headed by Chou En-lai. There is, as indicated above, no long-term evidence of discord between Lin and Chou, and there is no evidence that Chou headed a "faction" or group at all, much less one that would, without Mao's backing, be strong enough to oust Lin. Nor is it Chou's political style to attempt to play the political game so directly as to tilt frontally with Lin, just as it has never been Chou's predeliction to strive to be Mao's successor or even the titular leader at any time in the Chinese Communist movement. It is true that, with Lin's passing from the stage, Chou became "number two" behind Mao and in this sense "replaced" Lin, and it is true that Chou may have experienced serious opposition to his foreign policy moves, especially those related to the Nixon visit. For these reasons, the possibility that a power struggle did ensue between Lin and Chou cannot be excluded from consideration. However, other elements of a very serious sort must be added to make plausible a life-and-death combat between colleagues who had never before experienced major political differences. At this writing, these elements are not clear.

A more likely explanation stems from Lin's delicate political position between his (sometime extreme) army colleagues and the members of non-Fourth Field Army regional and central command structures, on the one hand, and the central leadership and Mao, on the other. Lin may well have been pressured from below to push for a change in established policies on such foreign policy questions as China's role in the India-Pakistan conflict over Bangladesh, the Sino-Soviet border problem, relations with Japan, and the Nixon visit. He may also have found it difficult to maneuver among army factions at the provincial level, some of which were known to be unfriendly to him. It is, finally, possible that the Chief-of-Staff, Haung Yung-sheng, was presenting, by his very activism and dynamism, an alternative to Lin that the latter could not afford to let go unchallenged—especially when it is considered that Lin might have again become ill and thus made it appear to many that Haung, not Lin, was more suitable as Mao's eventual successor. It is even possible that Haung, because of his very activism, had adopted policies that either were unknown to the possible bed-ridden Lin until they were irreversible (who then would have had no choice but to go along) or had carried out Lin's general directives to lengths beyond what Lin desired.

At this point, another critical element, Mao's geriatric megalomania, may have come into play as the Chairman perceived his policies, ordered into effect through Lin and Chou, either sabotaged, in his eyes, or applied differentially by those under Lin and those under Chou. Suspecting that political goings-on were taking place behind his back and noting that Chou seemed to be innocent of obvious wrong-doing, Mao may have concluded, however erroneously, that Lin was attempting to seize power from him, or even trying to do away with him. Although this may have been farthest from Lin's mind, he may have been caught up in the situation and felt it necessary to protect his credibility with his subordinates and opponents within the army to the extent of making certain political moves (as did Liu Shao-ch'i before him) that merely assured Mao that his suspicions were correct. The drama at that point, possibly in July-August, 1971, may have accelerated because of the necessity to make important foreign policy decisions (say, with regard to Bangladesh and the Soviet-India Treaty or with regard to the question whether to go through with the Nixon visit) and, like a Greek tragedy, moved after August inexorably to its conclusion.

Lin's political ouster obviously carries the most serious implications for the future of Chinese politics and, hence, for Chinese foreign policy. Not only is the question of the Maoist succession reopened at a very late (and, in view of the delicate foreign policy climate, embarrassing) time; the very stability of the Chinese political system is also in doubt. Of perhaps equal importance is the attitude of the rank and file of the CCP, to say nothing of the PLA, toward high political authority and toward the hitherto apparently sacrosanct person of Mao Tse-tung. Rampant cynicism and apathy can be the only product of the Lin affair, and a general increase of these kinds of feelings throughout the Chinese political system must lead, if unchecked, to severe modification of the Maoist style of political action, depending as it does on voluntarism and political enthusiasm.

Feelings within the PLA, and the role of the PLA as a whole in the system, depend as much on the scenario and the causes of Lin's ouster as on subsequent developments and Maoist plans for PLA-CCP relations. If, for instance, Lin was ousted because he really did plot against Mao in some manner, serious PLA-CCP differences can probably be minimized by a careful and truthful explanation of what went on and why. If, on the other hand, Lin was removed because of an intra-PLA struggle among field army heads or regionally based military factions, there will undoubtedly be a large-scale reshuffling and purge of Lin's erstwhile supporters in the Fourth Field Army system as well as those in central positions of authority. At this writing (early 1972), there is as yet little evidence of such a purge. If, finally, Lin was removed because of PLA-CCP differences (or, more likely, differences between personalities and on issues, some in each institution lined up on each side), continued political tensions can be expected, culminating at some point in a new showdown between factions, as the Lin followers attempt to recoup their losses or protect themselves from further attack.

Thus, the possibilities range all the way from a generally agreed-upon covering-over of the Lin affair to acute PLA-CCP tensions. It must be remembered, however, that the September events partook of the nature of palace politics and did not involve the masses or even large numbers in the CCP and the PLA. Thus, it appears that Lin's removal, taken alone, is unlikely to be of central importance to Chinese politics and to PLA-CCP relations in the long run. On the other hand, it could become a major factor in the politics of the Maoist succession, that is, in the narrow sense of the political struggle sure to follow upon Mao's death—though it must be remembered that Chinese politics as a whole, from 1966, have revolved around the question of policy and personalities that will prevail after Mao's death. Especially would

this be the case if Mao were to leave the scene in the next year or two
or if some crisis were to force the various factions into major de-
partures from policies now agreed upon.

Finally, Lin's ouster calls for a reevaluation of the relationship
between Lin and Mao in the past. Though the answer depends in large
measure on the facts of the power struggle of the summer and autumn
of 1971, it seems to this writer that, while politics at the top of a
political heirarchy do much to change bonds long maintained, the ties
of trust and confidence that these two men had established so early,
to say nothing of the leader-follower, father-son relationship between
them, all militate in favor of continuation of a similar relationship
down to the very end. That is to say, Lin's removal may have been
against Mao's wishes and therefore the very essence of anti-Maoism.
If that proves to be the case, we shall have to reevaluate, not Lin's
relationship with Mao, but the strength of Mao's rule itself.

5

THE NEW
GUN-BARREL
ELITE
John D. Simmonds

The Cultural Revolution has had a varied if generally remarkable effect on foreign observers. It has taught some of them to think of China as being under the rule of a kind of Chinese junta; for some time China had almost gone back to the warlord days. It has retaught some of the older ones that it was only fifteen to twenty years ago that a similar situation prevailed. It reminded those who may have forgotten that the vast majority of the ruling "civilian" elite had been soldiers. It has tended to lead some analysts to the conclusion that there is now a military dictatorship in China and that this is something new and wonderful to behold.

The fact is, however, that it is not new. Soldiers, of a kind, have always ruled: ultimate authority in Communist China has always rested with the armed forces. It was so before the regime was established, during the war against the Japanese and the Nationalists. It has been so ever since. Its most obvious form, visible negatively in the pages of the PLA Work Bulletin (Kung-tso Tung-hsun), showed Peking's concern over the reliability of its peasant-based armed forces during the famines of 1960-61.

The administrative structure of the regime has, with variations, always been one of interlocking parallel systems. In the early 1950s,

––––––––––––––
––––––––––––––

This was originally prepared in more detailed form for presentation to the Banff Conference on Chinese Elites sponsored by the Social Science Research Council and held at Banff, Canada, in August, 1970.

this was particularly clear. With the institution of regular civil government, it became somewhat less clear—perhaps more parallel but less obviously interlocking. The post-Cultural Revolution form, despite its differences, resembles the early 1950s. Though the membership of the central MAC is unknown, it can probably be safely assumed to be drawn exclusively from the CC. One may consequently assume its standing committee to reflect closely the membership of the Politburo.

This duality of Party-military role is nowhere more evident than at the provincial level. The newly instituted Provincial Party Committees and RCs have very strong military representation: virtually all the de facto leading positions are held concurrently by the most senior provincial military-district officers. Less well known, but equally certain, is the personal relationship between the special district (multi-hsien) RCs, of which there are something in the order of 200, and their exactly parallel military subdistricts.[1] A similar parallel is in existence at the level of municipality; this applied also for the hsien, which number over 2,000.[2] As the hsien is the basic unit of formal government and has remained so for well over 2,000 years, the integration of the PLA at this level indicates the degree of control exercised by the military throughout the land.[3]

It would not be too much of an exaggeration to state that, rather than one, there are twenty-six Chinas—twenty-nine, if the three major cities are included, each one of which is ruled from the relevant capital but through the hsien and down to the village. And it is at all these levels, even at that of the village, by means of armed forces or militia departments, that the military is ruling.

The difference about the situation today, where politics are seen to emerge from the barrel of a gun, is that this relationship was at best only implicit in the decade before the Cultural Revolution. Nevertheless, two points must be emphasized. In the first place, the regime has conducted direct gun-barrel politics for as long as it has dispensed with them. Second, even during the decade of nonmilitary rule, the parallel or alternative apparatus—the ultimate coercion— was always there like another gear in reserve. It is as though the military structure was a permanent alternative, comprehensive administrative system. What the Cultural Revolution did was to shift gears, to cause this alternative system to be used once again directly.

If this is so, and the evidence suggests that it is, then any reorganization of the PLA just prior to 1966 would probably relate specifically to the Cultural Revolution purges. If no such causal relationship existed, it would be difficult to explain the failure of important and powerful civil officials to protect themselves. That these men were powerful is beyond question, but their power bases had generally been restricted to the civil sector. With some notable exceptions, they had no direct control of military force, apart from internal provincial troops of marginal capability. Yet even those who did exercise direct command functions appear to have put up little or no resistance.

It is this curious phenomenon of the Cultural Revolution that will now be examined primarily for the purpose of answering the question, "Are the loyalties and perspectives of the new gun-barrel elite pro-Maoist, leftist, and centrist, or are they professional, rightest, and localist?" The time span will be from the tenth Plenum (1962) to early 1966 because it was during this period that the most important leadership shifts occurred. Though Lin Piao commenced his journey back to power in 1958, replaced P'eng Teh-huai in 1959, and then systematically started to purge the PLA operational forces as opposed to central command and administrative structures, it was only after the Chinese victory over the Indians in late 1962 that the real counteroffensive began.

REORGANIZATION OF THE PLA, 1962-66

The underlying assumption in this chapter is that Mao would never have launched the Cultural Revolution, which entailed purging a large number of powerful officials, without first being sure of his ability to conduct the purge. If that is so, given the fact that the Cultural Revolution commenced overtly at about the end of 1965, it follows that the analysis must begin with events preceding this date.

It is important to distinguish between what might be termed the two PLAs.[4] The first, and by far the more significant in the present context of purge and coup, consists of the operational armies. These are the "front-line," highly trained, and well-equipped armies (including eleven military-region headquarters) that are located strategically throughout China for the purposes of repelling or deterring invasion. It was the demonstrated control of some of these operational units that ensured periodic Maoist victory against certain provincial Party bosses during the earliest phases of the Cultural Revolution.* The second comprises the province-level commands,

*Some of the best examples of this are seen in the activities

principally those of the twenty-nine provincial military districts.
This PLA could be called the People's War branch, being concerned
primarily with administering local defense forces, militia recruitment, and the like. Although subordinate ultimately to Peking, these
local forces traditionally have come directly under military-district
command and, through political-commissar appointments, under
Provincial Party Committee rule.

After Lin Piao became Minister of Defense, he conducted a
general rectification campaign in the PLA, particularly, it seems,
in the ranks of the operational armies.[5] This was ostensibly to
counter defeatist or deviationist tendencies due to the failure of the
Great Leap Forward and to the leadership of P'eng Teh-huai. It had
as its immediate end the carefully devised and executed short war
against India. The purpose of this was not only to put the Indians in
their place and demonstrate to the world a real capability for defense
after the Great Leap Forward fiasco, but, at least equally important,
it was also a demonstration to the people of China of PLA power and
reliability plus Maoist infallibility. Following their swift victories,
the PLA became the idol of the people, the society-wide object of
emulation. Within a few months, PLA propagandists from the GPD,
still under a degree of direct military control, started moving into
a new political-department structure that was in the process of
enveloping the normal civil-government apparatus. This may have
been the beginning of the direct and active campaign to overthrow
the opposition. Or it may merely have reflected the by then overriding
and all-encompassing effort to revivify and resubject the nation.
Whatever the case, and the facts are too few to allow for decisiveness,
China's internal revolution was on the move again.*

The first period of Lin Piao's reorganization of the PLA was
in 1963 and witnessed a fair number of personnel changes. A few
occurred in the central organs, in the navy and signals corps.
Hsieh Fu-chih may have taken over command of the Public Security

---

of Li Yuan, 6900 unit (47 Army) in Hunan; Nan P'ing, 6409 unit (20
Army) in Chekiang; and Li Teh-sheng, 6408 unit (12 Army) in Anhwei.

*One difficulty in any thesis that argues that the establishment
of these political departments in early 1963 led to a Maoist victory
in 1968 lies in the fact that, if this had been intended as a direct move
against Mao's opposition, why were all the identified senior political-
department officials purged in the Cultural Revolution?

troops, probably at the time of the Indian war. A vice-minister of Public Security was also dismissed at about this time. The commander of the Peking garrison was removed, and, possibly, those of Hopei and Shansi military districts. If such were the case, as it seems to have been, then it is a clear indication that preparations were being made to guarantee the military reliability of the capital city and its surrounding provincial military districts. Nanking Military Region was also affected in 1963. There were at least three new appointments, and one man was "kicked upstairs." A few other moves were made in a number of military regions. There is some evidence to suggest that new appointments were made to several military districts, including those of Kwangtung, Kwangsi, Shantung, Yunnan, and Tibet.

It would appear that a second period, from about February, 1964, to June, 1965, inclusive, was in fact a time of considerably greater activity. Not many new appointments seem to have been made in the first half of the period. In the central organs and Peking Military Region, for example, none was noted. Kiangsi appears to have received a new commander. Liu Ch'ung-kuei was recalled from Vietnam to Kwangsi. Three military-district command changes were effected in Kwangtung, and in Hupeh a new commander was appointed. Faraway in the northeast, an additional deputy political commissar seems to have gone from an army unit in Kirin to the military-district headquarters, and the political commissar of Heilungkiang was dismissed and replaced by Wang Huai-hsiang. In the northwest, Huang Ching-yao took over command of Shensi Military District between September, 1963 and the following February. It is in the second half of the second period—that is, from about September, 1964, to June, 1965—that several important events took place and a relatively large number of significant appointments were made.

To enable the military moves noted in this chapter to be placed in context, it is necessary to refer to Cultural Revolution sources. Although these are in many cases suspect, if not obviously useless as source material, in other cases they are invaluable. Only salient points will be referred to here.[6] In September, 1964, Liu Shao-ch'i is alleged to have authored a socialist-education policy document, the "Later Ten Points." It is not known whether this document had been approved by Mao or, if not, whether he had stopped its dissemination. In fact, leadership views on the subject of the socialist-education campaign cannot be ascertained with any degree of confidence. What is clear, however, is that within a month of its being drawn up, the regime launched a major onslaught against domestic revisionism.

October, 1964, was indeed a highly significant time. While, almost precisely two years earlier, the nation had been finally called to advance after the post-Great Leap Forward retreat and the PLA had defeated the Indians, the call in 1964 was at least as dramatic. The war in Vietnam had seriously escalated; October 14 had seen the dismissal of Mao's enemy Khrushchev; two days later, China, "poor and blank," (Mao's characterization of the peasantry in the 1930s) had exploded its first nuclear device. From this moment on, the great movement was in a direction away from domestic revisionism, away from the national low posture. It was a heroic period, a time for histrionics.

Cultural Revolution sources further reveal that the Party General-Secretary, Teng Hsiao-p'ing, was criticized by Mao for having an "independent kingdom" and that this occurred at the end of 1964.[7] It is not possible to tell what truth there is in this allegation, but in view of other events at that time it does not seem improbable. There is, as well, Mao's oft-quoted account of his retreat to the second line until after the 23 Articles were drawn up, when he became greatly concerned over his inability to control affairs, particularly in Peking.[8] Assuming this to be correct, the date when Mao criticized Teng Hsiao-p'ing would have been in late December, 1964. This reasoning is based on the fact that a Politburo meeting is known to have been held in the last ten days of December; furthermore, virtually all key leaders were in Peking at this time. It is also known that the 23 Article program was formally discussed by a CC conference on January 14, 1965; this presupposes an earlier preparation of the document.

This was certainly a critical time. The National People's Congress sat on December 21 and did not finally break up until January 4, 1965. It was at this meeting that Lin Piao's election to the position of First Vice Premier was announced, apparently to the disgust of Lo Jui-ch'ing.[9] The Supreme State Conference, a prestigious body very seldom convened, unprecedentedly met twice on December 18 and 30. A week later, the National Defense Council sat in plenary session, thus strongly suggesting that the vastly more important body, the MAC, was convened at about the same time. A twenty-day, apparently highly significant PLA GPD meeting was also held in January.

The great campaign, which this chapter claims began in October, had gotten under way. The 23 Article program demanded that socialist education be conducted according to up-to-date Marxist-Leninist criteria. It further warned of the rectification of errant officials regardless of status. In this respect, specific mention was made of provincial and CC levels. With the conclusion of these high-level conferences, there was a gradual and partial exodus from Peking. Eventually, Mao himself left. He appeared on February 22, then again on March 4 and 14, after which he seems to have remained out of Peking until June 29.

In the months immediately following that meeting, there was a spate of changes at the regional-bureau and provincial-committee levels. In Shanghai, there was a reorganization. It was atypical, however, being concerned with the question of the succession to K'o Ch'ing-shih in a city obviously well controlled by military forces loyal to Mao. The other civil changes related specifically to the two areas one can now say could not have been safely assumed to be pro-Maoist: the central-south/southwest regions and North China.

In the central-south, Kwangtung First Secretary T'ao Chu was elevated to a vice-premiership, ostensibly in January, 1965, and replaced by one of his close associates. In addition, presumably with the intention of strengthening the hold of T'ao, another of his associates was appointed second secretary of Kwangsi by May. In Hupeh, on the other hand, Chang T'i-hsueh became prominent at the end of June as second secretary. This move probably was calculated to weaken control of the province by Wang Jen-ch'ung and T'ao. The end result of T'ao's elevation must have been the slight diminution in his control of his power base, though this maneuver was not consumated until he moved to Peking as vice-premier shortly before his purge.

The most significant moves were made in the southwest. As in the case of T'ao, Li Ching-ch'uan, the overlord of the region, was released from his Szechwan first secretaryship at the beginning of 1965. He, too, was replaced by his protégé. It is unlikely, however, that he thereby was sufficiently separated from his base of power. In the lesser province of Kweichow, Chou Lin was dismissed by the third week in February and replaced by another of Li Ching-ch'uan's men. At the same time, however, Li Li was brought in from Kwangtung as a new Kweichow secretary. He survived the subsequent purges. In neighboring Yunnan, with the Kunming Military Region headquarters, Yen Hung-yen's Party control seems to have been weakened at the beginning of 1965 by the introduction of Secretary Chou Hsing, a man with a long Public Security record and an ability to survive. He appears to have taken over the post of first political commissar of the Yunnan Provincial Military District very soon after arriving. Although falling outside the period under consideration, in August,

1965, Chang Kuo-hua was made first secretary of the newly created Tibet Autonomous Region, presumably in a bid to strengthen his position and prestige in the southwest area vis-à-vis Li Ching-ch'uan. The net effect of these moves may have been a lessening of Li's political power outside Szechwan; within the province, however, his political power remained virtually intact.

In Peking, Lin Piao's election to the position of first vice-premier, though insignificant in terms of power by comparison with his other posts, certainly gave him added status and influence nationally. There were also a number of significant moves in the North China provinces. T'ao Lu-chia was removed from his power base in Shensi in early 1965, though he was replaced by a man who also later was purged. The position of Lin T'ieh is less clear. It does seem, however, that he too might have been dislodged at the beginning of the year, and that the decision to do this was taken by the Politburo in December. Lin was not reported in news media between March 20 and May 11; he appeared once more publicly six days later and twice again at unspecified places in June and July. If he was not officially purged until much later, it nevertheless seems to be the case that he was effectively negated in the spring. Ulanfu's position in Inner Mongolia is impossible to judge. Although appearing infrequently in the first half of the year, he may well have preserved his basis of political power in Inner Mongolia until the Cultural Revolution really got under way. But his power base was of the flimsiest nature relative to that surrounding it, and his purge was not long delayed or difficult to accomplish.

Regarding military changes, it was in the second half of the second period that a great many occurred. It is possible if not probable that the decision to effect the majority of these was taken by the MAC on instructions from the Politburo and that the date for this followed closely on the Politburo meeting of late December, 1964. In all probability, the MAC was convened in plenary session around the time of the National Defense Council plenum, held on January 8, 1965. At the central level, a probable result of this was the appointment of Han Hsien-ch'u as deputy chief of staff. In the vital operations subdepartment of the General Staff Department, the director, Wang Shang-jung, dropped out of sight at this time precisely when some publicity was given to his ultimate replacement, Su Ching. Coincidentally, the end of the second period saw the last of Yang Cheng-wu for a while; he did not return to the limelight until after the fall of his superior, Lo Jui-ch'ing. This suggests that he was intimately connected with the preparations for Lo's downfall. It was in this period, too, that the top command of the navy was largely reorganized. Although the political commissar remained unscathed for some time and the commander survived the purges, the three officers who became prominent in the Cultural Revolution all received new posts by the beginning of 1965. The reorganization of the Public Security machine, which had started in 1963, resulted in the dismissal of two vice-ministers and their replacement by three others, apparently in October, 1964. Only one of these, Yu Sang, survived the Cultural Revolution.

In the military regions and districts, there were quite a number of changes in the latter half of the second period. Several men seem to have been affected in Peking (Shi Chih-pen, Wu Tai, and Liu Shao-wen) and in Hopei (Hsiao Ssu-ming). More occurred in the general area of the Nanking Military Region. Due probably to K'o Ching-shih's long and grave illness, Chang Ch'un-ch'iao was made secretary of Shanghai and Chang Chi-hou and Ch'en Shih-fa seem to have been added to the garrison. Liu Wen-hsueh may also have been promoted to garrison political commissar in this period, though no proof of this is available until November.

In Foochow Military Region, there were not many changes at all; most appear to have been made in the last few months of 1964 and first few months of the next year. Yeh Fei, who was commander and political commissar of the region and first secretary of Fukien, dramatically dropped out of the public eye after February, though he did not apparently fall until much later. Several new appointments seem to have been made in the Canton Military Region. Two operational army men appear to have moved into Canton city from Huiyang, and Liu Hsing-yuan was apparently promoted to second political commissar during the period. The latter's promotion was not certain until September. Possibly in this same general span of time, T'an Wen-pang became second political commissar of Hunan Military District. It may well have been in this period—that is, by June, 1965— that Ch'en Kuei-ch'ang was appointed first deputy commander of Honan; he certainly had been by September.

In the northeast, no moves of significance were made in the period, while in the northwest, Ting Sheng and P'ei Chou-yu may have moved in from the Chengtu and Peking Military Regions, respectively. Kweichow, where the Party apparatus was purged by the beginning of 1965, had its commander relocated to the military-region headquarters in Yunnan. Commander T'ien Wei-yang had left by August, 1965, having probably gone some months earlier; he did not survive the purges. In Tibet, which Chang Kuo-hua had formally taken over in August, 1965, Wang Ch'eng-han turned up from

Nanking Military Region together with Jen Jung from Peking. In addition, an existing deputy commander, Li Chueh, seems to have been dismissed at this time; he was last reported in November, 1964. Possibly also at the end of the second period, but certainly by August, 1965, one of the first Maoist military moves was made against Li Ching-ch'uan when one of Chang Kuo-hua's associates, Teng Shao-tung, transferred to Chengtu Military Region.

The picture that emerges from these post-1963 data falls into natural patterns. The first is related to October, 1964, and marks the beginning of an acute phase in Chinese domestic politics. This led to the second—the December, 1964, Politburo meeting, the 23 Articles program, and decisions on a society-wide series of appointments and dismissals. The third indicates an appointments trend immediately after October, 1964, reflecting an attempt to strengthen Maoist control of the central military machine. Fourth, an effort was made to weaken non-Maoist political power in North China, the central-south, and the southwest. In "reliable" military regions and districts of the northeastern, northern, and eastern regions, there was an over-all Maoist consolidation of Military power. Inner Mongolia may have remained largely untouched at this stage, but was, in any case, probably militarily insignificant. This consolidation also applies generally to Canton, Lanchow, and Tibet military regions. In addition, Kunming Military Region, once Kweichow was reorganized, and Honan Military District seem to have been secured for the Maoists in this period. It would appear that the areas still unsecured militarily, in varying degrees, at that time were Sinkiang and Wuhan military regions, Hupeh Military District, and probably the least secure of all, Chengtu Military Region and District.

By the end of June, 1965, therefore, the stage seems to have been set. With the exception of a few high-ranking officers, the pre-Cultural Revolution reorganization of the PLA had been completed. In this category, two new men were appointed to the General Rear Services Department (GRSD), and Hsiang Chung-hua was replaced by Huang Chih-yung in the armored corps. In the Public Security machine, two of the three 1964 appointees were presumably purged, and T'an Fu-jen took over the Military Court. In Peking garrison, it is speculated, Fu Ch'ung-pi and Teng Hai-ch'ing moved in at this time; they were definitely there shortly after the Cultural Revolution started. Coincidentally, with the end of general preparations, Mao returned to the public eye. He publicly unveiled himself in Hangchow on June 10 and made a dramatic reappearance in the capital on June 29. It was also at the end of June that the future chief of staff, Yang Cheng-wu, slipped out of view in order probably to prepare for the removal of the remaining key generals.

It is not possible to know precisely what took place at this time. Nevertheless, as Mao had presumably spent the previous three months in contemplation and investigation, it is not improbable that he had by then made up his mind to launch the Cultural Revolution. Though this goes against evidence from Maoist sources to the effect that it was not until September-October that he mapped out the "great strategic plan," he had certainly issued a Cultural Revolution type directive on education in July.[10] In addition, as he seems to have recognized the need for high-level purges at the end of September, it is not unlikely that he had, therefore, foreseen the need for the Cultural Revolution itself.[11]

Be that as it may, the leadership was summoned to an enlarged Politburo conference in Peking that lasted from at least September 28 until October 2, 1965, if not until October 4. It was at this meeting that Mao is supposed to have raised the problem of revisionism in the CC and the effects of this on the provinces, together with the question of cultural divergence or worse on the part of Wu Han. The meeting provided the occasion for calling away from their power bases many of the provincial Party and military leaders who were later to fall. Just over a fortnight passed, and Mao once more dropped out of sight, where he remained until well after the commencement of the Cultural Revolution. In all probability, he spent most of his time in his Hangchow, East China sanctuary.[12]

There was a general exodus from Peking at about the same time. The commander of Peking Military Region, Yang Yung, went to Korea for nine days; Vice-Minister of Defense Liao Han-sheng was last seen on October 17. Already noted were the activities of the commander of the armored corps, Hsü Kuang-ta, who made no public appearance from the beginning of September until late November, when he went touring the provinces. Lo Jui-ch'ing was last recorded in Peking on October 25 and seems to have gone to South China with his wife; he appears not to have returned until about a month later. Liu Shao-ch'i dropped out of sight on November 27 for a period of seven weeks. Ho Lung went to Sinkiang, where he remained from September 27 until October 13, thus missing the big Party meetings. After his return to the capital, he made only rare public appearances and then seems to have gone to Canton in late December. The director of the General Office of the CC, Yang Shang-k'un, another prominent target of the Cultural Revolution, dropped out of the news after November 29, but had in any case made only two publicized appearances between October 31 and that date. An even more important man, General-Secretary Teng Hsiao-p'ing, made only rare appearances after the conclusion of the Politburo conference: once in Peking on November 1, with Li Ching-ch'uan and Po I-po in Chungking on November 18, and then not again until December 22.

By December, the Cultural Revolution had started. Mao, it is said, had allocated the task of bringing down Wu Han to the reorganized Shanghai administration on October 10. Concerning these events, it is tantalizing to speculate on the activities of the non-Maoist leaders. Although not susceptible of proof, it is just possible that a belated effort was being made to protect themselves from the blow that was to come. Ho Lung, when he went to Sinkiang, had gone to one of his old First Field Army base areas; he may have tried to enlist support from his old wartime colleagues. Shortly thereafter, Teng Hsiao-p'ing and Po I-po, reputedly an associate of his and of Ho Lung, visited the southwest. Teng had been political commissar of the Second Field Army and the senior Party official in the southwest area in the 1950s; some of this army's units had subsequently been stationed in the area. There, conceivably, with the connivance of Ho Lung and active support of Ho's protégé, Li Ching-ch'uan, they may have plotted to protect themselves. This would have been on or about November 18. Whether the activities of Hsü Kuang-ta and Liao Han-sheng after September 3 were related to this postulated plot is quite unknown. Both were in the First Field Army, and Liao is alleged by Red Guard publications to have been Ho Lung's nephew. It is not impossible that they were related; at least Hsü probably had the opportunity to discuss matters with Li Ching-ch'uan eleven days after Teng Hsiao-p'ing's visit.

Whether or not there was such a northwest-southwest protective effort based primarily on old First Field Army loyalties plus assistance from Second Field Army elements may never be known. All that is certain for the moment is that these men and a considerable number of others did not survive the blow when it came. It is probably too early to attempt to write the final account: there are still men to bring down, probably even in the new CC; others will be given face but denied power; others again will be reeducated and returned to the public view. Although very many details remain to be revealed and some of what has been depicted here may be proven wrong, the evidence nevertheless strongly suggests that there was no hope of escaping the purges when they came. As Hobbes put it, "When nothing else is turned up, clubs are trumps."[13]

To summarize, the foundation structure of formal civil administration in China has little changed from that obtaining over 2,000 years ago. Upon this structure, the Communists grafted Party and military parallel substructures. For years, these existed together with the historical system, though government was exercised after 1954 by the Party through its administrative civil bureaucracy. With the Great Leap Forward experiment, the top leadership was subjected to stress. Subsequently, Mao joined with Lin Piao and others in an effort to overthrow Liu Shao-ch'i and a large number of the ruling elite. Before the purge could be accomplished, however, it was necessary to ensure the support of the PLA From the moment of his assumption of military command, Lin reorganized the armed forces and purged a number of his predecessor's associates. From about 1962 on, he then reshuffled the central armed forces' headquarters and certain unreliable military regions and districts. Furthermore, he tried to assert virtually complete control over the operational armies located strategically throughout the land. This protracted and extensive reorganization was fundamentally, if only partially, completed by the end of June, 1965. The Cultural Revolution that followed, consequently, merely reflected the successful earlier coup. This being the case, an analysis must now be made of this new Cultural Revolution elite.

THE NEW GUN-BARREL ELITE

A Maoist concept has been adopted here as a means of describing the present form of government as economically and evocatively as possible. The new ruling gun-barrel elite has in one form or another been in existence since before the regime was established. One tends to forget that the little general-secretary who so dearly loved to play bridge was once the political commissar of the mighty Second Field Army, that the late Politburo's agricultural chief was a Third Field Army commander, and that all this was not really so long ago. Using an earlier analogy, the military apparatus exactly paralleling the civil Party and government structure from the top to the bottom is the gear in reserve. This has in effect been a permanent alternative form of government.

In this sense, the Communist Chinese political system seems to be neither a military oligarchy nor a mobilization system. It is fundamentally different from the former, and it seems to be much more than the latter, as it cannot be circumvented nor its power curtailed and made a mere dependent organ of the body politic. It is neither a question of a simple militarized society nor of a merely paramilitary revolutionized mobilization system.[14] The standard categorization does not fully or even adequately correspond.

The gun-barrel polity is a highly systemized Sino-Leninist form. One of its essential features is the manner in which a preselected military bureaucratic alternative has been built into the system. It is in this respect alone that its fundamental difference requires that a new political category be devised to comprehend the Chinese system. To revert to the Cultural Revolution, Mao does not seem to have attempted to destroy the actual system itself. Instead, he called in the permanent reserve to purge the system's old bureaucratic segment. The changes effected in this permanent military alternative, as has been seen, were marginal by comparison with those the military themselves effected in the old bureaucracy. For the permanent military alternative to be maintained always ready and capable of exercising its societal role, it must itself undergo permanent or frequent purge. In more than one way, therefore, this alternating utilization of the gun-barrel elite leads to permanent but controlled revolution.

This military elite, however, is not specifically designed to rule anything but itself. It is not trained, equipped, or even large enough to govern the civil masses.[15] Its very elitist nature and discipline make it comparatively easy to control. It can be employed in its normal role to counter external and internal threats; it can be used to overthrow ruling bureaucracies; and it can even rule, for a while. It cannot, however, rule permanently without losing its identify, esprit, discipline, and force. Though civilianized soldiers can revert to military roles, they seldom do. Long periods of civil employment usually turn soldiers into civilians of a sort and, more important, provide them with strong vested interests in the civil sector. If used judiciously and in a controlled manner, the gun-barrel alternative can overthrow, select, and train a new bureaucracy leavened with its own hitherto promotion-blocked men and then return to its proper place.

The only serious weakness in this system, which would otherwise be both original and efficacious, is the possibility that a military leader might perform his purge duties and then refuse to give up his special powers. The best antidote to such a scenario seems to lie in the deliberate fractionization of military power among a number of central commands and service arms, among regional commands and operational units, and by changing personnel and unit locations. By such means, together with the existence of distinct garrison commands and fully militarized Public Security troops, the regime scatters military power. In addition, all are subject to the pervasive scrutiny of the normal Party and state control agencies.

Finally, this Chinese political system seems to offer an additional benefit: a solution of sorts to the very real and universal phenomenon of the "Red vs. Expert" dichotomy. The gun-barrel elite is both Red and expert for the simple reason that it is neither in comparative terms. This is not to assert that the PLA has escaped or will always escape the commissar-commander or Red-expert problem; it has not and will not. But in the PLA such a problem is relatively controllable. Certainly, it is much less of a problem for the military than for the two alternative parallel systems of Party and government, each innately either Red or expert.

If China is a gun-barrel polity ruled at the moment by a particular gun-barrel elite, the question that must now be posed and answered is whether this elite differs from the one of the previous decade and, if so, in what manner. One way in which to begin answering this is to define China's present developmental stage. If C. E. Black's periodization is employed as a rough guide, China would seem to be basically in phase two—the consolidation of the modernizing leadership—while concurrently in the early part of phase three—economic and social transformation.[16] Given this, how is it related to the hypothesized new elite? The first point to make is very similar to that made by William Quandt: perhaps the chief characteristic of the new Politburo is not so much the preponderance of what may be termed purely military men as the "decline in number of cosmopolitan, well-educated political leaders."[17]

A brief examination of the educational level of this Politburo is mandatory if one is to try to understand the new military leadership, which forms about half of its total. Compared with the educational level of the Politburo in existence from 1958 on, particularly relating to formal tertiary or "westernized" training, qualifications have fallen by something in the region of 70 percent Politburo members who have had university to normal school education have dropped from about 17 persons (8th Politburo) to about 5 (9th Politburo). There is no doubt that this is significant, but it can also be misleading, for how much of the old higher education is suitable today? Put another way, is it possible that much of the more pedestrian or pragmatic training given the new gun-barrel elite, in higher military institutions or commonplace military technical and educational programs, is of greater use even at the highest levels of political leadership? In addition, there is the t'ung-hsüeh (schoolmate) factor, which, as ever, is of considerable importance. On the other hand, today it may well be that a new factor, wu-hsüeh (without formal education), binds many of the new military leaders together far more tightly than one may suspect in the intelligentsia-ridden Chinese society.[18]

Nevertheless, it is not only in education that the new elite differs from the old. If the pre-Cultural Revolution Politburo could be projected into 1970 and its average age compared with that of the present top group (minus two whose date of birth is unknown), today's average would be some six or seven years less. The new eleven-man gun-barrel elite within the present Politburo actually seems to be even younger; its average age is approximately 60 years.* A further point of interest is revealed when the birthplaces of the old leadership are compared with those of the new. Whereas eight of the old came from Hunan and three from Hupeh, now seven to nine come from Hupeh and only Mao and possibly one other come from Hunan.** Even more striking and with implications for future leadership composition and competence is the fact that so many of the new gun-barrel elite both come from Hupeh and have had little or no formal education.

These conclusions would not in themselves be so compelling were it not for the fact that the important t'ung-hsiang (same birth-place) factor is reflected in the make-up of the rest of this new elite. It would be going too far to state that being a Hupeh man has become the passport to success, but obviously it has helped. Nonetheless, it must be pointed out that some of the notable purges of the Cultural Revolution have been of Lin Piao's fellow provincials, not excluding his Mach'eng neighbors.

An additional factor of considerable consequence in the make-up of this new elite, and particularly of the new military leadership, is that of wartime association or common membership in field armies and their antecedent subunits. La Dany has rightly questioned over-reliance on the association factor,[19] and the Cultural Revolution has provided much evidence to support such a position. Yet, this does not mean that past association should be discounted as an important factor in human relations. It can provide valuable insights into such

---

*The average is approximately two years less. The group comprises Lin Piao, Huang Yung-sheng, Hsü Shih-yu, Ch'en Hsi-lien, Li Hsien-nien, Li Tso-p'eng, Ch'iu Hui-tso, Wu Fa-hsien, Hsieh Fu-chih, and Li Teh-sheng. Chang Ch'un-ch'iao was tentatively included, as he appears to have been born in Hupeh.

**All three doubtful men could come from Kiangsi; in addition, three new Politburo men have unknown places of birth. The Hupeh contingent comes mostly from the Huang An-Huang Kang area (the radius is about 50 miles).

relationships. As an example of the value obtainable by means of
these methods, Chinese analysts in Hong Kong and Taiwan have for
many years studied the Peking leadership in terms of their pre-1949
field-army associations.* The best non-Chinese example of this is
provided by William Whitson in his excellent account of civil-war
field-army affiliations.[20]

As a general rule, by the summer of 1971, there had been a
marked decrease of First Field Army representation in the top levels
of the central military apparatus. This was perhaps to be expected,
considering the prominent parts played or supposedly played by P'eng
Teh-huai and Ho Lung over the years. This decline seemed to prevail
at the military-region and military-district levels, though it was by
no means so marked. Much less clear was the position of the second
and third field armies and of those units who came under direct
central-government control (the Fifth Field Army). There is a
suggestion that, relative to the whole, the numbers of officers traceable
to all three were thinning out somewhat. Nevertheless, since Hsü
Shih-yu and Li Teh-sheng, not to mention Chang Ch'un-ch'iao, appear
to have played such prominent roles in ensuring the success of the
Cultural Revolution, it did not seem likely that the Third Field Army
men were due for imminent purge. Indeed, the good standing of the
Third Field Army seemed to be reflected in the nonpurge of Su Yu
and, to a lesser degree, Ch'en Yi, though both seemed to be without
any real power in the hiararchy before the summer of 1971.

It was the Fourth Field Army, however, that had made such
remarkable headway. In the central military organs, this was nowhere
more notable than in the General Staff. Of the ten deputy chiefs added
after 1958, seven came from the old Fourth Field Army and one was
born in Hupeh; these eight were all members of the new CC. One of
the pre-1958 deputy chiefs had remained in the CC; since he came
from the suspect First Field Army, it is probable that he had been
permitted to retain face in order to facilitate the completion of the
process of purging the First Field Army group of its unhealthy
elements and the PLA of its First Field Army group. (The cases of
Wang En-mao and Chang Ta-chih illustrate this well.) Although the
Fourth Field Army preponderence in the other branches of the central
military machine was not so obvious, it still applied. The Minister of

---

*The methodology is as applicable to the study of Ch'ing and
Republican elites as it is to the Communist period and is, of course,
valuable for any period of Chinese (or other) history.

Defense and his chief of staff came from the Fourth Field Army, as did the following: Su Ching, in the operations subdepartment, both the director and the political commissar of the GRSD, what appeared to be the new director of the Political Department, the commander of the air force, and the commander and first political commissar of the navy. This pattern, however, did not seem to apply at all to the lesser arms such as the artillery and amor corps, at least not yet. Minister of Public Security and Commander of Public Security troops Hsieh Fu-chih comes from the Second Field Army, but was born in Hupeh.*

This picture of dominance by the Fourth Field Army probably typified the over-all national trend during the Cultural Revolution. Of the twenty-two military-region commanders and first political commissars, fourteen came from the Fourth Field Army. In the three most important regions—Peking, Nanking, and Mukden—control seemed to be in the hands of men of the second and third field-armies. Nevertheless, in each case the commanding officer came from Hupeh, as did the political commissar of Peking** and Nanking military regions and the commander of the Peking garrison. Hsien Heng-han, the long-standing political commissar of Lanchow Military Region, hails from both Hunan and the First Field Army; he should, therefore, not remain in position for long. For this reason the personnel in both positions in the Lanchow Military Region are regarded here as unknown; also unknown are the two positions in Inner Mongolia and the political-commissar posts in the military regions of Kunming and Sinkiang. Finally, the Wuhan regional political commissar, though from the Second Field Army, was born in Hupeh.

In sum, the general picture in the summer of 1971 was one of strong reliance at the military-region level on men from the original Fourth Field Army or from Hupeh. There may be exceptions to this rule, but if there are, they are few. Unfortunately, such a clear picture does not emerge for the military-district level, for the simple reason that there are insufficient data. Furthermore, the position is obscured, as it also must be for the military regions, by the presence and power of the operational armies and divisions, whose leaders are generally completely unknown, let alone possessing traceable field-

---

*Liu Po-ch'eng is the figurehead representative of the Second Field Army in the Politburo.

**Assuming this to be Hsieh Fu-chih, of which there may be some doubt.

army associations. There is, nonetheless, some suggestion, if an uncertain one, of a trend to Fourth Field Army men at the level of the provincial military district.

Minimal deductions of low reliability can be drawn from such a flimsy data base. This chapter may only have served to raise questions, not to solve them. Nevertheless, the evidence does seem to indicate some patterns. It suggests that the central core of the present leadership may not be the Standing Committee of the Politburo as much as a small group elsewhere in the Politburo. It suggests that this group is quite a cohesive one bound by a number of common backgrounds and experiences, not the least important of which is the role they played in making possible or executing the Cultural Revolution. The particularly significant common denominator comprises three factors: fairly low formal educational level, Hupeh origin, and service in the Fourth Field Army.

There is another point that seems to emerge from the data. It is that, just as in earlier days, some in the top Party bodies have been given prestige and denied power. The corollary to this is that some men outside these top bodies have more power, at least in an executive sense, than others in them. Related to this is the additional fact that wielders of power must be more than a group of unconnected individuals; they must form an integrated unit.

For this reason, the four top power positions in China today, and the most sensitive ones, probably comprise the team of the Defense Minister, his chief of staff, the latter's director of operations, and the whole group's protector, the commander of the Peking garrison. All four men are in the CC, but only the first two rate the Politburo, and of these Lin Piao alone is in its Standing Committee. All this suggests that it may well be less useful to consider who the post-Mao leader will be as to bear in mind the fact that the succession may have already been effected and that, in any case, in the gun-barrel polity whoever is selected as ruler will depend less on his mandate or the will of heaven than on the sanction of the new gun-barrel elite.

Whereas many senior members of that elite have clearly been drawn from the Fourth Field Army group, the events of the last four months of 1971 underscored the continuing viability of a balance-of-power political process in China and the determination of senior leaders in the Second Field Army and Third Field Army groups to protect their own collective power equities. Other chapters in this book will discuss some of the differences in viewpoint and style among the various field-army groups. But, above all, changes over the final months of 1971 emphasized the difficulties of predicting specific leadership appointments and changes.

Nevertheless, though the implications for future policy are not clear, the indications are that the Cultural Revolution has produced a new ruling elite that may well be better attuned to the twentieth-century needs of the Chinese people than might first appear to be the case. The attitude this elite adopts to the outside world cannot be accurately predicted. The evidence from the recent past indicates that if elitist behavior in theory allows for a range of choices, these are in the final analysis limited by structure. China is still and for some time will remain a basically agrarian society ruled by a particular elite—that of the gun-barrel. It is consequently a largely introspective, Sinocentric elite. Its foreign policy and international relations, therefore, cannot but be governed basically by domestic Chinese considerations.[21]

NOTES

1. See, for example, BBC's Survey of World Broadcasts, Far East 3388/BII/2-5 and /3397/BII/9-10.

2. BBC's Survey of World Brodcasts, Far East 3397/BII/5; and 3393/BII/11.

3. See H. G. Creel, JAS, Vol. XXIII, February, 1964, pp. 171, 183; also A. Doak Barnett and Ezra Vogel, Cadres, Bureaucracy and Political Power in Communist China (New York: Columbia University Press, 1967), pp. 124, 129-32, 249.

4. Harbin Radio, October 6, 1967.

5. For additional details of this and subsequent statements, see J. D. Simmonds, China: Evolution of a Revolution, 1959-1966, Working Paper No. 9 (Canberra: Department of International Relations, Australian National University, 1968).

6. Simmonds, Evolution of a Revolution, pp. 62-74.

7. Chung-kung Yen-chiu [Studies of Chinese Communism], (Taipei), Noll 1969, JPRS 49899 Translations on Communist China, No. 91, p. 16.

8. Mao CB, No. 891, October 25, 1966, p. 75.

9. See SCMM, No. 641, January 20, 1969, p. 9.

10. "Outline of Struggle Between Two Lines," CB, No. 884, October, 1969, pp. 25, 26; Mao, CB, No. 891, July 3, 1965, p. 50.

11. Ibid., No. 884, July, 1969, pp. 25-26.

12. For the basis of this and the following paragraph, see Simmonds, Evolution of a Revolution, pp. 80-83.

13. Quoted in Dankwart Rustow, A World of Nations (Washington, D.C.: The Brookings Institution, 1967), p. 170.

14. David E. Apter, The Politics of Modernization (Chicago: University of Chicago Press, 1965), pp. 371, 406.

15. S. P. Huntingdon, Political Order in Changing Societies (New Haven: Yale University Press, 1968) pp. 225, 243; Apter, Politics of Modernization, p. 135; and Janowitz quoted by Apter, ibid., p. 264.

16. C. E. Black, The Dynamics of Modernization (New York: Harper and Row, 1966), pp. 67-68.

17. William B. Quandt, The Comparative Study of Political Elites, P-4172 (Santa Monica, Cal.: The Rand Corporation, September, 1969). This preponderance is even more marked when compared with the strong civilian bias in the Politburo composition in 1949.

18. Compare with South Korea, in Robert A. Scalapino, "Which Route for Korea?," Asian Survey, II, 7, (September, 1962), 11.

19. CNA, No. 799, May 1, 1970, p. 2.

20. China Quarterly, No. 37, January-March, 1969, pp. 1-30.

21. This is the general theme of my book, China's World, the Foreign Policy of a Developing State (New York: Columbia University Press, 1970).

THE EMERGENT
MILITARY CLASS
Ting Wang

Judging by his position and absolute authority, Mao Tse-tung is like an emperor. The group of people who are especially close to him, including his wife, his confidential secretaries, guards, and the party theorists who do the agitprop work for him are unquestionably elements of the "royalist faction." They act as if they are boundlessly loyal to the "emperor" and push on with the "left-adventurist" line. The royalist faction or "palace faction" refers to those who are commonly known as the left-adventurist group or "ultra-leftist faction" within the CCP. Representative of this group of people are Chiang Ch'ing, Ch'en Po-ta, K'ang Sheng, Wang Tung-hsing, Chang Ch'un-ch'iao, and Yao Wen-yuan.

Attempts by the royalists in Peking to set up a Paris Commune type of government have met with complete failure, and professional soldiers, backed by the power of their guns, have set up a new form of government by military dictatorship. This new system of government is unique in that professional soldiers not only dominate the central and local party and government organs of leadership, but also have extended their power to control the industrial and mining enterprises throughout the country. Their position and their authority are unmatched by anyone who has held office and power in China over the past twenty years.

It is very difficult to make a precise definition of "professional soldiers" in Communist China. Any of the following cadres can be regarded as professional soldiers:

1. Those who held military ranks before the abolition of the system of military ranks and served primarily in military organs;

2. Full-time military personnel after the abolition of military ranks—those who held military ranks before but
   have not been engaged in military work for a long time,
   such as Chu Teh, are excluded;

3. Full-time political workers of the armed forces, such
   as political commissars and deputy political commissars, directors and deputy directors of political departments, political instructors, and so on (those falling
   within this category are Liu Feng of Wuhan, Yuan Sheng-
   p'ing of Tsinan, and Tseng Shao-shan of Shenyang, but
   those who hold concurrent office as political commissar,
   such as Hsieh Hsueh-kung of Tientsin, Chang Ch'un-
   ch'iao of Nanking, and Liu Chien-hsun of Wuhan are not
   counted as professional soldiers);

4. Members of the MAC of the CCP Central Committee
   (Mao Tse-tung would be more suitably classified as a
   career government official); and

5. Those serving in the ministries of national-defense industries under the State Council (such as the second,
   third, fourth, fifth, sixth, and seventh ministries of
   machine-building industries) while retaining their military status.

Since 1967, these powerful army men have been carrying out
a struggle against certain key figures of the royalist faction, such as
Ch'en Po-ta. Through this political struggle they have attempted
to rectify the mistakes of left-adventurism committed by the royalists
during The Cultural Revolution so as to stabilize the internal situation,
introduce a comparatively moderate political line, and heal the wounds
inflicted upon China's political and economic fabric by the Cultural
Revolution. In line with the requirements of their anti-Soviet strategy,
they are also trying to improve relations with the West.

Under the evolving system of military dictatorship, the professional soldiers in present-day China are wielding political influence
that reaches principally to the cities, towns, and rural areas. But
beyond the national boundary, in the next three to five years Peking
should assume a still more weighty role in international affairs. But
this does not mean that they are eager to realize expansionist and
aggressive intentions.

THE POLITICAL STATUS AND AUTHORITY OF
PROFESSIONAL SOLDIERS BEFORE AND
AFTER THE CULTURAL REVOLUTION

As Allen S. Whiting has pointed out, the PLA is the only state "instrument of national authority presently exercising power" in the whole country.[1] The universality of military participation in the management of state affairs can be seen at first glance from the present personnel situation in the central and local organs of leadership.

Of the twenty-five members and alternate members of the policy-making Politburo of the CCP's ninth CC, thirteen are military men, accounting for 52 percent of the total.* This is striking when compared with the membership of the Politburo of the CCP's eighth CC (elected at the end of 1956), which was composed of six military men (26.6 percent), and compared with the composition of the Politburo of the CC of the Soviet Communist Party, which included only one military man.[2] The prominent role played by military men in the political affairs of present-day China is evident from the figures given in Table 1 below.

A comparison of the above figures with the relevant situations before the Cultural Revolution bears out the spectacular advance made by professional soldiers in their standing and power. Take the membership of the Party's CC for example. Of the 90 members of the eighth CC, formed in 1966, 26 (26.8 percent) were military men and of the 73 alternate members, 22 (30.13 percent) were military men. At the same time, the ratio of military men among the members and alternate members of the CC of the Soviet Communist Party was only 7.69 percent and 10.9 percent, respectively.[3] This indicates that the ninth CC of the CCP is heavily tinged with the colors of a "military party committee."

Before the Cultural Revolution, the CCP CC issued a call in 1963 for "the whole country to learn from the Liberation Army." Subsequent to this call, large numbers of PLA officers and men retired from the services and took up new positions of leadership in party and government

---

*These thirteen professional soldiers are: Lin Piao, Huang Yung-sheng, Liu Po-ch'eng, Yeh Chien-ying, Yeh Ch'un, Ch'en Hsi-lien, Hsu Shih-yu, Hsieh Fu-chih, Wu Fa-hsien, Li Tso-p'eng, Ch'iu Hui-tso, Wang Tung-hsing, and Li Teh-sheng.

TABLE 1

Positions Presently Held by Military Men
in Organs of Power at Various Levels

Description of Position	Total	Number of Military Men	Military Men as Percent of Total
Members of CCP ninth CC	170	77	45.30
Alternate members of CCP ninth CC	109	55	45.87
First and second secretaries of Provincial Party Committees	36	26	72.22
Secretaries and deputy secretaries of new Provincial Party Committees	96	50	52.07
Directors of province-level RC	29	20	69.00
Deputy directors of province-level RC	290	100	34.48
New ministers of State Council	25	20	80.00

Note: The figures in this table are compiled from fragmentary personnel information available from the Chinese Communist press. "New ministers of State Council" include those who have not been formally designated as "minister," but hold offices with similar authority and responsibilities as a minister.

offices and industrial and mining enterprises. In those days, however, they were not like the military men of today, who retain their military status and position while taking up concurrent duties in the Party organs and government offices. Moreover, most of them only occupied secondary posts in the Provincial Party Committees and government organs; very few became members of the leadership cores. Their main duty was to assist government officials in carrying out activities of political education; their influence on the decisions on local affairs was rather limited.

The facts are that in those days, among the forty-five first and second secretaries of the Provincial Party Committees, only Wang En-mao of Sinkiang, Chang Kuo-hua of Tibet, and Ulanfu of Inner Mongolia were "semiprofessional soldiers." Strictly speaking, they were not purely military men, as they had participated in Party and government leadership work for a long time. Among the nearly 400 secretaries and alternate secretaries, only two were professional soldiers (Kunming Military Region Commander Ch'in Chi-wei and Kunming Military Region Political Commissar Li Ch'eng-mao of Yunnan). Among the standing committees of the Provincial Party Committees (9 to 15 members), usually only one was a military man.* As to the province-level government leaders, among the 400-odd governors and vice-governors of provinces, mayors and vice-mayors of the municipalities under the direct jurisdiction of the central government (Peking and Shanghai), and chairmen and vice-chairmen of the autonomous regions, only three were "semiprofessional soldiers" retaining their military status (Ulanfu, chairman of Inner Mongolia Autonomous Region and commander of Inner Mongolia Military Region; Major General Wang Lan-hsi, vice-governor of Kwangtung and deputy director of the Political Department of Canton Military Region; and Major General Chang Kai-ching, vice-governor of Kirin and cadre leader of Shenyang Military Region).

In contrast and worthy of special attention, in 1971 military men were not only participating in government administration on an extensive scale, but were also holding power of unusual magnitude. Before

---

*Usually, the commander or one of the full-time political commissars of a military district served as a standing committee member of the Provincial Party Committee—e.g., Chang Shu-chih (military-district commander) of Honan, Lung Shu-chin (military-district commander) of Hunan, Ch'en Te (military-district political commissar) of Kwangtung.

the Cultural Revolution, the Peking authorities stressed "collective leadership" and "division of labor between Party and government." Political power at the central or provincial level was thus diversified at least in form. In other words, Party power, government power, and military power were basically held by different persons among the leading hierarchy and were not concentrated in one person. In most places, the first secretary of a local Party committee usually did not hold concurrent office as head of the local government or as the military commander or political commissar (with actual responsibilities and special training as such) of that particular area.* The magnitude of their power, therefore, was far from being comparable to that of the local leaders at present.**

MILITARY MEN AND STATE OFFICIALS
OUST ROYALISTS

A military dictatorship is a product of national disorder. Paris H. Chang is correct in saying, "The political turmoil and breakdown of public order brought on by the Great Proletarian Cultural Revolution had as their end result the rise of the PLA to an unprecedented position of political ascendancy in Communist China."[4]

---

*For example, in Shansi Province, Wei Heng was first secretary of the Provincial Party Committee, Wang Ch'ien was governor, Ch'en Chin-yu was commander of the military district, and Chang Jih-ch'ing was political commissar of the military district. With the exception of the autonomous regions of minority nationalities, such as Inner Mongolia, Sinkiang, Tibet, and Kwangsi, similar situations existed in other provinces and municipalities.

**At present, most of the local leaders monopolize Party, government, and military powers in their respective localities. A typical case in Chekiang Province. Nan P'ing, political commissar of the military district, is concurrently first secretary of the Provincial Party Committee and chairman of the provincial RC, while Hsiung Ying-t'ang, commander of the military district, and Ch'en Li-yün, "a responsible person," are both concurrently secretary of the Provincial Party Committee, and vice-chairman, respectively, of the RC. Before the Cultural Revolution, Chiang Hua was first secretary of the Provincial Party Committee, but he was neither the provincial governor nor the full-time political commissar of the military district. Consequently, his powers were not as broad as Nan P'ing's at the present time.

Much of the power now held by military men was taken from the hands of career government officials. Yet, these military men are enjoying a certain measure of support from the civil service. The army men and government officials, in establishing a subtle relationship as "partners," have one common objective: to oust the rebels so as to consolidate their power and introduce a comparatively conservative political line.

Besides, more often than not the army men and the officials had had some indirect working relationships in the past, and, since they were both targets of attack during the time when the royalists were on the rampage, they tended to feel closer to each other. Moreover, because of their longer association with the CCP, they felt more attached to their occupation and resented the radical line of the ultra-left royalists. They stressed the practical interests of national defense and economy and had a common desire to settle the instable situation and restore normal social order. These are the factors that brought them together, although there were and are differences between them in certain respects.

For the last two years, army men and government officials have joined hands to attack the royalists from all sides, thus driving the royalists into a critical position. The most striking example is that in the two years subsequent to the Ninth Party Congress, a total of 107 vice-chairmen were added to the RCs at the provincial level, of which army men accounted for 49 (45.8 percent), while "representatives of the masses" (rebels) accounted for only 18.7 percent.[5] Of these "representatives of the masses," very few were actually associated with and influenced by the royalists. Most of them were political instruments nurtured and manipulated by the military or "labor models" who had not been detached from production jobs and therefore could not regularly participate in the leadership functions of the RCs.* They now have no real authority; they have scarcely any influence on the decisions of the RCs, nor can they interfere with its administrative affairs. Under these circumstances, what is supposed to be a "three-in-one" organ of leadership has become the joint operations headquarters of army men and government officials.

------

*Typical of such men are Chang Fu-kuei of Shantung and Lü Yü-lan of Hopei. The People's Daily reported on October 6, 1969, and April 29, 1971, that Chang Fu-kuei had engaged in labor in the countryside.

In late 1971, the presence of royalists on the new Provincial
Party Committees, which rank above the RCs, was even more insignificant. This was yet another indication that the royalists and the rebel
masses under them were being excluded from positions of power by
army men and government officials. By August, 1971, the twenty-five
newly established Provincial Party Committees had altogether 132
principal leading members. Of these, only 8 (6.06 percent) were
"representatives of the masses."[6] Moreover, most of the latter did
not really follow the political line of the royalists. Leadership power
in their respective localities had been lost by many of the trusted
lieutenants of the royalist group, Red Guard leaders, and other well-
known people (including ultra-leftist army men and government officials)
who vigorously pursued their own political line, including Nieh Yuan-
tzu, who was personally praised by Mao Tse-tung, Wang Hsiao-yü of
Shantung, and Li Ts'ai-han of Kweichow.*

Of course, the army men and government officials have not been
content with having thrust aside royalist elements and representatives
of rebel masses in the local organs of leadership; they have also directed the spearhead of struggle at the key figures of the royalist clique,
such as Ch'en Po-ta. They set their propaganda machinery in motion
after March, 1971, to launch an attack on Ch'en Po-ta, denouncing him
as a "sham Marxist political swindler."[7] This political campaign

---

*Nieh Yuan-tzu was a Red Guard leader of Peking University.
In May, 1966, she put up the first "big-character poster" attacking
Lu P'ing, then president of the university. Mao Tse-tung praised her
poster as "the first Marxist-Leninist poster in the whole country"
(Mao's comment was later published in the journal Red Flag, No. 13,
1967). Since then, she was closely associated with Chiang Ch'ing and
Ch'en Po-ta and actively supported their left-adventurist line.

After Wang Hsiao-yü, Li Ts'ai-han, and their like lost their
power, former government officials who were onced branded as "capitalist roaders" or "counterrevolutionaries" resumed their activities
forthwith and became secretaries of the new Party committees. Examples are Chang P'ing-hua, former first secretary of the Hunan
Provincial Party Committee, whom Chiang Ch'ing "hated beyond the
limit of forbearance" (see Tzu-liao Chuan-chi [Collection of Documents]
(Canton), No. 3, May, 1968), and Chao Tzu-yang, former first secretary
of the Kwangtung Provincial Party Committee, who was criticized by
name in a document of the CCP CC.

against the nucleus of the "royalists" could have been directed behind the scenes by Chou En-lai and Huang Yung-sheng.*

The royalists were thus doomed to complete failure because of popular resentment against their left-adventurist line and their lack of a power base and of support from the cadres. This is an important turning point in the political affairs of Communist China.

THE OUTLOOK

The political situation in China at present is quite similar to that in the early days after the establishment of the Communist regime. The administration and the economy, both badly battered by the "revolution," are in the process of recovery. This historic change will create a new situation in China.

Lifting of Military Control and Restoration of Party Committee System of Leadership

Military control is a transitional form of government brought on by the breakdown of public order and is bound to be abandoned sooner

---

*In 1967, the May 16 Corps (Peking), with the support of Chiang Ch'ing and Ch'en Po-ta, took Chou En-lai, Li Fu-ch'un, Ch'en Yi, Li Hsien-nien, Nieh Jung-chen, T'an Chen-lin, Hsieh Fu-chih (all leaders of the State Council), and Huang Yung-sheng (then commander of the Canton Military Region) as the main targets of their struggle. They attempted to overthrow these government and military leaders so as to seize power from the State Council and the local military commands. Their attempt, however, ended in failure in the face of strong resistance by Chou En-lai and his followers in conjunction with the local military leaders (headed by Huang Yung-sheng). The Corps' organizers, Wang Li, Kuan Feng, and Chi Pen-yu (all members of the CRG under the CCP CC and trusted lieutenants of Chiang Ch'ing and Ch'en Po-ta), were dismissed. Ch'en Po-ta's loss of power is believed to be connected with the May 16 Corps. It is quite possible that Chou En-lai and Huang Yung-sheng are directing the purge of Ch'en Po-ta and other left-adventurist elements so as to undermine his reputation and advance their own conservative political line.

or later. The reestablishment of local Party committees paves the
way for the lifting of military control.

Military leaders in various localities are playing an active part
in rebuilding a system of Party organizations. In the capacity of "head
of the Party core group" of a provincial RC, most of the regional
military commanders and full-time political commissars have assumed
the responsibility of rebuilding a Party committee in their respective
localities. They have provided the motivating force for the establishment of new Party committees in most of the provinces and counties.
And they are continuing their efforts to expedite the establishment of
Party committees at the special-district and commune-level Party
organizations. It will not be long before a complete system of Party
committees will be established to assume complete leadership.

The lifting of military control certainly will not weaken the power
of the professional soldiers. Since the local military leaders took
charge of and participated in the rebuilding of the Party committee
system of leadership, naturally they would not neglect their own basic
interests. On the contrary, this would legalize their de facto status
of leadership over the Party and the government. The reason is that
when they and their supporters become responsible members of local
Party committees (actually most of them are now heads of local Party
committees), they will have abandoned their status as purely military
men and will have become Party committee cadres holding concurrent
military offices. As heads of Party committees, they are in a legal
position to exercise leadership over the army and the government.

After the military-dominated Party committee system of leadership has been fully restored, it will be able to exercise effectively its
organizational functions. The army men will be able to make use of
these legal ruling organs to dominate all. By then, military control
will not be so visible.

The establishment of a complete leadership network of Party
committees will go a long way toward restoring the prestige of the
CCP, which was damaged by the Cultural Revolution, and toward
stabilizing the situation.

The Unified-Leadership System and
Its Contingencies

The formation of a "Party-government-military unified leadership" system (i.e., a military-control system) provides the army men

broad opportunities to participate in government administration. Many people doubt the ability of the army to handle government work and fear that their participation may lead to confusion. Such fears are probably ill founded. Only by looking into the history of the development of the CCP over the past fifty years can one understand the true meaning of military participation in politics.

Right from their inception in the late 1920s, the Chinese Communist armed forces had close connections with the "Soviet governments," the Communist governments in Central and South China base areas ("Soviets"). The system of "Party-government-military unified leadership" is nothing new; it was enforced as early as the creation in 1928 of armed-forces bases. The Kiangsi base, for example, was founded in the early 1930s; the officers and men of the armed forces there, while taking part in the "anti-encirclement campaigns," on the one hand, often were leaders or functionaries of the local government, on the other. During the war against Japan (1937-45), almost all of the cadres of the armed forces in the Shansi-Chahar-Hopei, Shensi-Kansu, and Shansi-Chahar-Shantung bases were concurrently members of local Party committees or cadres of local governments. They held the "gun" (military power) in one hand and the "official seal" (political power) in the other. Consequently, they all had practical experience in mobilizing the masses, carrying out political movements, and setting up and consolidating organs of political power.

When the Chinese Communists first seized political power on the mainland, military control was instituted in all parts of the country. At that time, all political organs and cultural and educational establishments were controlled by military men. Then, they were gradually reorganized and turned into regular government organs. When government organs at various levels were competent enough to carry out their regular functions, the "military and administrative committees" in the large administrative areas and the "military control committees" in the provinces and municipalities were replaced by regular government organs. Some of the military personnel then changed their profession to become full-time administrative cadres, while most of them went back to the troop units to which they belonged. Precisely because it has been a historical tradition for army cadres to take part in government work, those army cadres participating in government work today should not find it too difficult at all.

On the other hand, because the Chinese Communist government was established after many years of armed struggle, an overwhelming majority of the government cadres came from the armed forces; they were transferred from the army to the government to serve as administrative cadres. Important government leaders, such as Vice-Premier of the State Council and Minister of Finance Li Hsien-nien, Vice-Chairman of the State Planning Commission and Minister of the Petroleum Industry Yü Ch'iu-li, former Vice-Premier of the State Council T'ao Chu, and Vice-Minister of Geology Sung Ying, were all from the armed forces. Probing into this historical question, it becomes quite evident that the participation in government work by a large number of army men today is quite similar to the situation in 1949. Such a situation is the inevitable result of political turmoil. Like Li Hsien-nien, T'ao Chu, Yü Ch'iu-li, and others in the past, these army men are basically competent to lead the government organs.[8] The only difference between the present unified-leadership system and its counterpart in the past is that today military men hold the leading positions, whereas in the past Party secretaries formed the nucleus.

This system of unified leadership will remain in force for most of the 1970s. Then, it will head toward a revived division of labor and professionalism. Since the present system of unified leadership puts stress on the leading role of the army, army men will form the nucleus of leadership in the organs of power at all levels. With the passing of the age of "revolutionary rebellion," however, Peking will face new demands in construction (the fourth five-year plan will begin in 1972) and army men will find it impossible to control everything as they did earlier. They will have to share some of their power with other officials, making the necessary divisions of work and manpower.

After the state machinery has become normalized, it is only natural that a division of labor should be gradually put into effect. Along with the establishment of Party committees throughout the country, RCs, which were, once the provisional combined headquarters of the Party, the government, and the military when the situation was in utter disorder, will gradually become purely administrative organs. The new draft constitution drawn up by the Peking authorities in 1970 declares that the RC is a "local organ of state power."[9] This means that the RC is similar to the former local "people's council," which possesses the character and powers of a local government.

After a complete system of Party committee leadership is rebuilt, government and military organs should once again exist independently. It should then become necessary to divide their responsibilities. Of course, there is no clear-cut bureaucratic formula whereby the army and government cadres may share power and divide responsibilities. Different arrangements will have to be made in different regions according to different social conditions. Whatever the arrangements, the division of labor will probably seek to save manpower, to define clearly responsibilities, to heighten efficiency, and to play up the prestige of the army.

Regarding the goal of increased professionalism, the principal stress has been on the leading Party and government organs at the central level. At present, quite a number of PLA personnel have been transferred from various local military commands to important posts under the CCP CC or the State Council. Representative of these are newly appointed Minister of the First Machine Building Industry Li Shui-ch'ing, Minister of Foreign Trade Pai Hsiang-kuo, and Jen Yün-chung, a member of the International Liaison Department of the CCP CC.

After assuming office at the State Council or at the CCP CC, these people have found it difficult to manage their military duties as well, owing to the heavy administrative burdens and occasional requirements of their presence at diplomatic functions. Even if they keep their names on the army register for the time being, eventually they will have to give up their military status and become full-time administrative officers. This was exactly what happened to the military personnel holding offices in the central government between 1949 and 1954.

More Conservative and Flexible Domestic Policies

Present indications are that both army men and government officials have a desire to create a peaceful environment in the country. They will probably handle domestic social and economic problems with discretion and adopt a comparatively conservative and flexible policy to win the support of cadres at large so as to enhance their political prestige. Their somewhat conservative policies would probably embrace the following:

1. To restore the system of Party committee leadership as soon as possible and consolidate the organization of the central and local governments, so as to normalize the state machinery and social order and make the people at large feel that Cultural Revolution turmoil is over; to lead the people in the development of industrial and agricultural production and in the building of national defense

2. To maintain the basic urban and rural policies that were in force during the reign of Liu Shao-ch'i and, in particular,

no change would be contemplated in the system of ownership of means of production at the present stage; peasants would be allowed to keep their private plots for a
certain period of time; "free markets" would remain
open and no attempt would be made to launch a new
"great leap forward" movement

3. To adopt a more lenient attitude in dealing with the high-
    ranking cadres purged during the Cultural Revolution;
    to "liberate" more cadres and absorb them into leading
    Party and government organs at the appropriate time
    and by appropriate means, so as to put their political
    skills to use

4. To gradually rehabilitate the intellectuals who were
    formerly targets of attack and encourage them to make
    new contributions in science and technology

To army and government officials are likely to push on with these
and other conservative policies. While they will not wish to expand
the influence of Liu Shao-ch'i's "revisionist" line, they realize that
those revisionist policies are more popular than the left-adventurist
line pushed by the royalists. These policies not only benefit the people
to some extent, but also conform to the long-term interests of the
Party and moderate the contradictions between the people and the
government. By adhering to these policies, they can win over the
hearts of the people and isolate the royalists, thus consolidating their
own power and position.

Meanwhile, as a possible military confrontation still exists
between China and the Soviet Union, the power-holders in Peking must
strengthen internal security and stability so that they can concentrate
on the anti-Soviet struggle and mobilize maximum resources to carry
out economic and national defense construction, to provide the material
base for the anti-Soviet struggle, and to support the "world revolution."

In the name of mobilization, one can expect to see the Chinese
people subjected to even more rigorous control in the future. The
authorities will probably tighten the ban on "rebel organizations" and
their activities and expand the "production and construction corps"
to absorb unemployed and out-of-school Red Guards and to place them
under more effective supervision and management. They may also
deal with the discontented elements in society more forcefully through
courts and prisons so as to maintain their ruling foundation.

Judging from the above, Peking's two-faced policy—smiles on one side, frowns on the other—may have some significance in achieving temporary stability and economic progress, but it cannot lead China to true liberal democracy. Even the political freedom pursued in Czechoslovakia is unlikely to appear in a China under the control of the "guns" before the death of Mao Tse-tung.

Continued Support of Chou En-lai's Diplomatic Offensive

The effect of the inflation of PLA power on Peking's foreign policy is a matter of common interest. Many people fear that the ascendancy of PLA power would lead to expansionistic and aggressive tendencies. Such trends are unlikely. Most of the PLA men now holding key positions at the central and local levels took part in the Korean War, and many of them received professional training at higher military schools and academies. They know quite well the consequences of a modern war, be it conventional or nuclear. Since the Korean War, they have shown a certain degree of prudence and restraint in coping with the clashes on the Sino-Indian and Sino-Soviet borders. In the future, for a considerable length of time, they will probably avoid the political risk of any diplomatic line that smacks of militarism. On the contrary, they should continue to support Chou En-lai's "smile diplomacy."

Such a tendency is not hard to understand. In the first place, the military tension on the Sino-Soviet border is not going to change in the near future. Even if this situation eases, China would still have to maintain a high degree of vigilance against possible surprise attacks by the Soviet Union. In these circumstances, PLA commanders at the upper level will be inclined to consider the question of foreign policy from the viewpoint of national defense. They would not fail to see that hasty outward expansion would give the Soviet Union an excuse to launch an invasion, whereas improvement of relations with the West would bring greater pressure to bear on the Soviet Union and enable the deployment of more forces in preparation for an anti-Soviet war.

Second, in order to isolate the royalists and justify their own power status, it will be necessary for professional military men to accent foreign threats, both American and Soviet, the emphasis on an external threat varying among the army, navy, and air force. Controversy over which of several is the main external threat should generate a more flexible foreign policy, involving China increasingly in world affairs.

Another factor is the army's sense of responsibility in economic affairs. Their extensive participation in government work and in directing the industrial and mining enterprises since the Cultural Revolution makes them better understand the need for developing the national economy and improving industrial technology. They have become aware of the significance and urgency of strengthening contacts and technical cooperation with other countries and of expanding foreign trade.

Still another important factor is that the PLA men at the upper levels may have been influenced politically by Chou En-lai. Since 1968, the most active among the PLA elite were Huang Yung-sheng, Li Tso-p'eng, and Ch'iu Hui-tso. They often participated in diplomatic activities in company with Chou En-lai and had unusual working relationships with Chou. For example, when Li Tso-p'eng and Ch'iu Hui-tso were in charge of the administrative unit of the MAC of the CC between 1967 and 1968, they often took orders directly from Chou to deal with concrete problems. When Chou went to Canton during the Cultural Revolution to deal with the problem of political instability in Kwangtung, he did his best to shield Huang Yung-sheng. In short, whenever Huang and others were in political distress, Chou came to their assistance. This must have left a deep impression on the PLA generals. Moreover, in the last two years, because of the requirements of their work, they have had frequent contacts with Chou and numerous opportunities to consult one another. Besides, they all have a common desire to free themselves from interference by the royalists. All this tends to indicate that Chou En-lai may continue to exert considerable influence on them in making foreign-policy decisions.

Another point of note is that, although PLA leaders have established themselves in positions of importance, the latent influence of the royalists and their followers—the rebel masses—has not been completely wiped out, and there is still a possibility of their making a counterattack. For this reason, as far as the PLA leaders are concerned, they will regard coping with any interference from the royalists and preserving their power and position as more important than expanding their influence abroad.

After Mao's Death: The PLA's Role in the Political Struggle

As long as Mao Tse-tung lives, it is unlikely that a violent political storm would again occur in Peking. A struggle to seize power from Mao, who will be 80 very soon, is hardly conceivable. But this

political stability is temporary; there are all kinds of social contradictions hidden behind it.

Once Mao Tse-tung passes away, Peking cannot possibly solve
the question of leadership through a parliamentary-style democratic
election. People will have to acquire power through a merciless
political struggle. In this future struggle, only the PLA has solid
power, especially those who have extensive influence among the field
armies, such as Huang Yung-sheng, Hsü Shih-yu, Ch'en Hsi-lien, and
other reputable local military leaders. They will play the most important role.[10] The royalist elements, such as Chiang Ch'ing and Yao
Wen-yuan, who are active on the political stage solely by relying on
the prestige of Mao Tse-tung, are simply not the equals of the army.
As Mao Tse-tung himself put it in his famous saying, "Political power
grows out of the barrel of a gun!"

NOTES

1. Allen S. Whiting, "China's Ninth Party Congress: 'A Unity
of Opposites,' " Mainichi Shimbun English edition (Tokyo), Ft. I, June
1, 1969.

2. For a comparison between the CCP ninth CC and the CCP
eighth CC and the CC of the Soviet Communist Party, see Ting Wang,
"A Preliminary Appraisal of the Personnel of the New CCP Central
Committee," Chinese Law and Government (New York), No. 2, 1970.

3. Ibid.

4. Parris H. Chang, "The Second Decade of Maoist Rule," Problems of Communism, November-December, 1969, p. 7.

5. Compiled from personnel files held in the archives of the
Contemporary China Research Institute, Hong Kong.

6. Compiled from namelists published in JMJP between December, 1970, and June, 1971.

7. Articles criticizing Ch'en Po-ta appeared here and there in
Red Flag, the Kuang-ming Daily, and the People's Daily. Since Ch'en
was not attacked by name, however, and the words used were rather
ambiguous—they had to do with the history of the left-wing literary
and art movement in China in the 1930s—it was not easy for ordinary
observers to see the true picture. The author was the first outside

of China to expose the Ch'en Po-ta incident and came to the conclusion long ago that Ch'en Po-ta's political life was at stake. See the articles by Ting Wang about Ch'en's case, namely, "The 'Pigtail' of Ch'en Po-ta," "Peking Openly Criticizes Ch'en Po-ta," and "The Background of Ch'en Po-ta's Failure," Ming Pao (Hong Kong), May 12, June 28, and June 29, 1971, respectively.

8. See Ting Wang, The Question of Organization and Personnel in the Chinese Communist Cultural Revolution Movement (Hong Kong: Contemporary China Research Institute, 1970).

9. See Study of Chinese Communism (Taipei), October, 1970.

10. William Whitson pointed out in "The Field Army in Chinese Communist Military Politics," China Quarterly, January-March, 1969, that, because of historical factors, Communist China's regional military leaders have displayed a certain degree of independence.

PART

THE ORGANIZATION
OF MILITARY POWER
IN CHINA

7

**REGIONAL
AND PARAMILITARY
GROUND FORCES**

Harvey Nelsen

What Peking dubs "regional forces" are comprised of militia, "independent" divisions and regiments (including garrison and public security units), and traditionally the production/construction corps. This seeming hodgepodge is treated together for two reasons. First, these forces are controlled by the provincial military-district and military-region commands. Organizationally, the regional forces therefore belong together. Second, they serve a common strategic role. Mao Tse-tung has explained the wartime function of regional forces in China's national defense as follows:

> This army is powerful because of its division into two parts, the main forces and the regional forces, with the former available for operations in any region whenever necessary and the latter concentrating on defending their own localities and attacking the enemy there in conjunction with local militia. . .[1]

This chapter discusses historical, organizational, and strategic aspects of the regional forces, excluding the production corps, which are treated separately at the conclusion.

_____

The author expresses gratitude for the suggestions of his fellow doctoral candidate at George Washington University and student of the PLA Reed Probst.

135

THE MILITIA

A description of the regional-forces components is a necessary preamble to any further analysis. Starting with the best known, the militia is a paramilitary and production force organized around occupational enterprises. It is a part-time "volunteer" service with all members working at their regular production and service jobs. Both men and women from about ages sixteen to fifty are eligible. Entrance requirements for this general organization have always been loose, with acceptance the general rule for all who are physically fit and not branded as "landlord," "reactionary," or criminal elements. It is doubtful that anyone knows precisely how many workers in communes, factories, and offices and students in schools nominally belong to the militia. Current estimates range from 30 to perhaps 100 million. Fortunately, the numbers are of little importance.

The "common militia," which comprise at least 75 percent of the total, receive virtually no military training and need not be considered as part of China's military strength, except as a labor and manpower pool. The "basic militia" are a subgroup of perhaps 12 to 15 million persons who do receive individual and small-unit military training for several days each year. The age group in this category is more restricted—about eighteen to forty—and women constitute a small minority. Within this group, there is a still smaller elite of perhaps 5 to 7 million "armed militia." These are the politically screened basic militiamen who carry arms on coastal- and border-defense patrols and assist in maintaining public security. While basic and common militia must satisfy themselves with intangible rewards, armed militia receive some compensation for their more arduous and time-consuming duties. The best organized and most active of the armed militia are in border and coastal provinces.

Self-sufficiency is encouraged for all regional forces. The financing of the militia, for instance, is done at local and provincial levels. Militia units theoretically range in size from division level down to squads, but the company is the basic unit. In 1961, the Ministry of National Defense ordered that each militia battalion was to have one basic or "backbone" company. It is doubtful that this goal has been achieved a decade later. The order also stated that basic militia units were to be no larger than company size.[2] Armed militia patrols are usually of platoon size, and to this writer's knowledge paramilitary activities are not carried out by militia units above the company level (i.e., about 130 men). Larger units are merely for organizational convenience.

Demobilized and retired army men serve as cadres and provide routine drill and military training for the basic and armed militia. Cadres from the PLA provide more formal training for a few days each year, stretching to perhaps a few weeks for armed militia in strategic areas. Ideal militia relations with the PLA are described in the following example:

> After the establishment of the militia in 1958 in a Peking factory, we set up connections with units of the PLA and learned from them. We sent militiamen to army units on observation tours and selected and sent militia cadres to learn in army units. We organized all the militiamen of the factory to visit exhibitions of all types sponsored by the PLA. We invited heroic models of the . . . PLA to make reports in the factory . . . During the past few years, concretely guided and helped by higher level military offices and army units stationed in Peking, we overcame difficulties in respect to time, teaching materials and training apparatuses, and carried out military training on a regular basis.[3]

Naturally, such shining examples were and are rarities. Training was in fact sharply curtailed during the Cultural Revolution, but was largely regained during the 1969-70 Sino-Soviet border crisis and Peking's war-preparations campaign.

The present military capabilities of the militia are purely defensive. Its military readiness varies greatly from region to region. Coastal provinces opposite Taiwan contain the militia elite. Since the heyday of the Cultural Revolution, much effort has been devoted to improving the organization of the militia; still, the interior provinces would probably have difficulty in mobilizing their militia for a paramilitary role without considerable delay and confusion. Little is known of the militia quality along China's northern borders, but it probably falls somewhere between the two extremes.

Should an invasion occur, the militia could not fight battles in the conventional sense. Its arms are few and almost totally rifles, side arms, and hand grenades. Mao Tse-tung made an offhand remark in 1967 that the militia had "three million guns."[4] While that figure is certainly low now, there are today probably no more than two rifles for every three armed militiamen. Thus, military activities would be restricted to hit-and-run surprise attacks, military intelligence, and harassment behind enemy lines.

Basic and common militia are not equipped with firearms, although a few arms for such units are held in arsenals for training purposes. Their role would be to provide logistics and intelligence services to the regular forces and guerillas. Most common militia would remain at their production jobs. If an invading army were to penetrate deeply into China, especially through the densely populated provinces of the south and east, militia harassment would become an increasingly critical problem to the invaders. The enemy might eventually be forced into a complete withdrawal or reduction to a small-perimeter holding operation.

INDEPENDENT UNITS

Clearly, the militia could not wage such an effective protracted war without assistance. This is where the "independent units" play their role. They are regular army units, but are smaller and more lightly equipped than equivalent echelons in the main forces.[5] The largest independent unit is the division, while many are regiments. These units have no heavy artillery or armor, some anti-tank guns, and many automatic small arms. During peacetime, they serve as garrison units providing public security; engaging in construction projects, land reclamation, and the farming of PLA lands; and assisting the communes in their busy seasons. The number of such units is un-clear, but they comprise about 30 to 40 percent of the ground forces.* Should China be invaded, these troops would probably defend their provinces partly as units and partly as cadres for armed militia and upgraded basic militia.

The key organs of command and control are the military regions and their immediate subordinates, the provincial military districts. Regional commanders probably maintain control over independent divisions and the garrisons of large cities. The military-district

---

*This assertion may raise doubts among other students of the PLA. Prior to and during the Cultural Revolution, however, units formerly belonging to the Public Security forces were subsumed into the PLA as garrison and independent units, thus removing them from the command of the Ministry of Public Security. These troops alone numbered at least 500,000, and many other independent divisions and regiments have been in existence for years. About 1.5 million men are in the thirty-five army corps. With a ground force of around 3 million, the 30-to-40-percent figure for independent and garrison forces would seem a safe estimate.

level certainly commands the militia in the provinces and also controls
some independent units—at least regiments and smaller garrisons.
The military districts also supervise "people's armed departments"
at local, county, and provincial levels; these are the organs directly
responsible for militia control. Although the partitioning of command
powers between provincial-district and military-region headquarters
is foggy, it is probable that all forces here considered are commanded
at the local level, whereas the main force units—the army corps and
naval and air forces—are primarily controlled at the national level.
Both in peace and war, regional forces are probably intended to serve
only their own areas.

HISTORICAL ROLES AND MISSIONS

While the foregoing organizational concepts have remained
relatively stable since 1949, the political history of the regional
forces has been hectic. The militia evolved from Red Guards who
were peasant fighters and supporters of Communist forces in their
mountain strongholds during the early 1930s. (The name was revived
in the Cultural Revolution and officially applied to the student "re-
voluntionaries.") The "War of Resistance" against Japan (1937-45)
saw the development of vast Communist base areas and a concomitant growth in guerilla troops and militia. These were based around
village "self-defense corps," which, like the common militia today,
had little fighting power in themselves. Part of each self-defense
corps, however, was organized into a small militia unit equipped
with a few captured small arms. Full-time local guerilla troops,
better equipped and quite mobile, would use the militia as auxiliary
forces as needed. By the 1947-49 period, the system was well
established and as many as 5 million militia were supporting or
fighting together with the PLA on the battlefields.[6]

The establishment of the PRC in October, 1949, changed the
militia from a battlefield instrument into a political football. Those
leaders of the PLA and CCP who favored a close alliance with the
Soviet Union in order to achieve rapid modernization of the armed
forces and national economic development through borrowed technology favored reducing the militia drastically or even abolishing it. So
far as policy directives about the regional forces were concerned,
however, Mao and the traditionalists won the first battle. The
People's Daily announced in November, 1950, a national goal of a
militia numbering 5 percent of the total population—i.e., about 24
million.[7]

During the Korean conflict, the militia was used as the main conscription pool. Independent units recruited young, able-bodied men, and these units in turn remanned the depleted main forces in Korea. This function of the militia was probably one reason that the organizational concept survived the Politburo battles during those early years.

In 1954-55, a reorganization and regularization of the armed forces was undertaken. A national conscription service was begun, thus ending that role for the militia. A more-formalized reserve system was also launched, only loosely tied to the militia. Modernization was a key word in the armed forces. The Minister of Defense, P'eng Teh-huai was later quoted as having said that "the militia system is outmoded."[8] Indeed, difficulties in the system were serious. People were reluctant to join the militia because it meant extra work without remuneration. When training was taken seriously, it detracted from production. These problems have never been totally resolved. From 1954-57 on, the militia was not emphasized, and little was heard of regional forces.

Mao and his political allies made a stunning comeback in late 1957 and launched the Great Leap Forward in 1958. The basic principles behind the movement were self-sufficiency and rapid economic development through massive mobilization of manpower. Reliance on the Soviet Union was rejected. The militia was suddenly vaulted into a position of unprecedented importance. Its ranks reportedly swelled to 150 to 200 million—a figure commensurate with equally unreliable, inflated statistics of that period. The militia became a principal production organization under the new commune system.

The failure of the Great Leap Forward does not require recounting here. Suffice it to say that the militia was retrenched along with the most ambitious of the commune programs. A political power struggle ensued in the wake of the policy disaster. Mao largely lost control of the Party, but was able to effect the removal of his military rival P'eng Teh-huai in 1959. Under Lin Piao, the new Minister of Defense, the program of military self-sufficiency and the building-up of regional forces continued, although on a much smaller scale than during the halcyon days of 1958.

Captured secret documents from 1960-61 showed the militia system riddled with corruption and paper units; there were even cases of militia groups turning to banditry with their arms.[9] Under Lin's reorganized MAC, the supreme military decision-making body,

the provincial military districts were ordered to devote virtually
their entire resources to rebuilding the militia structure. Rather
than sheer numbers, organizational soundness was emphasized—a
policy that holds true today. Mao's explicit militia-building priorities
were organization, than politics, and finally military training.[10] As
an initial step, the formal military reserve program was quitely
dropped in favor of requiring demobilized PLA veterans to serve as
militia cadres.

In 1960, Mao suggested that several divisions of the main forces
devote themselves entirely to strengthening the militia in coastal
areas.[11] Over the next five years, however, the Chief of General
Staff, presumably with the backing of other top leaders, resisted
implementing Mao's proposal. (The reaction of Chinese professionals
was comparable to what one might expect in the Pentagon should the
President propose breaking up several well-established army and
marine divisions and using their components to train and develop
the National Guard!) In effect, Mao was seeking to convert a still-
larger percent of the army into regional forces. In 1965-66, a way
was finally found to satisfy his cherished project. This was done
largely through the Public Security Forces.

PUBLIC SECURITY FORCES

In 1949, a portion of the regular army forces had become
public-security units. At that time, quite intentionally, control was
not centralized over these new forces at the national level. China
had no desire to repeat Russia's experience with Committee for
State Security (USSR) units. Instead, local and provincial Party
committees controlled these troops for service in their own areas.
Further precautions were taken in the mid-1950s against the security
forces becoming a Frankenstein's monster. Following the precept
"divide and rule," other security forces were created under diverse
lines of control. The railway and communications systems, for
example, had their own police units. The People's Armed Police were
created at about the same time. This force of perhaps 500,000 was
also regionally controlled.

The Minister of Public Security from 1949-59, Lo Jui-ch'ing,
was later accused of attempting to centralize command of these
diverse forces.[12] Lo's efforts failed, but his idea did not; the army
gradually subsumed the miscellaneous security troops. Most of the
original Public Security force changed into PLA garrison units in
1958. Sometime in the mid-1960s, a similar fate befell the People's

Armed Police. Some units were disbanded, while the remainder were amalgamated into the PLA in 1966-67.

Not to be confused with the armed Public Security units, the police administration—the Public Security Bureau—as also taken over by the PLA in 1967. Apparently, none of the troops absorbed were converted to main-force elements; rather, they continued to serve in their old localities as independent units. Other such forces had descended from local guerilla columns of the civil-war period or were individual units formed from remnants of large demobilized forces. These regiments and divisions have always had the mission of security, militia work, and production/construction assistance. This is the dirty work required of the PLA. The officers of independent units are in dead-end careers, and the forces receive little in resource allocation. Regional forces are at the bottom of the PLA totem pole.

THE CULTURAL REVOLUTION

Several features of independent and garrison units proved of great political importance during the Cultural Revolution. Due to the local nature of their mission, such troops were largely the servants of the provincial, county, and city Party committees. The close relationship was institutionalized at the military-district level through the concurrent appointment of the leading provincial Party official as first political commissar of the provincial military district. This practice was often followed at military-region and subprovince administrative levels as well. Since the primary peacetime role of the militia is production, the Party directly controlled routine militia activities through what were called "Peoples Armed Department Headquarters" at commune-level. True, the People's Armed Departments remained subordinate to the military districts, but most orders to militia came from the Party committees directly to the People's Armed Departments.[13]

This coziness among the Party, independent units, and militia would have contributed to Mao's plan for militia building and generally facilitated governing China's provinces. Also, with the conversion of Public Security units into PLA forces, enough new troops would have been available to undertake a full-scale program of building up the militia organization and providing much-improved military training. Such developments in the provinces are only now beginning to occur. The Cultural Revolution delayed the program of revitalizing the regional forces.

During its initial phase (in the first half of 1966), the Cultural Revolution had little effect on militia and local forces. After the inauguration of the Red Guards in August and the attacks on regional Party leaders in September, 1966, however, the situation changed markedly. The threatened Party leaders were generally able to use their influence over the military districts and their virtual control of the militia and local police to stand off Red Guard attacks. The scale of the conflict grew as Party men in the provinces used militia and other channels to foment conflict between "radical" Red Guards and status-quo-oriented workers and peasants. By the end of 1966, the "revolutionaries," if not losing, were far from winning the battle against the Party bureaucracies in the provinces.

In order to break the stalemate, the Maoist leadership launched the "seize power" phase of the Cultural Revolution in January, 1967. The Red Guards were to occupy physically and supervise the running of local political organs at the province level and below. For this to be successfully accomplished, the badly outnumbered radicals required assistance. In the same month, January, 1967, the PLA was ordered to "support the left" in their power seizures. The burden was cast upon the military regions, districts, and garrison commands. Initially, the main-force units did not participate except through emissaries from their political departments. The following provides an example of the way things were supposed to function:

> Through the People's Armed Departments, militia organ-
> izations, garrison units and dependents of servicemen
> [the Heilungkiang Military District Command], had a
> good grasp of the [Red Guard and Cultural Revolution]
> activities in various spheres . . . The military district
> kept close coordination with armed forces units stationed
> locally and exchanged information with them.[14]

The purpose of this intelligence work was to sort out the genuine leftists from conservative mass organizations masquerading as revolutionary rebels while actually influenced or led by the extant Party power-holders. Once the political apparatus had been seized by the left with military support, "three-way alliances" were to be formed at local and provincial levels, consisting of Red Guards, military or militia cadres, and Maoist Party officials. This in turn would lead to the formation of the new governing bodies—the RCs.

Initially, the scheme was a failure. In many provinces, the Red Guards were too weak to attempt a power seizure. Of those seizures that did occur, many were not recognized by the Peking

leadership, as they suspected conservative forces of putting up a
sham performance. A primary reason for the January, 1967, power-
seizure failures was the behavior of the military districts, garrison
units, and militia. Instead of finding the left and supporting it, more
often they found the left but supported the right.[15] The reason has
already been suggested. Local military forces and militia were
tightly tied to the Party machinery in their home areas. The destruction of the existing local polities threatened their own status. A
leader of the Heilungkiang Military District provided one of many
examples of this Party/regional-forces relationship that bulked so
large in early 1967.

> The handful of leaders in the Provincial Party Committee
> taking the capitalist road said . . . that the Provincial
> Military District was not a part of the national defense
> army, and that its task was mainly concerned with the
> localities, and its principal leadership was the Provincial
> Party Committee.[16]

The Party leaders were speaking with considerable accuracy.
In retrospect, it is not surprising that only four provinces (Shansi,
Heilungkiang, Kweichow, and Shantung) managed to implement a
recognized power seizure with military assistance. In some areas,
military leaders were blatant in their opposition to the revolutionary
rebels; for example, in Szechwan Province 35,000 persons were
arrested in January, 1967. The Minister of Public Security was later
to claim that, nationwide, 100 percent of all urban and 80 percent of
all rural Public Security Bureaus had supported the "conservatives."
He stated further that 80 percent of the People's Armed Departments
were also guilty of favoring the "wrong side."[17] It might also have
been added that at least 75 percent of the military districts were
guilty of leaning to the right.

Peking did not accept such provincial military disobedience
without reacting. The spring of 1967 saw purges or transfers in
five military regions (Chengtu, Inner Mongolia, Peking, Sinkiang,
and Lanchow) and in seven military districts (Honan, Tsinghai, Kirin,
Shansi, Kiangsu, and Chekiang).[18] Still more momentous, centrally
controlled main-force units were dispatched in large numbers to
"support the left" and "exercise military control." The political
power of the regional forces was thus intentionally weakened.

The militia, which had been touted to play a major role in grass-
roots level triple alliances and small-scale military control projects,
largely disappeared from provincial broadcasts after March, 1967.

Nevertheless, the commune-level People's Armed Departments remained convenient organizations through which to exercise military control. Such control was imposed following the collapse or paralysis of the local and provincial Party machinery and the failure of the January, 1967, power seizures. This extensive use of the militia administrative organs received virtually no publicity.

One major reason for the silence was continued poor political performance by the militia, as revealed in an August 6, 1967, issue of the Liberation Army Daily.

> We must see that the handful of power holders in the Party
> and Army who take the capitalist road are adopting sinister
> means of hoodwinking, deceiving, threatening and inciting
> the people in order to prevent their doom. They vainly
> attempt to drag some cadres responsible for militia work
> and some militiamen to the bourgeois reactionary line and
> turn them into tools for protecting themselves and en-
> forcing the bourgeois reactionary line. They use militia
> to arrest, assault and detain the people and incite the
> militiamen to go to the cities to suppress the proletarian
> revolutionaries. They even go to the extent of instigating
> the militiamen to sabotage production and communications
> and upset the social order.[19]

The newspaper might have added that most of the arms used by Red Guards in their factional fighting were stolen from poorly protected militia arsenals supervised by the People's Armed Departments. In other cases, these departments quietly supplied arms to mass organizations in their favor. Small wonder that the radical left described the militia as "only a facade behind which the bureaucrats control the armed strength of the people."[20]

While the militia was thus distinguishing itself, what of the independent and garrison units? Their performance after January-February, 1967, was little improved. In July, 1967, an independent division of the Wuhan garrison was directly involved in kidnapping two leaders of the CRG. This was one incident too many. Over the next several weeks, Peking ordered main-force "central-support-the-left" units to take over several military districts (Among them, Hunan, Chekiang, Kiangsi, Sinkiang, Honan, and Anhwei) and ordered vast numbers of military cadres to Peking for "Mao-Thought study classes." Mao personally ordered that the first to come were to be cadres from the People's Armed Departments.[21] They were immediately followed by other military district and garrison officers.

Independent units also received early attention at such study sessions.
Through the remainder of the Cultural Revolution, China's regional
forces operated under reduced political authority. Several military
districts and independent units, however, persisted in supporting
Red Guard groups opposed by main-force units in their localities.
Friction between regional forces and "central-support-the-left" units
was a major mode of military factionalism from mid-1967 through
1969. The study sessions in Peking proved an insufficient curative
for the army's political ills.

Despite the poor political performance, Mao did not lose faith
in the concept of regional forces. In September, 1967, in the wake of
a series of fiascos capped by the Wuhan incident, the best Mao could
say was, "An independent unit can change for the better after some
training."[22] (He was referring to the Mao-Thought study sessions
in particular.) By April, 1968, however, Mao's defense of the regional
forces was more positive.

> Since the number of local armed units including indepen-
> dent divisions and regiments in our country is large, the
> various Military Regions, provincial Military Districts
> and armies [i.e., the 35 army corps of the main forces]
> should have the duty to help these armed units to rectify
> their mistakes, publicly commend their achievements,
> and regard them as brother units.[23]

While such a statement can hardly be construed as praise, it does
strongly indicate that Mao had no idea of abandoning the local forces
and militia.

A revival of the militia was begun in 1968. The PLA was over-
extended in administering military control and sought relief through
the creation of "mass dictatorship organs." These appeared in most
of China's larger cities and were composed primarily of urban
militia from factories. They inaugurated street patrols and generally
helped the army to maintain order. After August, 1968, they faded
from view, since the crackdown order executed by the military against
the revolutionary rebels proved most effective. Supplementary ad hoc
security organizations were no longer needed. The Sino-Soviet confrontation touched off by the border incidents of March-June, 1969,
brought on a massive war-preparations campaign that saw the militia
and the PLA return to a normal military training program.

THE FUTURE

At this writing, both regional forces and militia seem to have returned to an ante-bellum status quo, except that the old Public Security forces remain an integral part of the PLA. Mao's long-nurtured plans for strengthening militia organization are now being implemented. The governmental responsibilities borne by officers of municipal garrisons and independent units and many militia cadres have not markedly impaired the military posture of the regional forces. The political embarassment incurred during the Cultural Revolution has been more than offset by the political power wielded by the military leaders in their local RCs. This is particularly true of commanders and political commissars in the military garrisons. The main-force units have generally been withdrawn from the political arena, rotated to new areas, and are once again devoting themselves to their primary mission of national defense. The regional forces are thus no longer engaged in factional battles with their big brothers.

From the standpoint of American policy interests, the regional forces might be considered a bellwether. As long as regional forces and militia continue to receive emphasis, Peking will probably be concerned primarily with the defense of its own territory, increasing agricultural production, and satisfying the needs of the provinces. Should the regional-forces concept be dropped and the independent units converted into main-force divisions and army corps, then China might be setting a more aggressive course. Under such circumstances, a land invasion into a neighboring country would become a greater possibility.

It might be argued that, after Mao's demise, new leadership could, without intentions of international aggression, abolish the regional-forces concept as simply unworkable and useless in the nuclear era. The entire regional-forces concept is predicated on a repeat of China's experience in World War II—i.e., protracted conflict against a large invading army. In the 1970s, however, China could be ruined by nuclear weapons without a foreign invader setting foot on its territory. In light of this, China's military bureaucrats might simply scrap the regional forces as outmoded in the 1970s.

Such a possibility seems remote to this writer. The militia is of considerable value to peacetime production and social control.

Some similar institution would be needed to mobilize the population for a war effort and to serve as a manpower pool, regardless of whether the conflict were conventional or nuclear. The independent units and garrisons are the mainstay of public security. They are valuable to the provinces as mobile labor pools in public-works construction and agricultural assistance. The cost of such units is low because of their own side-line production. Regional forces supply much of their own food and also engage in some light manufacturing. Even that inveterate systematizer and modernizer of the armed forces, P'eng Teh-huai, is not recorded as having opposed independent units.

In the post-Mao era, some reorganization of local troops may occur. For example, a separate public-security force might again be built to offset the omnipresence of the PLA in the provinces. The Maoist concept of regional forces, however, will likely survive because it is useful. If mobile striking forces are heavily emphasized as opposed to the defensive and reserve roles of regional forces, it will be at the sacrifice of military leaders' current focus on China's domestic interests. Thus, if the 1970s sees the downgrading or abolition of regional forces, it would behoove the United States to watch for hostile intent.

In the 1960s, regional forces—especially the militia—were viewed in the West as another sort of indicator. As long as the People's War strategy of defense was receiving major emphasis and the organizational efforts in militia work were going strong, the likelihood of a Sino-Soviet détente was viewed as very slim. The concept behind this analysis was simple; a protracted war-defense policy meant that China was planning on going it alone. Should national policy deemphasize the militia and seek the modernization of the regular forces as a first priority, then a renewal of Sino-Soviet cooperation would be necessary in order to obtain the necessary military technology and industry. That this was a valid analytical conception was proven by the Cultural Revolution revelations concerning the Mao Tse-tung/P'eng Teh-huai political battles of 1958-59. P'eng advocated a continued Soviet alliance to provide rapid modernization of forces and would accept Soviet conditions to obtain nuclear weaponry. Mao's People's War implied national independence from the Soviet bloc and a gradual modernization of forces on a basis of self-reliance.

During the coming decade, this use of regional forces and militia as a barometer of Sino-Soviet relations will be of little value. China's own military industries have made surprisingly rapid progress during the 1960s. Virtually any military program desired by the

Peking leadership can be provided from China's own technology, given sufficient lead time and unstinting resource allocations. As for advanced weapons systems beyond China's capability, a renewal of the Sino-Soviet alliance would be valueless. The Soviet leadership would not provide a fractional-orbit-bombardment missile system to the dearest of international allies, much less to a prodigal son. China may or may not seek varying degrees of accomodation with the Soviet Union, but the status of regional forces and militia in the 1970s will no longer provide clues to such decisions.

A NOTE ON
PRODUCTION-CONSTRUCTION CORPS

The production-construction corps were initially to be treated integrally in this chapter as one more component of regional forces. The decision to do otherwise arose from confusion about the present command structure of the production-construction corps.

The original corps, the Sinkiang Production Construction Army Group, was founded in 1950, with PLA veterans serving as cadres over the rank and file, composed mostly of former KMT officers and other "undesirables." During its first decade, the corps evolved into an important unit in terms of land reclamation, reforestation, and the general economic health of Sinkiang. Unlike the militia, corps members devote full time to state projects. The size of the Sinkiang organization was relatively stable for many years at around 250,000 to 300,000 men. The 1969-70 campaign to re-locate massive numbers of urban population to the countryside, however, is believed to have doubled the size of the Sinkiang corps. In the mid-1960s, mention was made of a similar (though smaller) unit in Heilungkiang, the history of which is obscure. Such corps have some arms, including mortars and heavy machine guns. Only a small proportion of the corps personnel carry arms. In terms of potential military effectiveness, the Sinkiang unit would probably fall somewhere between the armed militia and independent units.

Early in 1967, confusion arose concerning the organizational structure. A central directive established the Capital Construction Engineering Corps as an integral part of the PLA. The order did not reveal the precise mission of the new organ, but it did state that the Capital Construction Engineering Corps was "drawn from the Ministry of Industry and Communications" of the State Council, (i.e., the national-government complex).[24] In spring, 1968, it was revealed that the State Planning Commission's "industry and communications unit" had been abolished.[25] In late 1968 and throughout 1969, Chinese media began to mention new production-construction corps in provinces all over China. These units may be the work force for the Capital Construction Engineering Corps. While the size of the new provincial corps was not mentioned, the 1967 national directive, cited above, made mention of self-defense and security units, so presumably the newly formed corps will also have a paramilitary role. It would seem safe to assert that the national total of production-construction corps members is now in the millions.

In view of these developments, there seems a distinct possibility that the PLA is now taking a major role in both the planning and execution of capital construction in China. It further seems that the large number of production-construction corps may be centrally directed labor forces, working on nationally established projects. An example might have been the war-preparations shelter-building campaign of 1969-70. If this speculation is valid, then the production-construction units are no longer regional forces in the Maoist sense. In that instance, the PLA will have strengthened its position in the continuous battle over resource allocations and will have a greater influence than before on the broad question of the proper paths for China's national development.

NOTES

1. JMJP, September 15, 1967. The quote comes from Mao's 1945 article "On Coalition Government," but is frequently invoked today in support of the "protracted war" defense policy.

2. Chester Cheng, ed., PLA Kung-tso Tung-hsun: The Politics of the Chinese Red Army (Stanford, Cal.: Hoover Institution on War, Revolution, and Peace, 1966), p. 47.

3. SCMM (American Consulate General, Hong Kong), No. 570, April, 1967, pp. 11-12.

4. SCMP (American Consulate General, Hong Kong), No. 4070, November 30, 1967, p. 10.

5. Cheng Mien-chih, "The Organization and Equipment of Chinese Communist Infantry," Issues and Studies (Institute of International Relations, Taipei), III, No. 10 (July, 1967). The article, based on captured documents, is authoritative. An independent division might number from 8,000-10,000 men, whereas a division

of an army corps would be in excess of 12,000. Independent divisions are "type C" in Mr. Cheng's presentation.

6. Nan-fang Jih-pao (Canton), October 25, 1950. The figure is quoted in Ting Li, Militia of Communist China (Hong Kong: Union Research Institute, 1954), p. 42.

7. JMJP, November 25, 1950.

8. SCMM, No. 615, February 19, 1968, p. 4.

9. Chester Cheng, Kung-tso Tung-hsun, pp. 117-25.

10. Communist China Digest, No. 193, January 8, 1968 (Joint Publications Research Service, U.S. Department of Commerce, No. 43903), p. 74.

11. Issues and Studies, V, 11 (Aug., 1969), 90.

12. Ibid., V, No. 11 (August, 1969), 95. The charge against Lo is quite plausible in terms of power politics and administrative efficiency.

13. Chester Cheng, Kung-tso Tung-hsun, pp. 374-75.

14. SCMP, No. 3924, April 24, 1967, p. 14 (quoting the People's Daily of April 10).

15. Jürgen Domes, "The Role of the Military in the Formation of Revolutionary Committees," China Quarterly, No. 44, October-December, 1970. Domes provides a province-by-province survey of the behavior of the military-district commands in January-March, 1967.

16. Harbin Radio, October 6, 1967.

17. SCMP, No. 4139, March 15, 1968, pp. 5-7. Hsieh Fu-chih is quoted therein. The same source also provided the Szechwan arrest figure.

18. Chu Wen-lin, "An Analysis of Recent Peiping Military Personnel Changes," East Asia Quaterly, (Taipei), II, No. 2, (February, 1970).

19. SCMP, No. 4009, August 25, 1967, p. 8.

20. Ibid., No. 4190, June 4, 1968, p. 10.

21. Ibid., No. 4070, November 30, 1967, p. 8.

22. Ibid.

23. Ibid., No. 4169, May 8, 1968, p. 1.

24. CB (American Consulate General, Hong Kong), No. 852, May 6, 1968, pp. 76-77.

25. SCMP, No. 4189, June 3, 1968, p. 8.

8

THE
GROUND
FORCES

Joseph Heinlein

This chapter will focus on the current status and near-term capabilities of Communist China's ground forces. Following a brief discussion of their origin and development, certain characteristics of leadership perspectives and organizational routine that have influenced the capabilities and potential of the forces will be isolated.

The ground forces, as differentiated from the naval and airforce components, constitute the majority of the PLA (some 2 million of the estimated 2.3-million PLA manpower are ground units—see Figure 1).[1] Ground-force units are widely deployed; they represent and embody the traditions of revolutionary development in China; and they are the source of the majority of military and political leadership. For these reasons, one should be conscious of the history of ground combat in the PLA.

Thanks to its short history, the ground forces cannot escape a distinctive set of still vivid traditions, organizational loyalties, and learned principles, scarcely forty years old. Unlike the ground commanders of many countries where military customs, traditions, and prevailing philosophies are centuries old, having been preserved by one generation after another of military leadership, a large proportion of China's ground-force (and political) leaders have lived through the formation of the PLA, seen its inception, tasted its battles, and created its lore. Indeed, this army's past is so recent that many

---

Views expressed in this chapter are solely those of the author and do not represent approval of any agency of the U.S. government.

FIGURE 1

China's Ground Forces

Strength: Approximately 2 million

Combat Divisions: More than 120 total, of which at least 110 are
infantry, about 6 armored, and a few horse cavalry; in addition,
there are border-defense and public-security forces that could be
used for combat; separate artillery divisions, both gun and howitzer,
available for support of armored and infantry divisions

Firepower: Most units short of heavier artillery; small arms probably
available in adequate quantity; ammunition stockpile is probably
well dispersed for contingencies and of extensive quantity; armored
units deficient in tanks, especially more modern types (Soviet-type
T34 is mainstay)

Disposition: Uneven geographic dispersion generally follows population and industrial pattern; most forces deployed in northeast and
along coastal agricultural sectors southward to Kwangsi and then
inland to Yunnan

Mobility: Generally poor; some motorized infantry may have full
complement of vehicles; no more than half of armored divisions
fully equipped; some Soviet-type armored personnel carriers in
use; for strategic moves, the divisions are rail-bound; tactical foot
mobility could be expected to be excellent

Training/Readiness: Uneven in quality throughout; certain elite units
(perhaps a strategic reserve) may maintain higher standards; combined arms exercises probably not as frequent or effective as needed
due to nonmilitary activities

Logistics: Logistical system tied to fixed rail and road nets; no
modern organic capability adequate to satisfy large scale maneuver;
probably would rely on prior stockpiling and local acquisition;
based on Korean War experience, only 8 to 10 pounds per man per
day would need replenishment, as opposed to 60 pounds per man
per day for a U.S. force

Tactical Organization: Triangular concept of 3 regiments to each
division; number of divisions per region (U.S. corps equivalent)

varies widely at present; divisions light in both men and firepower
by modern standards with about 14,000 men in an infantry division
and about 10,000 in an armored division

Sources: Samuel B. Griffith II, The Chinese People's Liberation
Army (New York: McGraw-Hill, 1967), pp. 219-21; and John Gittings,
The Role of the Chinese Army (New York: Oxford University Press,
1967), pp. 305, 308.

current leaders participated in the entire history now being emulated
as tradition. As a consequence, intervening generations have probably
had only marginal influence on the modification of these "elders" professional attitudes formed by first-hand experience.

ARMY TRADITIONS AND PERSPECTIVES

Perhaps the most striking feature of the ground-force tradition
in China has been its routine involvement in domestic political affairs.
The army has always been recognized by both military and civil leaders
as an instrument for the implementation of domestic policy. Its senior
leaders, far from being isolated from politics, have been encouraged
to participate directly in the melee of domestic policy formulation
and implementation. As in most developing social and economic en-
vironments, control and/or allegiance of the army has been and is
likely to remain a prerequisite to national leadership. Time and
again Peking's political leadership has relied on the military as a
model for and implementor of political and economic policy: "learn
from the PLA" was still a slogan in 1971; military efforts each harvest
season to assist with the vital crop are traditional; distribution of
products and resources with army transportation has been common.
The peak in institutionalizing the PLA as a political institution occurred in the tripartite ruling bodies of cadre, Party, and army members (with military preeminence), which actually undertook governing
China during and after the Cultural Revolution. These facts argue
that political, social, and economic involvement has necessarily been
viewed by senior army commanders as a usual role, especially among
the ground forces. This "political-army syndrome" is, then, a long-
standing facet of Chinese Communist military philosophy.

A second significant aspect of the development of the PLA was
the early and persistent conscious commitment to social revolution
and to Leninist organizational techniques and political philosophy.
Many early ground commanders enjoyed a direct association with

the Russian revolutionary experience or learned from the widespread
influx of Soviet military doctrine and technique through the latter's
advisers and training. Beginning in 1924, Russian advisers at the
Whampoa Military Academy deeply influenced the early formation of
today's Nationalist and Communist Chinese military establishment
in the Soviet image.

A corollary of their personal involvement in and commitment
to social revolution has been the ground commanders' lifelong exposure to political commissars and political training. In the mid-
1920s, commissars were made a part of the military organization
and remain so today. Ideology provided one set of motivations and
missions in opposition to purely professional values—namely, military
involvement in nonmilitary, economic, and social functions of government. It must be remembered that exhortation of the masses to emulate the military as the socialist model of altruism for the good of
the state was introduced to China in the Whampoa classroom.[2]

A fourth tradition, which perhaps summarizes the first three
is the current high-command perception of war as "total war." In
Kiangsi, when the Chinese Soviet Republic was resisting Chiang Kai-
shek's attempts to exterminate it for almost seven years, the differentiation among Party, government, and military was moot in
terms of personalities and functions. The Long March, essentially
a military operation, took with it the Party and government apparatus
of the Soviet Republic. During the Yenan resistance days of World
War II, the military mission was preeminent, but Party and government frameworks were integrated with it to form a totality that maintained at best a theoretical, though not a practical, distinction among
the three.

Again, in practical terms, the post-World War II years of civil
war in China had the Communist ground forces acting as a chief
instrument for implementation of policy, in most situation providing
the only visible evidence of a Communist Party or government. Until
1949, waging total war was a way of life for the majority of the current senior generation of ground-force commanders. Political administration, economic process, and even Party activity were tied
to the organization and operations of the army in a way that made a
real distinction of functions virtually impossible. While the Korean
War allowed for such a distinction with Chinese forces in Korea, the
armies remaining in China continued to represent the Communist
government and Party in the regions they occupied.

Fifth, with respect to the strategic military application of power,
there has been a consistent focus (with the possible exception of the

venture into Korea) on the application of military force either within
or on the immediate periphery of China's borders. The need to plan
and develop forces for far-reaching, sustained ground operations
beyond China's borders has not been a traditional military exercise.
The employment of the ground forces has always been limited geographically and directed at either protecting or recovering Chinese
territory (at least the Chinese rationale would see it this way). The
bulk of early experience consisted of warring with the Chinese Nationalists in a contest for control of Chinese territory. The formative
years, from about 1924 to 1939, as well as the Sino-Japan War gave
the PLA no horizon beyond Chinese territory. The Korean War saw
large forces deployed across the Yalu, but their timely withdrawal
upon cessation of hostilities could attest to limited ambition and
certainly did not establish as doctrine the use of massive ground
forces abroad.

Thus, while the idea of aggressive military action beyond China's
borders may not be anathema to the Chinese military mind, it probably does not constitute part of the basic military philosophy in Peking,
even though the occupation of Tibet may have provided useful practical
experience. Instead, virtue has been found in the necessity to rely
on the army's vast manpower resources for the formulation of national-defense strategy; an invading force would be "swallowed up"
by China's masses led by the PLA.

A sixth feature of PLA ground-commander perspectives and
organizational routines has been their familiarity with the small-
units tactics of guerrilla warfare. As mentioned above, the early
history of the Chinese Red Army was spent fighting within China.
Until the Korean War, ground-force operations were for the most
part characterized by hit-and-run tactics, considerable localized
maneuver by forced march, and striking at a time and place of their
own choosing against an adversary's weak points. This was the work-
shop for the now-famous Maoist tactics of guerilla warfare (which
many prefer to ascribe to Chu Teh rather than to Mao). These tactics
frustrated far superior numbers of better-equipped KMT forces for
six years in Kiangsi before the Red Army had to yield and begin the
retreat now known as the Long March. It is Mao's contention that
failure to apply these tactics, not a failure of doctrine per se, gave
Chiang the edge in the last Kiangsi campaign.[3]

During the Sino-Japan War, these same tactics were used with
considerable success, allowing the enemy to occupy the cities while
Communist forces made persistent forays against vulnerable lines
of communication and isolated installations. A combination of factors

made this an ideal strategy: the Red Army was consistently faced
with a superior force, the terrain was generally suitable for cover
and concealment, the population at large was sympathetic, and Communist forces were operating in familiar areas where they had established an infrastructure of control.

In contrast with these six characteristics, a professional
syndrome has also demanded attention. The Korean experience and
the close association with Soviet military thinking through the 1950s
gave cause for serious reflection on the efficacy of the strategy, tactics, and principles learned in pre-1946 quasi-guerrilla actions. As
Alexander George points out, despite initial success in Korea through
capitalizing on a manpower advantage and applying appropriate tactics,
Chinese forces soon discovered that the UN force was able to hold a
line across the peninsula, rolling with the Communist thrusts, but
never snapping under the pressure.[4] The enemy's weak points were
not discernible; recourse to a safe haven after an engagement was
not feasible. Heavy losses and ultimate failure necessarily gave cause
for Chinese military leaders to appreciate the need for modernization
of their forces to contend with future wars of this sort. The honey-
moon with Soviet aid and advisers did in fact bring about much in the
way of the modernizing and rethinking of strategy and tactics during
the 1950s. Much of the equipment so cherished by military men as
the concrete substance of their capability was provided by the USSR,
and for a time it appeared that certain military elements of their political-military tradition would be relegated to the museum in favor
of conventional military philosophy, organization, and training.

The Sino-Soviet split of the late 1950s, however, brought, inter
alia, an overwhelming Maoist revulsion toward this modern, conventional tack then being so well advanced within the armed forces. It
was most pronounced in bitter debates over strategy and tactics: was
China to develop conventional forces appropriately equipped to contend
with an adversary in terms of modern warfare, denying an invader a
foothold on Chinese territory, or was reliance to be placed on the
dogma generated by years of guerrilla warfare, inviting the adversary
to destruction within Chinese territory through an envelopment that
would bring overwhelming manpower and unique mobility to bear in
a guerilla war? The former thesis not only implied continued reliance on the Soviet Union, it might also necessarily have the attendant
effect of making a new type of military leader preeminent.

In attempting to resolve these questions, intra-Party debate
labeled P'eng Teh-huai (in 1959) and Lo Jui-ch'ing (in 1966) as "bourgeois military, revisionist Soviet lackeys" and gave led to the rise of

Lin Piao and a movement to rebalance red and expert factions in the PLA. According to Franz Schurmann, "From a sociological standpoint, the red and expert contradiction is the most important in China today."[5] This issue is more than Maoist vs. professional. Its resolution will ultimately reflect a generation gap among all chinese military leaders. Younger military cadre, trained in Soviet military technique in the 1950s, probably came to appreciate the value of rapid doctrinal and material military modernization. They probably share such views with a few older leaders who remember the lessons learned in Korea. All of these men certainly have reason for concern about the adverse effects of the "Red vs. Expert" conflict on ground-force military readiness, training, and operational methods. Conversely, the "Red vs. Expert" military conflict has served to entrench many other senior leaders dedicated to their early revolutionary experience and their domestic positions of relative power within both the civil and military bureaucracy. As long as they retain such perspectives and power, advancement of those who would innovate must be delayed.

In a force in which manpower dominates unsophisticated mobility and communications systems, middle- and low-level leadership will be paramount for progressive development, modernization, and efficient military operations. Yet, these levels of leadership in the Chinese ground forces are likely to remain stifled by outmoded doctrine and by the burden of political responsibility at least until the mid-1970s. The duration and intensity of the Cultural Revolution and the extent of ground-force involvement will probably provide a residue of "Redness" that will not soon be overcome.

No doubt the PLA, and especially the ground forces, have gained considerable prestige and dominance on the domestic scene both in the provinces and at the national level as a result of the Cultural Revolution. But this new-found role is not a military role. While ground force leaders at all levels may have basked in their prominence on the RCs and may enjoy flexing their organizational muscle in the midst of government and party bureaucratic disorder, any serious thought of the consequences for purely military responsiveness could not be reassuring. Should this prominence prove so satisfying to cadres at middle and low levels that it obscures the military role of the force, ill effects could accrue. There is some danger that this over-involvement in governing could, either by continuation or recurrence, become the rule rather than the exception and atrophy the modern war-waging potential of the ground forces.

ORGANIZATIONAL ROUTINES

First, it is important to recall the geographic location of ground-force units. In tracing the origins of China's Red Army, William Whitson identifies five distinct "streams" of organizational and "informal power systems" that emanated from the Kiangsi era of the early 1930s.[6] (Two, however, were geographically separate from the Kiangsi Soviet: Ho Lung's forces in northwest Hunan and Chang Kuo-t'ao's troops in Anhwei.) These streams eventually took shape as the PLA's five field armies, each of which operated throughout World War II and up until 1949 in its own geographic area. While the Korean War drew about two thirds of these units across the Yalu, upon cessation of hostilities most returned to the same locality where they had been stationed in 1949. Whitson reinforces his point of a likely affinity between units and geographic regions: "to date . . . the regular Corps have all remained in positions to which they returned after the Korean war."[7]

These are, of course, the most visible indications of "informal power systems"—webs of interpersonal relations and political dynamics that have fostered the entrenchment of military units in a given locale for decades. While recent evidence and traditional Chinese style would sustain the thesis that factions have evolve for the purpose of preserving power and influence along regional lines, the evidence is not sufficient to suggest that the military responsiveness of the ground forces to direction from Peking would break down. It is more likely that a give-and-take arrangement exists among military regions and between the regions and Peking.[8]

Prior to the Cultural Revolution, the formal organization within which these compromises were theoretically accomplished was the typical two-headed Communist model: ostensible direction by organs of government and actual direction by the Party hierarchy. (See Figure 2.) The senior military headquarters on the governmental side was (and remains) the Ministry of National Defense (PLA general headquarters). On the Party side, it was and still is the powerful MAC of the CCP CC (Currently Lin Piao, Mao's appointed heir, heads both). The twin chain of command extends downward from the Ministry of National Defense and the MAC directly to the professional staff and Party committee* at the military-region level. Before the Cultural

---

*This Party committee is a part of the political system <u>within</u> the military, <u>not</u> the civilian equivalent. Party committees are

FIGURE 2

Strategic Military Organization

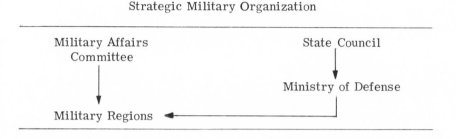

Revolution there were thirteen military regions (see Figure 3).* Those
regions having two or more provinces are divided into districts that
usually coincide with provincial boundaries. The civilian administrative districts within the provinces generally serve also as military
subdistricts.

Here, one can see that even the organization of the ground forces
is defined in geographic terms of region, district, and subdistrict,
reaffirming the notion of regional ties. A purely defensive engagement could permit retention of this terrain-bound organization, but
would not facilitate extensive maneuver or redeployment of large
forces. For this reason, reorganization of military regions as field
armies similar to the organization used during the Korean War would
be necessary if the ground forces were to engage in combat on a scale
requiring considerable movement, especially beyond Chinese borders.

THE IMPACT OF THE CULTURAL REVOLUTION

Even the present formal organization described here may have
little relevance in the aftermath of the Cultural Revolution. The

---

present down to regimental level; there are branches at battalion and
company levels and cells at the platoon level. [For further discussion
of the system, see Chapter 9.—Ed.]

*As noted in other chapters, there were probably only eleven
military regions in 1971, Iuner Mongolia having been subdivided
among Lauchow, Peking, and Shenyang military regions and Tibet
having fallen under the Chengtu Military Region.—Ed.

FIGURE 3

Military Regions and Districts

Regions	Districts
Canton	Kwangtung Kwangsi Hunan
Chengtu	Szechuan
Foochow	Fukien Kiangsi
Kunming	Kweichow Yunnan
Lanchow	Chinghai Kansu Ninghsia Shensi
Nanking	Chekiang Anhwei Kiangsu
Peking	Hopei Shansi
Shenyang	Kirin Liaoning Heilungkiang
Tsinan	Shantung
Wuhan	Honan Hupeh
Inner Mongolia, Autonomous Region	
Sinkiang Autonomous Region	
Tibet Autonomous Region	

effective demise of the Party apparatus and the PLA's GPD could
sound the beginnings of new and different organizational lines of communication and responsiveness.

With the ground forces dominating, the PLA played a paramount
role in the Cultural Revolution. Despite the fact that it remained
generally responsive to Peking, in retrospect a particularly military
attitude toward policy and events was evident. Neither radical nor
conservative factions could ignore this military view. There was a
voice for this military attitude in Peking and also in the provinces as
the PLA became the principal implementor of policy. The ultimate
ascendancy of reason over the choas of Red Guard "power seizures"
was in large measure due to the weight of this military perspective
and the influence it had on the central leadership in Peking.

Despite the fact that Mao, through his chief lieutenant Lin Piao,
had attempted for some ten years to tailor the military as his model
of revolutionary zeal and base of power vis-à-vis the Party bureaucrats who favored more conservative policies, in the final analysis
the weight of the PLA gravitated to the side of these conservatives.
It would be difficult to argue that this was a deliberate ploy by military leaders. It was probably more the product of policy ambiguity
at the center matched by chaos in the provinces.

The unstable state of power at the center caused by the give-and-
take between conservative and radical factions resulted in ambiguous
policy directives. Although the military was charged with "supporting
the left," the Red Guards were primarily responsible for the chaos.
Because the PLA was simultaneously directed to maintain economic,
political, and administrative stability, local commanders in general
opted for stability, in most cases through omission rather than commission, not by contravening directives but by interpreting them to
their own satisfaction. Local ground-commander influence was thus
a restraining factor on the radical rebels. When open clashes between Red Guards and the Party apparatus occurred, the highly politicized ground forces tended to favor the Party elements, especially
at local levels—not an unlikely response given long personal association with counterparts in local administration and a mutual interest
in stability within their regions.* This preference for stability on the
part of the military was to cause a reaction from Peking.

---

*See Chapter 7 for a more detailed discussion of local-force
behavior during the Cultural Revolution.—Ed.

When revolutionary rebels proved incapable of either seizing or managing power, the PLA was directed to implement the RC concept. In doing so, the military again acted in the interest of stability, despite clear direction to assist the rebels. The "triple alliances" of the RCs disguised this PLA preference for order in a way that initially precluded leftist criticism. Nonetheless, radical reaction did come in April, 1967, in the form of a directive effectively telling the PLA "hands off" the Red Guards.

The discipline apparent in the response of local military commanders to this directive is quite amazing. With the exception of the Wuhan incident, in which the military-region commander openly backed conservative factions and was consequently dismissed, the PLA ostensibly complied. There are some indications that military commanders tacitly favored conservative factions, but no great trend of outright dissent developed. But the PLA did become the object of radical attack, and military patience was probably wearing thin.

An appreciation of the military view in Peking was undoubtedly instrumental in a policy reversal that shifted the balance of influence to the conservative factions in the central leadership in the fall of 1967 (this, of course, in the context of rampant chaos in China at the time, does not imply that the military view was the only factor in causing the shift). As a result, not only was the PLA again emulated, it was now empowered to restore order. This it began to do, but Red Guard excesses in the summer of 1968 saw the PLA adopt the tactic of "sit and wait" while radical elements vying for recognition "shot it out." In late 1968, it became evident even to Mao that order was needed. He personally sounded the death knell of the Red Guards by calling for the dissolution of their organizations. The PLA reacted efficiently and effectively, established RCs throughout China, and restored stability. What remains after the Cultural Revolution is in fact a new power structure that has the PLA, and especially the ground forces, as its core. Military domination of the RCs and new Party committees is one foundation for PLA strength in this structure. Just as important is the greatly increased military presence on councils of leadership in Peking. Indeed, a military man, Lin Piao, is Mao's appointed heir.[9]

While one could argue that policy formulation in Peking remains in the hands of a select few who are not necessarily military or military oriented, there is no doubt that implementation of policy is dependent upon an administrative structure almost totally subject to ground-force influence.[10] In the absence of a viably reconstituted Party, left in shambles by the Cultural Revolution, the PLA and particularly the ground force will continue to wield this influence. In addition, ground-force commanders occupying positions of regional power within the new structure are clearly influencing the reconstruction of the local Party apparatus to a degree that must cause concern among the left-leaning factions in Peking.

The salient characteristics of the pre-Cultural Revolution development of the ground forces have been reinforced. That is, the ground forces still accent activities within China; their political involvement has reached a new peak. Although diverse leadership attitudes remain apparent, they have been better defined (especially in the professional/political dichotomy as it relates to strategic military policy). The historical affinity between ground forces and geographic regions has necessarily been bolstered by the PLA's governing functions on the RCs. Military participation in high-level leadership has been further institutionalized.

CURRENT AND FUTURE CAPABILITIES

How do these considerations translate into more practical terms of current and projected capabilities of Chinese ground forces? Regarding the principle of domestic political roles, some Chinese military leaders have recognized the adverse effects that political, social, and economic involvement can have on the PLA. From the viewpoint of its purely military mission and functions, distraction from training can only have an adverse effect upon ground-force readiness and capabilities.

Yet, it would appear, based on historical precedent, that until the mid- to late 1970s, the ground forces will continue to be so involved. And that involvement should continue to be a professional distraction in the sense that the Peking leadership will need to rely on the resources, organization, and responsiveness of the army when necessary to implement and/or enforce domestic policy.

Depending on the extent of this involvement, ground-force capabilities and especially readiness will be more or less effective. A repeat performance of the Cultural Revolution could render them virtually ineffective in terms of large-scale deployments or engagements on China's periphery. For the ground forces especially, there appears to be no near-term prospect for a total respite from the political role that would permit complete concentration on military training and activities. This prospect alone could adversely affect efficiency in the sense that units will be ever conscious of the added requirement and concerned about meeting the task effectively.

Traditional ground-force deployments are unlikely to change. China's ground forces are for the most part disposed in a way that finds units and strengths coincidental with population distribution. It is likely that this pattern of disposition will continue unchanged for a number of reasons: population concentrations naturally coincide with the most economically important geographic areas, be they agriculturally fertile, industrially developed, or commercially prominent. It follows that military presence lends stability and security; the military's unique role as an adjunct to the economic apparatus dictates colocation with agricultural and industrial enterprises. The traditional and current role of the PLA as a political instrument reinforces this rationale for colocation of ground forces with population concentrations. Furthermore, both economic and military real-property infrastructure, e.g., rail nets and military-base training facilities and schools, have a measure of permanence that would suggest their continued use (unless massive relocations are undertaken at great cost), since ground-force mobility demands reliance on railroads for strategic moves and road nets would not easily accomodate large-scale wheeled or track motor troop transport and supply even if organic means of mobility were somehow developed. Finally, vested interest on the part of the military in maintaining the long-standing ties with localities in which the forces are based may not be easily overcome if the decision to reorient the ground forces was for some reason deemed appropriate.

The regional command and control organization of the ground forces is also unlikely to change. Only a major war might reorganize the ground forces or, at a minimum, the military-region headquarters or elements thereof into something similar to a field army if deployments to another locality were required to meet a conventional military threat. Historic defense strategy is unlikely to change. Current strategy probably does not call for a reorganization of forces into field armies, in part because the People's War doctrine of defense postulates inviting the enemy into a given military region and engaging his forces in guerrilla-type warfare. The logic in this strategy not only befits the Sinocentric experience of earlier wars; it is also an ideal "quick-fix" solution to China's inability to proceed with a wide range of military production programs simultaneously. It would follow that conventional ground forces will receive the lowest priority in the allocation of resources to modernizing ground-force weapons programs. Ground-force improvements in firepower and mobility will probably be slow in coming.

This is not to say that refinements of the ground-force posture will not be undertaken. The so-called bourgeois military line and the modernization of the armed forces along conventional lines was discredited by the Maoists initially in 1959 because of the implication for continued acceptance of both Soviet military aid and military doctrine, with an attendant professionalization of the military. Yet, that military line was in many ways a sound approach to the defense of China's industrially developed sectors, e.g., Manchuria. The Maoist notion of "swallowing up" an invading force with a People's War strategy has consistently failed to acknowledge the importance of China's economic and industrial bases. Indeed, the professional strategy for defending northeast China against Soviet ground-force invasion would call for the use of conventional military force to stop the invader at the first obstacle (the Greater and Lesser Khingan mountain ranges in the northeast) and preclude his disruption or destruction of industrial centers. People's War would not be adequate for the defense of such an industrial complex unless leaders were willing to sacrifice the capacity for production.

This same logic applies to any real or perceived threat from the Korean peninsula. Assuming the Peking leadership values this industrial base, it follows that the ground forces, in the Shenyang Military Region at least, will be better equipped and trained along conventional lines during the next decade in order to meet this contingency. Such logic, of course, also implies that similar modernization would be applied to the remainder of the military regions once the capacity to produce appropriate material and equipment has peaked.

Assuming that the present influence of the PLA in political affairs continues, ground-force commanders will be in a particularly good position to have their views about ground-force modernization heard. Given their dominant influence because of their more intense and widespread involvement in the post-Cultural Revolution political system at local levels and in Peking, it would follow that their share of the political pie will be greater. It is not unreasonable to speculate that their gains will be at the expense of other programs and perhaps other PLA services.

Concerning the balance of power among military regions, one should anticipate an imbalance in distribution of military hardware among the military regions. Some ground-force commanders will certainly be able to extract political concessions from Peking in return for services or resources held within their regions. None of this implies that a particular region will be likely to revert to a totally independent stance akin to warlordism (though Kao Kang stands as something of a precedent in Manchuria). Such a political system has apparently been precluded in a military sense: resources, research and development and means of production of sophisticated hardware have spread throughout the country, with the consequence that no one satrap could achieve self-sufficiency.*

Given the foregoing and the earlier assertions by military leaders that a more professional, better-equipped, and better-trained army was a desirable goal, it is conceivable that ground-force commanders could alter the direction of policy, planning, and strategic thinking to focus on this goal.

It is also conceivable that, having established itself as a nuclear power, Peking will find satisfaction in a token nuclear force and will apply more resources toward developing a viable conventional ground force. Nonetheless, for perhaps the remainder of the decade, any improvements would only bring the ground forces up to standards defined by current organization (that is, make available equipment and means of mobility that would bring present forces up to strengths called for by current organization). Given continued Soviet and U.S. sophisticated conventional forces, Chinese ground forces will remain well behind their super-competitors on a relative scale. An early policy move toward improved conventional forces however, could give Peking considerable room for maneuver in dealing with the U.S. and USSR and certainly vis-á-vis its smaller neighbors. Some feeling of security below the nuclear threshold would surely accrue in relation to Japan's economic and political presence (and military potential) in Asia. Thus, conventional modernization might be a desirable addition to Chinese force posture options available in 1971, given the lightweight status of China's nuclear capability.

An immediate and striking conclusion that one can draw from this analysis is that the ground forces are at best only prepared to undertake a defensive war against a modern army. Deficiencies in mobility, firepower, and command and control can all be rationalized in terms of a People's War strategy of defense. Persistence in this strategy would strongly imply that the PLA is incapable of conducting a more conventional defense of China and that offensive capabilities are probably quite limited. While the ground forces will remain capable of maintaining internal security and domestic order through the 1970s, these forces will be no match for U.S. or Soviet conventional forces. While Chinese ground forces could muster a credible defense of the mainland, they probably could not maintain large-scale, sustained conventional operations for very long against a determined

---

*See Chapter 11 for a more detailed discussion of this point.—Ed.

Soviet or U.S. effort. If the combat arena were beyond China's borders, even a lesser foe, such as the much-improved (since 1962) Indian Army, could probably contend with China's ground forces.

NOTES

1. Samuel B. Griffith II, The Chinese People's Liberation Army (New York: McGraw-Hill, 1967), pp. 219-20.

2. Roderick L. MacFarquahar, "The Whampoa Military Academy," in East Asia Program of the Committee on Regional Studies, Harvard University, Papers on China, IX (Cambridge, Mass., 1955), pp. 150-51 (mimeographed).

3. Edgar Snow, Red Star Over China (New York: Grove Press, 1968), p. 180.

4. Alexander L. George, The Chinese Communist Army in Action (New York: Columbia University Press, 1967), pp. 172-73.

5. Quoted in ibid., p. 197.

6. William Whitson, "The Field Army in Chinese Communist Military Politics," China Quarterly, January-March, 1969, p. 3.

7. Ibid., p. 7.

8. Ibid., p. 23.

9. Ellis Joffe, "The Chinese Army in the Cultural Revolution: The Politics of Intervention," Current Scene, December 7, 1970, p. 23.

10. Ibid., pp. 23-24.

9

THE GENERAL
POLITICAL
DEPARTMENT
Glenn G. Dick

INTRODUCTION

Before the Cultural Revolution, the importance of the GPD lay in two areas: the role it played in guaranteeing Party control of the PLA and the influence it effected in shaping the thought and behavior of PLA personnel. From the early days of the CCP's armed forces (1927-28), there probably has been a staff or organization executing functions similar to those carried out by the GPD. Thus, virtually all PLA general officers, most field-grade officers, and senior non-commissioned officers have been intimately affected by the GPD or its predecessor organizations.

But the future of the GPD—and the role it will play in the 1970s—is clouded by uncertainty. During the Cultural Revolution, it dropped completely out of sight for over two years. Since its return as a functioning bureaucracy in late 1969, it has apparently had only a shadow of its former power. Whether it will be able to reestablish itself as a major element of PLA headquarters in Peking and resume its influence among PLA personnel is still unclear.

This chapter will briefly review the history of the GPD and describe how the GPD operated within the political context of the PLA. It will then discuss what appears to be the key variables that will determine the GPD's role in the 1970s and suggest some specific

---

Views expressed in this chapter are solely those of the author and do not represent the official position of any agency of the U.S. government.

ways in which the GPD may affect forseeable developments during the coming decade.

BACKGROUND

Political control and indoctrination have been fundamental parts of Chinese Communist military life from its beginnings. Many of the Communists' first officers had been members of Chiang Kai-shek's KMT army and had been exposed to political indoctrination under the party-control system that Sun Yat-sen and Chiang had adopted from their Soviet advisers.[1]

From the Nanch'ang Uprising in early August, 1927,* until March, 1928, scattered Communist armed bands were too concerned with mere survival to do much political work. During this period, however, Mao managed to form "soldiers' committees" in units under his influence.[2] The CCP CC established a Politburo-level military committee in September, 1928, during its Sixth Congress.[3] This military bureau, or military department as it was called, was ordered "to consolidate the Party's leadership of the army; . . . train military personnel in the Party, and raise the most reliable officers from workers and Party members.[4] The Party, presumably through this military bureau, directed its officials to make sure that local conditions were favorable before initiating military action, if the situation was favorable, the Party was to ensure that the anticipated action was "well prepared, well organized, [and] well planned," and that "suitable tactics" were employed.[5]

This predecessor to the present-day MAC probably was not very effective since the CC remained underground in Shanghai after returning from the Sixth Congress, which had been held in Moscow. This first military bureau probably became more active after the CC moved to Mao's mountain stronghold in Kiangsi in 1931. It probably was not until after the Long March ended in 1935, however, that the CC's military department was able to set up a stable and effective staff to execute wide-ranging political, educational, and propaganda programs.

During the second civil war (1945-49), the MAC's political staff was apparently developed as the counterpart to the General Staff.

---

*August 1, 1927, is celebrated as the founding of the PLA.

The GPD, the General Staff Department, and the General Rear Services Department (GRSD) have since remained the three principal staff components of the PLA from the governmental reorganization in 1954 until the GPD dropped from sight in 1967.[6]

THE GPD IN THE PLA[7]

To understand how the GPD functioned before the Cultural Revolution, it is necessay to digress briefly into the way in which the PLA was controlled. The PLA's system of leadership differed fundamentally from other major armed forces. Instead of a unitary chain of command, the PLA was controlled through a heirarchy of Party Committees that served as the "core of unified leadership" of each combat unit, school, or organization. The 1963 "Regulations" spell out the functions of these committees:

> On handling all important questions . . . , except during a state of emergency when responsible persons may act on their own discretion, the Party Committee must hold a full discussion of the question and arrive at a decision in accordance with the system of democratic centralism of the Party; if it concerns military matters, the troop commander should be responsible for carrying it out; if it concerns political matters, the political commissar should be responsible for carrying it out. Both the political commissar and the military commander are leading officers of the unit; they are mutually responsible for the work of their unit. Under ordinary conditions, the political commissar is in charge of the daily routine of the Party committee.

The last sentence of the above quote is the key to the pre-Cultural Revolution PLA command and control system. The political commissar normally was the Party committee's secretary and thus, by definition, the unit's most powerful leader. This system tended to relegate the commander to the role of a technician. It was a cumbersome system because operational orders, to be binding, normally had to be countersigned by the political commissar. Many students of the PLA believe that the Party committee command system was a major source of tension between the PLA's political and professional soldiers.

Atop the heirarchy was the MAC, which established over-all military policies and disseminated directives to be implemented by the three general departments (GPD, General Staff Department, and GRSD). The MAC also seemed to have a "skip echelon" prerogative that enabled it to communicate orders directly to virtually any level or organization. In 1968, for instance, members of the newly formed MAC administration group were instructed to become personally acquainted with division-level commanders and commissars in order to effectively supervise and evaluate them.[8]

Before being swept away during the Cultural Revolution, the GPD stood one echelon below the MAC in the Party's system for controlling the PLA. Its job was to put forward general political tasks and basic political requirements for the PLA, to review the execution of these political tasks, to carry out investigations and studies, and to publicize the deeds of model soldiers. It was to relay its findings to the MAC and to seek instructions from and report its activities to the MAC. Specific duties included the following:[9]

supervising all indoctrination of the PLA

supervising the building of Party committees at all levels

propagating policies pertaining to training "so that the troops will always maintain sound combat readiness"

raising the military learning, tactical, and technical levels of the troops

reviewing officers' performance and selecting those to be promoted, reassigned, or demoted

supervising demobilization procedures for the PLA and providing for suitable civilan employment for retired officers

exercising leadership over political security work and supervising procuratorates and the military courts

supervising PLA cultural, entertainment, and sports activities

publishing PLA newspapers and other publications

overseeing relations between military units and their surrounding civilian population

leading military efforts in political warfare and
subversion against enemy forces in time of war

exercising leadership over political work in
scientific research organizations for national defense "to
ensure successes and produce men of ability"

exercising leadership over political work and political education in PLA schools in order to "bring up cadres
who are both red and expert"

overseeing political activities of the militia

supervising political work related to conscription
and wartime mobilization

caring for the welfare of PLA personnel (especially
those who have been disabled), their dependents, and the
dependents of those killed in the line of duty

carrying out liaison with friendly foreign military
forces.

Thus, the GPD exercised broad authority over political and
indoctrinational activities of lower-echelon military Party committees
and their supporting political departments. Its scope went beyond
strictly "political" activities, however, and entered "professional"
areas of assessing combat readiness, overseeing military research
and development, and evaluating professional officers' performance.

In fulfilling these missions, the GPD worked closely with both
the Party committees and each committee's attached political department. These departments provided each unit's Party committee
(down to the regimental level) with appropriate staff support. The
unit's political department director was normally the lowest-ranking
member of the unit's Party committee. So much indoctrination,
political evaluation, political counterintelligence, and record-keeping
is required that "political work" long ago became a highly professional-
ized specialty. There are a series of political staff schools that train
officers for this activity; officers choosing this branch of service are
normally expected to continue in it throughout their careers.

Before the Cultural Revolution, the GPD performed functions
for the MAC somewhat analogous to those of the political departments
of lower echelon Party committees—carrying out general and specific

MAC directives, examining the effectiveness of PLA political programs, and supervising lower-echelon Party committees and their respective political departments. Much remains unknown about the GPD: its size, political controversy within its halls, cliques and factions among its personnel, and its relationship to the larger political scene in China. These unknowns have added to the mystery surrounding the GPD's disappearance during the Cultural Revolution.

THE GPD AND THE CULTURAL REVOLUTION

It may have been that the GPD identified too closely with the other large Party bureaucracies in Peking, such as Teng Hsiao-p'ing's secretariat of the Party CC. If so, the GPD may have reflected the Party's opposition to or bewilderment over the direction and scope of Mao's Cultural Revolution. Or, it may have been that the GPD was too enthusiastic and efficient in implementing the radical programs of the Politburo's first CRG. It also may have been overzealous in carrying out the purge of senior PLA officers that began in late 1965 with the fall of former Chief of the General Staff Lo Jui-ch'ing and continued until about mid-1967. The GPD may have moved too bruskly to settle scores that perhaps had accumulated since 1959 when Mao replaced former Defense Minister P'eng Teh-huai with Lin Piao. Lin's vigorous promotion of the status and power of the GPD may have generated many a feud within the upper echelons of the PLA.

Perhaps it is not simply coincidental that the GPD disappeared shortly after the Wuhan incident of July, 1967, when the commander of the Wuhan Military Region, Ch'en Tsai-tao, opposed the Peking leaders and was immediately cashiered. Japanese reporters in Peking at that time reported that there was a strong movement afoot to make Ch'en the central figure in a campaign against military opposition. The campaign to "strike down Ch'en" never materialized, however, and GPD Director Hsiao Hua came under heavy criticism by Lin Piao in August and dropped from sight in September, 1967. One may never know why the GPD dropped from sight, but the timing of its disappearance strongly suggests that it was unable to change directions when, in early August, 1967, the Politburo shifted abruptly away from permitting "revolutionary" violence to run virtually unchecked to a policy of using the PLA to curb Red Guards and others who were seeking to exploit the situation for their own good.

Curiously, the disappearance of the GPD did not seem to adversely affect the PLA's political directors, for their departments operated throughout the Cultural Revolution. It seems that the MAC assumed GPD functions. It may have absorbed its middle- and lower-level staff, its files, and its supporting personnel as well. If so, the MAC simply shortened the chain of command for even routine political control and direction of political activities by eliminating the GPD echelon. In the swirl of the fast-moving events of 1967, many of which required immediate military and political decisions at the highest levels, it may have been that the GPD simply got in the way and that it was expedient to bypass it, whether or not its personnel had committed specific errors.

THE GPD IN 1971

If the disappearance of the GPD is a mystery, its renascence is an enigma. Judging from the official press reports, by late 1971, it seems that the GPD had regained only part of the institutional profile it had before 1968. Besides its new director, only two deputy directors could be identified. From 1970 to September, 1971, only a handful of other personnel, whose positions had not yet been announced, were listed with the new director or his deputies during national holiday appearances of Peking's senior military officials. The GPD has issued only a few routine directives and its identifiable personnel have shown up mostly at fêtes for foreign visitors. Finally, the fact that the current GPD director, Li Teh-sheng had dual responsibilities —as secretary of the newly formed Anhwei Party Committee and GPD director—suggests that his Peking job may not have required his full attention. So far, these indicators, plus the fact that the regime has chosen to be very uninformative about the new GPD, raises questions as to whether the MAC intends to rebuild the GPD along its former lines.

THE GPD IN THE 1970s

Until more is known about the new GPD's scope of activities or until there is some hint of the MAC's intentions for it, projections of GPD influence on decisions and events during the coming decade must carry a relatively low level of confidence.

The attitude of the MAC will be the key to the GPD's future status. Personnel appointments to the GPD so far suggest that the MAC wants to bring in an entirely new team—younger men, some without much experience in the upper military echelons in Peking. Li Teh-sheng, as noted above, has both national and provincial responsibilities. He was promoted to his present job from the position of commander of the Anhwei Military District (about a one-star general's position) to head of a PLA general department (probably equivalent to a three-star general's post). In making this promotion, the MAC must have passed over many general officers, especially political officers, senior to Li. Of the two known deputy directors, one has been political commissar of the artillery troops for several years, and the other was a deputy commissar of the Shenyang Military Region. Nothing is known of the backgrounds of the other personnel associated with the new GPD.

One explanation for this choice of a younger, relatively inexperienced GPD leadership may be that the MAC intends to cut back radically on the reorganized GPD's area of activity. The MAC may intend to assign only routine indoctrination, political programs, liaison with friendly foreign armed forces, or other less-sensitive tasks. This would leave the MAC free to continue to exercise more critical functions, such as the evaluation of officers' performance and loyalty (perhaps at the colonel level and above), evaluation of unit combat readiness and training, monitoring of political reliability and effectiveness of senior personnel in the military research and development field, and other tasks that MAC officers might be reluctant to turn back over to the GPD.

If this is the case, as it seems to be, then one will have to look to the MAC not only for the formation of basic military policy during the 1970s, but also for the implementation of at least the more critical and sensitive aspects of political policy and control of the PLA. Circumstances may arise during the decade, however, that could change the MAC's attitude toward the GPD.

There are a number of variables that may influence the MAC's approach to its own role during the 1970s and thus, by extension, have a bearing on the GPD's scope of activities and on its impact on the PLA. One of these variables will be the level of any foreign military threat to the PRC. This includes both the primary threat posed by Soviet forces on China's frontier and the potential military threat posed by the nature and rate of Japanese rearmament. A prolonged, high Soviet threat level and a rapidly mounting Japanese naval and/or missile capability would tend to keep the MAC's attention focused on the more traditional military concerns of generating military capabilities to counter foreign threats. Such a development could create circumstances in which the GPD could play a larger role, e.g., that of assisting the MAC with the software side of the PLA while the MAC concentrated on improving the hardware. The senior field grade and lower-ranking general officers in the MAC, who may now be reluctant to relinquish the functions they acquired during the Cultural Revolution, might then be free to handle more glamorous, politically less hazardous tasks of improving PLA combat capabilities.

Another variable that will affect the GPD is the tone set by the Politburo under Mao and his successor(s) should Mao retire or die during the decade. If an intensely political or suspicious Stalinesque atmosphere develops, the MAC may simply have to do more career evaluation and counterintelligence than it can handle and may be forced to concentrate its attention on the upper levels of the PLA, leaving the middle and lower levels of the officer corps to the GPD staff.

An intriguing area of speculation centers on what role the GPD might play in consolidating the position of Mao's successor or successors. Transition of power in Communist regimes, as in most other autocratic governments, is an unstable process, and predicting the outcome is a risky business. Forseeing who and what will follow Mao is doubly difficult since probably less is known about Chinese politics than about that of any other great power. China-watchers generally agree that some sort of coalition between Mao's designated heir, Lin Piao, and Premier Chou En-lai (or between some other key military and government leaders) will rule after Mao. This estimate is based on the following assumptions: Chou's fabulous powers as administrator, politician, and statesman will continue to make him an indispensible man; Lin's uncertain health, his lack of a power base outside the military, and his minimal experience in politics will prevent him from establishing himself as dictator; and as Mao fades, Chou and Lin will work together because they share a predominently nationalistic, pragmatic outlook.

Under a Lin-Chou coalition, the GPD would probably be used to strengthen the PLA's capabilities to implement both military and civil policies. The GPD would also be used to strengthen the nation's loyalty to the coalition. The Lin-Chou coalition, however, may be short-lived or may never get off the gound. Lin could make a bid for supreme power, or Chou could attempt to substitute a less-formidable military figure for Lin Piao. In either of these cases, the role of the GPD could be important, depending on how vigorously it carried out MAC directives. The GPD would probably be less than enthusiastic about supporting anyone who threatened to downgrade the status of the PLA or undermine the political soldier's importance. Conversely, the GPD would probably gladly support a leader who promised to guarantee the political officer his accustomed status and maintain the PLA as a prominent (if not dominant) Chinese institution. Since the GPD is a creature of the MAC, it would take its basic direction from the MAC.

Aside from these questions of the personalities of future leaders lies an institutional problem that is almost certain to develop during the decade. Whoever follows Mao will have to develop an institutional counterweight to the PLA bureaucracy unless he wishes to become deeply beholden to it. Traditional Chinese governments maintained a check-and-balance system between two or more state bureaucracies. From 1950 until the Cultural Revolution, Mao more or less successfully counterpoised the regime's three main bodies—the Party, the government, and the PLA. The Cultural Revolution, however, left the PLA predominant. Between two thirds and three fourths of the key positions in China today are held by military officers. Whoever follows Mao probably will seek to diminish the present pervasive scope of military activity and influence.

When the post-Mao leadership decides to reestablish the bureaucratic balance, the GPD may find itself in a curious position. It may be competing with whichever institution is chosen to counterbalance the PLA's influence. This situation would be especially ironic if, for instance, Lin Piao opts for this course of action. In such a situation, the GPD could be caught up in a riptide of conflicting interests, since it would find itself trying to fight a rear-guard struggle to preserve the status of the PLA in disagreement with the very man who has guided the PLA to unprecedented power and influence. A by-product of such a conflict could be another purge of the PLA in which many of those who have headed the PLA for the past two decades would be eased out of authority. (These would be officers who joined the Communist forces before 1934 and are veterans of the Long March.) They would probably be replaced by younger men who made most of their important career associations after the Long March (i.e., after 1935).

After the passing of the Long March Veterans, PLA leaders may well be more professional in their outlook. They will have spent a larger portion of their careers with conventionally trained and equipped forces than the Long March Veterans. They also may be more willing to see the PLA take a secondary role in running the country than would the generation of officers now in command of the PLA. Also, since they have a longer career ahead of them, they may take a longer view of China's development prospects and be willing to accept smaller defense budgets in return for higher levels of investment in long-term economic development. They would probably favor retaining the GPD and the Party committee system of leadership, however, since Party soldiers will continue to play a vital role as spokesmen for the PLA in Party councils. The post-Long March generation is thoroughly familiar with the political-control system and would probably find it easier to work within the system than to oppose it.

Great issues of national and international military-political strategy may be debated during the decade. The GPD would certainly be active in these discussions. In 1965, such a debate took place over how to meet the threat posed by the increasing U.S. presence in Southeast Asia. Lin Piao closed that discussion with his famous article "Long Live the Victory of the People's War," which argued that the Vietnamese should carry the burden of the war and which spoke against Peking's making hasty military preparations to counter the escalating American threat. There probably would have been a similar debate in 1969 over how to prepare against the Soviet danger had not a major war seemed so imminent as virtually to preclude discussion of alternative strategies.

Debates of major significance during the decade undoubtedly will be exploited by ambitious officers to advance their careers, and it is impossible to foresee the players, much less the game. One of the great discussions, however, may turn on national economic strategy—how available GNP surpluses should be divided between military outlays and economic development. Although no accurate measure of the Chinese military burden exists, it is reasonable to assume that Peking is stepping onto the strategic-weapons cost escalator—the accumulating cost of deploying or improving costly weapons that have already been developed while at the same time having to continue research and development of new weapons. On one side may well be those who believe that the threat facing China is so great and immediate that all other needs must be placed second to military requirements. On the other side probably will be those who would prefer to divert resources from military programs to build the economy, perhaps arguing that a faster-growing economy would be able to bear heavier future defense outlays.

Another issue may be the balance between central and regional or provincial authority. The present trend toward greater decentralization of the economy and civil administration (education, health care, and so on) will probably reach its outer limit sometime during the decade, and Peking will have to set the bounds of permissible regionalism. If so, the GPD is likely to support strongly a reassertion of central authority (unless the status of the PLA were threatened).

There can be little doubt that the GPD will play a role in these discussions. What that role will be, however, will depend on many variables, including those mentioned above. If the post-Mao leadership wants to cut back on military influence and spending, it would use the GPD as an instrument for gaining acceptance of its views. Again, if the leadership after Mao is a military-civilian coalition, the GPD may act as a propagandizer and lobbyist for the PLA's special interests. If senior PLA leaders feel that the military threat to China is not receiving sufficient recognition, the GPD may instinctively drag its feet on programs that it would judge to have an adverse effect on the PLA as an institution.

CONCLUSIONS

The key to the GPD's role in the coming decade rests in the hands of the Politburo and the MAC. Looking forward, there seem to be two main courses for the GPD: a continuation of the GPD's current low profile or reassertion of the GPD's pre-Cultural Revolution authority and influence.

If the current, dimished stature continues through the decade, the GPD may be little more than an implementor of routine political programs and policies. Its role will be a rather minor one, influencing some developments within the PLA, but not projecting its will much beyond the military establishment.

On the other hand, if Mao or his successor(s) chose to rebuild the GPD, it will not only recover its pre-1967 functions and power within the military, but also will probably have an impact on the whole nation. Among developments that the GPD will affect may be a readjustment in the PLA's relationship to the Party and government, a reduction in the military's role in national life, and a possible reformulation of national economic and military strategies. If the GPD is rebuilt, it will have a definite, if difficult to estimate, impact on the 1970s.

NOTES

1. For a useful description of the development and function of the political control system, see John Gittings, The Role of the Chinese Army (New York: Oxford University Press, 1967), pp. 99-118; and C. Martin Wilbur and Julie Lien-ying How, Documents on Communism, Nationalism, and Soviet Adviser in China, 1918-27 (New York: Columbia University Press, 1956).

2. Mao Tse-tung, Selected Military Writings of Mao Tse-tung, (Peking: Foreign Languages Press, 1963), p. 21.

3. Conrad Brandt et al., A Documentary History of Chinese Communism (Cambridge, Mass.: Harvard University Press, 1959), p. 35.

4. From the "Political Resolution [of the Sixth National Congress of the CCP, September, 1928]," ibid., p. 154.

5. Ibid., pp. 162-63.

6. See Gittings The Role of the Chinese Army, pp. 261-302, for further details on PLA headquarters organization from 1949 to 1965.

7. The following discussion is based on the 1963 "Regulations Governing Political Work in the PLA," published in summary form in LAD, May 8, 1963, and in JMJP, May 10, 1963. A summary of the 1963 regulations was translated in SCMP (American Consulate General, Hong Kong), No. 2984, May, 1963. Another invaluable source of information on political control of the PLA is the Kung-tso Tung-hsun (Bulletin of Activities), of which the only available issues are from January 1 through August 26, 1961 (translated in Chester Cheng, ed., PLA Kung-tso Tung-hsun: The Politics of the Chinese Red Army (Stanford, Cal.: Hoover Institute on War, Revolution, and Peace, 1966). Highlights from the Kung-tso Tung-hsun are available in Ralph Powell, Politico-Military Relationships in Communist China (Washington, D.C.: Bureau of Intelligence and Research, Department of State, October, 1963), and in Powell "The Military Affairs Committee and Party Control of the Military in China," Asian Survey, III, 7 (July, 1963), 347-56.

8. "Talks by Vice Chairman Lin [et al.], at a Reception Given to Comrads . . . of the Military Commission," Wen-i Chan-pao [Literary and Art Combat News], No. 11, March 9, 1968, translated in SCMP, No. 4148, March 28, 1968.

9. "Regulations Governing the Work of the General Political Department of the Chinese People's Liberation Army" in "Regulations Governing Political Work in the PLA."

10

THE GENERAL
REAR SERVICES
DEPARTMENT

Richard E. Gillespie
John C. Sims, Jr.

In the armed forces of developing countries, logistics has consistently been the slowest component to develop. Yet, logistics tends to provide one of the greatest constraints upon the buildup of these forces beyond a certain development point. Modern China has proven no exception. Logistics represented a central weakness of the Nationalist military establishment, with its leadership never fully understanding its importance or according it sufficient attention. Communist military forces, on the other hand, appreciated more fully the role of resupply in military operations, and this comprehension proved an important factor in their victory over the Nationalists. The PLA leadership's awareness of logistics factors was demonstrated on the rear-services organization it constructed after 1950.

Each major era in the history of the PLA left its mark on the rear services. Participation as part of a politicized military force during the Chinese civil war, creation of a modernized logistics structure during and after the Korean War with Soviet assistance, and involvement in advanced-weapons development and in the Cultural Revolution in the 1960s generated significant changes in rear-services organization. These phenomena also affected its capabilities and helped create a distinctive perspective among the leadership of the GRSD—the component now charged with over-all supervision of the PLA logistics function—toward its roles and missions.

––––––––––––––

Views expressed in this chapter are solely those of the authors and should not be considered the official position of any agencies of the U.S. Government.

GENESIS OF THE REAR SERVICES

The origin of the PLA's rear services dates back at least to
the early 1930s. Each of the major guerrilla forces evolved early its
own rudimentary logistics system. The O-Yü-Wan (Honan-Hupeh
Anhwei) Soviet, for example, designated a portion of each hsiang as
public land (kung-t'ien) for army support, with the village-level Soviet
governments contributing the required labor and equipment to till it.[1]
The extensive reorganization of the Red Army undertaken after 1932
saw some division of labor with regard to logistics implemented at
major echelons, with selected staff elements assigned specific responsibility for that function. A department handling supply and services
was noted on the Revolutionary Military Council of the Central (Kiangsi)
Soviet, and most major subordinate commands seem to have included
logistics departments during the Kiangsi period.[2]   Most of the functions
that have come today to be included within the GRSD's purview—supply
(procurement, storage, and distribution), transportation, medical,
and maintenance—were being assumed by these staff agencies before
the Sino-Japan War (1937-45).

PERFORMANCE OF LOGISTICS FUNCTIONS
DURING SINO-JAPAN- AND CIVIL-
WAR PERIODS

The logistics organization of the Red Army, while still rudimentary, was developed further during the war with Japan. Starting with
a rear-services headquarters operating directly under that of the
Red Army, logistics staff sections by 1945 had appeared in all army
operational sectors, each of which corresponded with specific "liberated areas." Service bureaus materialized in each division staff,
with supply offices handling resupply and taxes serving as its principal
component. Most regimental headquarters contained supply platoons,
while economic committees appeared at the company level charged
with supervising company production, conservation, and supply.[3]
Cadre specialization in logistics remained strictly limited, however.

The economic crisis that materialized within the Red Army
base areas following the Communist 100-Regiments Offensive against
the Japanese in 1940 and the subsequent tight KMT and Japanese
blockades of Communist areas forced Red Army logistics to assume
certain unique forms. Procurement of supplies and equipment for
the next eight years was effected through three primary means:
capture of Japanese or Nationalist stocks, requisition or taxation in

kind, and Red Army production. The effectiveness of the logistics system was distinctly limited prior to 1945, principally because the Japanese did not surrender their food and material easily and the KMT blockade worked reasonably well. Thus, the Red Army remained poorly supplied and equipped prior to the Japanese surrender.

Under the Red Army doctrines of self-sufficiency that prevailed in the liberated areas after 1941, requisition and production in the Communist base areas rather than captured Japanese stocks constituted the primary supply source. The Maoist precept that the army's support should be derived chiefly from the people's taxes and the troops' production activities was implemented vigorously: Party and government organs set up in each liberated area took as a primary mission supply of the Red Army, with military-affairs bureaus being formed in all echelons down to the hsien level and below to handle this work.[4] Examples of peasant logistics support for the Red Army are legion: the peasantry of Shantung, for example, were mobilized to produce clothing materials, the use of civilians on piecework support projects was widespread and organization of the farmers into Peace Preservation Corps became a popular means of supplying the armed forces. Taxation in kind proved a reasonably effective way of requisitioning supplies, and the Red Army also purchased such items as radio spare parts and medicines covertly from the cities occupied by the Japanese.[5] Requisition and taxation in kind proved essential to Communist military operations.

Next to requisition and taxation, Red Army production came to constitute its major means of support. Self-sufficiency programs also called for Red Army units to operate cooperatives, factories, and mills; to reclaim wasteland; to raise livestock; and to manufacture such commodities as shoes, socks, gloves, and even weapons and ammunition. Military participation in production varied considerably by area. In some places units confined their activities to protecting the peasants who were engaged in production; in other liberated areas, military activity was much more extensive. Soldiers and militia were required to farm when not fighting. Troops in the sparsely settled Shensi-Kansu-Ninghsia area reportedly were required to supply 80 percent of all logistics materials other than food and clothing, while troops in Shantung undertook more than 50 percent of their own support in 1944. One brigade, at Nanyiwan (near Yenan), seems to have engaged solely in production activities during the winter, the normal training period for that unit. Light, portable radios were manufactured in some installations.[6]

Procurement of weapons and ammunition constituted a special problem for the Red Army. With regard to the commodities, the

Japanese and Chinese puppet armies provided the most fruitful sources.
By the war's end, however, the Red Army had constructed a series of
small arsenals in all base areas. Mobile arsenals were also reported
to have been formed and attached to each division within the New
Fourth Army.[7] While manufacturing techniques were rudimentary,
the output of these arsenals ranged from small-arms ammunition
to grenades, land mines, and light (pack) artillery. Although considerable progress was recorded in this area, the Communists still had no
capability for manufacturing heavy weapons in 1945.[8]

No uniform system of distribution of supplies and equipment
emerged during the Sino-Japan War. With the Red Army lacking an
adequate logistics organization, captured enemy material was usually
allocated among those units capturing it, with the excess left hap-
hazardly behind for the militia and other Communist paramilitary
organizations. Some small centralization over distribution was evident,
however, for there are reports of Ch'en Yi's New Fourth Army pro-
curing grain in excess of its needs from the rich Shanghi area for
shipment to Yenan.[9]

The Red Army organized simply to handle its transportation
and medical functions. Its transportation organization was skeletal
and the military relied primarily upon coolie labor for their requirements in this area. Peasant transport did suffice, however, because
the undeveloped road network rendered speed unimportant. Its medical
organization was slightly more elaborate, with medical-aid stations
down to the battalion level, fixed hospitals down to the division level;
and medical schools, factories, and nursing schools at the military-region level—all under the control of the 8th Route Army medical
department. The medical organization was highly decentralized,
however. Treatment was simple, much of it being accomplished in
civilian homes.

Since the Red Army's light equipment posed minimal requirements for servicing, no maintenance organization was developed.[10]
The absence of a maintenance capability was reported to have hampered the Red Army on only one specific occasion—the Communist
defeat of the Japanese in P'inghsingkuan (Shensi) in 1937. The substantial quantity of trucks captured in the battle had to be destroyed
because the Red Army could not maintain them.

Logistics constrained Red Army operations materially. Commanders apparently had to limit their fighting in many instances to
those places where Communist troops could obtain a decision with
minimum ammunition expenditure. Operations were normally limited

to short forays to battlefields close to their bases. On many occasions, the Communists surrounded but could not annihilate Japanese forces because they could not afford the ammunition expenditure.[11]

The civil-war period witnessed the buildup of a large conventional Communist army; with it emerged an expanded logistics establishment. The logistics problem assumed new dimensions following the capture of large stocks of Japanese and Nationalist equipment. Red Army firepower was improved with the 300,000 rifles, 4,836 machine guns, 1,226 artillery pieces, and 2,300 vehicles taken from the Japanese Kuantung Army stocks in late 1945. Armor was acquired from the Nationalists in the battle of Changchun (April, 1946), while the seizure of two arsenals in Mukden in 1948 led to the incorporation of anti-aircraft weapons.[12] The Red Army by 1949 was equipped with a variety of modern weapons.

The expansion of the Red Army after 1946 to incorporate some 75,000 troops from the former puppet Nanking government plus approximately 1.5 million demobilized Nationalist soldiers further compounded Communist logistics problems. Feeding, clothing, and equipping their troops absorbed an increasing share of the commanders' time, and they undertook a more active and independent role in resupply activities while they consolidated new areas. As field armies began conducting campaigns in areas encompassing two or more civil-government regions, leaders were forced to concentrate more on logistics matters because of the lack of a single centralized government to handle these affairs. More complex logistics organizations were therefore needed to assist the commander in the performance of this function: each field ultimately included a transportation regiment and ordnance units were formed after 1946.[13] The medical organization was improved late in the war. Since the supply organization still remained inadequate for the tasks required, commanders looked increasingly to their commissars, who concerned themselves with mobilizing the populace, for organization of the peasantry to augment the system. Thus, Red Army logistics activities came increasingly to be supervised by the political-commissar apparatus.

The Red Army during the civil war exploited most aggressively three sources of supply: captured enemy material, requisition and taxation in kind, and their own production. Communist operations were often planned with the goal of replenishing their stocks by the capture of enemy arms and proved highly successful. Communist official claims of captured equipment from 1946-50 include 3,161,912 small arms, 319,958 machine guns, 54,430 artillery pieces, 622 tanks, 389 armored cars, and 189 military aircraft plus extensive supplies.[14]

Approximately 60 percent of all U.S. material supplied the Nationalists reportedly gravitated into the hands of Communist forces. The Red Army has been aptly depicted as being the only army in modern times to equip itself predominantly with captured material.[15]

Requisition and taxation in kind reaped an increasingly rich harvest. The Red Army used United Nations Relief and Rehabilitation Agency (UNRRA) stocks and medical supplies procured locally; they also resorted to such homemade implements as hemostats, forceps, centrifuges, and traction sets for operations, acquiring modern medical treatment facilities only after the major cities were taken late in the war. Relying on such organizations as the Self-Preservation Corps, Lin Piao's Fourth Field Army conscripted some 300,000 peasants, 460,000 horses, and 120,000 horsecarts to support his forces in North China. Ch'en I's commissars mobilized approximately 1 million farmers for logistics support of his Second Field Army during the critical Huai-Hai Campaign. The Red Army grew more adept in this technique as the peasantry became increasingly committed to the Communist cause.

Red Army production increased, with those units not engaged in fighting furnishing a larger share of their own food and clothing. Capture of several Mukden arsenals enabled the Red Army to manufacture weapons and munitions sufficient to sustain six to ten divisions in combat. By 1948, there were some seventy small arsenals scattered throughout Communist-controlled regions producing about 50 percent of the Red Army's small-arms ammunition requirements.[16] Red Army production, despite these improvements, fell short of its needs and continued to limit Communist military effectiveness. Little progress was made in improving the distribution system for supplies. Consequently, unit equipment fluctuated constantly, depending on the material of the KMT units the Red Army was facing.[17] Development of uniform tables of equipment proved impossible.

Red Army transportation changed materially only during the final stages of the civil war. By 1949, the various field armies came to operate over broad areas far removed from their sources of supply, and this served as a catalyst for turning to new modes of water, rail, and motor transport. Reliance on porterage was reduced and highways and railroads were exploited to the maximum, with the PLA constructing and repairing these facilities as soon as they felt assured of controlling them permanently. By October, 1949, the Red Army controlled 21,742 miles of railroad, 17,314 miles of which they had rebuilt. More than 200,000 miles of highway was included under their control in November of that year, 26,264 miles of which they had repaired.[18]

The shift to rail and motor transport increased the Red Army logistics capability greatly. Its maintenance capability similarly expanded to service its new equipment.

These improvement were taken in the context of a decentralized logistics system. The five field armies that ultimately defeated the Nationalist forces were expected to be self-sufficient, and the supply structures their commanders built up operated relatively unfettered from higher headquarters. There existed very little centralized control in the logistics field.

The Red Army in 1949 was still a poorly equipped and supplied force despite its accumulation of Japanese and Nationalist equipment, and this colored its perspective toward logistics. Rations were meager throughout the war with Japan; soldiers operated continually under severe ammunition constraints in combat, and clothing and uniforms often were inadequate.[19] Despite progress in all these areas during the civil war, the experience of perpetual shortage made the Red Army cadre much more conscious of logistics than their KMT adversaries.

While there was little system in their logistics operations prior to 1950, Red Army leaders did display supply-consciousness throughout the Sino-Japan and civil wars. A cardinal principle of Red Army operations came to be that its strength should never exceed what the economy of the particular liberated area could support. When this occurred, excess personnel were required to be self-supporting. Anna Louise Strong recorded this viewpoint from a commander during her visit to a Red Army liberated area in 1946 as follows:

"We may have to defend the area for a long time and we have fixed on four hundred thousand as the number we can sustain without injuring the area's economic progress. . . . We could raise a larger army, but we could not feed it indefinitely. We have chosen a size that is large enough to defend our basic farming and eventually take back our cities."[20]

There existed a definite connection between the adherence of the Red Army cadre to sound logistics principles and the development of a fighting force superior to that of Chiang Kai-shek: Red Army commanders catered more to the needs of their soldiers than did their Nationalist counterparts. The fact that Communist soldiers were better fed and equipped did contribute to their superiority in battle.[21] A greater attention to logistics matters was noticable after 1950 as the PLA accorded high priority to modernizing their rear services.

EARLY REAR-SERVICES LEADERSHIP

Early leadership for the rear services derived in large measure from the regular pool of Communist commanders and commissars. In line with the general lack of staff specialization that marked the Red Army's early history, commanders attended to logistics matters in much the same fashion as other facets of their command duties. As successive Red Army reorganizations came to delineate duties between staff sections, however, a corps of specialists dealing with supply, transportation, and maintenance matters slowly emerged. It was primarily personnel within the political commissar apparatus, as mentioned earlier, who came to concern themselves with logistics during the Sino-Japan- and civil-war periods. Maoist military doctrine required active popular support for Communist operations, and it befell the commissars to mobilize the peasantry to furnish this support. A large proportion of top cadre in the GRSD today served earlier under the GPD.

Examination of the biographies of the first four directors of the GRSD, formed in the early 1950s, illustrates vividly the prevalence of commissar backgrounds. Yang Li-san (1949-54), the Red Army's principal logistics expert up through the civil war, doubled on occasion during that period as a political representative. During the Sino-Japan War, for example, he served as both commissar and head of the Yenan supply depot. Huang Ko-cheng (1954-56), a Hunanese graduate of the Whampoa Military Academy and early protege of P'eng Teh-huai, appears to have rotated command, commissar, and logistics assignments during early and mid-career. Assigned as head of the rear-services staff element in the 8th Route Army headquarters, he subsequently served in the political department of Ch'en I's New Fourth Army in the civil war. Hung Hsueh-chih (1956-59), another P'eng protege who also affiliated with Lin Piao and Huang Yung-sheng in the civil war, incorporated a commissar background. Ch'iu Hui-tso (1959-), who assumed the post of GRSD director after Hung's purge along with P'eng Teh-huai, was promoted through a series of increasingly important commissar positions after 1945—chief political representative in the 8th Column of Lin Piao's Northeast Field Army in 1947-48 and later commissar of the 45th Army. Chiu emerged from this service as a dual protege of Lin Piao and Huang Yung-sheng. Chang Tien-yun, a current deputy director, worked in a command position within Lin Piao's 115th Division prior to 1945 and later in Lin's Fourth Field Army.[22] The above officers seem also to have favored officers with similar backgrounds in their promotion systems.

This pattern of early assignments helped evolve two unique phenomena within the early GRSD leadership: a more-or-less uniform perspective toward the functions of the logistics structure, especially the degree
of centralization and politicization; and the development of affiliations
in consonance with the elite factionalism that marked the Red Army
leadership.

SOVIETIZATION AND MODERNIZATION OF THE REAR SERVICES, 1950-71

When the Chinese entered the Korean War in 1950, the substantial Soviet military advisery and material assistance wrought a profound metamorphosis in the PLA logistics structure and doctrine.
While the PLA's logistics doctrine continued to accent battlefield
salvage, capture of equipment, and human and animal porterage for
resupply, a greatly changed system was required to support Red Army
operations against the U.S. 8th Army. Yang Li-san, the director of
the PLA's logistics from 1949-54, directed these very necessary and
far-reaching changes with Soviet advisery and material support. By
1953, supply for the CPR volunteers in Korea had been greatly improved
and PLA logistics was modernized sufficiently to support a force of
1 million personnel.[23] For the first time, the PLA had a logistics
system adequate to support its forces outside of China's borders.[24]

The supply and logistics system accelerated its adoption to
current realities after the Korean truce. Much of this change was
direct fallout following the promulgation of the constitution in 1954,
wherein the PLA became a duly constituted body having a legal basis
for standardization and modernization. No longer was logistics handled
principally as an additional duty for political commissars. Instead,
a full-time logistics apparatus was created, patterned increasingly
on the rear-services establishment of the Soviet Red Army. The new
rear-services organization, one of three primary branches of the
Ministry of National Defense, called for a cadre of full-time logisticians, which was accomplished in large measure through incorporation
of former GPD personnel with previous logistical experience. Drastic
changes were undertaken during 1954-55, including the establishment
of the General Rear Services, General Ordnance, and Finance Departments, among others, under the Ministry of National Defense. Another
reorganization in 1958 amalgamated all logistics functions under the
GRSD. The rear-services structure by 1958 resembled the Soviet
system closely; this structure has continued to the present with only
minor changes.

Since 1958, the PLA logistics system appears to have included a regularized hierarchy of uniform logistics components at all echelons from the Ministry of National Defense down to and including the regiment. The PLA's topmost logistics staff, the GRSD, comprises a sizable number of subdepartments and bureaus, each concerned with specific aspects of supply, research, procurement, testing, and distribution.[25] For the ground forces, it is assumed here that the national-level rear-services organization has been duplicated on a smaller scale at the military-region and lower levels.

Names of the GRSD subdepartments have been difficult to obtain. At the Second National Conference of Representatives of Activists in the Rear Services of the PLA in May, 1959, there were 540 activists and representatives from the various subdepartments, including medical service, supply, transportation, ordnance, finance, and production.[26] It is assumed that these six subdepartments would carry out the functions that their name implies. In 1961, the Barracks Subdepartment was identified as being responsible for the care and issue of materiel in storehouses as well as maintaining depot stocks of heavy equipment.[27] In 1967, the Petroleum-Oils-Lubricants (POL) Subdepartment was identified;[28] 1970 saw the Equipment Subdepartment mentioned in official publications.[29] In 1971, the Subdepartment of Enterprises was identified, but its functions are not clear.[30] Other subdepartments and bureaus may also have been established to perform specialized functions. While the identity of the various subdepartments are given by date, it is probable that they were all established about the same time, but information only became available at a later date.

Delineation of responsibility by echelon appears to have been established by 1959. At the national level, the PLA GRSD is presumably charged with the responsibility for centralized logistics planning procurement, a complex mission in view of the turbulent history of the PLA during the 1960s. The GRSD's function of managing the procurement of defense items for the armed services has required it to coordinate closely with the State Council, which has over-all responsibility for national production planning. The GRSD mission was rendered doubly difficult by the PLA's modernization and its ever-widening role in response to the constantly changing requirements of the regime.

How much centralization wartime PLA logistics doctrine calls for is problematical. Since supply impetus is from the rear to the front, the senior wartime tactical echelon—the theater—would logically seem to serve as the principal logistics link between the combat unit and national sources of material. Division of logistics responsibility within the theater is unknown.

Wartime operation for air-force and naval organizations operating either directly under the central military authorities or under the theater command are also difficult to discern. Procurement, storage, allocation, and distribution would probably be subjected to greater centralization than for the ground forces in view of the divergent nature of their missions, operations, and command structure.

How closely logistics doctrine is being followed in peacetime, or would be adhered to in wartime, remains obscure.[31] There are indications that current operations are in actuality decentralized to a great degree in certain respects. Procurement of rations serves as a typical example. In consonance with their long-standing tradition, the PLA has continued to grow as much of its food as possible. Rations procurement apparently is also being handled at the lowest echelon possible, PLA units normally purchasing their food directly on the local civilian market.[32] Procedures appear to be analagous for the acquisition of organizational clothing. In consonance with the central military authorities' recent (1967-69) attempts to curtail the power of many military-region and military-district commanders over their subordinate units, some aspects of logistics were centralized, particularly transportation. Whether or not this centralization will be permanent must await further research. The question of how much guidance theater commanders could expect to receive from the Ministry of National Defense during a conflict—how much freedom they would be allowed—remains unanswered.

The bare outlines of the organization and functions of the GRSD and other logistics organizations of the PLA that have been pieced together leave several other crucial questions unanswered. First among them is the involvement of the GRSD in China's advanced-weapons programs. The PLA was reportedly drawn increasingly into this field after 1960.[33] Undoubtedly, this involved the GRSD in support of nuclear testing, missile research and development, and submarine and surface-ship development, as well as all other aspects of advanced-weapons development. Its participation, especially in nuclear weaponry, seems to have increased during the Cultural Revolution, as will be discussed later. The forms and dimensions of this participation remain obscure, however.

Another issue concerns the relationship of the GRSD with conventional weapons and armaments development under the numbered ministries of the machine-building industry.* In 1952, two ministries

---

*For a more detailed discussion of the conventional arms industry, see Chapter 11.—Ed.

of machine-building industry were created, the second ministry apparently specializing in military production. Between 1960-64, the number of machine-building industries was increased from two to eight, with the second through the seventh industries concerned with military equipment. Military men were designated in many cases as ministers, and the GRSD was undoubtedly deeply involved with the machine-building industries. By 1970, the GRSD was reportedly monitoring production in civilian-operated defense industries and physically running a number of factories manufacturing high-priority military hardware and software.

A final obscurity relates to the responsiveness of the GRSD to the demands of the services. The top-level GRSD leaders have continued to manifest a strong degree of localism in their perspective and in their promotion of junior officers. The mandate for modernization, however, has undoubtedly begun to erode that outlook gradually in favor of viewpoints more closely attuned to national needs. A younger generation of "technocrats" seems to have emerged within the middle and lower echelons of the logistics system by the 1960s. These officers, many of whom received training in the Rear Services College in Peking, have increasingly emphasized efficiency in production and distribution above all else. Yet, to date there has emerged no discernible core of career logistics officers, a fact that has made performance of logistics functions by the apparatus difficult. The increased assertiveness of the younger professionally and technically inclined cadre bred a disunity within the rear services that was felt in the military politics of the PLA.[34]

MILITARY POLITICS OF THE GRSD,
1950-71

The PLA leaders handling logistics were drawn into the military politics of the Red Army prior to 1949, through their affiliation with senior Red Army commanders.[35] After 1950, Red Army politics embraced the following four phenomena:

1. The issue of professionalism versus politicization of the PLA

2. The question as to what extent the PLA should be modeled after the Soviet military and how closely Peking should ally with Moscow in pursuit of its goals

3. The issue of allocation of resources between military
   and civilian needs

4. Continued cadre factionalism within the PLA.

Policies and programs of the GRSD changed and individual rear-services
leaders rose and fell with the military politics that attended the Korean
War, the Great Leap Forward, and the Cultural Revolution.

As mentioned previously, the Korean War and its aftermath
witnessed a sweeping reorganization within the rear services, as the
substantial Soviet military aid to the PLA together with the presence
of large numbers of Soviet advisers helped evolve a Soviet-style
logistics system within the PLA. The impetus for this program derived
from the influential and logistics-conscious Marshal P'eng Teh-huai.
This Russian-modeled logistics system was aggressively instituted
by all three of the initial directors of the GRSD—Yang Li-san, Huang
Ko-cheng, and Hung Hsueh-chih, the latter two directors being P'eng
proteges. The acceleration of Soviet-style regularization and modernization reached its zenith in the period just preceding the Great Leap
Forward, when Huang promoted P'eng's programs as chief of staff of
the PLA while Hung served as Director of the GRSD.[36] Accompanying
this regularization came a greater PLA concentration on military as
compared to political work and allocation of substantial funds to
modernize the military.

Some of these programs generated strong opposition from Mao
and the more politically oriented officers during the Great Leap
Forward, however. Mao's deeply rooted commitment to the policy
of the "mass-line"—involving the populace as enthusiastic and active
participants in party programs—demanded a politicized rather than a
narrowly professional military establishment. Logistics units, like
other PLA components, were soon drawn into Great Leap Forward
political programs. In furtherance of Maoist economy programs reminiscent of the Yenan period, rear-services units engaged more extensively in such nonmilitary activities as reclaiming wasteland, growing
foodstuffs, and raising livestock. Reports recount that the GRSD
contributed several thousand vehicles and motor cars to support steel
production and other construction, while its medical teams treated
nearly 3 million civilians during 1958.[37] Mao's anti-Soviet orientation
after 1958 also required a dismantling of the Russian alliance and
eradication of Soviet features within the PLA structure. Disputes
between the professionally and politically oriented officers toward

regularization, military doctrine, the size of the armed forces, the
feasibility of borrowing from Soviet experience and practice, the use
of the PLA as a labor force, and the desirability of professionalism
arose repeatedly after the Korean War.[38]

Promotion of new Maoist doctrines for the armed forces, a
phenomenom that accompanied the Great Leap Forward, provoked a
vigorous challenge to Mao and his programs at the Lushan CC Plenary
Session (North Kiangsi) in mid-1959 by P'eng Teh-huai. P'eng on this
occasion evidently rebuked Mao for his insistence on PLA participation
in labor projects and other political activities and also for the loosening
of the Sino-Soviet alliance at a time when Russian assistance was
badly needed for military modernization. Mao nonetheless withstood
this challenge successfully and P'eng, Huang Ko-cheng, and their
adherents were purged. P'eng's purge involved a number of the top
leadership of the GRSD.

Hung Hsueh-chih, as director, was the senior officer dismissed,
his removal being effected one month after P'eng in October, 1959.
The nature of Hung's heresy was subsequently revealed in the 1960-61
issues of the Bulletin of Activities (Kung-tso Tung-hsun), published
in 1963. Linked with P'eng and Huang, he was specifically criticized
for his "simple military viewpoint" and "militarist" practices. As a
key member in P'eng's military contingent of Mao's mission to Moscow in November-December, 1957, Hung had also played a crucial
role in the negotiations with the Russians over military assistance.[39]
Hung thus bore a large share of the censure for the "dogmatism"—
indiscriminate borrowing from Soviet experience—that Maoists
heaped upon P'eng's associate's at the time of purge.[40] The Bulletin
Activities specifically rebuked Hung for his disruption of the Maoist
"anti-dogmatism movement" of 1958 and also his "liquidationaism"—
blindly instituting big reductions and cancellations that resulted in
inefficiencies (in rules and systems) and a "confusion of ideology and
knowledge" in the logistics system.[41] The accusations attending
Hung's purge reveal the presence of a core of logistics officers
supporting P'eng's viewpoint, which was committed to emulation
of Soviet supply models, a closer relationship with Moscow, and a
desire to concentrate PLA efforts more narrowly on military activities. This movement was temporarily delayed.[42]

Marshal Lin Piao's elevation to the posts of de facto head of
the MAC and also to Minister of National Defense, ushered in sweeping
changes in military programs that were felt strongly within the rear
services. As part of his successful attempt to raise the political-
ideological standards of the PLA, Lin chose the GPD as his primary

vehicle, a decision that led to an extensive reorganization of that department and to an increase in the power and status of its commissars.*

It was probably Ch'iu Hui-tso's commissar background that prompted Lin Piao to select this relatively obscure protege for the post of GRSD director in 1959. A commissar undoubtedly seemed best qualified to fashion the GRSD into a reliable political instrument. The record of Ch'iu's performance over the past decade defies his clear-cut categorization as a Maoist or a member of Mao's opposition. Throughout the pre-Cultural Revolution period, Ch'iu appears to have promoted Mao's mass-line programs vigorously within the GRSD. To effect this, new blood was injected into the GRSD top leadership, principally through promotion of a number of politically oriented cadre who had developed no close affiliation with P'eng Teh-huai or Hung Hsueh-chih. Chang Ling-pin, a deputy director prior to 1959 who was retained by Ch'iu, provides a typical example. As a deputy director, Chang had become actively involved in GRSD political work and could well have disputed Hung over this issue.[43] It was still through an older generation and an orthodox leadership, however, that Ch'iu sought to transform the orientation and character of the logistics apparatus after 1959, and many of his top lieutenants were professionals.

The years 1960-65 witnessed the implementation of new political programs within the rear services in accordance with Lin Piao's dictum "Let Politics Take Command," while the PLA was simultaneously discarding some of the Soviet features in its logistics system. Under the scrutiny of rear-service commissars, political training was not only accorded greater priority, but units were also required to undertake more extensively Mao's Yenan-style economic programs to raise more of their own food and otherwise curtail their expenses.[44] How much the logistics apparatus could be cleansed of its Russian bureaucratic characteristics in light of the PLA's continuing modernization is debatable, so the changes made there would seem to have been more in style and perspective than in organization and technique. The rear-services cadre, which now included within its middle and lower ranks more and more management- and technically oriented officers, witnessed these new programs with a mixed perspective. The younger "technocrats" approached political work differently from the senior cadre, treating it as an unwarranted diversion from their "professional" mission.

---

*See Chapter 9 for a more detailed discussion of the GPD.—Ed.

Criticism of Maoist programs remained muted as long as these programs involved only indoctrination and did not involve cadres in political promotional ventures outside of the military. The nature of Lin Piao's politicization of the PLA—raising political standards but not neglecting the view of military professionals—was such that full compliance with political demands was not demanded and a delicate balance was maintained between political and professional requirements (at least until 1965).[45] Thus, Lin's programs included many features that some professionals could support: the military leadership's emphasis on regular forces over militia; PLA participation in nuclear-weapons development; the continued high rate of investment in missiles, aircraft, and other conventional weaponry; the military's enhanced role in the management of national defense industries; and the renewed status accorded to "experts."[46] These developments enabled Ch'iu Hui-tso to maintain unity within the GRSD officer ranks.

Mao's attempts to employ the PLA to reform the Party, begun in his February, 1964 "learn from the PLA" campaign, generated disharmony within the GRSD, as in other PLA components. Although manning the new political departments was accomplished primarily with commissars, widespread support was manifested within the rear services for PLA Chief of Staff Lo Jui-ch'ing's attempt in 1965 to redress the extreme politicization of the PLA when the danger of China's involvement in a war with the United States over Vietnam loomed great. While Lo's dismissal from his post and the purge of those leaders sharing his views restored a semblance of unity within the military leadership at the top, diversion of effort toward political work constituted a continuing source of great resentment among lower-rank officers.

The Cultural Revolution created greater turbulence within the GRSD ranks.[47] Mao, increasingly dissatisfied with the political system's implementation of his revolutionary policies, searched after 1960 for organized support to effect a "revolution from below" against the CCP, which he held primarily responsible for obstructing his pro-grams. By 1966, he was apparently convinced that he had found this support within the PLA, whom he viewed as "the most faithful curator of his revolutionary virtues."[48] Mao launched the Cultural Revolution early that same year, employing an extra-party mass organization (the Red Guards) at first to compel the Party to rectify itself and later to purge it. Mao's assessment of the military proved accurate initially, for it was the united stand of the top military leadership that proved one of Mao's main sources of strength during the early stages of the Cultural Revolution.

The exact motivations for the PLA high command's strong initial support for Mao are not known, but this support probably derived from a desire to keep the military out of the Cultural Revolution and to keep the Cultural Revolution, at least its most militant features, out of the PLA. As long as the military remained free of interference in its internal affairs by Mao's CRG, its support was assured. As the revolution waxed more violent in early 1967, with the militant Red Guards undertaking "power seizures" against those refusing to accept the new revolutionary order, the PLA was ordered to take an active part in promoting the Cultural Revolution. Once the PLA was directed to intervene in the political struggle in early 1967, a serious rift materialized between the PLA high command and the Maoist leadership.[49]

This hiatus between the military command and the radical wing in the central leadership continued while the PLA worked from February, 1967, to September, 1968, to create provisional organs to rule China's major administrative areas—the RCs, composed of youthful Maoists, veteran Party cadre, and the PLA. Responding to conflicting directives emanating from a shifting leadership coalition increasingly polarized between radical and moderate wings, the military proved unable to implement the Maoist revolutionary programs. PLA intervention usually was undertaken to reestablish order; military influence in forming the new alliances tended to favor moderate elements promoting order over revolution. The history of the RCs indicates that they came early under military domination, while the PLA's pivotal role in administration, agriculture, industry, public security, the operation of essential services, and control of mass media showed that its nonmilitary functions grew more extensive than they had been at any time since 1949.[50]

Attempts of the radical wing of the Maoist leadership to impose control over the military and intensify the Cultural Revolution within it led to extension of the revolutionary purge to the PLA. The purge within the PLA generally paralleled that of the Party and government, generating periodic spurts of intensity, and continued until the specter of conflict with the USSR in 1968 led the party center to order the PLA to terminate the Cultural Revolution and disband all rebellious factions.

Conduct of the purge within the PLA was assigned to the GPD under the direction of the MAC. A careful weeding out of unreliable cadre had begun as early as 1964, as commissars teamed up with young Maoists to erode the power of old-time Party and military leaders. Confused and on the defensive until mid-1967, senior military

leaders finally rallied and compelled Mao and his militant associates
to dismantle the GPD.* Before the moderate leadership could be
effectively reasserted within the PLA, however, the purge there had
assumed substantial dimensions.

The rear services were inevitably drawn into the Cultural Revolution, with its leadership carrying out Maoist programs and also suffer-
ing its share of casualties. There is some evidence to show that the
central leadership attempted to exempt certain rear-services activities
from the Cultural Revolution. A joint directive of the CCP CC and the
State Council on February 4, 1967, for example, prohibited Red Guards
from interfering with factories, research and design institutes, and
basic construction units under the supervision of the second to the
seventh ministries of the machine-building industry, labeling these
as vital national-defense industries.[51] While the leadership attempted
to adhere to this directive, the Cultural Revolution reached most
rear-services components sooner or later. GRSD director Ch'iu
Hui-tso entered the Cultural Revolution in a strong position, his
earlier implementation of structural changes and Maoist political
indoctrination within the rear services having placed him in good
stead with Lin Piao. The GRSD cadre, particularly its commissars,
apparently promoted revolutionary programs vigorously after 1966.
Red Guard organizations were soon organized in the schools, units,
and facilities associated with the rear services. GRSD activists also
seem to have played varying roles in the formation of the RCs. On
at least one occasion, their judicious blanding of threats and persuasion
in order to bring about the necessary coalition was officially commended.[52]

While evidence as to the exact nature of the rear-services
participation in the Cultural Revolution is meager and often contradic-
tory, this evidence does show that it was extensive and varied. During
the most violent phases of the Cultural Revolution in 1967-68, when
Red Guard activities came to pose a grave threat to the regime's
stability, logistics units joined other PLA components in assisting
the militia and public-security forces to secure defense-related
facilities. The question of arming the Red Guards drew the GRSD
early into controversy with the PLA's assuming direct control over
China's arms industry in the spring of 1967.

---

*The reader should note that other authors in this book disagree
with this interpretation. The editor is in complete agreement with
Gillespie and Sims on this point.—Ed.

As rival factions contested power in the provinces with weapons often looted from logistics depots, it is logical to assume that the GRSD became deeply involved in controlling these weapons and protecting arms depots.[53] When revolutionary violence later threatened the advanced-weapons program and Chinese support for the North Vietnamese war effort, the GRSD apparently was charged with the mission of securing key lines of communication. The military took control of the Yangtze River Transport Bureau in June, 1967, and the railroads later in the year. Transporting better than 50 million Red Guards around the country from 1966-68 together with keeping the system operational against the disruptions caused by rival groups of railroad workers proved a monumental feat.[54] The political power of the PLA within the various ministries, through the MAC, grew substantial and involved the military in ministry politics. The GRSD presumably labored for a long period to end the serious disruptions that plagued several departments of the ministries of machine building, especially the sixth and seventh ministries, and caused a general slow-down in defense-related production in the second half of 1968.[55]

That the disruption did not extend further within the machine-building ministries probably was attributable to the negotiating acumen of GRSD leaders. By the end of the Cultural Revolution, GRSD leaders apparently were deeply engrossed in ensuring continuity in the advanced-weapons programs, defense production, and aid for Vietnam. At lower levels, rear-services cadre assisted in building the RCs (and later the new provincial Party organs) while logistics units were being used to guard defense industries, communications facilities, civil air installations, warehouses, and transportation facilities. In view of the turbulence that attended formation of the RCs the GRSD undertook these assignments with the greatest reluctance. Performance of these duties brought logistics activists and cadre into the crossfire between power-holders and power-seekers, both claiming Maoist credentials, and this exposure only served to intensify the purge within the GRSD.

The dimensions of the purge within the GRSD remains obscure, but it was undoubtedly substantial. Despite the support the GRSD presumably rendered Red Guard groups initially, it soon drew Maoist censure. Although rear-services commissars supported revolutionary programs, director Ch'iu Hui-tso seems to have lined up with moderate PLA leaders trying to limit military involvement in the Cultural Revolution. Because of this stance, Ch'iu underwent severe censure for his conservatism during the early stages. In early November, 1966, the Revolutionary Rebel Corps at the Second Military Medical University accused him of suppressing the Cultural Revolution in the military medical schools. Red Guard groups organized within the GRSD soon

after the revolutionary "power seizures" were launched intensified
their attacks on Ch'iu in January and February, 1967, linking him with
the disgraced Marshal Ho Lung, who apparently also resisted PLA
political intervention. These attacks continued during the spring,
possibly connected in some way with the assault on Chou En-lai by the
Maoist May 16 Corps, and Ch'iu was reportedly subjected on at least
one occasion to public denunciation. As late as November of that same
year, the Revolutionary Rebel Corps of the Second Military Medical
University was still rebuking the GRSD director for his alleged suppression of Maoist programs within the logistics system. It reportedly
took Lin Piao's personal intervention in the summer to save him.
The principal theme in Lin Piao's directive of August 9 to senior
military cadre, in which he praised as well as criticized the GRSD
(among others) for its political work, was a caution against rash action;
this undoubtedly strengthened Ch'iu's position.[56]

   Ch'iu Hui-tso's subsequent activities reveal him as one of the
more order-oriented members of the military high command, a
stance that was to serve him well during the latter stages of the
Cultural Revolution, which saw the ascendancy of moderate commanders
in the PLA at the expense of the radicals. The reshuffling of the
CRG in the fall of 1967 saw his appointment as deputy chief; when a new
organization was created to replace it, he was again designated to a
key position. Not being closely affiliated with PLA Chief of Staff
Yang Cheng-wu, Ch'iu survived the latter's purge in the spring of
1968, in spite of his probable approval of many of Yang's programs.[57]
Yang's dismissal, in fact, worked to Ch'iu's advantage. With Huang
Yung-sheng's elevation to the chief-of-staff post, Ch'iu, as a dual
Lin-Huang protege, was promoted to deputy chief of staff while retaining
the GRSD directorship. The presence of Mao, Lin, Ch'iu, and other
senior military figures at the concluding meeting of the second congress
of GRSD activities (a thirty-day study session) probably concerned
policies for ending the violence that afflicted the nation's railroads at
that time.[58] In any event, Ch'iu undoubtedly received a large share
of the credit for keeping the transportation system operational. His
handiwork was also discernible in the directives emanating from
Peking in July, 1968, calling for factions to surrender their weapons
to the PLA and in the GRSD implementation of this decision.[59] All
of these actions facilitated his career.

   Ch'iu's election in April, 1969, to the Presidium of the Ninth
National Party Congress and also to the CC and its Politburo later
in the month indicate clearly that his performance during the Cultural
Revolution had merited incorporation within the top Party and military
leadership. That he has remained in favor with the central leadership

is shown by his frequent public appearances over the past two years and his selection to handle highly sensitive assignments. Ch'iu, for example, accompanied Chou En-lai and Yeh Chien-ying in an important visit to Hanoi during the South Vietnamese incursion into Laos in March, 1971 to demonstrate Peking's support for the North Vietnamese. Chiu in his multiple roles as GRSD chief, CRG member, deputy PLA chief of staff, and Politburo member exhibited considerable political acumen as well as professional competence, reconciling the demands of the purge and other Maoist programs with those requirements for order, military development, and support for the Vietnam conflict.[60]

Ch'iu nevertheless lent some measure of support to the continuing purge within the GRSD, which brought down at least three of his top lieutenants. Li Chu-k'uei, GRSD senior commissar since at least 1962, was demoted in October, 1967, possibly a casualty of Ch'iu's efforts to reinvigorate the department's prosecution of Maoist programs. Deputy directors Jao Cheng-hsi and T'ang Tien-chi both seem to have been removed by the fall of 1969, Jao reportedly disappearing along with PLA Chief of Staff Yang Cheng-wu. Rear-services officers affiliated with other key central and regional military figures who were purged presumably suffered demotion or rectification along with their mentors. As elsewhere in the PLA, commissars ultimately suffered the brunt of the military purge.

Ch'iu, more firmly ensconced than ever as GRSD director at the end of the Cultural Revolution, appears to have pruned his associates rigorously, retaining those who had proven the most loyal while also injecting new blood into the leadership. A New China News Analysis listing of top GRSD leaders on July 1, 1971, reveals four deputy directors of long standing—Chang Ch'ih-ming, Chang Hsien-yueh, Chang Ling-pin, and Chang Tien-yun—all surviving the revolution. Chang Ch'ih-ming has been promoted to Li Chu-k'uei's position as commissar, while the other three all retained their deputy directorships. The seven current deputy directors include as new members Ch'en Pang, Feng Yung-shun, Wang Hsi-kuo, and Yen Chun, all presumably Ch'iu proteges.[61] Two new second echelon figures—Tai Chih-chuan, deputy political commissar, and Yuan Hua-ping, chief of the equipment subdepartment—have appeared with unusual frequency in public ceremonies during 1970-71, signifying possible influence rivaling that of some of the deputy directors.[62] A goodly amount of continuity seems to have been maintained with the rear-services ranks.

THE OUTLOOK FOR THE 1970s

The Red Army's unique history has left its imprint upon the rear-services organization. Three dominant stains have been present in its development. The first strain was the politicization evident in its pre-1949 history. It was this Red Army politicization that proved a decisive factor in bringing the Communist regime to power. The Red Army commanders paid closer attention to logistical factors than did their Nationalist counterparts, explainable probably because of their lack of access to military resources up until at least 1946. The fact that logistics staffs remained small and rudimentary, with most logistics functions being handled by commissars as an additional duty, helped evolve a peculiar perspective toward logistics on the part of the Red Army elite. The emphasis on Red Army production, the stress on battlefield recovery and capture of enemy equipment, and the concentration on civilian procurement and civilian logistical support all combined to evolve a unique operational code for PLA logistics.

The Sovietization of the rear-services system beginning with the Korean War provided another crucial component in rear-services development. Important organizational changes were introduced into the PLA logistics system during the 1950s that have survived attempts by Maoists during the 1960s to discard them. The modernization of the PLA, while proceeding spasmodically, has represented an inexorable process, and modernization has meant retention of many Soviet features. Increased Soviet influence has meant a stronger professional and bureaucratic orientation.

The over-all effect of the involvement of the GRSD in the Cultural Revolution is as yet unknown. Efforts to exempt certain rear-services activities seem to have been only partially successful. Disruptions within machine-Building industries were felt in a number of sensitive fields. The noticeable slowdown in nuclear testing in 1968 may well have reflected the downgrading of Russian-trained engineers and technicians and their forced participation in lengthy manual labor and political indoctrination programs. While it is generally agreed that the defense-related industry suffered less damage than other basic industries, one expert's estimate that defense industry, particularly its nuclear programs, suffered a setback of from one to two years could well be accurate.[63] That this and other setbacks were no greater was undoubtedly due in large measure to the work of the GRSD.

Only tentative conclusions can be drawn as to any changes in perspective that the Cultural Revolution may have generated within the GRSD cadre ranks. What impact participation in political indoctrination or forced manual labor may have had on logistics leaders is not known. Most of the cadre, especially the technocrats and managers, outlasted the purge, probably due to the essential work in which they were involved. While many older cadre survived primarily through affiliation with regional military and political leaders and thus retained locally oriented views, the perspective of the logistics cadre as a whole has without doubt become increasingly professional and more in line with the central elite's perception of priorities, as these logisticians worked on advanced-weapons development and the perfection of more complex conventional weaponry. The Cultural Revolution exercised the PLA logistics system more extensively than in the past, and one can reasonably assume that greater centralization and control over such functions as transportation, storage, and distribution generated by this experience also affected the leadership's outlook. With moderate leadership now in charge at both central and regional levels, any ideological disagreements remaining between professionally and politically oriented officers and between regionally and centrally motivated cadre may be muted in the 1970s. Ch'iu Hui-tso seems to have reestablished a united logistics, albeit less revolutionary, leadership. One should expect the perspective of the rear-services elite to wax increasingly technocratic and national as the PLA logistics system becomes more sophisticated.

Professionally speaking, the PLA rear services retains many deficiencies. By U.S. standards, the system is still rudimentary and constrains Chinese Communist military capabilities. The PLA lacks modern as well as standardized equipment. It has developed a "system" to its logistics, however, and has gradually moved away from what Robert Riggs two decades ago termed its "parasite philosophy" of too much reliance on captured equipment.[64] How well it could sustain the PLA in case of invasion or in an operation outside of China's borders is a moot point. With the disruption of the Cultural Revolution being overcome and with renewed interest by the Peking leadership in upgrading their military readiness and equipment, one could logially forecast substantial improvements in the performance of all logistical functions over the next decade. Nonetheless, two dominant strains in the history of the rear services—the politicization of the organization before 1950 and after 1964 and the Sovietization of the system during the 1960s—represent contrasting tendencies. How these tendencies will be balanced during the GRSD's future development represents a subject that deserves close attention.

NOTES

1. Ilpyong J. Kim, "Mass Mobilization Policies and Techniques," in Doak Barnett, ed., Chinese Communist Politics in Action (Seattle: University of Washington Press, 1969), p. 86.

2. "Personalities: Chiu Hui-tso," Issues and Studies, February, 1961, p. 71; and Donald W. Klein and Anne B. Clark, Biographic Dictionary of Chinese Communism (Cambridge, Mass.: Harvard University Press, 1971), p. 981.

3. Lyman P. Van Slyke, ed., The Chinese Communist Movement, A report of the United States War Department, July 1945 (Stanford, Cal.: Stanford University Press, 1968), pp 132-33, Chart 1, and p. 188, Chart 3.

4. Evans Fordice Carlson, The Chinese Communist Army: Its Organization and Efficiency (New York: Institute of Pacific Relations, 1940), p. 39.

5. Ibid, p. 37; Mao Tse-tung, On Guerrilla Warfare, Trans. by Brigadier General Samuel B. Griffith (New York: Frederick A. Praeger, 1961)), p. 80; and Robert B. Riggs, Red China's Fighting Hordes (Harrisburg, Pa.: The Military Services Publishing Co, 1951 and 1952), p. 289.

6. 18th Army Group, Political Department, K'ang-chou pa-nien lai ti pa-lu-chün yu [The 8th Route and New Fourth Armies in the Eight Years War of Resistance], March, 1945, p. 163. U.S. military intelligence (Van Slyke, Chinese Communist Movement, p. 145) estimated that army, government, and Party members were actually producing 64 percent of their food and clothing in Shensi-Kansu-Ninghsia in 1945.

7. Van Slyke, Chinese Communist Movement, p. 151.

8. Riggs, Fighting Hordes, p. 297; and Van Slyke, Chinese Communist Movement, p. 199.

9. Riggs, Fighting Hordes, pp 290-92; and Van Slyke, Chinese Communist Movement, pp. 45, 152-53, 173-75, and 199-205.

10. Research and Analysis Report No. 892, National Archives Building, Records of the Office of Strategic Services, Records Group 59; and Van Slyke, Chinese Communist Movement, p. 193.

11. Frederick F. Liu, A Military History of Modern China, 1924-1949 (Princeton, N.J.: Princeton University Press, 1956), p. 228; and Riggs, Fighting Hordes, pp. 103, 277.

12. China Handbook (Taipei: China Publishing Co., 1951), pp. 374-75.

13. Riggs, Fighting Hordes, pp. 10, 76, and 84. Page 84 discusses briefly Second Field Army Commander Ho lung's use of his rear ser- vices.

14. Hu Chiao-mu, Thirty Years of the Communist Party of China, An Outline History (London: Lawrence & Wisehart, 1951), p. 30; and Riggs, Fighting Hordes, p. 255.

15. U.S., Department of State, "A Summary of American Chinese Relations," letter from Secretary of State Dean Acheson to the Presi- dent of the United States transmitting the record of U.S. Relations with China (Washington, 1949), p. 35; and Graham Peck, Two Kinds of Time (Boston: Houghton-Mifflin, 1950), p. 682.

16. Riggs, Fighting Hordes, pp. 285-86, 297-98.

17. Jack Beldon, China Shakes-the World (New York: Harpers, 1949), p. 335. Anna Louise Strong, in her book The Chinese Conquer China (New York: Doubleday and Co, 1949), pp. 209-10, states that the Red Army sought out the better-U.S.-equipped forces for conflict for this purpose.

18. China Handbook, pp. 379-80; Shanghai, Ta Kung-pao (news- paper), October 23, 1949; and Hong Kong Ta Kung-pao (newspaper), Sept 26, 1959.

19. Riggs, Fighting Hordes, p. 14. The military ration in the Shansi-Hopeh-Chahar border region during the Sino-Japanese War was 22 ounces of vegetables daily and 2.5 ounces of meat monthly. In Shantung, soldiers frequently went without shoes in the winter and were forced to wear thick, padded uniforms in the summer. See Van Slyke, Chinese Communist Movement, p. 148, Table 2, for further data.

20. Anna Louise Strong, The Chinese Conquer China (New York: Doubleday and Co., 1949), p. 197.

21. Riggs, Fighting Hordes, p. 284.

22. "Chiu Hui-tso," p. 72; Klein and Clark, Biographic Dictionary, pp. 397, 981.

23. Ray E. Appleman, South to the Naktong, North to the Yala (Washington, D.C.: Office of the Chief of Military History, 1961), p. 719; and Riggs, Fighting Hordes, pp. 298-300.

24. Riggs, Fighting Hordes, pp. 299, 301-3.

25. Samuel B. Griffith II, The Chinese People's Liberation Army (New York: McGraw-Hill, 1967), foldout entitled "National Defense Organization, People's Republic of China."

26. JMJP, May 13, 1959.

27. Chester J. Cheng, PLA Kung-tso Tung-hsun: The Politics of the Chinese Red Army (Stanford, Cal.: Hoover Institute on War, Revolution, and Peace, 1966), p. 747.

28. NCNA, October 13, 1967.

29. Ibid., November 16, 1970.

30. JMJP, June 15, 1971.

31. Rear-services rules, regulations, and teaching materials are contained in the PLA's Rear Services Operational Manual. A copy of this document, however, is not available for study. See Cheng, Kung-tso Tung-hsun, p. 198.

32. Ibid., pp. 46, 195-99.

33. Ralph C. Powell, "The Increasing Power of Lin Piao and the Party Soldiers, 1959-66," China Quarterly, XXXIV, 48 (April-June, 1968), p. 43; and Cheng, Kung-tso Tung-hsun, p. 194. The Military Service Academy was instructed by the MAC in January, 1961, to undertake research on selected military topics. This represented one of the first indications of PLA involvement in this field.

34. Cheng, Kung-tso Tung-hsun, pp. 751-52.

35. See William Whitson, "The Field Army in Chinese Communist Military Politics," China Quarterly, January-March, 1969, pp. 1-30, for the most scholarly discussion to date of PLA factionalism.

36. Klein and Clark, Biographic Dictionary, p. 409; and Riggs, Fighting Hordes, p. 41.

37. JMJP, May 13, 1959.

38. Powell, "Increasing Power," p. 43.

39. Klein and Clark, Biographic Dictionary, p. 408.

40. Ellis Joffe, Professionalism and Political Control in the Chinese Officer Corps, 1949-1964. (Cambridge, Mass.: East Asian Research Center, Harvard University, 1965), p. 138.

41. Kung-tso Tung-hsun [Bulletin of Activities], Publication No. 2, December 16, 1950, pp. 17-18. [Hereafter cited as Bulletin of Activities.]

42. For a fuller account of P'eng's purge and also that of his chief associates, see: "Make our Army a Great School of Mao Tse-tung's Thought," LAD, editorial, August 1, 1960, and in PR, No. 32 August 5, 1966, p. 9; NCNA, "CCP Resolution Condemns P'eng Te-huai Clique" [in English], August 15, 1967; HC, editorial, November 13, 1967, and in SCMP, No. 590 August 28, 1967, pp. 1-4; Li Hsin-kung, "Settle Accounts with P'eng Te-huai, etc.," PR, No. 36 September 1, 1967, pp. 12-14; David Charles, "The Dismissal of Marshal P'eng Te-huai," China Quarterly, VIII, 8 (October-December, 1961), 63-76; and J. N. Simmonds, "P'eng Te-huai: A Chronological Re-examination," China Quarterly, January-March, 1969, pp. 120-38.

43. JMJP, May 13, 1959.

44. Bulletin of Activities, pp. 45, 50. The Bulletin lauded Chiu for instituting the "three-eight" working style within the GRSD, which accented political work. He was also commended for achieving closer GRSD adherence to Party directives.

45. Ellis Joffe, "The Chinese Army in the Cultural Revolution: The Politics of Intervention," Current Scene, VIII, 18 (December 7, 1970), p. 4.

46. Powell, "Increasing Power," p. 43.

47. For a detailed analysis of the PLA's role in the Cultural Revolution up to late 1969, see William Whitson The Chinese Communist High Command, 1927-1970: A History of Military Politics (New York: Praeger Publishers, 1972), Chapter 7.

48. Joffe, "Politics of Intervention," p. 3.

49. Ibid., p. 9.

50. Philip Bridgham, "Mao's Cultural Revolution in 1967: The Struggle to Seize Power," China Quarterly, XXIV, April-June, 1968, pp. 13-23; Joffe, "The Chinese Army in the Cultural Revolution," p. 13 and Tang Tsou, "The Cultural Revolution and the Chinese Political System," China Quarterly, XXXVIII, (April-June, 1969, p. 86.

51. Chu-Yuan Cheng, "Growth and Structural Changes in the Chinese Machine-Building Industry, 1952-1966," China Quarterly, XXXI, January-March, 1970, p. 28.

52. NCNA, January 19, 1968.

53. Joffe, "Politics of Intervention." p. 15.

54. Cheng, "Machine-Building Industry," p. 3; and Whitson, The Chinese Communist High Command, chap. 7.

55. Cheng, "Machine-Building Industry," p. 9.

56. Chu-ying Tung-fang-hung [Pearl (River) Film Studio East-Is-Red, a Canton Red Guard newspaper], September 13, 1967; translated partially in SCMP, No. 4036, October, 1967, pp. 1-6. Ch'iu was seen frequently in public throughout this critical phase of the Cultural Revolution: National Day (1966), the Peking Red Guard Rally of November 3, 1966, the May Day 1967 festivities; and at the welcoming ceremony at the Peking Airport (July 23, 1967) for Hsieh Fu-chih and Wang Li after the Wuhan incident. These appearances would seem to indicate that he retained strong support from Mao and Lin Piao.

57. For Lin Piao's explanation of Yang Cheng-wu's dismissal to senior military leaders, see "An Important Speech by Vice-Chairman Lin at Reception for Army Cadres on March 25," Kung-lien (Workers Federation, Canton), April, 1968; translated in SCMP, No. 4173, May, 1968, pp. 1-5. Sankee (September 2, 1967) and the Tokyo Shimbum (September 3, 1967) reported Ch'iu's appointment to the All-PLA CRG.

58. British Broadcast, Summary of World Broadcasts, Part III, No. 2677. Cited in "Quarterly Chronicle and Documentation," China Quarterly, XXXIV, (April-June, 1968), p. 167; and NCNA, February 28, 1968, and February 15, 1969.

59. "Notice of the CCP Central Committee, State Council, Military Affairs (Commission of the Central Committee and Cultural Revolution Group," Chung-hsueh Hung-wei-ping [Middle School Red Guards, Canton], July, 1968; translated by SCMP, No. 4232, Sept., 1968, pp. 1-3.

60. "Chiu Hui-tso," Issues, pp. 73-74; Ts'an-k'ao Tsu-liao [Reference Material], July 1968, translated in SCMP, No. 4222, July, 1968, p. 7; "Quarterly Chronicle and Documentation," China Quarterly, XXXXV (January-March, 1971), p. 197: and "Quarterly Chronicle and Documentation," China Quarterly, 46: 407 (April-June, 1971). Ch'iu was designated as one of the ten military representatives to the twenty-five-man Politburo in 1969. He was also reportedly appointed to a reorganized administrative unit within the MAC. A listing in the Peoples' Daily on October 25, 1970, of those senior leaders attending a reception marking the entry of Chinese volunteers into the Korean War ranked Ch'iu as fourteenth in the order of precedence.

61. NCNA, July 1, 1971.

62. NCNA has reported 104 public appearances for Yuan from May, 1970, to May, 1971, which represents more than Ch'iu Hui-tso himself. See also NCNA, December 16, 1969, and July 23 and October 12, 1970.

63. Cheng, "Machine-Building Industry," pp. 10-11, 13.

64. Riggs, Fighting Hordes, p. 282.

THE PRODUCTION
OF CONVENTIONAL
WEAPONS

James R. Blaker

Prior to the early 1950s, the Chinese Communist military forces relied primarily on weapons captured from the KMT armies, taken over from the Japanese, or, to a much lesser extent, received from the Soviet Union. Of these sources, the Nationalist forces were probably the most important in terms of quantity.

The U.S. White Paper on China, referring to a U.S.-embassy report of November, 1948, states that in four battles alone—Tsian, the Liaoning Corridor, Changchun, and Mukden—the Nationalists lost 230,000 rifles in addition to other military materiel. In December, 1948, the U.S. military attaché at Nanking reported that the Communist had probably captured at least 80 percent of all U.S. equipment supplied to 17 divisions.[1] These figures tend to justify the July, 1949, claim by PLA headquarters that it had captured 60,000 pieces of artillery, 250,000 machine guns, 2 million small arms, and over 500 tanks during the previous four years.[2]

The exact types and amounts of Japanese equipment gained by the Communists in Manchuria have never been determined with much precision, but it is probably fair to say that these stocks, combined with those captured from the retreating Nationalists, provided the Communists with a conventional-arms arsenal that was then about the fourth or fifth largest in the world. But the equipment possessed

---

Views expressed in this chapter are solely those of the author and do not represent the official position of any agencies of the U.S. government.

by the new PRC at the end of the civil war was a mixture of U.S.,
Japanese, and Russian materiel of widely varying age and efficiency.[3]
The Chinese had an aging, mismatched arsenal, impressive in numbers,
but lacking the depth provided by a well-founded, comprehensive
indigenous productive capability.

In terms of the indigenous production of conventional weapons,
three post-1950 general periods can be discerned. While it would be
a mistake to argue that these periods reflect a comprehensive prior
planning effort, there is clearly a historical continuity that runs through
the last two decades and outlines an obvious effort by the Chinese to
build upon what existed earlier. One can, therefore, talk of "stages"
in the Chinese production of conventional weapons, and, for the purposes
of discussion, identify these stages as the "postwar restoration period,"
the "era of Soviet assistance" and the "era of self-sufficiency." The
precise time frames associated with each stage are difficult to pin
down, but the first probably ran from the end of the civil war through
1951, the second from about 1951 to 1960, and the third from the withdrawal of Soviet technicians in mid-1960 to the present.

There were, of course, deeper roots to the production of conventional weapons in China than implied by the timing of the first stage.
During the war against Japan, the Chinese Nationalists developed 15
major small-arms and ammunition arsenals in addition to 5 smaller
arsenals, the total capable of producing enough small ammunition to
supply the Generalisimo's forces.[4] There were reports of some
arsenals producing both small arms and ammunition in Communist-
held areas as early as 1942, but the industry as it exists today did
not really begin until the end of the civil war in 1949. Probably all
the plants that have produced armaments since 1950 were built, expanded, or reequipped with the aid of Soviet technicians.

THE POSTWAR RESTORATION PERIOD, 1949-51

Although the Communists had assumed control of Nationalist
arsenals, during the postwar restoration period they concentrated
primarily on the restoration of the Japanese industrial complex in
Manchuria and its associated weapons-production facilities. Many
of these facilities had been damaged or stripped of equipment. The
Communists were able to restore them to partial productive use
within about a year after the KMT forces had been defeated. But production was limited primarily to ammunition and small arms; artillery
production was restricted to less than 100 mm pieces, a factor that
was to limit Chinese combat effectiveness in the Korean conflict.

As late as the autumn of 1951, the bulk of the military materiel used by the Chinese People's Volunteer Forces consisted of ex-KMT weapons. It was common to find several different kinds of rifles of varying origin and caliber in the same regiment.[5] The People's Volunteers formal order of battle included an artillery battalion with every division, but studies of the Korean War suggest that this arrangement was "theoretical rather than actual as far as Korean operations of 1950 were concerned.[6] These limitations probably contributed to the tactics adopted by the Chinese in Korea, as they necessitated the reliance on foot mobility and mass to compensate for the U.S. superiority in firepower. The losses sustained by the use of such tactics just as surely underlined the criticalness of establishing a self-sufficient armaments industry in China and, in the interim, paying the political and economic price for Soviet aid.

THE ERA OF SOVIET ASSISTANCE, 1951-60

The era of Soviet assistance began, verbally at least, as early as September, 1949. Article 22 of the People's Political Consultative Conference called for developing industries devoted to national defense. Indeed, one of the major themes of the October, 1951, conference was the high priority that had to be placed on national defense. Chou En-lai reportedly insisted that all production should point toward the strengthening of the military. A month later, Ch'en Yun, at that time minister of heavy industry, indicated that investment funds were being diverted from nonmilitary industrial goals toward defense industries and Li Fu-ch'un, then vice-chairman of the Finance and Economic Committee, stated that heavy industries connected with defense would receive the highest priority in terms of the allocation of funds. The models and technical expertise for the effort were to be supplied by the USSR.

Soviet aid to China increased rapidly after Stalin's death in March, 1953. Within three months of his death, the Soviets promised to undertake the design and construction of ninety-one industrial plants in addition to the fifty already begun.[7] The allocation of this aid in China indicated a clear preference for the development of heavy industrial sites, some of which had already been associated with armaments production. Soviet assistance went to projects in Mukden, Shanghai, Peking, Tsingtao, and Anshan, several of which were centers of armaments production under either the Nationalists or Japanese. Assuming that many of the early Soviet aid projects were related to Chinese defense industries, it is likely that the new industrial centers of Pao-t'ou in Inner Mongolia and Chengtu in Szechwan and the expansion of the industrial base in Hsian, all of

which received extensive Soviet assistance between 1951 and 1959,
may have added additional conventional-weapons production facilities
to the Chinese inventory.

Although there were already cracks in the Sino-Soviet alliance,
the scale of Soviet aid to China increased sharply in 1957 and 1958.
A Sino-Soviet agreement on new technology for national defense was
signed on October 15, 1957, in which, according to subsequent Chinese
claims, the Soviets promised to provide nuclear-weapons data.[8]
Khrushchev's visit to Peking in August, 1958, was highlighted by an
agreement to build an additional forty-seven industrial plants, some
of which undoubtedly were related to the defense industry.[9] But in
the same month, the concept of a Great Leap Forward was announced
in a resolution of the CCP calling for the organization of the communes;
the deterioration of Sino-Soviet relations was on the way to becoming
a public affair.

THE ERA OF SELF-SUFFICIENCY, 1961-71

Soviet aid ended in 1960 with the final withdrawal of the military
advisers and technicians. There are some indications, however, that
the construction and modernization programs associated with conventional weapons had either been completed or were at levels where
the Chinese could complete them by themselves by the early 1960s.
As early as November, 1956, the Liberation Army Daily had suggested
the Chinese would soon be able to produce the entire range of new
weapons introduced in the 1950s. Some western authors credit the
Chinese with self-sufficient production of light and medium weaponry
in the early 1960s.[10]

But while the production facilities may have been ready, actual
production undoubtedly slipped downward as a result of the withdrawal
of Soviet technicians. The Bulletin of Activities (Kung-tso Tung-hsun)
of 1961 alludes to the production of weapons and related items falling
behind requirements,[11] and most studies of the Chinese economy
share the view that nearly all productive sectors experienced a decline
in the early 1960s.

There is no evidence that the Chinese have improved or expanded
significantly the production base begun during the period of Soviet
assistance. The Bulletin of Activieties alludes to the effort to build
new military installations away from main urban and industrial centers
as a means of decreasing the vulnerability to nuclear attack, but
definitive analyses of Chinese industrial complexes indicate that the

Chinese have preferred to develop the base they had begun with Soviet assistance in the 1950s rather than begin industrial ventures in new areas.[12] Since the defense industries are embedded within the more general Chinese industrial complex, the Bulletin of Activities references to dispersion probably refer strictly to barracks, training areas, and other operational installations, rather than to production facilities.

PRODUCTION

Every major type of Chinese infantry weapon appears to have entered production for the first time during the last two decades. It is difficult to determine precisely when the Chinese began producing the family of weapons that now arm their forces, but photographs of military personnel armed with the assault rifle based on the Soviet AK-47 design began appearing in Peking Review and other Chinese publications as early as 1957. In view of the statements in 1956 about being able to produce such weapons in China, it is likely that many of the weapons in the current Chinese inventory—all of which appear to be based on designs that were introduced to the Soviet Army in the early 1950s—entered Chinese production prior to 1960.

One can only guess at the level of output. Assuming that the production of the present family of conventional weapons followed the same general pattern as Chinese industrial output, production may have reached a peak in 1958 or 1959, slipped downward in the early 1960s, and then subsequently experienced a general upward trend at least until the disruption associated with the Cultural Revolution in the late 1960s. There is a hint that the production of infantry weapons and perhaps tanks was considered by some Chinese leaders to be more than sufficient for their own needs as early as 1966; the Chinese were willing by that date to export infantry weapons to Vietnam.

THE DISTRIBUTION OF PRODUCTION FACILITIES

Before World War II, modern industry in China, to which the production of nonnuclear weaponry is tied, was confined largely to the great seaports—Shanghai and Tientsin in particular—and to Japanese-held Manchuria. As late as 1948, only 18 cities in 13 provinces (excluding Manchuria) had sufficient manufacturing capacity to be considered even modest industrial centers; 10 of China's 26 provinces and autonomous regions had no modern industrial complexes. East and North China together accounted for about 80 percent of the factories and industrial employment in China proper.[13]

The Communists saw this as irrational and, during the first five-year plan, announced a major effort to develop new industrial regions and bases. Active construction was to proceed in a number of new industrial bases, including T'ai-yuan, Shih-chia-chuang, Lo-yang, Cheng-chan, Chu-chan, Meng-yang, Lanchow, and Hsian, and bases for major iron and steel complexes were to be laid at Pao-t'ou in Inner Mongolia and at Wuhan.

The effort to move industrial complexes westward and modify the excessive reliance on Manchuria and the coastal provinces was only partially successful as of the late 1960s. The initial exuberance of the first five-year plan concerning the westward march of industry was replaced as early as June, 1956, by a retrenchment and shift in investment back toward established industrial complexes. Li Fu-ch'un argued at the third session of the first National People's Congress that greater reliance had to be placed on existing industrial bases. By the mid-1960s, the older industrial bases were clearly being given priority for investment. In retrospect, the policies and programs of the 1950s and 1960s had the affect of industrializing Honan, Hunan, Anhwei, Shansi, and Inner Mongolia, but, at the same time, increasing greatly the level of industrialization in the older centers of modern industry. As of the late 1960s, there were nine large industrial centers in China; with the exception of Pao-t'ou in Inner Mongolia and Wuhan in Hupeh province, these centers were located in the same areas of modern industry that had existed at the end of World War II.[14]

As Table 2 indicates, these nine industrial centers constitute roughly 60 percent of China's total industrial capacity. The remaining 40 percent is distributed among 119 other cities, of which T'ai-yuan's 1.35 percent is the highest percent for a single city. The concentration of industrial capacity in China is demonstrated by functional output also. Over 70 percent of all steel and steel products are, for example, turned out by five complexes; Anshan, Chungking, Shanghai, Pao-t'ou, and Wuhan. In terms of the provincial distribution of industrial capacity, over half can be found in the three provinces of Kiangsu, Hopeh, and Liaoning. (34, 11, and 9 percent, respectively). If Szechwan, Hupeh, Kuangtung, and Inner Mongolia are added to the list, the seven provinces account for about 75 percent of China's total industrial capacity. Thus, about three fourths of the Chinese industrial capacity is located in about one fourth of China's provinces.

Translating this distribution of industrial capacity to the military-region context, it becomes clear that, in terms of capacity, there is a marked difference between military regions. As Table 3 indicates, over one third of China's industrial capacity is located in the Nanking

TABLE 2

Industrial Cities Ranked by Industrial Capacity

Industrial Area	Percent of Total Chinese Industrial Capacity*
Shanghai	30
Tientsin	6
Wuhan	5
Anshan	4
Chungking	3
Nanking	3
Peking	3
Pao-t'ou	3
Canton	3

*Rounded to nearest percent.

Military Region, and, taken together, the Nanking, Peking, Shenyang, and Wuhan military regions have nearly 75 percent of China's entire industrial capacity within their borders.

This has all, of course, been in reference to over-all industrial capacity. It should be noted that the distribution of industrial capacity is only indirect evidence of the regional distribution of conventional-weapons-production facilities. It seems likely, however, that the Chinese would locate their conventional weapons production facilities as closely as possible to the major industrial complexes, if for no other reason than to cut down on transportation costs. Likewise, the early association of plant expansion and construction with defense production tends to support the view that conventional-weapons-pro-duction facilities parallel major industrial complexes. What this means, of course, is that the regional concentration of industrial capa-city reflects at least as great a concentration of the capability to pro-duce conventional weapons in about five of China's thirteen military regions.

This is not to say that other military regions do not have

TABLE 3

Military Regions Ranked by Industrial Capacity

Military Region	Percent of Total Industrial Capacity	Province	Percent of Total Industrial Capacity
Nanking	38	Chekiang	1
		Anhwei	3
		Kiangsu	34
Peking	14	Hopeh	11
		Shansi	3
Shenyang	12	Heilungkiang	1
		Kirin	2
		Liaoning	9
Wuhan	7	Honan	2
		Hupeh	5
Canton	7	Kwangtung	4
		Kwangsi	1
		Hunan	2
Chengtu	6	Szechwan	6
Inner Mongolia	4	Inner Mongolia	4
Foochow	4	Forien Kiangsi	4
Lanchow	3.2	Shensi	1
		Kansu	2
		Ninghsia	0.1
		Chinghai	0.1
Tsinan	3	Shantung	3
Kunming	1	Kweichow	0.2
		Yunnan	0.7
Sinkiang	1	Sinkiang	1
Tibet	-	Tibet	-

conventional-weapons-production facilities within their borders. All of China's military regions possess some industrial plants within their borders that are either now producing arms or ammunition or, with some modification, could produce armaments (fertilizer plants can usually be made to produce gunpowder). But the distribution of major industrial complexes and the concentration of industrial capacity support the contention that less than half of China's military regions have the capacity to produce a wide range of weaponry.

If one breaks down conventional military equipment into the three functional areas of transportation, firepower, and communications and then makes some inferences based on what is known about the production facilities in each military region, it appears that only a few military regions have the capacity to produce all the materiel usually needed to carry on military operations within their own boundaries. Shenyang, Nanking, and Peking military regions seem to come off the best in this respect, having the kind of industrial complexes that may now or could easily be called upon to produce almost the entire spectrum of conventional military equipment. In contrast, Tibet, Sinkiang, Kunming, Foochow, and Lanchow military regions appear to possess relatively limited capabilities, perhaps limited to the production of only the less-sophisticated items of but one of the three general categories mentioned above. Wuhan, Chengtu, Canton, Tsinan, and Inner Mongolia seem to fall somewhere between these two extremes. Each of these five regions possesses significant industrial potential, but in several cases (Pao-t'ou in Inner Mongolia, the tricity at Wuhan, and the complex at Chengtu) these are new industrial complexes about which relatively little is known. For the purpose of comparison the classification in Table 4 seems applicable.

This overview suggests that there are gaps in the production of conventional weapons in China. In terms of production facilities, the Chinese do not appear to have had much success in creating a regionally based system in which each military region has the capacity to produce all or nearly all the weapons possessed by the troops within its borders. Indeed, if the Chinese adhere to the same pattern in the production of conventional weapons as they do in the production of other goods, the gaps may be even greater than the distribution of industrial capacity suggests.

Several studies of Chinese industry have pointed out that the production of relatively sophisticated end-items is often concentrated in only a few factories. A great deal of specialization appears to exist in the production of vehicles and electronic equipment, for example, at least in the sense that the total output of the more-

TABLE 4

Production Capability by Function

Military Region	Transportation	Firepower	Communication
Shenyang ⎫ Nanking ⎬ Peking ⎭	Probably capable of producing entire range of materiel		
Wuhan ⎫ Chengtu ⎬ Canton ⎭	Unknown	Entire Range	Entire range
Tsinan	Motor vehicles	Small arms	Unsophisticated Components
Inner Mongolia	Motor and tracked vehicles	Artillery and small arms	Unsophisticated Components
Foochow ⎫ Lanchow ⎬	Unknown	Artillery and small arms	Unsophisticated components
Sinkiang ⎫ Kunming ⎬ Tibet ⎭	Little if any	Artillery and small arms	Unsophisticated components

complicated pieces can be traced to a single industrial complex and in some cases a single factory.

If the same phenomenon occurs in the production of conventional weapons, then it may be that even those three or four military regions that appear to have the capacity to produce the entire range of conventional weapons do not. Assuming that this is the case—that aircraft, tanks, or other major items or equipment are produced in only one or two of the major Chinese industrial complexes—the overview one gets from the distribution of industrial capacity may not be the full picture. If specialization characterizes the production of conventional weapons, Shenyang, Nanking, and Wuhan military regions may not be as self-sufficient as their industrial capacity might suggest.

CONCLUSIONS

The picture one gains from this is of regional interdependency rather than regional self-sufficiency. In one sense, there is a general equality among military regions—they may all share the inability to produce the entire spectrum of conventional weaponry. As such, the Chinese may have a national system in which there is a rough parity among military regions, even though some of the regions, Shenyang and Nanking in particular, have the potential to become far superior. Each may actually be dependent upon others for a complete equipping of the forces stationed within it.

This, in turn, may tell us something about the thinking of the Chinese elite. It suggests that Chinese planners do not place a high priority on maintaining the military security of individual military regions and that military regions are not the basis for security planning against external threats. The distribution of production centers suggests the opposite, or rather that a concerted effort has been made to avoid giving any single military region the capability to sustain combat should it be isolated from other military regions. Only a few—Nanking, Shenyang, and perhaps Wuhan—appear to possess the capacity to produce all the conventional weaponry required for troops within their borders. If the production of important end-items is concentrated in single, well-dispersed centers, even these military regions could be hurt badly by the loss or isolation of other, less industrially potent regions.

Thus, the distribution of production facilities does not appear to have been a result of the rationale of a group of planners who were highly concerned about external threats, particularly nuclear in nature.

Rhetoric devoted to survival in a nuclear war aside, what the Chinese may have developed is a system of production that is highly susceptible to disruption; if it relies upon a relatively few production centers, it could be immobilized by the destruction of a small number of centers.

There is a startling logic to the system if the distribution of production facilities is view in the context of a priority concern for internal threats and internal power arrangements, however, for the system appears to place the balance of power in the hands of a central "balancer." Thus, without central control in the allocation of resources and planning, the supply of materiel to each military region would, with the possible exceptions of the Shenyang and Nanking military regions, probably fall apart. This factor necessarily emphasizes the superior status of central vs. local regional elites, or of the center vs. most regional coalitions, in the production and allocation of conventional weapons, especially for relatively advanced systems such as artillery, armor, and electronics.

NOTES

1. U.S., Department of State, United States Relations with China, with Special Reference to the Period 1944-1949, Department of State Publication 3573, Far Eastern Series 30 (August, 1949), p. 357.

2. PLA GHQ, "Three Comminque's on Achievements in the Civil War," Summary of World Broadcasts, Part V: "The Far East," No. 51 (July 15, 1949).

3. John Gittings, The Role of The Chinese Army (New York: Oxford University Press, 1967) p. 133. See also, Robert B. Riggs, Red China's Fighting Hordes (Harrisburg, Pa: The Military Services Publishing Co., 1951), p. 100.

4. United States Relations with China, p. 358.

5. Gittings, The Chinese Army, p. 134.

6. Ibid.

7. David Floyd, Mao Against Khrushchev: A Short History of the Sino-Soviet Conflict (New York: Praeger, 1963), p. 19.

8. JMJP, "The Origin and Development of the Differences Between the Leadership of the CPSU and Ourselves," September 6,

1963. For the English translation, see Peking Review, September 13, 1963.

9. JMJP, "Communique: August 4, 1958."

10. See, for example, Samuel B. Griffith II, "The Military Potential of China," in Alastair Buchan, ed., China and the Peace of Asia (London: 1965), p. 73.

11. See "Bulletin of Activities," in J. Chester Cheng, ed., PLA Kung-tso Tung-hsun: The Politics of the Chinese Red Army (Stanford, Cal.: The Hoover Institution on War, Revolution, and Peace, 1966), pp. 19-25.

12. The references in the Bulletin of Activities can be found in ibid., pp. 689-92. For arguments regarding the failure of the initial effort to disperse industry, see Yuan-li Wu, The Spatial Economy of Communist China (New York: Praeger, 1967), pp. 18-19.

13. Wu, Spatial Economy, pp. 8-10. See also Yuan-li Wu, An Economic Survey of Communist China (New York: Bookman Associates, 1956), p. 34. Wu's data was derived from a Chinese Nationalist study published in 1949, Industrial Survey of Principal Cities in China, Preliminary Report (Nanking: National Economic Commission, 1949).

14. Wu, Spatial Economy, pp. 56-66.

THE PRODUCTION
OF NUCLEAR
WEAPONS

Charles Horner

THE CONSTRAINTS OF HISTORY

For more than a century, the Chinese have faced the problem of adapting advanced Western technology to their national needs.[1] As with other countries of the non-Western world, one cost of technological backwardness was military defeat. Thus, the first efforts at modernization were invariably carried out in the military sector. In China, the immediate reaction to a series of reverses in the mid-nineteenth century was the assumption that the mere acquisition of ships and guns would alter the Sino-Western military balance. It was then possible to believe that this one aspect of Western technology could be grafted onto Chinese society without fundamental social or political alterations. Another defeat in the Sino-Japan War shattered this view. Indeed, one could date the beginning of the Chinese "revolution" from the time when influential thinkers reached the conclusion that the mere ownership of modern weapons could contribute little to China's defenses. What was needed, according to this newer view, were new organizations to make and employ the weapons, new military concepts to govern their use, and a new over-all social outlook that would allow such innovations to succeed.

But some of the results of this conceptual change were unintended. Western arms, training procedures, and staff organizations resulted in new "model" armies whose major contribution to Chinese life was a generation of warlordism. The same arms, employed in different ways for different ends, gave rise to a revolutionary army that overturned the social order altogether. Even today, the highest Chinese authorities indicate their concern that a change in attitude toward technology within the PLA could result in a qualitative change in the nature of the military institution itself. Indeed, this seems to be one of the axioms in the continuing debate over the "two military lines."

This chapter will consider but one instance of the ongoing interaction between technological advancement and political behavior in
China. The object in question will be the latest Western intrusion into
the lives of Chinese defense planners—the atomic bomb. Nuclear
technology has created whole new possibilities; politics will decide
how they will be exploited. By considering how the Chinese political
system has responded to the options that the development of Chinese
technology has placed before it, one may be able to speculate about
future decisions in this important area. And by applying what little is
known about the decision-making process to future technological options
as they are capable of being forecast, one may gain some insight as
to what a particular kind of nuclear-weapons program will imply for
China's behavior as an international power.

To be sure, a Chinese decision to produce and deploy nuclear
weapons (as distinct from some future decision to engage in a nuclear
war) does not seem to imply consequences as far-reaching as those
that resulted from an earlier effort at military modernization. But
it is reasonably certain that the Chinese will continue to encounter
theoretical and bureaucratic problems similar to those that accompanied
the large-scale introduction of nuclear weapons into the arsenals of
the other major powers.

THE CHINESE BUREAUCRATIC FACTOR

In recent years, understanding of political behavior in regard
to strategic problems has been enriched by refinements in organization
theory, by development of more complex models of bureaucratic politics, and the like. In particular, the internal dynamics of any country's
weapons-acquisition process has come to be appreciated in a way that
casts doubt on the action-reaction character of the arms race; strategic
doctrines are expounded, vast amounts of money are invested, and
debates are carried out in what appears to be a bureaucratically self-
contained atmosphere. In short, there is a tendency to the somewhat
more cynical view that conceptions of national interest are often put
forward to protect and promote parochial bureaucratic interests.

If this is the case, the development of theories of explanation
has far outstripped the availability of data to apply them. This is
particularly true in the Chinese case. It is now realized that close
scrutiny of Chinese public statements is only one operation to be
carried out in attempting to fathom the future of the Chinese strategic
program. For other data, one is dependent upon the few items of "hard"
intelligence from Western sources that manage to find their way into

the public press. From time to time, internal stress within China leads to sensational disclosures, the veracity of which must always be questioned. Nor is an examination of ideology the best solution, for it is possible, as shall later be seen to derive from the official military canon entirely different strategic deployment concepts with radically different international consequences.

Employing the political language currently in vogue in China to define the major problem, it would seem that the Maoists would deny that the nation must choose between the technological sophistication necessary to enhance Chinese power in international society and the ideologically-motivated people's army necessary to preserve "genuine" Communist power at home. But from time to time, other Chinese Marxists are known to have opposed Mao by implying that his views are irrelevant, that they may be nothing but the superstructure generated during a more primitive time. It is true, of course, that Chairman Mao's teachings are the product of an era that predates extraordinarily complex and expensive weaponry. To state that the Party commands the gun is to say that it ought to command the gun, not that it always will. Indeed, in the post-Cultural Revolution era, military power appears easily translatable into political power at every level, and, in looking toward the future, one can observe that in countries more advanced militarily shifting alliances between the military services, defense intellectuals, scientists, and economic managers have become important in resolving concrete questions of policy. It is therefore still an open question whether the CCP will be able—in General Eisenhower's phrase—to "guard against the acquisition of unwarranted influence . . . by the military-industrial complex."

CHINESE COMMUNIST PERCEPTIONS OF SCIENCE AND SCIENTISTS

The Chinese Communists have always attached great importance to scientific development. The Chinese Academy of Sciences was organized the same month the CPR was proclaimed. As the successor to the Nationalists' Peiping Academy and the Academia Sinica, the academy was charged with establishing an academic and scientific leadership group for the country, fostering cooperation within the Chinese scientific community, and following scientific developments in foreign countries.

Outside assistance was provided by the Soviet Union, though the bulk of it seems to have been technical assistance related to various industrial projects.[2] The two countries agreed to exchange scientific and technical information in 1954. In 1956, a delegation of Soviet scientists arrived in Peking to aid in the preparation of a twelve-year "master plan" for the development of Chinese science and technology. Presumably, this plan would have established scientific priorities through 1968 and defined the future Soviet role in Chinese scientific programs. The Soviets, however, terminated almost all their scientific assistance by 1961. But the public discussion of the plan emphasized broad policy guidelines rather than specific scientific and/or techno-logical targets.

Significantly, this question of the proper role of science and scientists was raised at a time when a larger debate was unfolding. Mao's "hundred flowers" speech of 1957, for example, seemed to hold forth to Chinese intellectuals the promise of greater freedom. But in 1958, this policy of relaxation was dramatically reversed, the Great Leap Forward was launched, and greater emphasis seems to have been placed on applied rather than pure science. The effects of these rapid and arbitrary shifts in the Party line on intellectual work—particularly on those elite members of the scientific community who had been trained in a different atmosphere in the West—can only be guessed at. Their privileged status, however, may have brought them a certain degree of immunity.

(The problem of the impact of mass-mobilization campaigns, rectification movements, and the like on the rate of Chinese scientific progress is a speculative one. Indeed, this may have been one factor the leadership took into consideration before deciding to launch them. In the earlier phases of the Cultural Revolution, certain elite scientific personnel were specifically exempted from "reeducation." The sci-entific establishment, on the other hand, has been subjected to periodic shakeups and humiliations, not only at the policy level, but in conjunc-tion with reforms carried out in the area of higher education. For example, reports filed by Western correspondents at the time of the Chinese tour of the American table-tennis team in early 1971, indicated that the sizes of the student bodies at elite universities had been drastically cut back and that entrance was being determined on the basis of "class background." The long-term effects of this remain to be seen. In regard to scientists themselves, official statements, also originating in early 1971, can be interpreted as moderate ones. Though scientific research is another area where the struggle between the two lines is said to continue, the appeal is for greater cooperation between scientific and technical personnel and ordinary workers. The former are supposed to serve "workers, peasants, and soldiers wholehearted-ly"; it may or may not be significant that scientists are not specifically exhorted to <u>learn</u> from them. Indeed, "ideas such as 'there is no

future in scientific research work,' and 'use your hands more and
your head less,'" two plausible lessons of the Cultural Revolution, are
specifically repudiated. More significant, perhaps, is the subdued
tone of the threats. "If those people who still have the gravely erroneous
idea of 'private ownership of knowledge' today fail to speed up the
remolding of their ideology, they will definitely be useless to the proletariat and will eventually be abandoned by the people." This is a
milder fate, say, than being ground into dust and swept into the dustbin
of history.[3])

    The origins of the nuclear program can also be traced to the
early years of the regime. While little is known about the motivations
underlying the initial nuclear-research efforts, it is hardly conceivable
that scientific planners did not foresee a time when the knowledge and
skills gained from the program would be applied to nuclear-weapons
development. The Soviet Union played an important role in Chinese
plans. In April, 1955, a joint agreement was reached for the building
of an atomic reactor and a cyclotron in China. Chinese were given
access to the research facilities at the Joint Institute of Nuclear
Research near Moscow. In the Chinese polemics directed against the
Soviet Union in the early 1960s, it was revealed that, in 1957, the
Soviets had pledged to provide a prototype of a nuclear weapon and
certain details about how to make it, though not necessarily the materials needed to manufacture it. The Soviets are said to have reneged
on this pledge.

    In retrospect, however, it appears that the reservoir of outstand-
ing scientific talent created through training in Western countries
prior to 1949 was of a long-term significance at least equal to that
of the ad hoc assistance of the Soviet Union. Many of the people occupying key scientific (as distinct from managerial) positions in both
the nuclear-weapons and strategic-missiles programs were trained
in the West. These men are of even greater long-term value as teachers of a subsequent generation of Chinese scientists. Indeed, their
extended exposure to Western influence during a formative period of
their lives may make them one easily identifiable interest group that
would have a minimum of difficulty communicating with Americans
in some future period of improved Sino-Western relations.*

---

    *In May 1971, the New China News Agency reported that two
American scientists had arrived in China for a visit. The National
Science Foundation has also expressed interest in instituting high-
level scientific exchange.

(In an appendix to The China Cloud, a rather florid book about
the Chinese strategic program ["The ancient ghosts of Lop have re-
appeared. . . . A great fireball seared the autumn sky . . . casting
an eerie purple glow across the bleak flats of the Takla Maken desert
. . .], William L. Ryan and Sam Summerlin have collated biographical
data about these important scientists.[4] Of the 15 people they say were
most important in the development of nuclear weapons, 13 were educated in the West, 6 of these in the United States. Of the 5 leading scientists in the missile program, 4 were trained in the United States
and 1 in Britain. The best-known case is that of Ch'ien Hsueh-shen,
director of the Institute of Mechanics of the Chinese Academy of
Sciences and a graduate of both M.I.T. and the California Institute of
Technology. After being active in the early phases of the American
missile program, Ch'ien was the subject of a "loyalty investigation"
in 1950 and was deported to China in 1955. In April, 1968, Radio
Moscow offered the view that Ch'ien's repatriation had been arranged
at the Sino-American talks in Warsaw; the broadcast drew sinister
implications about the presence of so many American-trained scientists in the Chinese weapons program. It seems implausible however,
that the American government should be credited with the great degree
of foresight that would have led to a conclusion, in 1955, that a Chinese
nuclear capability would ultimately redound to American interests.
Of course, transfer of political loyalties is not uncommon in the history
of strategic weapons, for many non-Americans contributed to such
programs in the United States. One cannot help but recall the verse
by Tom Lehrer: "Once the rocket goes up, / Who cares where it comes
down, / That's not my department," says Wernher von Braun.)

THE DECISION TO DEVELOP NUCLEAR
WEAPONS

In May, 1958, Foreign Minister Chen Yi revealed China's intention
to acquire nuclear weapons. Obviously, a decision to proceed with the
manufacture of the bomb would have to have been made some time
previously, but it is not known when. It is highly unlikely that this
decision was the outcome of an abstract debate over possession of
nuclear weapons. Whether or not there had ever been a suggestion
that China foreswear nuclear weapons altogether, the nuclear-energy
program had a built-in bias toward acquiring the weapon "sooner or
later." Indeed, that issue had probably been resolved—if it arose at
all—well before the Soviet offer of a sample atomic bomb in 1957. The
real question must have concerned the priority of a nuclear-weapons
program—more specifically, whether the bomb should be produced on
a crash basis.

There is a consensus among Western analysts that 1958 was indeed the year when the nuclear-weapons program shifted to a higher gear. Many of them, in retrospect, relate the timing of the decision to the failure of the Soviet Union to place its own nuclear arsenal squarely behind Chinese political aims, particularly those related to the Taiwan straits. Soviet vacillation, in this view was an indication to the Chinese that their major ally was unreliable in times of crisis.[5] Just as some in France had concluded, after Suez, that the United States would not risk nuclear war with the Soviet Union over a "European" interest—one possible contributor to France's 1958 decision to acquire nuclear weapons—the Chinese, too, may have decided that an "independent deterrent" was a political necessity.

Less attention seems to have been paid to purely internal pressures that may have been leading to nuclear acquisition. The pre-1958 period was one when large numbers of Chinese officers were exposed to Soviet influence. They were no doubt aware of the emerging body of Soviet doctrine about the ways in which nuclear weapons had altered the character of warfare. They were witnesses to the modernization of Soviet ground forces and the ways in which nuclear weapons were being integrated into them. Mao himself indicated that the development of Soviet strategic rocketry had altered the world balance of power. These influences might have won out regardless of the diplomatic behavior of ally and adversary.

If the Chinese were being exposed to one body of Western doctrine regarding the "war-fighting" role of nuclear weapons, a more subtle debate was being carried out in the West about the ultimate value of nuclear weaponry. But one can only wonder what, if anything, the Chinese absorbed from it. Some parties to the debate in China no doubt realized that a Chinese atomic bomb would be viewed as highly "provocative" by both the United States and the Soviet Union. Moreover, the scientific establishment must have been aware that it would be years (if ever) before China would acquire a nuclear striking force sufficient, in and of itself, to contribute to deterrence by being able to survive an enemy's first strike. It may be significant in anticipating the reaction of other countries to antiacquisition arguments that the Chinese obviously did not buy the classical case against proliferation and the distinction between first- and second-strike forces upon which it rested. Indeed, the Chinese, like the French (and like the Indians or the Japanese?) may have thought the argument irrelevant for their purposes.

Even if the Chinese realized that they needed "all" in order to contemplate using nuclear weapons in a general war, the alternative to "all" did not have to be "nothing." If one could be reasonably confident that neither the United States nor the Soviet Union would interfere militarily with a Chinese nuclear-weapons program, the period of maximum vulnerability might be survived. The Soviet Union was itself an example, for it had endured years of nuclear inferiority yet had escaped an American nuclear attack. China's ability to deter an American and/or Soviet nuclear attack could, in any case, depend on factors other than the size of its own nuclear inventory, especially if the Soviet example of not neglecting general-purpose forces was heeded.*

Thus, from the Chinese perspective, it is difficult to see how they could have viewed themselves as being worse off by attempting to acquire nuclear weapons. At the least, the symbolic and phychological value of the weapon might be operable in some future crisis, even though in the computational sense Chinese weapons might not be able to limit damage if deterrence failed. Moreover, an analysis of Soviet diplomacy of the mid-1950s might have been very revealing, for the West (and the Chinese themselves) had appeared to be highly impressed by essentially symbolic military demonstrations such as Sputnik.

In any case, the decision to proceed with the manufacture of the weapon must have involved a quantum jump in the effort devoted to the nuclear program. By 1958, manufacturing an atomic bomb was essentially an engineering problem; the theoretical problems had long since been solved.[6] The Chinese had the advantage of knowing, at least in general, how both the United States and the Soviet Union had overcome various technical obstacles. Even so, decisions had to be made as to whether the first weapon should be made in a manner that would allow more rapid progress toward a thermonuclear weapon, even though the appearance of China's first bomb might be significantly delayed.

---

*In this connection, it is interesting to ponder the rumors of late 1969 that the Soviets were planning a "disarming" attack against China. If in fact they were entertaining such ideas, why were they discarded? China's nuclear forces lacked the characteristics associated with credible deterrent, yet deterrence of a sort may have been operating. Of what, then, did it consist? It may be that the Chinese have concluded that there are numerous considerations that contribute to a decision to launch a first nuclear strike, aside from its technical feasibility. This does not mean, of course, that Chinese behavior is not seriously restrained by a lack of a second-strike capability.

TECHNOLOGICAL CONSTRAINTS

A poor country cannot usually afford to follow parallel paths in developing a new weapon and then choose the best alternative that emerges, thereby writing off the investment made in the other programs. An initial decision has the air of irrevocability, especially when technological and economic constraints are severe. Choices have to be made in regard to each piece of hardware that will ultimately become part of a weapons system. For the Chinese, it must have been difficult to decide whether technological obstacles would appear in the initial phase of the program that would preclude the final product as envisioned. Indeed, it is safe to theorize that the final product as envisioned. Indeed, it is safe to theorize that the final product itself may well be the outcome of a series of small decisions whose overall cumulative effects will only be known over time.[7] In this connection, it may be useful to consider the technical problems (and their larger implications) that may have been involved at each stage of the Chinese strategic program.

If one envisions a long-range missile system, one sine qua non is a thermonuclear warhead light enough in weight to be delivered by a rocket and large enough in yield to be worth sending. On the other hand, if one envisions the employment of nuclear weapons by general-purpose forces, a different problem arises, for one must produce a large number of warheads not only low in weight, but low in yield. The design and production of warheads for these two extremes of the weapons spectrum are technically the most difficult. The characteristics of the warhead itself will therefore influence the design of the system in which it will be used.* Design of a missile, for example, for which the warhead has not yet been produced is a calculated risk for a poor country, and it is possible that the Chinese were reluctant to commit themselves to various types of missile production until advances in warhead technology justified it.

The manufacture of an atomic bomb or of the triggering device of a hydrogen bomb begins, essentially, with the collection of fissionable material. Two metals are suitable for this purpose—the

---

*It has been suggested that the Soviets turned initially to the production of large, liquid-fueled rockets because they had been unable to "miniaturize" their warheads at the time they began their missile program.

synthetic element Plutonium and the so-called U-235 isotope of uranium.[8] Plutonium is produced when the most common form of natural uranium, so-called U-238, absorbs additional neutrons during the controlled chain reaction that occurs when an atomic pile is in operation. The plutonium then has to be separated from the U-238 in a reprocessing plant.

Relying upon plutonium has advantages and disadvantages as far as long-term weapons production is concerned. Past experience indicates, for example, that a reprocessing plant can be built for some tens, rather than hundreds, of millions of dollars. The principal disadvantage of plutonium, however, is that it is not well-suited for constructing the trigger for a thermonuclear weapon. Its principal advantage, on the other hand, is that a significantly smaller quantity of this metal (as against U-235) is required to manufacture a bomb. Simply put, plutonium is more desirable for extremely small bombs, U-235 for extremely large ones. A choice at the initial state of producing fissionable materials, therefore, is not an important one.

The other alternative is the manufacture of U-235. This metal is useful for both atomic and hydrogen warheads, can be used to fuel other reactors, and, once initial obstacles are overcome, can be produced in significantly larger quantities than can plutonium. Unfortunately, less than 1 percent of natural uranium exists in the form of U-235. In order to accumulate any significant amount of this material, the U-235 has to be refined out of its natural host. This process is usually called enrichment, that is, the creation of uranium that has a higher-than-natural percentage of U-235. This can be accomplished by a process called gaseous diffusion, but the technology required is far more complex and expensive than that required to manufacture plutonium.* Basically, uranium that has been previously refined from uranium ore is mixed with other materials, and turned into a gas, and is then passed through a large series of filters; a small quantity of U-235 is collected at each stage. Because the degree of enrichment is a function of the number of filters the gaseous mixture passes through, the process cannot be compressed. Rather, output is increased by enlarging the scale of the operation. Thus, in order to compensate for the remarkable inefficiency of this method, the

---

*France did not acquire such a plant until 1967; it is estimated to have cost almost a billion dollars to construct and put into operation. There are five such plants in the West, three of them in the United States.

manufacturer is forced to build an ever-larger factory if he wishes
to accumulate the material in any meaningful amounts. This requires
the manufacture (or purchase) of complex heating, cooling, and filtering
equipment, together with vast supplies of electricity.[9]

Based on what we now know about the timing of Chinese nuclear
tests, the lead times required to put various forms of technology into
operation, and the like, it is clear that the Chinese must have reached
a decision regarding the relative merits of plutonium and enriched
uranium about the same time they decided to proceed with the manufacture of their nuclear weapon. The only known nuclear installation
in China in 1958 was the Soviet-provided reactor near Peking. Theoretically, that reactor could have provided enough irradiated uranium
to make possible the extraction of five kilograms of plutonium by the
end of 1960, about the amount needed to manufacture a bomb. The
reprocessing would have required about six months, and enough
plutonium would have been available to explode a device some time
in 1961.[10] The problem with this approach would have been the dependence of this reactor upon Soviet-manufactured enriched uranium for
its fuel supply.

Two avenues of approach must have presented themselves. The
first was to build an atomic reactor that could be fueled with natural
uranium and from which a militarily usable supply of plutonium could
be extracted. Alternatively, the Chinese might have attempted the
technologically unfamiliar route of producing enriched uranium. While
the initial investment in this latter method would have been greater,
the costs might tend to even out as nuclear weapons entered into serial
production. Additionally, a capability to make enriched uranium would
provide the Chinese with enough fuel of their own to begin the process
of accumulating plutonium from their existing nuclear facilities. This
route might delay the first nuclear test, and might even impose a
specific sequence on weapons development. This might also have implications for the sequential development of weapons systems, strategic
doctrine, and the like.

The first Chinese nuclear test of October, 1964, used a device
made with enriched uranium. The uranium was the product of a gaseous
diffusion plant constructed at Lanchow in Kansu province. It is not
certain when construction began or whether Soviet assistance was
provided during the early stages of development. It is likely that the
Soviet contribution was minimal, since an independent Chinese capability to make enriched uranium could hardly be in the Soviet's interest.
The real costs of the enterprise must also remain speculative.[11] In
domestic economic terms, the center of the "nuclear industry" was
shifted from Peking far to the West.

Taken together with the construction of a weapons assembly plant and a testing facility, elements from the entire bureaucratic complex must have been involved: central and provincial officials, large numbers of "subcontractors" and skilled workers, an elaborate security apparatus, maintenance of elite morale during periods of national commotion, and so on. The Chinese have been very uncommunicative in describing the organization of the effort. Has the weapons program been split into separate components analogous to the American division of labor between the Atomic Energy Commission and the Department of Defense? What is the nature of the PLA role in terms of producing weapons designs? Does the nuclear industry operate within the normal five-year planning cycle? The answer to these and a host of other questions would allow one to define discrete bureaucratic interests. (One can only hope that the "struggle between the two lines" in this realm becomes to intense that the Chinese authorities will some day feel it worthwhile to reveal at least a portion of the program's internal conflicts.)

Considerations of the constraints imposed by the irrevocability of initial decisions and the gap between the ability to design and the ability to produce may be even more important in an examination of missile development. Because of the relative backwardness of the Chinese economy over-all, high-technology research and development must be a relatively self-contained operation. The manufacture of one or two prototypes is essentially a cottage-industry task, and a small number of missiles can probably be assembled with little drain on the nation's industrial capacity as a whole. Since improvements originating in the research-and-development sector can be generated at a higher rate than production facilities can absorb them, the gap between what could be made and what is actually made is likely to grow. From the point of view of the manager, any decision to "freeze" a design and place it into production should be avoided as long as possible. Countervailing pressures may originate from those bodies who want forces-in-being as soon as possible.

There are at least two conceivable ways to get out of this predicament. The first is by the adaptation of existing military hardware to nuclear weapons. The second is to bypass the intermediate state of the guaranteed obsolescence of any strategic system that can be deployed over the near term, prolong nuclear vulnerability, give up short-term prospects, and attempt to move into the next phase. Based on these alternatives alone, the first choice would imply an emphasis on a tactical nuclear-war capability, and the second would suggest maximum emphasis on the development of an intercontinental ballistic missile (ICBM). (In fact, the choice need not be so clear-cut, since thermonuclear warheads themselves can be produced more rapidly than the ballistic missiles to deliver them, thereby leaving a certain amount of fissionable material left over for other purposes.) While these two alternatives may not be mutually exclusive, the deemplasis of one or the other in favor of concentrated development of an inter-mediate-range ballistic missile (IRBM) would seem to make the least sense in accordance with the technological research-and-development industrial efficiency criteria under discussion. If, in fact, an IRBM does emerge as the preferred route over the near term, this would seem to indicate that political/military factors may be predominating over purely "technical" and "economic" considerations.

The limited information available about the Chinese missile program allows for a variety of plausible interpretations. The first linkage between nuclear warheads and rockets, according to the Chinese press, was in October, 1966, when a nuclear warhead was delivered to the test site by a "guided missile." Assuming that the missile was fired from the missile-testing facility at Shuangchengtzu and impacted near the nuclear test site near Lop Nor, this would imply a range of approximately 500 miles.

Greater insight into the Chinese rocket program is provided by the two satellite launchings. The first, in April, 1970, is presumed to have used a rocket analogous to an IRBM, though it may have been the test of an ICBM prototype.* A second satellite launching in March, 1971, revived speculation that the testing of an ICBM was imminent.[12] The Chinese inventory of missiles of shorter range is also speculative, as is the ability to deliver nuclear warheads by more conventional means. It is therefore an open question whether the Chinese strategic program should be praised for its progress since, say, 1958, or whether the Chinese have been less successful than they might have been under different organizational arrangements.[13]

THE CONSTRAINTS OF ALTERNATIVE STRATEGIES

Whatever the technical problems that have arisen during the course of missile development, it is also conceivable that the "delays"

---

*The problem is apparently one of accounting for the "eccentricity" of the orbit of the satellite, that is, whether it resulted from a malfunctioning IRBM prototype or a properly functioning proto-ICBM.

in deployment reflect the fact that fundamental problems of strategic doctrine have not yet been resolved. To the extent that such doctrines originate within the military services, one corollary is important: no military service has ever formulated a doctrine that concludes that its own relative share of resources should be reduced. Indeed, all bureaucracies are adept at defining the point at which the axes of self-interest and national interest intersect, as indeed they may do in some cases. In regard to PLA ground forces, such a doctrine could be built around the concepts of "maximum warfighting" and "minimum deterrence." The outlines of such a strategy can be found within the Maoist military canon itself.

Indeed, it may not be too far-fetched to envision a doctrine built upon the concept of "protracted nuclear war." Such a strategy would envision the widest possible dispersion of nuclear weapons and their employment with relatively short-range and simple systems. Proponents of this view would draw parallels to the historically demonstrated ability of the PLA to operate in self-contained units in coordinated fashion—the prerequisites of conducting a limited nuclear war. Such a force configuration would make nuclear weapons available for the more likely military contingency—massive Soviet attack.

Nuclear dispersal would deprive the Soviets of the opportunity to launch a "surgical" nuclear strike directed against the Chinese nuclear arsenal. It would force the Soviets (or indeed the Americans) to choose among a conventional armored invasion, a massive "counter-value" attack against the Chinese population, limited nuclear strikes, and so on, none of which could guarantee quick victory. Since any Chinese land-based missile system will be vulnerable to a Soviet disarming attack for the foreseeable future, its very presence might invite such a strike, thus leaving the Chinese population centers defenseless in any event.

Protracted nuclear war is, moreover, an unprovocative defensive strategy, and would seriously complicate Soviet planning. With minor adjustments, this deployment would also take other possibilities into account. Weapons in the low-kiloton range could be delivered on Taiwan or an invasion fleet originating from there, thus making it possible to redeploy some of the large troop concentrations from Fukien to other areas. Relatively primitive delivery systems would be credible against Indian defenses, against Soviet military targets in Mongolia or other areas adjacent to China, and even against Japan (given the small area and high population density of that country). Withal, Chinese technology is capable of fulfilling the requirements of this doctrine.[14]

The opposing argument would begin from the assumption that China cannot even begin to contemplate using nuclear weapons in a war with either of the major powers without the ability to inflict punitive damage on their territories. Nor can it hope to bargain with the major powers over such matters as arms control until its nuclear assets are housed in the containers that have come to symbolize strategic power. A doctrine embodying this view could be built up around the concepts of minimum warfighting and maximum deterrence. In such a view, the development of an assured second-strike capability would take precedence over other considerations. The solution to the problem would have to be technology intensive, emphasizing the survivability of the strategic-weapons system. In an ideal world, the best argument would be put forward by the Chinese navy, taking the Polaris-type system as an archetype.* The more likely response, however, is one employing an exotic system: e.g., mobile-based missiles on barges, railroad flatcars, and the like, and deployment of missiles in a large number of small units.

This could be justified as being in keeping with another tenet of the Chinese armed forces-deception. In larger political terms, such a force configuration holds forth the best prospect of genuine equality, at least in a formal sense, among the three major powers. The proponents would point to the possibility that an arms-control agreement between the United States and the Soviet Union could work to Chinese interests, especially if it results in the abandonment of "area" ABM defenses. To a greater or lesser extent, the argument for maximum deterrence might draw supporters from the more technologically oriented segments of the society (including economic managers and

---

*In fact, the problems involved in going to a submarine-based system would appear to be so severe as to preclude serious consideration of it for a long time. The U.S. experience is that a Polaris submarine costs about three times as much as a flight of a Minuteman and that the costs of operation are about three times greater. Without nuclear submarines, forward bases for the exchange of crews, complex communication equipment, and the like, the Chinese would lose much "on time" service from such submarines. Among the more exotic, and less likely, solutions to this problem must be mentioned the possibility of Chinese missiles based in other countries. But it is hard to envision the political changes that would make this possible. (A Pacific micro-state's agreeing to serve as a Chinese submarine base? Albania's agreeing to the installation of Chinese IRBMs?)

elements of the Air Force and from those concerned with international diplomatic problems (the Foreign Ministry?).

These are two ideal and extreme cases. Certain practical considerations may make this dichotomy far less explicit in the minds of Chinese planners. The first is the available military budget and its allocation between general-purpose and strategic forces. The measurement of Chinese military spending is, of course, an inexact science that seems to be strongly influenced by the procedures of astrology and alchemy.[15] This notwithstanding, the "conventional wisdom" assumes an annual military buget in the neighborhood of $5 billion, with about $1 billion devoted to the strategic program—about 20 percent of the total. (The proportions of the American military budget are about the same.) Even if these figures are only a rough approximation, the proportion of resources devoted to nuclear weaponry is not inordinately great. Moreover, there are indications of a powerful conventional weapons "lobby." The Chinese have modernized much of their conventional inventory, are known to have begun producing a new jet fighter (a modified MIG-19), a medium bomber, small naval craft, an improved tank, and modernized artillery—all in significant numbers. Thus, as far as strategic weapons are concerned, one is discussing perhaps but one quarter of Chinese military spending.

The second practical component is the actual political process involved in the formulation of defense plans. It is at this level that strategic abstractions will be translated into specific forces and organizations. Such decisions are likely to reflect the self-images and standard operating procedures of the various services, the ambitions of key leaders, and so on. Recent reevaluations of Chinese strategic debates and changes in the Chinese high command in recent years have offered a plausible view of "the extent to which domestic political considerations can affect strategy preferences and the Chinese leadership's determination of the armed forces mission."[16] Thus, whether the leadership chooses to diffuse nuclear weapons into the existing military organizations, to create new military organizations to receive them, or to enlarge some organizations at the expense of others is a problem that cannot be divorced from political considerations. But though much has been written on the subject, it is still not clear precisely what role Mao, say, actually ascribes to the military in the Chinese political process. It is even less clear how the Chinese leadership perceives the role that the military plays in affecting policy decisions. The participants probably do not view the situation in the same way an American China-watcher might, even though by some accident an outside observer should happen to be correct in his judgment in some objective sense. Thus, what one may consider to be major

political problems raised in the deployment of nuclear weapons, may
be considered trivial, if not ludicrous, by the Chinese themselves.

THE PROBLEM OF REGIONALISM

One immediate problem would be ensuring that, whenever nuclear
weapons are deployed, they serve only the interests and the purposes
of the highest central authorities. For this, a formal, if not legal,
procedure must be established and safeguards instituted so that the
system cannot be compromised. But whenever one considers nuclear
dispersal and large numbers of tactical warheads widely distributed
throughout the country, the technical and mechanical problems of
command and control become enormous. Under such an arrangement,
it is impossible to control the actual arming and detonation of a nuclear
warhead from a source not physically present on the scene.* One
must instead presume a high level of political stability within the country in general and a high degree of internal cohesion within the military
in particular. From the perspective of the leadership, it may be the
height of fantasy to envision "nuclear civil war," even during the most
severe periods of self-induced internal upheaval (the Great Leap
Forward and the Cultural Revolution). But even in "normal" times,
the relatively decentralized military organization that may have been
imposed on China for a variety of extramilitary reasons would still
present a not-insignificant problem.

For organizational purposes, China is divided into eleven military
regions, only two of which (Tibet and Sinkiang) are presumed to be
responsible directly to the civilian authorities in Peking, rather than
to the highest military authorities. Knowledge of the actual authority
of each regional commander is limited, nor is it known whether the
regions are actually "regional" in the sense that personnel are, as a

------

*The actual arming of the nuclear warheads of American land-
based strategic missiles can be controlled independently from the
launching of the rocket itself. This is accomplished by a so-called
permissive-linkage system, which allows the warhead to sit in readiness atop the missile, but prevents it from being armed until a specific
electronic message is received from another source. This is not a
practical proposition for other forms of delivery systems, especially
at the tactical level. There exists the possibility of storing the warheads separately from the missiles and keeping the storage facilities
under the control of a separate agency.

matter of policy, assigned to the same region from which they are recruited or whether each region is dependent upon "regional" as distinct from "central" supplies. It is believed, however, that each regional commander commands not only the regular PLA ground formations in his area but also any air, naval, or civilian-militia forces in his region. This arrangement makes a certain degree of sense in terms of the widely accepted belief about China's "defense-in-depth" strategy. But its applicability to a nuclear strategy can be and probably has been questioned by the central leadership.

Indeed, it would seem that the leadership has been extremely judicious in diffusing nuclear weapons within this system. Such weapons are under the control of the so-called Second Artillery units of the PLA, about which relatively little is known. This group was first mentioned in the Chinese press in March, 1965. People's Daily revealed the name of the political commissar of the Second Artillery (Li T'ien-huan) in January, 1968; his background in the Public Security forces has led to the assumption that elements from the Public Security division (the Peking garrison) served as the early organizational base for the Second Artillery.* Cadre for these units may have been drawn from the work forces of the defense industries. Over the years, the names of the key personnel in the command structure have never been made public, so that it is difficult to chart the internal history of the Second Artillery.

As the organization most closely identified with advanced weapons technology, however, the Second Artillery must have been involved in the debates and struggles related to the two military lines.[17] The increased political importance that regular PLA units acquired during and after the Cultural Revolution, and the prospect of near-term conflict with the Soviet Union (late 1969) may have turned both regional and central leaders' attention to conventional forces, for both their political and military manifestations. In fact, there seems to be little evidence that the nuclear weapons lobby was able to profit by the political instability and increase its organizational independence and/or its claim on resources, even though it may have been successful in resisting ad hoc proposals for the upgrading of PLA capabilities in the medium-technology area.[18]

---

*Armed forces under the organizational control of the Committee for State Security (KGB) were the earliest custodians of nuclear weaponry in the Soviet Union, so such an arrangement in the Chinese case does not seem implausible.

THE FUTURE

All this may suggest that, for a variety of political reasons, over-all Chinese military development may proceed along two independent routes that will become increasingly divergent over time. It may well be the aim of the leadership to ensure that the strategic-weapons program continues to develop in an atmosphere as divorced as possible from the ongoing process of military-bureaucratic politics. This would be in keeping with both the ideological and the practical considerations that enter into the formation of strategic policy. It would be in accordance with Maoist precepts about controlling the rate at which technology enters into the regular army, yet it would maintain the central leadership's undisputed control over nuclear assets.

If there is any plausibility to this view, it is not unlikely that the leadership will pursue organizational, production, and strategic policies designed to maximize the international effect and minimize the internal effect of Chinese nuclear weapons. This would imply the acquisition of weapons best adapted to an independent strategic-forces organization. The leadership may well recognize that such an arrangement is not the most desirable from the purely military point of view, but this would not have been the first time that "politics took command."

Ironically, such a development within China would coincide with the aims of those who wish to integrate China into international arms-control arrangements, for "strategic" weaponry is the only component of nuclear arsenals that seems susceptible to such agreements. Yet, the ability of the leadership to prevent a separate "rocket service" from one day aspiring to a leading position among the armed forces will also remain in doubt. It may be possible to control the discussion of military doctrine and to emphasize repeatedly that no new look based on nuclear weapons or other advanced technology can ever have any dialectical validity. The Maoists may even be expected to launch cultural revolutions on a periodic basis to break up lobbies and shatter old factional alignments. But to institutionalize uncertainty in this was is, paradoxically, to promote time-serving, careerism, bureaucratism, and so on, and to stifle the very imagination and creativity that the Maoists say they wish to promote.

Meanwhile, Chinese nuclear capability grows apace. Each new missile requires one more crew of experts who, in the nature of things, must devote more time to the technical manual and less to the Maoist book, at least when learning their jobs. The initial excitement of nuclear acquisition and the pressure of catching up with the advanced

nations may well give way to a time when nuclear weapons are but
another fact of Chinese life. At that point, the peculiar mathematics
of cost effectiveness and of the balance of terror could be internalized
even by the Chinese. Perhaps they will then recall Chairman Mao's
phrase of an earlier era: "We want to do business. . . ."

NOTES

1. We do not oppose learning advanced techniques from foreign
countries . . . We must take the initiative in learning and use what
we have learned to serve our purposes" ("Grasp Firmly the Struggle
Between the Two Lines to Deepen and Carry on the Revolution in
Designing," Radio Peking Domestic Service, April 19, 1971).

2. During 1950-59, "the majority of Soviet personnel sent to
China were technicians . . . Only about 8 percent of the 11,000 Soviet-
aid personnel were senior scientists, and they seldom stayed in Communist China longer than four months" (Chu-yuan Cheng, Scientific
and Engineering Manpower in Communist China, 1949-1963 [Washington,
D.C.: National Science Foundation, 1965], p. 187).

3. "In Scientific Research We Must Persevere in the Orientation
of Serving the Workers, Peasants, and Soldiers," "Thoroughly Repudiate
the Idea of 'Private Ownership of Knowledge,'" "The Doctrine of
'Knowledge Belongs to the Individual and Achievement Belongs to the
Public' Must be Repudiated," JMJP, March 19, 1971; translated in
SCMP, LXXI, 13, pp. 156-66.

4. William L. Ryan and Sam Summerlin, The China Cloud (Boston: Little, Brown, 1968).

5. In an interview with an American correspondent, Chou En-lai
is reported to have said that the explosion of a Chinese atomic bomb
was "thanks to Soviet behavior since Soviet experts had been withdrawn
and the Chinese were compelled to rely on their own strength" (New
York Times, May 21, 1971, p. 10).

6. Just how general this knowledge has become is suggested by
recent concern over the possibility of an international black market
in plutonium. The proliferation of nuclear reactors makes it conceivable that military-usuable fissionable material may fall into private
hands. It takes only five kilograms of plutonium to manufacture a
Hiroshima-type bomb. And "the technology and hardware are available
—many sources recommend the World Book as a good text on atomic-

bomb building" (Deborah Shapley, "Plutonium: Reactor Proliferation Threatens a Nuclear Black Market," Science, April 9, 1971, p. 144).

7. Though weapons "do not decide everything," they may decide more about a nation's future policies than is envisioned at the time they are developed. One student of the American military has observed, for example:

> Although development of the B-52 cost less than $500 million, the price of creating and maintaining a B-52 operational capability for the last fifteen years has exceeded $25 billion, and the continued presence of that aircraft in the strategic inventory has vitally influenced decisions on the composition of the national war plan, the character of the probable national response to nuclear attack, relations with various foreign powers (Spain and Japan, for instance), and the structure of the assured destruction strategy on which national defense policy has hinged. Had a different sort of bomber been introduced, or had the B-52 been phased out in the early 1960s, as was planned, the cost, structure, and operations of the entire defense establishment certainly would be different. The behavior of the military services and the character of the national-defense effort is directly related to the nature of system acquisition choices and development policies.

Adam Yarmolinsky, The Military Establishment (New York: Harper and Row, 1971), p. 260.

8. Both materials were used in the earliest American atomic bombs. The first bomb tested used plutonium; the one dropped on Hiroshima used enriched uranium. For a discussion of the problem of fissionable materials, see Institute of Strategic Studies, The Military Balance, 1970-1971 (London: Institute of Strategic Studies, 1971), pp. 121-126.

9. The three plants in the United States, if operated at full capacity, would consume more than 52 billion kilowatt hours of electricity per year, "which is approximately equal to the total electricity consumption of Australia." Institute of Strategic Studies, Military Balance, p. 123.

10. Leonard Beaton and John Maddox, The Spread of Nuclear Weapons (New York: Praeger Publishers 1962), p. 123. The authors

correctly predicted that China's first nuclear test would occur in the latter part of 1964.

11. There are no hard-and-fast estimates on the costs of acquiring a nuclear arsenal. Australian authorities, in estimating the costs of an Australian nuclear deterrent, concluded that it would require an initial capital investment of about $1 billion, the assignment of 1,000 scientists and technicians, and annual expenses of about $80 million per year. A hundred missiles with silos could be had for about $1.75 billion, with an additional $500 million for guidance and warning systems and about $100 million per year to maintain and operate the missile system. Australian Institute of International Affairs, "Nuclear Dispersal in Asia and the Indo-Pacific Region," (Canberra, February, 1965).

12. Official American predictions would seem to have underestimated the lead times involved in the Chinese missile program. In February, 1970, Dr. John Foster, Director of Defense Research and Engineering, reported that during 1969 the Chinese had built ICBM launching facilities and had reached the point where they were ready to conduct ICBM tests. In March, 1970, Secretary Laird said that an I CBM flight test was expected that year, and he went on to project a Chinese inventory of 10-25 ICBMs for 1975. In March, 1971, the Secretary stated that a "small number" of MRBMs would be deployed by mid-1971. An IRBM capability is projected by 1973, but the Chinese "probably could not have significant numbers of ICBMs deployed until late in the decade." (Statement Before the House Armed Services Committee, March 9, 1971.)

13. Comparisons in this area are dangerous and can be misleading. The only standard is that of France, but the geographical factors are very different, making the entire emphasis of the French program different. It was not until January, 1971, that France announced that it would proceed with the development of a hydrogen warhead. The largest warhead in the French inventory has an estimated yeild of 500 kilotons. The current French force consists of 36 Mirage 4A bombers in the 1,000-mile range, capable of delivering 60 kiloton free-fall warheads. The first Polaris-type submarine is due to enter service in early 1971 and to be joined by 4 others by 1975. In terms of land-based missiles, the first silo-based nine-missile unit is due to become operational by mid-1971, each missile having a range of about 1,800 miles. The French are also developing shorter-range systems designed to deliver tactical warheads. International Defense Review, February, 1971, pp. 19-20.

14. The detection of plutonium in 1969 nuclear tests, an underground test of the same year, and other related technical developments

may indicate that the Chinese are turning toward an emphasis on the "battlefield" use of nuclear weapons and are deemphasizing the development of a multimegaton warhead for long-range delivery. For an assessment of the evidence, see Alice Langley Hsieh, "China's Nuclear Missile Programme: Regional or Intercontinental?," China Quarterly, No. 45, January-March, 1971, pp. 85-99.

15. For example, the authoritative Institute of Strategic Studies observes: "As the Chinese Government has not made public any budget figures since 1960, China's defence expenditure can only be estimated. If one accepts the American view that China is spending 9-10 per cent of her GNP on defence (including defence R & D), and assuming that in 1970, the economy has at last move above the 1966 level, then Professor T. C. Liu's calculation of the GNP for late 1966 at 11.8 billion yuan indicates a defence expenditure figure of approximately 12.0 billion yuan today ($4,880,000,000). Calculation of the GNP in dollar purchasing power (about $80 billion) would indicate a rather higher defence expenditure." The Military Balance, 1970-1971, p.57.

16. Harry Harding and Melvin Gurtov, The Purge of Lo Jui-ch'ing: The Politics of Chinese Strategic Planning, Report R-548-PR (Santa Monica, Cal.: The Rand Corporation, February 1971), p. iii. The authors conclude, inter alia, that alternative defense policies can be evaluated to some extent "according to narrow bureaucratic interests," that the domestic implications of strategic postures are carefully considered, and that "the Maoists are reluctant to permit the national security functions of the PLA to take precedence . . . over its domestic political functions."

17. An article appearing in the December, 1967, issue of Chieh-fang-chun Wen-i [Literature of the People's Liberation Army] by Li T'ung-cheng of the Second Artillery's political department, mentioned that among the leadership of the Second Artillery there was a handful of "capitalist roaders" who were awaiting the opportunity to stage a comeback. This would seem to imply that a "reorganization" had taken place sometime previously. Cited in Chin Ch'ien-li, "Survey of Chinese Communist Artillery and 'Second Artillery,' " Hsing-tao Jih -pao [Hsingtao Daily], (Hongkong), December 30, 1970, p. 4. Translated by the Joint Publications Research Service, Translations on Communist China, No. 134, February 18, 1971, p. 10.

18. Prior to his removal, Chinese Chief of Staff Lo Jui-ch'ing had proposed such things as an upgrading of air defense in response to American escalation in Vietnam. Harding and Gurtov, Purge, p. 55 refer to Red Guard commentaries that suggested that Lo's proposals threatened the advanced-weapons program. Presumably, those

associated with the program would have been among those who "could be expected to be skeptical and critical of Lo's proposals."

13

THE ROLE
OF THE
CHINESE COMMUNIST
AIR FORCE
IN THE 1970s

Franz J. Mogdis

Any attempt to describe the development of the Chinese Communist air force over the last twenty years and, moreover, to project into the future what the 1970s hold for this arm of the PLA is faced with an almost insurmountable problem—the lack of reliable information and data.[1] Nevertheless, the importance today of this element of the PLA is such that an effort must be made to assess its present position and future development. This chapter will briefly trace the growth of the Chinese air force in the 1950s and 1960s, discuss its current status, and suggest what the future may hold.

HISTORICAL DEVELOPMENT

The Chinese Communist air force was formally organized late in 1949 under the command of General Liu Ya-lou, who had been up until that time the chief of staff of the Fourth Field Army. At its inception, the air force numbered no more than 100 usable aircraft, and this included civil transport. As Liu Ya-lou was to later relate, the modernization of the air force was to become an extremely difficult task. "The new China was just established, our national economy was in rags, our industrial foundation was very weak, and there was no aviation industry at all."[2] As a result of these constraints, the air force was to become the most dependent of all of the services upon Soviet military aid and upon rapid modernization of indigenous Chinese industries. Both of these dependencies and the pressures they created to opt for supportive domestic and foreign-policy positions were factors that were to have severe repercussions for many of the CCAF leaders in the late 1960s and early 1970s.

During this early period, the new air-force leadership, like that of the navy, was for the most part by necessity made up of personnel shifted from the ground forces. Although a few pilots had received training during World War II, the majority of the top leaders of the embryonic air force were nonrated; that is, they were not qualified as pilots for any type of aircraft. Thus, it became an unescapable fact of life that the buildup had to be carried out using not only Soviet equipment but also the guidance of Soviet advisers.

The Korean War was to alter this picture somewhat, however, and to provide the initial impetus to the growth of the air force, both in trained personnel and in equipment. In the area of personnel, the experience gained against UN forces in Korea provided a new generation of rated leaders who gradually assumed command of operational units. Between 1953 and 1971, these younger leaders were to move quickly into key positions in air armies and divisions. As a result, the air-force members of military-region staffs, for example, tended to be the youngest members of that staff. This factor created another reason for the friction that developed between the air force and other career channels within the PLA.

By late 1951, General Vandenburg, the U.S. Air Force chief of staff, was to note that, in terms of capability, "almost overnight China has become one of the major air powers of the world."[3] The greater part of Soviet assistance during this period consisted of modern jet aircraft, mainly MIG-15 jet fighters, but also included a smaller number of IL-28 twin-jet bombers. As reported by John Gittings, at the end of 1950 the Chinese probably had no more than 500 planes, the majority of which were propeller fighters.[4] By the end of 1951, this total had tripled to around 1,500, of which at least half were jets, and by the end of the war the air force's total strength was around 2,000 aircraft, with 900-1,000 of these jet fighters and bombers.

After the war ended, the attention of the air force—for that matter the entire PLA—shifted back to the southern coastal provinces of Kwangtung and Fukien opposite Taiwan. This attention resulted in the rapid construction of airfields and other logistic support facilities as well as redeployment from Manchuria to the south of the majority of the air force's aircraft. From 1953 until mid-1968, there seems to have been only minimal shifts in the location of any air-force units. The effect of this stability in location was to create a situation where over a fifteen-year period the air-force units at a particular location developed very strong ties to the military region at the expense of central control from Peking. Increasingly as time passed, the command and control of air units became more decentralized and directly tied to the military region within which the unit was located. In retrospect, it is evident that a lasting result of the Korean War was to place the air force in a position of being a competitor for limited funds and resources—funds and resources the air force felt should be directed to supporting the development of a modern air force and later an advanced-weapons program.

This feeling was reinforced by the air force's almost immediate problem after the war of rapidly aging aircraft because of a lack of spare parts for repairs. The air force also found itself severely limited because of a lack of sufficient high-octane aircraft fuel. The severity of these two problems—critical before 1960—grew even worse with the total withdrawal of Soviet assistance in 1960. The lack of spare parts and fuel resulted in a situation that inhibited both the satisfactory training of new pilots and the rapid expansion of the air force itself. This situation put great pressure on air-force leadership to guarantee that priority development be given to solving these two problems irrespective of cost.

Early in the game (perhaps as early as 1953), a decision was also made that the PLA, in general, and most certainly the air force would develop along defensive lines. This resulted in the emphasis being placed on priority development of fighter aircraft, radar, and other defensive systems, and not on the development of an offensive delivery capability. As indicated in Table 5, the strength of the air force has been and remains even today basically a defensive force. Indeed, today it is probable that the Chinese Communist air force could give a credible performance against conventional manned fighter and bomber attacks from external sources. It, however, has only minimal defensive capability against nuclear-tipped missiles. The development of the air force in this defensive mode is a fairly clear and unambiguous trend. Much less clear, however, is the developing political affiliations of the air force.

When Mao Tse-tung decided to go nuclear in the mid-1950s, it certainly was done at the expense of the ground forces—thus, giving a real boost to the air force. This decision was to reinforce strongly the air force's position of being a prime competitor for severely limited funds and resources. An increasingly large percentage of these resources were to go to the advanced-weapons program, and these were funds and resources that could only be obtained at the expense of other elements in the resource process, particularly in the army and civil sectors. It seems certain that across time there developed bitter and intense rivalries between the air-force and the

TABLE 5

Growth of Chinese Communist Air Force, 1950-70

Entry	1950	1955	1960	1965	1970
Manpower[a]	40,000	125,000	175,000	225,000	250,000
Jet fighters[b]	-	800	1,100	1,600	2,500
Piston fighters	400	200	-	-	-
Jet light bombers[c]	-	150	175	160	150
Piston light bombers	50	175	125	80	75
Medium bombers[d]	-	10	15	10	20
Piston light transport	50	100	120	150	400
Turbo transport	-	-	-	10	20
Jet reconnaissance	-	-	15	15	15
Helicopter	-	-	50	125	225

[a]Perhaps as many as 50 percent of current air-force personnel (1970) are assigned to radar, AAA, and SAM-2 air-defense units.

[b]The majority are MIG-15s and MIG-17s, but a growing number of Chinese produced MIG-19s (since 1964 or 1965) and a few MIG-21s.

[c]All of the light bombers are probably Russian IL-28s.

[d]Majority are TU-16s; China now has these in series production and is expected to have a significant force by mid-1972.

army leadership over who was to receive priority funding—rivalries that were to surface in the purges of 1968 and 1971.

A second factor that only served to reinforce the increasing rivalry between the two services was the question of elitism. As the advanced-weapons program progressed in its development and increased in size and as the regular air force modernized, the Chinese Communist air force became more and more specialized and technocratically oriented. Increasingly, the air force found itself in a position of having to defend itself against charges of putting elitism and technology ahead of ideology. Moreover, because of its very nature (a new, numerically expanding organization), opportunities for advancement were much greater in the air force than in any of the other services. Increasingly, the question of internal equity within the PLA was raised. The gap between the levels of possible attainment and the speed with which it could be reached for those in the air force and other services became wider and wider as time passed.

The civil sector also became an early competitor of the air force. The nature of air-force weaponry required expenditure of large amounts of limited resources for factories and development of production capabilities that contributed little to the over-all development of the Chinese economy. The highly sophisticated equipment and technology needed for advanced weapons, for fighter aircraft, and for radar could be and was produced only at very high costs. These costs were paid, but at the expense of support for basic industries that would have contributed to the long-term growth and expansion of the economy. Increasingly, the economic planners— those in the civil sector who realized that China required priority allocation of its limited resources to the expansion of basic industries if it was to ever extricate itself from the economic bottleneck with which it was confronted—found themselves siding with the army against the air force.

The issue that continually swung the pendulum in favor of the air force when priority decisions on allocation of resources were made was the air force's ability to point to a major external threat, In the 1950s, the threat was the United States. The United States as a nuclear power with sophisticated nuclear delivery systems and a noncontiguous border with China posed a threat that realistically could not be defended against using conventional ground forces. Although the decision to maintain a defensive posture continued, in order for this to be successful it was apparent that the defensive capability of the PLA needed to be upgraded so as to allow it to be able to defend against the capabilities of a threat that primarily

came from manned bombers and fighters. As the Sino-Soviet conflict
intensified in the early 1960s, and as the Vietnam War expanded in
size, the position of the air force became even stronger. Now, rather
than facing one major enemy, the air force could argue that a severe
threat existed from two—the Soviet Union and the United States—and
that the only way China could deal with two enemies was by even
greater and more rapid expansion of the air force and the advanced-
weapons programs. Moreover, in retrospect it seems probable that
the air force was also able in the mid-1960s to push successfully
for a modification of the existing defensive military posture being
pursued by China by arguing that an offensive capability was needed
so as to be able to credibly threaten retaliatory or preemptive
nuclear action against nations on China's periphery (in particular,
Japan, Indonesia, and India). This change in strategy was reflected
in increased priorities being assigned to the development of an
operational medium-range ballistic missile (MRBM) and a Chinese-
produced offensive bomber capable of delivering nuclear weapons.

Design, growth, and, for that matter, deployment of not only
air but also ground and naval units since the mid-1950s thus seems
to have reflected only limited concern with specific global military
and political issues. The dynamics of decision-making in this area
rather seem to have been a function of a more generally perceived
threat from the United States and from the Soviet Union and, moreover, was an outcome of internal debates over distribution of power
and status within the high command and between the military and
civil sectors over priority-setting in the allocation of China's
limited resources.

FROM THE CULTURAL REVOLUTION
TO THE PRESENT

Following the death of General Liu Ya-lou, commander-in-chief
of the air force (a post he had held since the formation of the air
force in 1949), in the late spring of 1965, Wu Fa-hsien was appointed
as the new head of the air force. This was a political appointment
that sidestepped Wang P'ing-cheng, Liu's former deputy commander
and then minister in charge of the seventh ministry of machine
building. This seemed to put the air force under full Party power
for the first time. Wu had been assigned to the air force in the
early 1950s as its deputy political commissar and became the full
political commissar during the purge of P'eng Teh-huai in 1959.
Although Wu was untrained in the management of air-force operations
and functions, his political connections gave him great powers, and
the air force seemed to become a model instrument of Party policies.

Almost immediately on the heels of Wu's official appointment as the new commander of the air force, the Cultural Revolution began in Shanghai in November, 1965. It would certainly seem probable that Wu's selection as the new head of the air force was made with forehand knowledge of the forthcoming Cultural Revolution and, indeed, that he was selected to lead the air force during this rectification campaign by the very leaders who were responsible for directing that the Cultural Revolution be carried out.

Until May, 1967, it looked as if the air force would remain relatively unaffected by the purges taking place across the country as an outgrowth of the Cultural Revolution. This, however, proved to be only the lull before the storm, for in May, 1967, Lin Piao personally initiated an attack on "anti-Mao personnel" in the armed forces, claiming that "malicious elements" had all but taken control of the air force. The first casualty was Chang Ting-fa, then deputy commander of the air force. Within a matter of months, the only air-force officers that still held their posts were the commander-in-chief, one deputy commander, and a deputy political commissar. The purges ended in late March, 1968, when the CCP leadership abruptly announced at a large Peking rally that acting PLA Chief of Staff Yang Cheng-wu, air force Political Commissar Yu Li-chin, and Peking garrison Commander Fu Ch'ung-pi were the "backstage bosses" of the entire May 16 conspiracy to overthrow the government and to usurp the leadership of the air force by overthrowing Wu Fa-hsien.

Within two and a half years after taking over as head of the air force, Wu was able to look around and see that with the exception of one or two leaders the entire hierarchy of the air force had been replaced with his choices. (See Table 6 for a listing of current key air-force personnel.) It is certain that this was only possible with the strongest of support from the very highest levels—in this case, Lin Piao and probably Huang Yung-sheng.

From the early spring of 1968 until 1971, it looked as if, at least in the air force's case, the problems that had caused dissension and conflict within the ranks that had been so evident during the Cultural Revolution were solved. Then came the dramatic reversal of Chinese policy vis-à-vis the United States, concurrent with a major shift in economic priorities in early 1971; indications of dissension within the highest levels of leadership in the summer of 1971; and the unusual events in China in the fall of 1971.

It seems quite certain that the Chinese Communist air force played a major role in the events that took place in China in

TABLE 6

Current Air-Force Personnel

Position	Name
Commander	Wu Fa-hsien*
Deputy commanders	Ch'ang Ch'ien-k'un Kuang Jen-nung T'an Chia-shu Ts'ao Li-huai Tseng Kuo-hua
Deputy political commissar	Wang Hui-ch'iu
Responsible persons of PLA units under air force	Chi Yao-yeh Chiao Ching-wen Chu Hsu-chih Ho Te-ch'uan Hsia Li Hsueh Shao-ch'ing Liang P'u Wang Yung-hua Yang Kao-ming Yuan Chi-choy

*Purged as of September, 1971.

Source: Directory of Chinese Communist Officials, A 71-14, (Washington, D.C.: Department of State, May, 1971).

September and in October, 1971. First, the CPR's domestic air services were mysteriously interrupted from September 13 to 15, and international flights were reported altered without explanation during this period. While civilian flights were resumed after the three-day stoppage, military air traffic over China continued into November to be marked by unusual flight patterns. Second, Japanese reports from Peking on September 22 stated that the PLA had canceled all furloughs and had called back all soldiers in the past few days to guard against any possible confusion that might occur when the government made an "important announcement." Third, Moscow radio reported on September 30 that a Chinese military aircraft

on a direct route from Peking had crashed 100 miles into Mongolia
on September 13, killing nine people. Fourth, a group of Japanese
parliamentarians who were due to meet Chou En-lai in Peking on
September 11 were told that the meeting was to be postponed until
September 16. From September 12 to 16, virtually all of the CCP
Politburo members and all of the top military leaders dropped out
of sight, suggesting an important CC meeting at that time. Finally,
on September 21, with preparations for the twenty-second anniversary
celebration of the founding of the CPR well underway, Peking in an
unprecedented move announced that the October 1 parade had been
canceled because of a "reform" and that the anniversary celebrations
would concentrate on the "concrete deeds" of the CPR. The following
week, diplomats in Peking were told that the banquet normally given
by Premier Chou En-lai on the eve of National Day had been downgraded to a reception to be hosted by the Foreign Ministry. Even
at the height of the chaos created by the Cultural Revolution such
restrictions had not occurred.

In the absence of any official explanation of these events in
China, it is only possible to speculate on the true situation in the
country, but it seems certain that an internal political conflict
developed during the spring and summer and that it reached crisis
stages in September. Moreover, it also seems certain that the crisis
was either precipitated by or involved the country's armed forces.
It would seem that a reasonable explanation for the events themselves and the causes that precipitated the crisis is that the CCP
Politburo was deadlocked in a dispute over funds for modernization
of the military, in particular, funds for the Chinese Communist air
force. As noted earlier, intense resentment had built up against the
air force since 1953—resentment from both the army and the civil
sector over the air force's success in obtaining money for their
programs, money obtained at the expense of the army's and the civil
sector's development. The reason for this success, as noted, was
the air force's ability to demonstrate a major threat from the United
States and the Soviet Union.

It seems apparent, however, that the moderates gained the
upper hand in the early spring of 1971, and perhaps even as early as
late 1970. As a result of their success, there was a new look at the
"real" threat from outside, and there seems to have been an acceptance of the view that the United States, in fact, presented no "real"
or realistic first-strike threat to China and that China's major
enemy and threat was the Soviet Union. (Although to outsiders this
seemed like a rapid and radical shift, the change in attitude had been
gradually taking place over the preceding four or five years. As

FIGURE 4

Chinese Evaluative Perceptions
of the United States and the Soviet Union
(Positive-Negative)

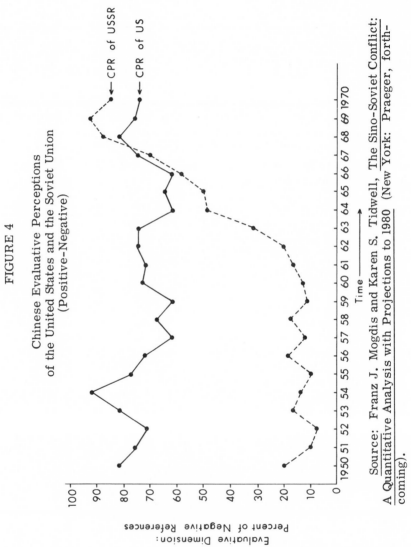

Source: Franz J. Mogdis and Karen S. Tidwell, The Sino-Soviet Conflict:
A Quantitative Analysis with Projections to 1980 (New York: Praeger, forthcoming).

262

Figure 4 shows, by 1967 the Soviet Union was seen more negatively and as a greater threat than was the United States.) Accepting this change in perception, however, meant that the air force's trump card had been taken away from it. It no longer could justify its budgetary demands in terms of a major threat from two enemies. Even more important, the key enemy in the air force's justification had been the one that was eliminated. Because the United States was noncontiguous to China, the air force could and had argued in the past that the army's ground forces were for the most part useless in defending against a U.S. attack, unless, of course, the United States invaded with ground forces, and everyone knew they had no intentions of fighting a land war on the mainland. The only way, therefore, to defend against such an attack was to increase the defensive capability of the air force and advanced-weapons program as rapidly as possible. When applied to the Soviet case, however, the same argument wasn't nearly as strong. The Soviets shared a 4,500-mile common border with China, and all of a sudden the army, with its ground forces and large numbers of personnel, became the most important element in defending China against a Soviet attack. Given the decision that Moscow, not Washington, was the major military threat to consider and plan for, roles had suddenly been reversed. Now the army found itself in the driver's seat, and the air force found itself on the outside.

What exactly transpired during the Politburo deliberations is still unclear, but it seems probable that final approval was given to a major reversal of economic priorities as outlined in the fourth five-year plan, to continuation of increased U.S.-CPR ties, and to China's acceptance of UN membership—all three, final defeats for the Lin Piao faction.[5] In the economic area, the five-year plan stressed the primary role of agriculture and light industry in providing the raw materials and surplus wealth for development of the heavy sector, with a reduction in spending on the armed forces. There are strong indications that the air force was to bear the brunt of the reduction in military spending; for example, the vital electronics industry (vital to the air force, that is) was drastically downgraded in priority, with the funds instead going to expand basic industries (e.g., steel). The goal, of course, was to expand the mechanize agriculture—that is, to use the increased steel production to increase the number of tractors produced yearly.[6]

It seems quite probable and certainly understandable that Air Force Commander Wu Fa-hsien was unwilling to accept these decisions gracefully. It is also reasonable that PLA Chief of Staff Huang Yung-sheng, formerly in command of air defense in South

China, was strongly opposed to a reduction in funds for modernization of the air force. These two, along with Lin, winners in 1968,
now faced the ultimate defeat and a loss of power to the moderate
faction headed by Chou En-lai. If so, and a planned coup failed, the
disappearance from view of Lin, Huang, and Wu, as well as many of
their colleagues, is easily explained.[7]

Irrespective of the exact sequence of events, it is clear that
the air force has suffered a severe blow to its power within the
Chinese decision-making apparatus in the last half of 1971. This is
a loss of power that will have a lasting impact on the future role and
development of the air force.

THE FUTURE

Unless there is a major shift in the Chinese perception of who
their primary enemy is, and such a shift seems highly unlikely,
there is little liklihood that the air force will again play a dominant
role in determining how economic priorities will be set and resources
allocated. As long as the Soviet Union remains the prime threat,
the army will play the major role in Chinese military strategy.
What this means is that even if the moderates were to lose out to
more radical leadership in the 1970s, it is doubtful that the air force's
power would be greatly increased. Thus, in the 1970s it seems
reasonable to anticipate a Chinese military strategy for their security
problems that is similar to the way the Soviets approached their
security problems in the 1950s. That is to say, rather than concerning themselves with excessive commitments of resources to
an ICBM program, it would seem more likely that ground-oriented
first and second-generation Chinese leaders will accent weapons
systems and political gambits aimed at placing major American and
Russian clients on China's borders in a hostage status.

It does not mean, however, that the Air Force will not continue
to expand and grow in the 1970s, for it most certainly will. The
direction and the rate of growth, however, will be different than one
would have expected or projected prior to the events of 1971. The
emphasis will probably be on continued but reduced levels of production of MIG-19s and an effort to put into series production a
Chinese version of the Soviet MIG-21. One can also expect a major
effort to upgrade existing jet fighters to an all-weather capability
(perhaps as few as 10 percent of Chinese aircraft currently have
that capability). The production of TU-16s also will probably continue, but again at reduced rates.

TABLE 7

Estimated Growth of Chinese Communist
Air Force, 1972-80

Entry	1972	1975	1980
Manpower	275,000	325,000	350,000
Jet aircraft	2,700	3,200	3,900
Jet light bombers	125	100	50
Piston light bombers	50	25	-
Medium bombers	30	50-75	100-200
ICBMs	-	5	15-25
MRBMs	5-10	50-75	200-300
IRBMs	2-5	25-40	100-250

The change of direction will certainly effect the advanced-weapons program. It will probably mean only a minimal effort to develop and deploy an operational ICBM (maximum range: approximately 6,500 miles) in the 1970s. The Chinese will probably also deploy a small number of MRBMs (maximum range: approximately 1,200 miles). The emphasis, however, will be on the development and deployment of an operational IRBM (maximum range: approximately 2,300 miles). This is to be used as an additional threat to the nations on the periphery of China (including the Soviet Union, but significantly not the United States). The IRBM will allow China to reach targets in the Soviet Union otherwise inaccessible to nuclear attack. Table 7 presents estimated levels of growth for the Chinese air force in the 1970s.

In the final analysis, the 1970s seem to hold for the Chinese Communist air force a future that includes limited growth, reduced visibility and prestige, and certainly reduced power in the decision-making process.

NOTES

1. The best single work on the Chinese Communist air force is Richard Bueschel, Communist Chinese Air Power (New York: Praeger, 1968). Also see John Gittings, The Role of the Chinese Army (New York: Oxford University Press, 1967); and Robert Futrell and Lawson Moseley, The United States Air Force in Korea: 1950-1953 (New York: Duell, Sloan and Pearce, 1961).

2. Liu Ya-lou, "The Young Air Force of the Chinese PLA," JMJP, July 31, 1957; translated in SCMP, No. 1596, Aug., 1957.

3. As reported in David Rees, Korea: The Limited War (New York: Macmillan, 1964), pp. 370-78.

4. Gittings, Chinese Army, pp. 136-41.

5. Washington Post, November 5, 1971, A-1.

6. Far Eastern Economic Review, October 9, 1971, p. 7.

7. One story, supposedly receiving wide circulation within China, is that in fact the demise of Lin Piao was due to his attempt to overthrow Mao, with the fellow conspirators being Huang Yung-sheng, and Wu Fa-hsien. The story continues that Lin, Huang, and Wu were killed in an air crash in Mongolia while trying to flee China. Far Eastern Economic Review, November 27, 1971, p. 5.

14

THE INTERNAL ROLE
OF THE MILITARY
Paul Elmquist

"Ample" is virtually all that need be said of the PLA's capability to handle any internal threats to the authority of the PRC. But this conclusion—based on the army's present stature in the country and within the CCP—may be simplistic, and is certainly open to challenge. It is, therefore, desirable to look deeper into the situation and to examine the PLA in some detail as a tool for political control.

In countering internal threats to the regime, the PLA has essentially two roles. It directs police and Public Security forces, which in turn are backed up by army regulars, and it exercises an important degree of political leadership, particularly through its interrelationships with the Party. This essay treats the PLA primarily in its second role, as a political-leadership force. The thesis is that the PLA politicization program—the source of a deep mutual involvement with the CCP—will be very hard to reverse.*

———————————

*There has never been a time when there was not PLA-CCP involvement, the leading figures of both often being the same persons. Institutionally, however, the 1950s saw a trend toward a division of labor between PLA and CCP that began to be reversed after 1959.

———————————

Views expressed in this chapter are solely those of the author and do not represent the official position of any U.S. government agency.

As the political-leadership role unfolded in the 1960s, three related tasks emerged. By 1964, the PLA was being drawn into Party reform by Mao's dissatisfaction with the CCP performance in political action. A second task of supporting political revolution materialized between mid-1965 and August, 1966. With the deterioration of public order thereafter, the PLA then shouldered a third task of directly supervising the organization of emergency government, beginning in January, 1967. In 1967 and 1968, however, the task of revolutionary support often took precedence over the keeping of the peace. Whether to support, suppress, or overlook and stand aside from the activities of specific local groups contending for power often called for a politically complex decision from a military-unit commander.

POLITICIZATION OF THE PLA

The Mission After 1959

A lengthy retrospective discourse, "Commemorate the 50th Anniversary of the Communist Party of China," was published on June 30, 1971.[1] It reiterated Mao's precept of 1938 (in "Problems of War and Strategy") that "Our principle is that the party commands the gun, and the gun must never be allowed to command the party."[2] The 1971 statement gave little space to the current political work of the PLA, but it succinctly summarized the PLA leadership contribution to the political tasks of emergency administration and provisional government during the Cultural Revolution. Invoking CCP history in support of Mao's concept of a revolutionary army, it reiterated the triple mission of the PLA: "Since the day of its founding our People's Liberation Army has been a fighting force . . ., a working force, and a production force, and it has more than 40 years experience in doing mass [political] work. That is why our armymen could easily become one with the masses . . ."

Awareness of the political mission had ebbed in the 1950s until Lin Piao became Minister of National Defense in September, 1959, and began to rebuild the political machinery in the spirit of Mao's 1938 statement. In it, Mao pictured the PLA political role much as it was to be realized in 1966-69:

> Our principle is that the party commands the gun, and the
> gun must never be allowed to command the party. Yet,
> having guns, we can create party organizations, . . . we
> can also create cadres, create schools, create culture,

> create mass movements . . . The army is the chief com-
> ponent of state power. Whoever wants to seize and re-
> tain political power must have a strong army . . . We
> are advocates of the omnipotence of revolutionary war.[3]

Intensive PLA involvement in nonmilitary work began with the
lengthy 1960 "Directive of the Enlarged Meeting of the Central
Military Affairs Commission on Ideological and Political Work in the
Armed Forces."[4] This document, the point of departure for the
politicization of the PLA, was received and adopted at a five-week-
long Enlarged Conference of the MAC in September-October, 1960.
The directive established guidelines, points of departure, and working
formulas. Its symbols were the "four firsts," the "three-eight work
style," the "five-good soldier," and, added a year later, the "four-
good company."[5] Without disparaging modernization, active defense,
and the "liberation of Taiwan," the document dwelt on how to "strengthen
the revolutionary process" and how to "persist in the current direction
of political work."

The leadership mentality idealized in the directive was to be
motivated by a sense of obligation and characterized by a flexible
readiness to serve. The army was told to identify with the people by
methods that would keep individuals in contact with other individuals
in the spirit of "leadership control and mass supervision," and
"collective leadership . . . with individual responsibility . . ." In
the various areas of political work with youth, militia, People's
Armed Police, and regular troops, the working elements—cadres,
political departments and their directors, Party committees and
branches, military units, and the military districts and subdistricts—
were furnished scores of specific suggestions for political work.

Preparation

The GPD of the PLA at a later annual all-PLA work conferences
formulated various lists of commandments: "The Ten Experiences
in Grasping Living Thought" (March, 1961); "Seven Measures for
Improving the Leadership of the Armed Forces Organizations over
Companies" (April, 1962); and "Twelve Basic Experiences in Improving the Work of Companies" (February, 1963).

The February, 1963, PLA political work conference adopted a
new set of "Regulations Governing Political Work in the People's
Liberation Army." They were promulgated by the CC on March 27,
1963, to replace a 1954 set of draft regulations. Set out in detail

was the entire mechanism of relationships between troop commanders,
political commissars, Party committees, and political departments
at all levels from the military region down. The regulations delineated
the GPD mission at the top and the characteristics that military Party
committees should have. They clarified the extensive local role of
People's Armed Forces Departments, which were to be closely
involved with local Party committees in recruitment and conscription,
militia development, cultivation of the Young Communist League, and
Party building.[6]

In 1964, the "learn from the PLA" movement to politicize the
economy and the society called for the creation of a climate of intense
mutual involvement crossing the ordinary protective barriers of
daily life. Mao's policies for the Party, at that time, contained

> the call . . . for the whole country to learn from the People's
> Liberation Army . . . the call for the whole party to grasp
> military affairs and for everybody to be a soldier . . . the
> call for the People's Liberation Army and all factories,
> villages, schools, commercial departments, service trades
> and party and government organizations to become great
> schools of revolution . . .[7]

After the January, 1964, work conference, the "learn from the
PLA" movement was instituted for the country. Its significance
was that Mao had turned to the PLA for help with the Party's problems
in reaching the people. The new movement stressed class-conscious-
ness, industriousness, and ideological self-strengthening. Ostensibly,
the PLA began to work for Party reform. A new apparatus of military-
type political departments utilizing PLA political officers and demobilized servicemen made its appearance in government in 1964.[8]
These departments were established alongside existing Party committees in the same way, apparently, as PLA units had political
departments associated with military Party committees. The intent
was to introduce PLA political-control techniques into the areas of
finance, trade, industry, and transportation. Such departments were
apparently established in the CC as well, and in more than 20 government ministries and bureaus.

The year 1964 was one of dispute between Mao and the CCP
high command, and the imposition of PLA political assistance on
nonmilitary organizations reflected the seriousness of the controversy.
Before 1964, the political indoctrination of PLA officers and men was
an ideological self-strengthening effort, the results of which could
conceivably have been channeled back into the Party to reinvigorate

it. From 1964 on, the PLA cadres were moved into a more exposed and visible political-support role, as though embarrassment to the Party leaders no longer mattered.

In 1965, the emergence of the PLA as a revolutionary force was symbolized by abolishing military ranks. This weakened professional careerism, emphasized the importance of politics, and broke with Soviet influence in rank structure, insignia, and uniforms. PLA personnel were divided into basic categories of commanders, commissars, and fighters. The positions or tasks to which they were assigned then further distinguished them.

Action

The shadow of the Cultural Revolution over the PLA-CCP relationship is likely to be a long one. PLA cadres at lower levels gained leadership experience during those years, a period in which the promotion and leadership experience of people in other occupational groupings were often retarded. The Cultural Revolution years also provided the PLA with experience in civil government and perhaps a taste for continued activity in the civil sphere.

The Cultural Revolution was launched by Mao and his radical helpers—the students—and the PLA over a fourteen-month period extending from November, 1965, when polemics began, to January, 1967, when political reconstruction was ordered to begin. For the PLA, these months were a stage in which the underlying demands for PLA political-leadership support did not change appreciably. The period was to end with the breakdown of the CCP organization, but at its outset the conventional subordination of PLA to CCP was vigorously restated at the January, 1966, GPD all-PLA political work conference. It called for the PLA to carry on and be helpful in political assistance, but to respect Party prerogatives. The conference report seemed to disclaim any PLA intent to outrun the CCP. Emphasizing PLA subordination, it stressed that "the decisive factor in putting politics first was party leadership" and that "the system of dual leadership by the military command and the local party committee under the unified leadership of the party's Central Committee must be resolutely enforced."[9]

From February to April, 1966, the PLA newspaper, Chieh-fang-chun Pao [Liberation Army Daily], published a series of editorials on the primacy of politics. From April on, spearheading the campaign, it initiated use of the term "Great Proletarian Cultural Revolution," and in a series of articles began to dispense ideological guidance. By May and June, thousands of PLA members were helping Red Guards get ready for the coming campaign. The Red Guards made their first unpublicized appearance late in May and were unleashed in August.

The violence soon to erupt found encouragement in Mao Tsetung's incendiary call to "bombard the [Party] headquarters" at the Central Committee's Eleventh Plenary Session in August, 1966. The August 8 "Decision . . . Concerning the Great Proletarian Cultural Revolution" had said, "The only method is for the masses to liberate themselves, and any method of doing things on their behalf [i.e., doing the job for them] must not be used . . . Respect their initiative. Cast out fear. Don't be afraid of disorder . . ."[10] Trouble began in several provinces in August, 1966. With the physical support of the PLA, eight mammoth rallies for 11 million Red Guards were staged in Peking between August and November, 1966. "Power seizures" were recommended to them. The PLA was restrained from interfering when order suffered, weapons were lost, and economic functions and services threatened.

In January, 1967 the PLA entered a new phase of activity when it was committed as a political force to assert leadership both in interim government and in completing the revolution. This enlargement of the political mission accompanied a step-up in the tempo and disruptiveness of the Cultural Revolution, which went into an eight-month period of factional dispute and fighting. Military government began: party-soldiers were moved into virtually every organization and enterprise as centralized controls faded and as provincial governments were overthrown. The governing burden fell on PLA leadership, chiefly using the local forces under military-district command.

The August 1966 Eleventh Party plenum had endorsed a radical dream, visualizing rapid seizures of Party and government power by revolutionary action followed quickly by general elections. This was the model of the 1871 Paris Commune, supposedly the world's first proletarian government. Obviously unworkable without disciplined leadership, it failed in January and February, 1967. Meanwhile, a relatively orderly method of combining factions with PLA assistance for the purpose of interim administration of government business appeared. This was the provincial RC. Heilungkiang formed one first, on January 31, 1967.

The RC was a "provisional organ of power." In it, three political interests were clustered, forming a "revolutionary three-way combination" of the army, the revolutionaries, and the Party and government cadres. It was a coalition to work out a provisional allocation of power. As a political mechanism, the provincial RC served incidentally to submerge factional goals in coalition politics. The real purpose in its makeup, however, was to bring together three interest groups: the PLA for order, the rebels for revolutionary enthusiasm, and the cadres for experience.

Reconstruction of government by this means began haltingly, and only the participation of the PLA permitted a successful conclusion. Establishment of the remaining twenty-eight province-level committees was to require an additional nineteen months, until September 5, 1968, when the last two committees were formed in Tibet and Sinkiang.

The Test

The PLA's conception of its political role in 1967 was confused. In each region and province, the problems took different shape: PLA forces were sometimes involved on the side of revolutionaries and sometimes on the side of established authority, sometimes to keep order and sometimes to influence the outcome. The "true Maoists" were hard to distinguish and harder yet to support, without encouraging fighting and destructiveness.[11]

When possible, the PLA sought neutrality. Disorder was kept in quarantine by province and military region until the new political machinery could be set up. The PLA would have moved sooner, more effectively, and with better-coordinated direction to suppress the sanguinary warfare had not a "higher" purpose prevailed in Peking to prolong the disorders. The Maoists at the center were intent on securing the most radical redistribution of political power that was possible within tolerable limits of disorder.

A torrent of orders, directives, speeches, editorials, and obiter dicta flowed from Peking in 1967. In particular, three directives, issued between late January and early September, symbolized the changing situation for the PLA in that period. Neutralism was abandoned on January 23, 1967, when the PLA was ordered into the turbulence to choose sides among competing, professedly Maoist factions, so as to begin consolidation of so-called power seizures by true leftists. Complying with an order of Mao to Lin, the MAC on that day ended the previous period of watchful waiting with instructions to "support the left."[12]

Military control committees were formed around expanded Party committees to take over key functions, such as Public Security Bureaus. Military government work was capsulized in a formula that is still in use, "Three Supports and Two Militaries." The formula means that in their political and administrative work, PLA cadres support the left, support industry, support agriculture, exercise military control directly where needed, and provide military and political training opportunities for young revolutionaries. These measures mitigated the chaos, even though by the end of February only five provincial RCs had been formed. Tsinghai had a small mutiny at the military-district headquarters in February, and the support-the-left movement began to run down against both military and civil opposition. The task of keeping the revolution going in January and February was seen as one of resisting power solutions in which nominally revolutionary takeovers from local Party committes might have conservative backing. Takeovers that did not meet Peking's standards of ideological sincerity were reversed.

By mid-February, the MAC was obliged to restrain "power seizures" within the PLA itself and to place the Public Security bureaus clearly under provincial military command. Because of their resistence to local "power seizures," PLA local forces and their Party committees came under increasing attack.

Peking added to radical pressures in March and April, lest the revolutionaries fail. On April 6 another landmark directive was issued through the MAC. Its purpose was to protect leftist action against suppression.[13] Having concluded that the PLA had not supported the left effectively in February and March, the Commission issued prohibitions against arrests, labeling of undesirable factions, and use of firearms against leftist mass organizations. This order blocked units seeking to quell conflict, and the PLA, being thus committed to nonresistance, soon came under attack itself.

In an incident that occurred at Wuhan on July 20, a dissident Public Security Division had the passive support of the military-region commander in detaining two senior Peking emissaries until Chou En-lai secured their release. The leading regional commanders were then assembled in Peking, and radical pressure mounted for a purge in the PLA. The military leadership became more tense, as the absurdity of inactivity enforced by directive in the face of a need to restrain disorder and carry on with government became more obvious.

In the tense month of August, 1967, radicals attacked the PLA itself but lost. The military leadership was severely lectured by Lin Piao on August 9, but at the same time he indicated he would not support another large-scale purge of the PLA. By the end of that month, Mao, Lin, and Chou En-lai were prepared to support the suppression of disorder. Chiang Ch'ing, Mao's wife, put herself alongside the PLA on September 5 in the course of addressing a delegation from the troubled province of Anhwei.[14]

Chou En-lai led the regime, at this time, in describing the PLA's supposed failings of 1967, for which the radicals were criticizing it. The PLA had lost weapons, had failed to support "correct" factions and groups of Peking's choice, had in some cases reinstated toppled leaders, and had often stood aside from intervention in support of the left. Chou asserted, however, that "to seize a handful within the PLA"—the radical slogan of late July and August, 1967, in calling for a purge within the PLA—was an ultra-leftist procedure. It would harm the Cultural Revolution by encouraging people who, "when they go to outside areas invariably support the faction which opposes the leadership."[15]

An order went to the PLA on September 5 endorsing its mission in restraint of lawlessness. This ended close to a year of inconclusive turmoil. The order focused almost entirely on recovery of lost weapons and other materiel and on preventing further losses. As necessary, force was authorized in making arrests. The order prohibited seizures or bestowals of weapons, vehicles, ammunition, stores, and the like by mass organizations or by errant PLA units. Forcible arrests and use of force in self-defense were authorized.[16]

Much more fighting was to follow, lasting into 1968, before the country would be pacified. But by September, 1967, it was established that the country would be pacified chiefly by local forces and not by regular field forces; that the local forces had turned in a mixed performance; that the full-scale use of the PLA to suppress disorder had been avoided; and that the PLA was able to avoid schism over issues related to peace-keeping.

In the winter of 1968-69, Party rebuilding was begun. The Ninth CCP Congress of April, 1969, elected CC weighted toward the PLA. The main burden of political leadership in reestablishing a form of Party life under Maoist auspices now fell to the PLA.

PARTY AND ARMY

The Party System and
Political Control in the PLA

The PLA is privileged, in large part, to manage its own side
of the CCP, utilizing a complex and essentially orderly, but imper-
fectly known system. What follows here is admittedly a model, based
primarily on available facts as to how the system operated until
1967, but rounded out with surmise on recent years.[17]

PLA Party committees in units and commands are distinct
from civil Party committees (although regulations require routine
lateral coordination with local Party committees at equivalent levels).
The PLA committees rise tier on tier from regiments to military
regions and exist in all service arms and units of the PLA headquarters, including the GPD the General Staff Department. The
highest level of military Party committee is the inner circle of the
MAC, the senior organ for the PLA.

The MAC, being a commission of the CCP CC, is in effect its
own Party committee, with the MAC standing committee presumably
being its core group (recent information on the makeup of that standing
committee is not available). The full membership roster of the MAC
is unknown, but it is reasonable to suppose that the MAC membership
includes most of the central military leaders and, if not most, at
least many of the commanders and first commissars of military
regions and districts. At the regional level, the command team,
consisting of the military-region commander and the first political
commissar, speaks for the military-region Party committee and
presumably may deal directly with the MAC.

The Chinese Communist system of dual command relies on a
pair of leaders, the unit troop commander and the unit political
commissar, to lead the unit Party committee and its working core,
the standing committee. An imprecise division of labor between
military and political matters permits them to share command of
the unit and leadership of its political activities. Two career traditions
meet in this twosome, harnessed together under the Party committee
system that requires collective leadership, without merging the lines
of military and political command. The unit commissar is not subordinate to the unit military commander, but he is subordinate to
both officers at the next-higher level.

Unified command necessarily must exist for the Minister of National Defense and for the PLA chief of staff to function, but the system is designed to tolerate tactical and administrative decentralization and flexibility in collective response to leadership. In political matters the commissars are required to take their guidance from many sources—the CCP CC, the MAC's administrative office, the GPD, their own unit party committee, and the Party committee, commander, commissar, and political department at the next-higher level. For problems created by multiple channels of communication and influence, the typical solution appears to be the meeting. One device that clears the air on a nationwide scale is the telephone conference. Several were convened in 1960-61 "as a means employed by senior leadership organs to transmit certain urgent directives or to explain certain problems."[18] Presumably, they continue to be used.

Just as the General Staff Department tops the regular line of military command, the GPD stands at the head of the line of political control, administering political work directly. The military-region first political commissar may deal directly with the GPD.

The GPD is an organ of the MAC, as it were, not of the Party as a whole, and it received special mention in the 1956 CCP constitution, serving to shield the PLA from direct CC interference.[19] Formally, the GPD is one department of the PLA headquarters under the Ministry of National Defense and, as such, is detached from the General Staff Department. The chief of staff gains his ascendancy over the director of the GPD through their respective MAC positions. Since early in the 1960s, and possibly down to the present, the chief of staff has been secretary-general of the MAC secretariat, and the GPD director, at least during Hsiao Hua's tenure down to 1967, was deputy Secretary-general.

Large and powerful, the old GPD under pre-Cultural Revolution regulations dealt both with unit commissars and with unit political departments and their directors and, through these and other channels, with Party committees. By these arrangements, the political department at each level, though a regular part of a unit headquarters, received guidance from many directions, especially from four principal sources: the CC, the MAC, the GPD, and, obviously, Chairman Mao. The balance, was provided by the MAC-connected subordination of the GPD director to the chief of staff on the MAC secretariat.

The closeness of the MAC-GPD connection permitted the MAC

to take control of essential GPD functions in 1967-68 after Hsiao
Hua had been purged. A new "administrative unit" made up mostly
of deputy chiefs of staff and headed by the chief of staff was set up
in late 1967 in the MAC to control cadres, political work, and the
Chieh-fang-chun Pao [Liberation Army Daily]. By fall, 1970, the
GPD had apparently been reconstituted to resume its former mission,
but in what form is not known.

PLA Strength in the CCP

The PLA political machine and its associated commanders now
serve in government through an array of administrative, monitoring,
peace-keeping, policy-making, propaganda, and governing committees.
PLA political strength is seen in the composition of the leading
organs beneath the Politburo Standing Committee, until mide-1971
the domain of Mao, Lin, and Chou En-lai. From the data in Chinese
press accounts, one can conclude that a majority of the Politburo
and 41 percent of the ninth CC are military. Twenty of the first
secretaries of the 29 new Provincial Party Committees and 60 percent of all 158 secretaries of those committees are career PLA
commanders or commissars. Regional commanders or first commissars pocketed the first secretaryships as concurrent posts in
nine provinces. Provincial military-district commanders and
commissars have, in eight provinces, extended their political authority
to include a first secretaryship. In three other provinces, the first
secretaries are military, but are of lesser career stature. In the
nine remaining units—Shanghai, Peking, Tientsin, and six provinces—
six first secretaries have acquired PLA affiliation and hold posts of
regional or district commissars.

This outcome places most provincial authority in military hands.
While such employment is a possible demilitarizing influence for key
PLA officers, it is more likely to mean further militarization of the
Party. It is also at least arguable that Party prestige is weakened
by such obvious dependence on the PLA. The Liaoning first secretaryship of Shenyang Regional Commander and Politburo member Ch'en
Hsi-lien is at best his third-most-important job and obviously its
duties must be carried out by associates on his behalf. One wonders
about the vitality of the Party leadership that Ch'en will contribute
under such an arrangement, given his other preoccupations.

At the lower levels of the CCP, the PLA influence is based
on its relatively steady emphasis on Party building since 1960 and,
by now, can scarcely be slight. Itself, the PLA is a relatively small

politico-military elite of under 3 million. But public-security and border troops and the paramilitary production and construction corps—a growing labor army of ex-military, ex-students, and urban-area deportees—may add a like number. With around half a million newly demobilized persons becoming available annually, the total of PLA-oriented men among militiamen and ex-soldiers may number around 10 million. The PLA's immediate circle of politically aware people is thus perhaps of the order of some 15 million persons, even before its influence is weighed in the extended militia organization, the schools, and the families of military-oriented persons.

The desire not to dilute quality has made difficult the maintenance of an adequate rate of Party growth in the past two decades, and the CCP seems undermanned. In the 1960s, it numbered about 2.5 percent of the population.* It had no choice but to be an overworked, elite party. In the 1960s, meanwhile, the PLA was energetically recruiting Party members through its conscripts, the militia, and the Young Communist League branches in the companies. Although Party members recruited through the civil CCP organization greatly out-number Party members recruited through the PLA, the Party members of PLA origins or affinities may now, in 1971, be a sufficiently large proportion to facilitate working control of the local-level CCP by the PLA, if the PLA cadres are energetic enough to take over.** The thought of the PLA capturing control of the CCP from within, before securing working control of Provincial Party Committees through secretaryships, is novel, but there is no reason why it should not have happened. Local Party committees became extensively dependent on military Party committees at the same level during the Cultural Revolution, and the strong PLA role in recent Party-building tends to perpetuate this dependence.

Present Party membership, even after a certain amount of

----

*The Communist Party of the Soviet Union comprises 5 to 6 percent of the population of the USSR. The Communist parties of North Vietnam and Mongolia include over 4 percent of the populations of those countries. In North Korea, the proportion is about 14 percent.

**By "control" is here meant the capability to elicit the needed or desired political response from the rank and file and to secure the interested and energetic response of senior local cadres. The use of Western-style democratic processes of free choice is not implied.

recent purge, is likely to be in the range of 18 to 20 million. If, over the past decade, even 5 million military-oriented persons have become members under PLA auspices, the PLA may have gained 25 percent, more or less, of the Party membership. With good leverage in standing committees, core groups, propaganda teams, and similar apparatus even a smaller fraction would suffice to give the PLA working-level control.

OUTLOOK

While the process of winding down the Cultural Revolution goes on, the future working environment of the PLA is unpredictable. What happens to the PLA in its internal role of protecting the regime depends chiefly on matters beyond the assigned limits of this chapter— the impact of foreign affairs, future power struggles within the Chinese leadership, the ebb and flow of internal politics within the PLA, the influence of such historical accidents as deaths within the leadership, and such natural accidents as bad crop years. In the following conservative speculations on the PLA-CCP relationship, on regional-central polarization, and on dissidence, it is suggested that the PLA will observe both the limitations and the opportunities of its role. The opinions, obviously, are those of the author and mostly await proof.

Implications of the Present PLA Position

The PLA preoccupation with politics threatens to be prolonged unless steps are again taken, as was done in 1954 when civil government was first established, to set the PLA and CCP apart from each other.

The partial role reversal of the 1960s amounted to a shift in emphasis from a conventional military force seeking the capability to fight a modern war to a uniquely Chinese Communist revolutionary force capable also of running a country. In the 1970s, these dual roles will necessarily persist, with continuing debate over their relative merits. A decisive return to the constraints of a predominantly professional combat role seems, in the short run, to be improbable; clear-cut PLA-CCP disengagement is unlikely. Two PLA's, so to speak, will be operating and, at times, their conflicting roles will create a dilemma for the high command in Peking.[20]

The degree of need for PLA-CCP disengagement is, however, arguable both ways. The Maoist concept of the national interest values internal political development very highly and seems to argue against disengagement until a new generation of leadership has become established. In this view, continuing PLA-CCP involvement, if necessary for effective internal political action, is a good thing and there need be no time pressure for disengagement. Institutional needs of the PLA and CCP, if they become urgent, should be met another way; a large part of the Chinese Communist leadership may reason thus.

The rub is that the Party needs to regain a life of its own, or so it seems. In conventional manner, the June 30, 1971, statement on the CCP* unrealistically stressed the present primacy of the Party over the army in its leading support role.[21] An innocent reader would mistakenly presume that the CCP has already regained the requisite vitality and confidence to take charge both of itself and of the PLA. As yet, however, the PLA, in late 1971 and after five years of political turmoil, lacks the support of a fully structured CCP system. The principal present achievement in Party-building has been establishment of the military-dominated Provincial Party Committees. Local Party reconstruction is considered to be incomplete, and the shape of the "compact and efficient" central organs promised in the new Party constitution of April, 1969 is not yet visible.[22]

No chief of staff or yet-unnamed Party general secretary can, however, totally ignore institutional obligations based on the need of members of an organization to have a clear sense of identity. The working needs of the PLA and the CCP, as institutions, probably argue for clear disengagement and establishment of a division of labor between military and political matters that will be comfortable for their personnel. The question, at the institutional level, is whether the PLA, as much as the CCP, does not need disengagement from immersion in nonmilitary activities for its own sake as a fighting force.

Because the PLA-CCP involvement is seemingly intensifying, the likelihood for disengagement is not great and any lingering professional dissatisfaction with that outcome will have to bide its time. Political and economic, as well as strictly military, issues will enter

---

*See above, p. 270

into intra-PLA conficts and rivalries as the involvement continues, increasing pressures at various points of possible tension.

The PLA, therefore, runs the risk of divisive internal conflict along a number of planes of cleavage that can be visualized. The ongoing role conflict between combat and political missions was brought to the surface when it was decided, for present purposes, that politics prevails, although preservation of a combat potential for defense retains a high priority. It left tensions within the PLA leadership—for example, competition for position—that may be confined and settled by purge, but also may erupt in the open. Conflict may materialize between PLA and CCP and divide the PLA. The divergence of purposes between operational forces and the protective local forces may enlarge. The ground forces may have differences with the other services. The central authorities and the military-region authorities may come to odds. Centrally dominated regions may find localism and provincialism a problem. Differing generations of military leadership may lose their rapport. The military commanders and the political commissars may draw apart. Preoccupation with political-leadership tasks in continuing close embrace with the CCP could have the result of aggravating all such potential cleavages within the PLA.

Examination of the contrasting case for disengagement, in view of its unlikelihood, is virtually academic. In practice, it would tend to encourage political polarization of Party and army as special-interest groups, although the successors of Lin and Mao, if talented enough, could conceivably succeed in the feat of disengagement without appreciable polarization. The traditional corrective is a sort of distributive multiple-hatting in appointments, to ensure that loyalties and responsibilities are well spread. The present trend in appointments is running instead toward concentration of appointments and responsibilities and tends to support continuation of mutual involvement.

Dissidence

Colorful reports of sometimes disruptive local dissidence are no novelty and they may increase in number as future contacts with China increase. Enforced population transfers, propaganda pressure exerted through the public media (not only the press, but also rediffusion), mass campaigns, reeducation camps, and unfulfilled economic expectations, together with such positive factors as gains in public health and in agricultural output, directly or indirectly contribute to stimulation of the independent thinking that breeds dissatisfaction leading to dissidence.

Such incidents of local rebelliousness as may occasionally flare need to be isolated and controlled. Cultural Revolution experience showed that most such dissidence is, indeed, suppressible if security forces are adequately motivated and led, know which way to turn politically, energetically protect stored weapons, and are not under undue restraint. Not all dissidence need be permanently destructive; the PLA will in the future be involved both in suppression and dissipation of harmful dissidence and in channeling other dissidence toward legitimate expression.

In repression, force backs up moral pressure on personal motivation of individuals through regular political indoctrination—now called "struggle-criticism-transformation." Self-policing under moral coercion is the basis of Chinese Communist internal security, supplemented by police control, reeducation, and punishments.

The internal security system of the decade past has comprised the civil Public Security Bureaus and their forces, usually called the People's Armed Police. The People's Armed Departments that operate within local governments but under higher military authority, mainly to run the militia and military recruitment; and the border defense and internal security divisions and regiments comprising the so-called Public Security forces.

Militia forces consist of a selective, partially armed basic militia and an almost inactive horde of ordinary militia. This is not all: the cities have used various types of urban militia of workers, students, and children, male and female. In some places, "workers' provost corps" were established during the Cultural Revolution under RCs; they controlled variously named "provost" units engaged in police work. Presently, the PLA is in full control of this extensive internal-security system. As long as this is so, it is unlikely that those forces will be allowed to lose their effectiveness at their primary task, providing they are not arbitrarily restrained from performing it, as occurred during the Cultural Revolution.

Regionalism and Provincialism

Circumstances are driving China toward increasing recognition of the administrative difficulties and political dangers of highly centralized rule. An inherited basis for regionalism in geographical differences is crudely reflected in the system of command of field forces and of military Party committees at the military-region and district (provincial) levels. The delegation or relinquishment of central authority and responsibility merits watching because it has the potential of encouraging de facto autonomy in specific administrative fields related to nonmilitary activities.

The years of the 1950s, when regionally based military commanders of the large field armies all had strong bases of personal power, ended in a purge chiefly affecting northeast China. In 1961-66, the Party utilized regional bureaus, as it had in 1949-54, to strengthen centralized control. From the mid-1950s on, reacting both against excessive regional strength for military commanders and against a supposedly cumbersome overcentralization of the civil bureaucracy, Mao and others have pressed toward decentralization of much non-strategic economic activity, despite its obvious economic cost. Edgar Snow recently learned from Chou En-lai that the decentralization policies now favored are intended to support simplification of administrative structure and intensification of regional and local self-sufficiency.[23] Chou displayed no concern, in his interview with Snow, over the military implications, and it may be that there is no threat. Local self-sufficiency, however, confers a degree of independence on military commanders to ignore the center if they choose, even though they do not support their own armies to the extent that the warlords once did.

It is likely that significant growth of political self-consciousness took place in the provinces over recent years; the Cultural Revolution did nothing to discourage provincialism from taking deeper root in Communist politics. The central authorities respected provincial needs in working out the 1967-68 provincial settlements according to each situation and not usually by blueprint. Continuation of factionalism in the provinces during up to four years of political change permitted self-examination among participants and observers and went on long enough for intraprovincial differences to harden.

Many influences work for and against the center, and the notion of regionalism as the antithesis of reliance on the center only offers a framework in which to evaluate developments outside the capital. If outside circumstances affect central-regional relationships, those of national emergency will probably tend to work in the favor of the regional commanders as a group responsible for defense of the country. Special circumstances appealing to national pride could favor the power of nationalistic leaders, usually those at the center. Deteriorating circumstances at the center could lead to strengthening of indigenous localism.

The danger to the regime is less a visible threat than a drain of strength. That loss could be less than it would be under a fully centralized system that is faltering. Accordingly, the real costs of decentralization and of permissive regionalization by plan are difficult to calculate. The dissidence and possible revolution resulting from a central breakdown could be more costly than even substantial loss of real authority to regionally based authorities.

CONCLUSIONS

Basic constitutional questions are at issue in China's domestic politics and the PLA-CCP relationship is one of them. The shape of future dissidence, leadership quarrels, and political-control problems depends on the new form of the government and how well it works. Indeed, it may be premature to speculate concerning future threats as long as current issues and their solutions remain undefined. One complicating factor is that time frames in China are often prolonged. The replacement of old Party committees with new ones consumed a period of almost five years. The shortest period between formation of a provincial RC and establishment of a Provincial Party Committee to complement it was two and a half years (for Kwangsi), and one province (Heilungkiang) required four and a half years. At such a pace, many of the decisions yet to be made could conceivably consume most of the next decade.

NOTES

1. Jointly published by <u>JMJP</u>, <u>HC</u>, Chieh-fang-chun Pao [Liberation Army Daily], July 1, 1971; NCNA, June 30, 1971; <u>FBIS</u>, I, July 1, 1961, B16. Also in <u>SCMP</u> (American Consulate General, Hong Kong), Nos. 709-10 (combined issue), August 3-9, 1971.

2. Stuart R. Schram, <u>The Political Thought of Mao Tse-tung</u> (New York: Praeger, 1969), p. 290; and Mao Tse-tung, <u>Selected Works of Mao Tse-tung</u>, 4 vols., II (Peking: Foreign Languages Press, 1965), 224-25.

3. <u>Ibid.</u>, pp. 224-25.

4. <u>Documents of Chinese Communist Party Central Committee, September 1956- April 1969</u>, Vol. I: <u>Documents</u> (Hong Kong: Union Research Institute, 1971), pp. 345-88; and J. Chester Cheng, ed., <u>PLA Kung-tso Tung-hsun</u>: <u>The Politics of the Chinese Red Army</u> (Stanford,

Cal.: Hoover Institution on War, Revolution, and Peace, 1966), pp. 66-94.

5. The four firsts concern the correct handling of four relation-ships (i.e., preferred choices) in PLA political work: men over weapons, political work over other work, ideological work over routine political work, and living ideas over book thinking. The three-eight work style is composed of the three phrases directing officers and men to keep a correct political orientation, to work hard and live plainly, and to be flexible in both strategy and tactics; and of the eight Chinese characters for the four words: unity, vigor, seriousness, and liveli-ness. The five-good soldier is the soldier who succeeds in becoming good in political thinking, good in military skills, good in the three-eight work style, good in performing tasks as assigned, and good in physical training. The four-good company is the company that is good in political work, good in the three-eight work style, good in military training, and good in management of the men's living arrangements. These definitions are slightly recast from "A Glossary of Chinese Communist Terms and Phrases (revised)," JPRS, October, 1969, pp. 6, 21-22, 40, 42.

6. For another summary, see John Gittings, The Role of the Chinese Army (New York: Oxford University Press, 1967), pp. 250-51.

7. "Communique of the 11th Plenary Session of the 8th Central Committee," August 12, 1966, Documents, I, p. 221.

8. Ralph L. Powell, "The Increasing Power of Lin Piao and the Party-Soldiers 1959-66," China Quarterly, No. 34, April-June, 1968, pp. 46-47; "Itinerary of the People's Republic, Part III: 1963-64," CNA, No. 640, December 9, 1966, p. 5; Victor C. Funnell, "Bureaucracy and the Chinese Communist Party," Current Scene, IX, 5 (May 7, 1971), pp. 9-10; Gittings, Chinese Army, pp. 256-58; Ellis Joffe, "The Chinese Army under Lin Piao: Prelude to Inter-vention," in John M. H. Lindbeck, ed., China: Management of a Revolutionary Society (Seattle: University of Washington Press, 1971), pp. 343-74.

9. The Great Cultural Revolution in China (Hong Kong: Asia Research Centre, 1967), p. 389.

10. Ibid., p. 398; and Documents, I, p. 210.

11. Two complementary accounts are: Philip Bridgham, "Mao's Cultural Revolution in 1967: The Struggle to Seize Power," China Quarterly, No. 34, April-June, 1968, pp. 6-37; and Jurgen Domes, "The Role of the Military in the Formation of Revolutionary Committees, 1967-68," ibid., No. 44, October-December, 1970, pp. 112-45.

12. The Great Power Struggle in China (Hong Kong: Asia Research Centre, 1969), pp. 311-13.

13. GPSC, pp. 318-320

14. GPSC, pp. 423-426

15. Ibid., pp. 426-28.

16. Ibid., pp. 405-7.

17. Available information is old and describes the GPD only through 1966. The GPD was presumably reorganized in 1968-70, and Director Li Teh-sheng probably utilizes different procedures from those of his predecessor, Hsiao Hua. For background, consult: Frederic H. Chaffee et al., Area Handbook for Communist China (Washington, D.C.: Government Printing Office, 1967), pp. 613-30; Gittings, Chinese Army, pp. 106-16, 280-91; Ellis Joffe, Party and Army: Professionalism and Political Control in the Chinese Officer Corps, 1949-64 (Cambridge, Mass.: East Asian Research Center, Harvard University, 1965), pp. 28, 29; Ralph L. Powell, Politico-Military Relationships in Communist China (Washington, D.C.: Department of State, 1963); Peter S. H. Tang and Joan M. Maloney, Communist China; The Domestic Scene 1949-1967 (South Orange, N.J.: Seton Hall University Press, 1967), pp. 432-38. Numerous Current Scene and CNA issues also contain helpful information.

18. Cheng, Kung-tso Tung-hsun, p. 698; see also pp. 31, 97, 136, 313, 405.

19. "Chinese Communist Party Constitution," CB (American Consulate General, Hong Kong), No. 417, October 10, 1956, p. 59: Article 35 . . . The General Political Department . . . shall administer the ideological and organizational work of the Party in the army under the leadership of the Central Committee."

20. Potential leadership conflicts and purges are not within the scope of this chapter. It has been suggested (A. Doak Barnett,

China After Mao (Princeton, N.J.: Princeton University Press, 1967), pp. 100-101) that in China the purge rate, so to speak, is slowly rising and is symptomatic of the growth of ideological and policy differences and conflicts of group interests. (The purges of Chief of Staff Lo Jui-ch'ing in 1965 and of Acting Chief of Staff Yang Cheng-wu in 1968 still lack full explanation, but seemingly had no negative effects on the rise of the politicized PLA to power.)

21. The organs of state power are the PLA, the Communist Youth League, and other revolutionary mass organizations—workers, poor and lower-middle peasants, and Red Guards. "Text of Chinese Communist Party Constitution," NCNA (Peking), April 28, 1969; FBIS Supplement, April 29, 1969, p. 33,

22. Ibid., p. 34.

23. "Snow Interview with Chou En-lai," FBIS, I, March 25, 1971, B10; Dwight Perkins, "Mao Tse-tung's Goals and China's Economic Performance," Current Scene, IX, 1 (January 7, 1971), 6.

15

CHINESE ALLIES
AND ADVERSARIES

Richard Wich

INTRODUCTION

A major determinant in the formation of defense policy and
international strategy is the structure of alliance and adversary relationships shaping the environment in which a strategy must operate.
A dominant feature of the post-World War II environment in which the
new Communist regime in China was born was the overarching bipolar
relationship that drew a global line of confrontation between the superpower rivals, the United States and the Soviet Union. This cold-war
rivalry engendered a series of centers of tension—such as Berlin,
Korea, Taiwan, and Indochina—where the line of confrontation, by
dividing countries or halting revolutionary movements short of their
territorial fulfillment, caused local problems to become polarized
within the global power struggle. As a result, these became focal
points of global conflict by virtue of their implications for the integrity
and credibility of great-power commitments. By the same token, they
became focal points for the testing of the internal-alliance relationships in which they were emmeshed.

The polarizing process led to the formation of alliances and blocs
embodying globally interdependent mutual-security expectations.
Perceiving the facts of international life from the perspective of the
time, Mao Tse-tung declared that his regime would "lean to one side"
by aligning itself with the Soviet bloc, though his Party's power base
owed little to direct Soviet support and, indeed, had often suffered

----

Views expressed in this chapter are solely those of the author and
do not represent the official position of any U.S. government agency.

from Soviet intervention into Chinese affairs. Accordingly, soon after the proclamation of the PRC in the autumn of 1949, Mao proceeded to Moscow for protracted negotiations leading to a Sino-Soviet treaty of alliance (dated February 14, 1950), thus formalizing the decision to lean to one side and shaping the cornerstone for an over-all Communist alliance system that would embrace a billion people astride the Eurasian land mass. In the two-camp worldview, this was "the socialist camp."

The 1945 treaty between the Soviet Union and Chiang Kai-shek's government had been directed against Japan: this was now updated in the new Sino-Soviet treaty to provide mutual defense against Japan or "any state allied" with Japan, a formulation taking account of the new bipolar setting. As in the case of central Europe, where the postwar lines of confrontation had already been tested in Berlin, the lines were drawn in northeast Asia between the Sino-Soviet alliance and the United States as the occupier of Japan and then as the guarantor of Japan's security. What remained fatefully ambiguous at this time, however, were the stakes and commitments of the major powers in Korea, a country bordering the two large Communist allies and divided along cold-war lines after having been occupied by the armies of the great-power rivals. Within months of the signing of the Sino-Soviet treaty, this ambiguity was being resolved by force of arms.

The United States proceeded quickly to delineate more sharply the boundaries along which the writ of the American commitment was intended to run in Asia. Two days after the outbreak of the Korean War, President Truman on June 27, 1950, in effect drew the lines of the global great-power continuum through the Taiwan Strait and defined a stronger U.S. commitment to the struggle in Indochina.* Later, the United States formalized its commitments by means of such instruments as the mutual-defense treaty with the Nationalist Chinese regime on Taiwan and the Southeast Asian Treaty Organization (SEATO).

Thus, the Korean War deepened the global lines of conflict in Asia and brought areas of vital interest to Peking into the bipolar continuum. Peking's vital interests—such as completion of the revolution to establish sovereignty over Taiwan, defense of China's borders as the overriding security interest, and an independent status especially in regional affairs—had been drawn deeply into the broader arena of East-West rivalry. The interplay between these interests and between

_____

*Peking marks the Truman order for the Seventh Fleet's interdiction of the Taiwan Strait as the beginning of the U.S. "occupation" of Taiwan.

those of the broader alliance relationships was destined to transform
the bipolar international environment and to fracture the Communist
alliance system along its Sino-Soviet axis. At two critical junctures,
in the late 1950s and in the middle of the 1960s, that alliance was subjected to major tests. By the end of its first decade, Mao's regime
had come to have serious doubts about the value of the alliance for its
own vital interests. By the mid-1960s, Mao decided in effect to withdraw
from the alliance despite strong pressures to close ranks against an
external threat. By the time the Maoist regime entered its third decade, it was in the process of devising a strategy for a vastly transformed environment of alliance and adversary relationships.

"THE SOCIALIST CAMP MUST HAVE A HEAD,"
1957-65

In the period after the Korean War, Soviet influence in China
stood at a high level, as reflected in a wide range of fields: trade and
aid relations, the "modernization and regularization" of the PLA along
Soviet lines and under Soviet guidance, and political coordination in
such matters as the 1954 Geneva agreements on Indochina. Nonetheless, in the international arena the alliance was not at this time a
major instrument in Peking's foreign initiatives. This was a period
in which Peking's foreign affairs were marked by conciliation and
accommodation across bloc lines, as in the cultivation of Afro-Asian
neutralist governments at the 1955 Bandung conference (under the
banner of the "five principles of peaceful coexistence") and the calls
for "peaceful liberation" of Taiwan. In bloc affairs, Peking sought to
play a mediatory role in the destalinization strains—culminating in
the Hungarian revolt in the autumn of 1956—that followed Khrushchev's
denunciation of Stalin early that year at the twentieth Communist Party
of the Soviet Union (CPSU) congress. It is true that in assuming such
a role, with its implicit criticism of Moscow's failure to exercise
proper leadership, Peking took a step toward what eventually became
a major challenge to Soviet hegemony in the Communist movement;
however, the first serious test of the stability of the alliance system
developed after Peking had made a sharp turn toward a hard line in
bloc affairs some time in mid-1957.

In this new phase, Peking's strong pressure in behalf of a disciplined and cohesive bloc—recorded in the demand that "the socialist
camp must have a head"—placed new emphasis on Communist unity
and correlatively on a sharply defined bipolar international system.*

---

*Moscow's position as the "head of the socialist camp" was
confirmed in the declaration of the ruling parties at the 1957 Moscow

Though the formula accrediting Moscow with leadership of the socialist camp was not new, what was significant was Peking's insistence on a strongly unitary line in bloc affairs, a line that meant abandonment by the Chinese of their mediatory role in intrabloc conflict resolution and the assumption of a new role as the most militant watchdogs of bloc discipline. At this important juncture, Mao went to Moscow for the first time since negotiating the Sino-Soviet treaty, on this occasion taking part in a Communist summit conference in late 1957. In addition to his insistence on a unitary bloc under firm Soviet leadership, Mao offered his famous judgment on "the East wind prevailing over the West wind, which he defined as meaning that "the socialist forces are overwhelmingly superior to the imperialist forces" as a result especially of Soviet technological breakthroughs that year. Putting the two factors in a new equation—tightened discipline in the socialist camp and significant technological advances (Soviet launchings of the first ICBM and sputniks)—Mao proclaimed "a new turning point in the relative strength of the two major camps."

Mao did not, of course, make a rare trip abroad simply to offer an abstract assessment of the existing balance of power. What Mao sought was to refashion the alliance that he had joined at the beginning of the decade into an instrument of a new forward strategy of greater risk-taking and stronger pressure on the forward presence of the United States. This strategy was intended to meet the challenge of a situation in which American-sponsored alliance structures and U.S. commitments in Asia circumscribed the projection of the PRC's influence, a situation that was particularly intolerable in that the Chinese Communist revolution remained visibly incomplete as long as the rival Chiang Kai-shek regime stayed entrenched on Taiwan behind an American shield. The importance of alliance politics in this strategy was reflected in the ideological assault launched by the Chinese against the Yugoslavs as a living challenge to tight bloc discipline and as proponents of détente policies that would blur the bipolar lines of global conflict. Significantly, the first issue of the new ideological journal Red Flag contained a vigorous denunciation of the Yugoslavs by Ch'en Po-ta for denying that "the most fundamental feature of the present world situation is the counterposing of two different social, political, and economic world systems and of the

---

conference. In 1961, after the Chinese had mounted their challenge to Soviet leadership, Khrushchev indicated that the Soviets had not desired the 1957 formula, but had acceded to Mao's insistence on this point.

<u>two camps</u> arising from these two different systems."1 The stage
was set for a testing of the integrity and credibility of Moscow's
commitments to the front lines of the socialist camp.

As the development of events demonstrated, and as subsequent
Chinese and Soviet accounts of the period confirmed, the Soviets were
unwilling to assume the role assigned to them by Mao to use their
power and leadership of the socialist camp as a guarantor of probes
of the West's global lines. Indeed, whatever Peking's original intentions, these probes served more to test Moscow's commitment to its
ally than to test corresponding commitments on the Western side. The
bipolar framework, at this time so sharply defined by Peking, served
to bring the divergent expectations of the Communist allies into sharper
focus and to reveal fundamental conflicts of interests that seriously
strained their relationship.

The results of the 1958 Taiwan Straits crisis, a particularly
sensitive test case, demonstrated to Peking that the Soviets placed
the interests of their relationship with the United States above their
commitment to Peking's fundamental goals. For Moscow, it was precisely because the Taiwan question had been drawn into the great-
power continuum that counsels of caution and restraint were imperative.
For this purpose, the Soviets desired a monopoly on foreign initiatives by the Communist camp, or at least close control over the scope
of moves by their allies. This was reflected, most notably, in Moscow's
decision to renege on a nuclear-sharing agreement with Peking.

In reviewing the origins of the Sino-Soviet conflict, the Chinese
have interpreted Moscow's moves during this period as dictated by a
desire for an accommodation with the United States in the interests
of stabilizing the international environment—at the very time when
Mao had undertaken a range of destabilizing initiatives at home and
abroad. Thus, the Chinese version goes, Moscow's decision to terminate the nuclear agreement with the PRC and its neutral position on
the Sino-Indian border dispute "were ceremonial gifts to Eisenhower
so as to curry favor with the U.S. imperialists and create the so-called
'spirit of Camp David.' "2 As for the Taiwan crisis, the Chinese have
accused the Soviets of having offered deterrent support only when they
were certain that no such need would arise. Moreover, the Chinese
viewed the Soviet counsels of restraint, on the ground of the two superpowers' commitments to their respective Chinese allies, as having
the effect of a "two-Chinas" policy, perpetuating the alienation of
Taiwan from the PRC in the interest of Soviet-American stability.
It was to counter that interest that Peking undertook to promote des-
tablizing moves wherever it had the power.

The Soviet version of these events betrays serious concern over Peking's goals, particularly in connection with its desire for nuclear weaponry. A Soviet statement in 1963, hinting at a withdrawal of the Soviet deterrent from the PRC, contended that "the very idea of the need to provide themselves with nuclear weapons could occur to the leaders of a country whose security is guaranteed by the entire might of the socialist camp only if they have developed some kind of special aims or interests that the socialist camp cannot support with its military force."[3] The statement claimed that Peking intentionally became embroiled in a border clash with India in 1959 in an attempt to torpedo the relaxation of global tension then taking place. Another Soviet account disclosed that the Chinese shelling of the offshore islands in 1958 was undertaken without consultation with the USSR as required by the Sino-Soviet treaty. Significantly, Moscow has charged that the Chinese probes in this period were undertaken in areas—such as the Taiwan Straits and the Sino-Indian border—that could be manipulated by Peking in an effort to assume control over the strategy and foreign policy of the entire socialist camp. Peking's calculation in making these moves was based on "the supposition that the Soviet Union would support the military actions of China" and abandon its efforts at détente with the United States.[4]

Whatever had been the precise calculations of the Communist allies at the 1957 Moscow conference, by the end of the decade their divergent expectations concerning the uses of the alliance had become plainly and painfully evident to each side. Khrushchev brought the message directly to the Chinese when, speaking in Peking after his visit to the United States (and bearing tidings of détente), he warned his hosts of a lack of support for attempts "to test by force the stability of the capitalist system."[5] What was really being tested, of course, was the stability of the Communist alliance system.

Having found that Moscow insisted on using its leadership of the alliance for its own interests, Peking proceeded in the early 1960s to mount a vigorous ideological and political challenge to Soviet hegemony in the international Communist movement. Its pressure on Moscow since 1957 having proved unavailing in scuttling Khrushchev's détente policies, Peking set out to assume leadership over the forces in the world that shared its impatience with the status quo and its resentment toward the superpowers' efforts to stabilize the international situation. Where previously the Chinese had stressed the bipolarity of international forces, they now took Moscow to task for focusing solely on the "contradiction" between the two camps to the exclusion of other "fundamental contradictions" of the era. Significantly, the Chinese now insisted that the various types of contradictions were "concentrated" in Asia, Africa, and Latin America and that the "whole" revolutionary cause "hinges on the outcome of the revolutionary struggles of the peoples of these areas." A major crack in the Communist alliance system had thus been introduced.

Although there were ebbs and flows in the competition for leadership of the international Communist movement, a pattern of deepening challenge and response put the two sides on a schismatic course, particularly in connection with Moscow's project of a new international Party conference that could only split the movement along an East-West axis of its own. It is not at all certain, however, that the development of events along this course, had other factors remained constant, would have passed beyond the stage of competition for leadership of a divided Communist movement—a stage at which rival sources of authority exercised influence in their respective spheres, Moscow as the ultimate guarantor of the socialist camp and Peking as promoter of the other "contradictions" to which it accorded priority in international strategy. Even in the conditions of a schism along ideological lines, the polarizing forces within the Communist movement might have been contained short of a final fracture of the socialist camp, preserving the defensive alliance commitments for purposes of deterrence vis-á-vis the United States. Indications of Khruschev's desire in 1964 to disengage from Indochina might have pointed to the sort of accommodation that would have contained the polarizing forces by reducing the areas of direct rivalry. Instead, Khrushchev's ouster from power and the challenge to the stability of the socialist camp posed by the rising level of hostilities in Vietnam brought this rivalry to a breaking point.

VIETNAM AND THE SOCIALIST CAMP, 1965-69

The major new developments that supervened on the ideological rivalry between Peking and Moscow were the attempt by Khrushchev's successors to reassert Soviet influence in the Asian wing of the movement, the serious intensification of the Vietnam conflict, and the concomitant pressures to close ranks in the Communist movement behind a member of the socialist camp under direct attack. The testing of the alliance posed by these interacting developments challenged Peking's decision-making on several levels: how to respond to the post-Khrushchev Soviet leadership's appeal for Communist unity, how to react to growing hostilities near the PRC's southern borders, and how, accordingly, to order priorities in determining the lines of Chinese strategy. A response on one of these levels entailed complementary responses on the others, and taken together they were translated into hard choices that the Chinese had to make about the future of the Communist alliance structure and, indeed, of the international system itself.

The new Soviet line called for "unity of action," a line designed to reduce the ideological strains in the Communist movement while seeking an accommodation based on mutual-security interests and defense of the socialist camp. At the same time, the new Kremlin leadership sought to demonstrate Moscow's bona fides as a guarantor of the camp's security by taking a marginally tougher line on East-West relations. Premier Kosygin was dispatched to Hanoi, Pyongyang, and Peking to propound the new line; the timeliness of his message was underscored by U.S. air raids on North Vietnam during his visit. The intensifying military actions in Vietnam provided the Soviets a concrete context for proposing measures in support of Hanoi that would require a degree of Chinese coordination, or at least Chinese acquiescence, in moves that would strengthen Moscow's hand in Indochina.

Increasingly, the Chinese were confronted with a dilemma in their decision-making: either to accept some level of accommodation with Moscow, and thus risk a reassertion of Soviet influence in an area where it had been seriously eroded by Peking's challenge, or to reject the Soviet proposals and risk isolation in the Communist movement. Ironically, Moscow's attempt to assume the role of alliance leader that Mao had assigned it in the late 1950s compelled the Chinese to rethink their place in the alliance under conditions in which the Soviets were in an improved position to influence events and thus to seek to determine the strategy of the Communist movement.

The course of this rethinking was marked by sharp shifts and clashes of line. At the time of the U.S. bombing raids on the Communist Democratic Republic of Vietnam (DRV) in February, 1965, Peking issued strong declarations of support for Hanoi in terms that later disappeared after fundamental decisions had been taken about the future of the alliance system. Thus, a PRC government statement on February 9 declared that the DRV "is a member of the socialist camp and all the other socialist countries have the unshirkable international obligation to support and assist it with actual deeds. . . . Aggression by the United States against the DRV means aggression against China; the 650 million Chinese people will definitely not stand idly by. . . ."[6] Significantly, the Chinese leaders' message to their Soviet counterparts on the 15th anniversary of the Sino-Soviet treaty (February 14, 1965) termed the bombing of the DRV "not only an aggression against

the DRV, but also an aggression against the entire socialist camp,"
thus broadening the mutual-security commitment to include the USSR
as well as the PRC.[7] A People's Daily editorial on the occasion spelled
this out further by asserting that China and the Soviet Union "will
inevitably fight shoulder to shoulder and wipe out . . . all aggressors
who venture to invade the socialist camp."[8]

If advocates of Communist unity were given hope by these statements, there also were disquieting signs. Ch'en I, speaking at a Soviet
embassy reception on the treaty anniversary, lectured his hosts that
peaceful coexistence with the United States "is out of the question"
and that "only in concrete action" against the Americans could the
alliance be tested and unity consolidated.[9] Similarly, the afore-
mentioned editorial on the occasion pointedly cited the programmatic
"general line" advanced in the CCP's landmark June 14, 1963, statement codifying Peking's challenge to Moscow as a source of international strategy.

That the Soviet line on unity was encountering trouble in Peking
became abundantly clear the following month when the Chinese seized
on the innocuous "consultative" conference of Communist parties in
Moscow in early March—which had shelved Khrushchev's schismatic
project for a new international Party conference and appealed for an
end to polemics within the movement—to denounce Khrushchev's
successors and to serve notice that their overtures were rejected
out of hand.[10] Clearly, an attempt was being made to fuel the ideological flames in a calculated effort to counter Moscow's appeal for a
cooling of the rivalry in the interest of the Vietnamese comrades
"standing on the southeastern outpost of the socialist camp." The
anti-Soviet hard-liners were increasingly concerned to sharpen the
issues in this rivalry and to undercut any tendency toward an accommodation based on alliance commitments. The second anniversary
of the June 14, 1963, statement of Peking's strategy for the Communist
movement afforded the occasion for posing these issues in the sharpest
possible form.

A People's Daily/Red Flag editorial on the anniversary reflected
concern over what it defensively viewed as the "more covert, more
cunning, and more dangerous" tactics being followed by the new Kremlin
leadership. In a striking passage running to the heart of the issues
facing Peking, the editorial posed the question of how the Chinese
should respond to the Soviet line: "The question confronting the
Chinese communists today," according to the editorial, was whether
to carry the fight "against Khrushchev revisionism to the end or
whether to stop halfway." In this context, the article took note of the

"honeyed" words about unity coming from Moscow and acknowledged
the pressure on the Chinese arising from the Vietnam War by warning
that the Soviets were seeking to capitalize on aspirations for "closer
unity of the revolutionary forces in face of the U.S. imperialists' rabid
aggression." The editorial observed that the Soviets were "pretending
to be quite accommodating," but "we should not be misled by the various
guises and tricks of Khrushchev's successors and give up our principled
struggle." Those advocating an accommodation with the Soviets were
given a stern lecture: "It would be wrong to exercise unprincipled
flexibility, to create ambiguity and confusion on questions of principle
on the pretext of flexibility." The editorial made it clear that the
stakes were high and the choices momentous. "If we were to abandon
our principled stand and accommodate ourselves or yield to the
Khrushchev revisionists . . . it would be a grave historical mistake.
. . . It is imperative to carry the struggle against Khrushchev revisionism through to the end."[11]

That revealing statement was remarkable both for its defensive-
ness regarding the pressures for Communist unity at that time and
its clear indications of divided councils among the "Chinese communists
today." As its polemical emphasis on "questions of principle" suggested,
there were those willing to blur the differences in the Communist movement and to exercise flexibility "in face of the U.S. imperialists' rabid
aggression" in Vietnam. In fact, during this period serious concern
was being expressed over the growing exercise of American power
near the PRC's borders, a concern that raised fundamental questions
regarding the country's preparedness for threats to its security and
the implications of its commitments within the alliance system. Not
surprisingly, it was the professional military establishment, the
institutional interest group most directly affected by these contingencies,
that expressed particular concern over the state of Chinese preparedness and the state of the alliance relationships affecting Chinese
security.*

The principal textual source of this expressed concern is a
major article by the chief spokesman of the professional military,
PLA Chief of Staff Lo Jui-ch'ing.[12] Giving a tendentious reading of
World War II on the twentieth anniversary of the defeat of Nazi Germany,
Lo elaborated a strategy for the current situation predicated on a

---

*Note that this was a period of serious strategy debates among
Chinese military leaders—notably the Chief of General Staff vs. the
Minister of Defense. See Chapter 18 for details—Ed.

need to meet the challenge of the U.S. intervention in Vietnam and to shore up the alliance at a time when its stability was being seriously tested. The question of a possible new Korea-type conflict had arisen when the United States carried the war in Vietnam to the north by its bombing raids. The Chinese declared that this move had erased the demarcation line dividing Vietnam and that the DRV thus had the right to take the initiative in the south. A PRC statement on the U.S. air attacks in February, 1965, pointedly recalled the Korean War, asking the United States if it wanted that "lesson repeated in Indochina."[13] It was in this context that Lo presented a strategy of "active defense" and "hot pursuit," justifying moves by the DRV to take on the Americans and their allies on a main-force level and preparing the Chinese for the risks of escalation inherent in such a strategy.

Concern over these risks was a central theme in Lo's reading of the situation, as reflected in his strong emphasis on military preparedness ("it makes a world of difference whether or not one is preprepared once war breaks out") and on the need to prepare "not only" for small-scale but also medium- or large-scale war involving nuclear as well as conventional weapons. The polemical tone of this "worst-case" analysis of the situation suggested demands being presented by the professional military that were being resisted in favor of competing priorities and programs.

The risks entailed by the strategy propounded by Lo also raised another sensitive matter of priorities, the "questions of principle" relating to Peking's alliance relations. Lo's discussion of these issues indicated that he placed a higher premium on the deterrent value of the alliance than on pressing the rivalry with the Soviets at a time of outside threat. Significantly, in taking account of the risks of the expanding Vietnam conflict, Lo invoked the deterrent of the socialist camp as a whole. The United States, he pointed out, was taking on "the socialist camp, which is a vast expanse of contiguous territories with a total population of one thousand million and many times stronger than the Soviet Union was in Hitler's time." It was not foolhardy, therefore, to meet the American challenge on its own terms.

But to invoke the alliance presupposed a unity of purpose that was conspicuously absent in Sino-Soviet relations at the time; on this point Lo was notably explicit, stressing that the United States could be deterred "provided that we are good at uniting the socialist camp" (emphasis added). Such a prescription implied the sort of flexibility that the anti-Soviet hard-liners were condemning as a grave misordering of priorities. An examination of Lo's article does, in fact, reveal an ambiguity on this sensitive issue that the major June 14

editorial later sharply denounced. Thus, Lo cautiously avoided a
direct attack on the post-Khrushchev Soviet leadership and its appeal
for unity, ambiguously referring to "revisionists like Khrushchev"
and taking care not to foreclose an accommodation with the mainstay
of the socialist camp. Indeed, he signaled an interest in such an
accommodation by effusively paying "high tribute" to the Soviet army
and expressing strong confidence that the Chinese and Soviets would
be united and "fight shoulder to shoulder" against the common enemy.[14]

The contrast between Lo's approach and that of other authoritative
pronouncements at the time was shown in sharp relief by a People's
Daily article that also was devoted to V-E Day. Again picking up the
ideological challenge to Moscow and explicitly rejecting the Soviet
leaders' proposals for unity, the article denounced the Soviet line as
a "swindle"—expressly attributing it to the "successors to Khrushchev"
—and as an offer of "sham unity" designed to serve the interests of
Soviet-U.S. collaboration at the expense of the Vietnamese. As for
the Communist alliance system, the article offhandedly noted the
existence of "a socialist camp consisting of a number of socialist
countries."[15]

Lo's approach was also challenged by the abolition, announced
that same month, of the military ranking system in the PLA.[16] This
development accentuated the army's role in guerrilla warfare and ran
counter to Lo's emphasis on conventional and nuclear capabilities; it
also signaled a reversal of the "modernization and regularization"
of the PLA begun ten years earlier and a perennial source of conflict
between the professional military and the Maoists. The attack on
military modernization was ideologically elaborated in a major article
on the August 1 anniversary of the army's founding that defensively
argued against demands for modernization and professionalism in
military affairs.[17]

It was in this setting, marked by a renewed emphasis on the
PLA's mission in guerrilla warfare and by insistent demands for an
inflexible anti-Soviet stand, that Lin Piao's celebrated tract on People's
War propounded a strategy in accord with Maoist priorities by assigning primacy to guerrilla warfare and accepting the risks of isolation
in preference to an accommodation with the Soviets.[18] This strategy
called for the Vietnamese Communists, facing an infusion of American
power into a situation where they had sensed imminent victory, to
dig in for protracted guerrilla warfare, thereby minimizing the risks
of an escalation into a Korean-type conflict. Seeking to lower the
PRC's commitment to the Vietnamese, Lin prescribed a policy of
self-reliance for the insurgents, putting them on notice that they must

be ready to carry on the fight independently "even when all material
aid from outside is cut off." All but spelling out the message, he added
a warning against relying on foreign aid even from socialist countries
"which persist in revolution," namely countries like the PRC.

Lin's strategy was designed to decouple the Vietnam conflict and
China's security, a move serving at once a low-risk policy militarily
and the political needs for complete independence of Soviet influence.
Significantly, Lin's tract omitted any mention of the socialist camp,
a remarkable but revealing omission of what had been a central—and,
for the Chinese in the late 1950s, the central—element in the articulation
of Communist strategy. In universalizing the doctrine of People's
War, he applied the strategy to Asia, Africa, and Latin America as
the "main battlefield" for the present anti-U.S. struggle. In dialectical
terms, this was the claim that "the contradiction between the revolutionary peoples of Asia, Africa, and Latin America and the imperialists headed by the United States is the principal contradiction
of the contemporary world."[19] To appreciate the extent to which the
evolution of Chinese thinking was accelerated in the eventful months
preceding Lin's tract one should recall how Peking's message to
Moscow—signed by Mao—on the anniversary of the Sino-Soviet treaty
in February invoked "the entire socialist camp" in connection with
the U.S. bombing of North Vietnam. In less than a year, the triumphant
Maoists, overriding those voices cautioning against the risks of isolation at a time of external threat, had thrown the alliance system to
the gathering winds of change and prepared to unleash the storms of
the Cultural Revolution.

Lo Jui-ch'ing was purged some time in late 1965. A major policy
statement on November 11 undertook to explain a situation in which
the struggle was especially sharp and "astonishingly abrupt changes"
were taking place.[20] Significantly, the statement was devoted to an
intransigent denunciation of Moscow's line of "united action," exhibiting
a vehemence and finality of tone that testified at once to the strength
of the Maoist impulse toward independence and to the force of the
appeal to international Communist unity at a time of stress. Signaling
a determination to foreclose categorically and irreparably any accommodation on this issue and any effort to mediate the schism,
Peking now demanded that "a clear line of demarcation both politically
and organizationally" be drawn between its supporters and those following or accommodating the Soviets, a demand that would severely
strain its relations with its Asian allies and plunge the Chinese into
deep isolation. With the process deepened by the dynamics of the
Cultural Revolution,[21] the Chinese entered a period of "great upheaval,
great division, and great reorganization" causing "drastic divisions
and realignments" of forces in the world."

REALIGNMENT AND RECONSTRUCTION,
1969-71

When the PRC emerged from this period of upheaval, its relationship with the Soviet Union having developed into a menacing confrontation across a severely troubled border, a situation arose in which the
adroit professionalism and flexibility of Chou En-lai could be brought
profitably into play. As the aftereffects of the Cultural Revolution
continued to send tremors through the Chinese body politic, the strength
of Chou's hand and the boldness of Chouist policy moves became increasingly evident. The startling announcement in mid-1971 that the
American President had been invited to Peking served dramatic notice
on the international community—and particularly on Moscow—that the
PRC had indeed returned to center stage in the world arena.

A salient dimension in Peking's new moves on this stage was
its effort to repair its alliance relations in Asia, an effort particularly
motivated by a desire to gain leverage against the Soviets. This effort
also reflected its definition of Chinese national interests in an essentially regional framework, as opposed to the global scope of the two
superpowers (discussed below). The reconstitution of the PRC's
alliance with North Korea provides a case study of Peking's reviving
foreign relations. Redressing the imbalance and damage resulting
from the ideological compulsions of the preceding phase, the Chinese
proceeded to secure a strategic flank against the Soviet Union by
strengthening their convergent interests with the North Koreans. In
particular, the Chinese have capitalized on Pyongyang's concern over
the potential impact of a more assertive Japan. Moreover, a movement
of "Asian revolutionary unity" embracing the Chinese, Korean, and
Indochinese Communists and their leftist allies has strengthened
Peking's influence in the region while tending to squeeze out the
Soviets. In a significant measure of Peking's success in cultivating
Pyongyang, the latter embraced the movement of Asian unity in place
of its once strong commitment to "the socialist camp"—the very com-
mitment that Pyongyang had formerly invoked in denouncing the
Chinese for failing to heed the calls for united action in behalf of the
DRV.

In rebuilding their alliance relations, however, the Chinese were
cautious in defining their commitments. Significantly, this caution
was most notably expressed by the PLA chief of staff on the twentieth
anniversary in October, 1970, of the Chinese entry into the Korean
War. In a major policy pronouncement characteristically using the
past to discuss the present, Huang Yung-sheng offered an unusually

explicit explanation for the Chinese intervention twenty years earlier.
He clearly distinguished between the period when the Chinese "supported and assisted" the Koreans in "their fatherland liberation war"
and the period of direct Chinese intervention after the U.S. had "fla-
grantly extended the flames of its aggressive war to the Yalu River
in disregard of the repeated stern warnings of the Chinese people and
gravely menaced the security of China." In assessing the present
situation, he used the low-risk formula of Chinese "support and assistance" to pledge backing for the North Koreans. The over-all implication was that the Chinese themselves were not committed to further
action until a high threshold of direct threat to their borders and
security was reached.[22] Also at this time, the Chinese began referring
for the first time in several years to "peaceful" unification of Korea,
as if to underscore their counsel of caution and to demonstrate their
readiness to countenance negotiations as an instrument of foreign
policy.[23]

A few months later, the strategic posture being enunciated by
Huang and others was confronted with an actual test of Peking's commitments to its allies. In February, 1971, South Vietnamese troops
with U.S. support launched an operation (Lam Son 719) in southern
Laos aimed at crippling the North Vietnamese supply trails passing
through that area. Peking reacted by issuing a government statement
on February 12 that for the first time in several years directly linked
China's security to military developments in Indochina. Claiming
that "U.S. imperialism's aggression against Laos is also a grave
menace to China," the statement warned that the Chinese "absolutely
will not remain indifferent to it."[24] The Chinese seemed sensitive
over the credibility of their warning, taking particular exception to
President Nixon's subsequent denial that the Laos operation posed a
threat to the PRC as an attempt "to tie the hands of the Chinese people
in giving support" to their friends in Indochina. In language reminiscent of Huang's account the previous October of the conditions triggering
Chinese intervention in Korea, an authoritative commentary claimed
that the United States was "spreading the flames of war to the door
of China" and lectured the President on the geographical realities of
a common PRC-Laotian border of several hundred kilometers.[25] At
this time, the Chinese in fact hinted at an analogy with Korea, though
taking care to avoid drawing the parallel on their own authority and
to limit their commitment to the pledge of continuing rear-area "support and assistance."

During the first few weeks of Lam Son 719, the North Vietnamese,
who were expressing concern over the possibility of further enemy
"military adventures" aimed directly at them, pointedly linked their

security interests with those of the Chinese in an evident effort to
obtain a stronger commitment from Peking. The Chinese finally responded in early March by dispatching a powerful delegation to Hanoi,
headed by Chou En-lai and including strong military representation.
As they had done the previous month in the case of Laos, the Chinese
for the first time in years directly coupled their security with that of
the DRV. A joint communiqué warned that the "new and extremely
grave war escalation" by the United States in Indochina "directly
menaces the security of the DRV and at the same time the security
of the PRC." It also declared that the two sides had "taken full account
of the recklessness and madness of the Nixon government" and reached
"completely identical views" on "how to deal with possible military
adventures" by the United States. For their part, the Chinese offered
the assurance that they would take "all necessary measures, not
flinching even from the greatest national sacrifices," to support their
allies in Indochina.[26]

Though with respect to the DRV as well as Laos the Chinese did
not indicate that they were contemplating measures beyond those of
rear-area support that they had undertaken for years, it was nonetheless
the case that, in reconstituting their relations with close neighbors,
they were projecting their security interests in terms of stronger
commitments than they had during the previous period dominated by
Lin Piao's isolationist strategy. That this move encountered resistance
is suggested by the appearance of a remarkable new "instruction" by
Mao, which Chou introduced in a speech on March 6 in Hanoi—the same
speech in which Chinese readiness for "the greatest national sacrifices"
was proclaimed.[27] Mao's instruction sanctioned support for the
Vietnamese in notably strong terms: "If anyone among us should say
that we cannot help the Vietnamese people in their struggle against
U.S. aggression and for national salvation, that means mutiny, that
means betrayal of the revolution." While the choice of Hanoi as the
venue for releasing this statement from the highest authority served
to dramatize Peking's commitment to the North Vietnamese, the
cutting edge of its warning seemed aimed at elements in Peking
reluctant to assume the firmer strategic posture. Though the relations
between reconstruction at home and realignment abroad remain murky,
it should be noted that Ch'en Po-ta, the fourth-ranking leader and a
figure closely associated with the radical policies of the Cultural
Revolution, had disappeared from view from the time of the Party
plenum held the previous August and September. Moreover, it was
during the spring of 1971 that the year's fourth issue of Red Flag
began a campaign against "idealist apriorism" that was clearly directed
at Ch'en and his policies. In the context of international affairs, this
campaign has been marked by an insistence on the need to undertake

readjustments and realignments in order to accommodate changing
conditions and new realities.

The demand for flexibility and the evolution of an increasingly
differentiated strategy, which have been reflected in Peking's policies
across a global range of expanding relations, is rooted primarily in
Peking's perception of its triangular relationship with the two superpowers. The new flexibility found dramatic expression in the July,
1971, announcement of the invitation to President Nixon to visit the
PRC. As in past major junctures in Peking's policy-making, such as
in 1957 and 1965, events had developed with notable rapidity. In early
March, the Chinese and their North Vietnamese allies were taking
account of "the recklessness and madness" of the Nixon Administration,
but shortly afterward Peking had pulled back from its characterization
of a threat to Chinese security in Indochina and pronounced the situation
there to be "unprecedentedly fine"—a judgment that justified greater
maneuverability to pursue its interests in a broader Asian context.

Characteristically, Peking again turned to the theory of "contradictions" and to an explication of alliance relations to account
for the new strategic line. Peking's explication confirmed that
its flexible moves in the international arena were highly purposive
and carefully designed to strengthen its hand in an environment that
it clearly now perceived as fundamentally multipolar. To sanction
this flexibility, the Chinese invoked the highest authority, canonical
works by Mao, which, among other uses, serves to justify new moves
as a continuation of tried-and-true practices of the past. Most notably,
the ninth issue of Red Flag in 1971, the first issue prepared after the
announcement of the invitation to the U.S. President, drew on the
authority of Mao's 1940 work "On Policy" to provide a guide for the
new "extremely complex situation."[28] Red Flag's analysis focused
on the need to identify "the main enemy," as distinguished from "the
enemy of secondary importance," and to make maximum use of
contradictions among adversaries and of "temporary allies or indirect
allies" in order to isolate the main enemy.

The Red Flag analysis deserves—as it was clearly intended to
receive—a close reading. In a crucial passage, recalling the period
of Mao's 1940 work, the article noted that the Chinese Party "opposes
all imperialism, but we made a distinction between Japanese imperialism then committing aggression against China and the imperialist powers which were not doing so at that time; and between
the imperialist powers which adopted different policies under different
circumstances at different times." The first distinction, if updated
to the current reality of the bitter Sino-Soviet confrontation across

a border that had become a battle line, clearly implies a need to concentrate on the Soviet Union as the primary threat today. Where the first distinction was taken directly from "On Policy," the second one telescoped a passage that includes explicit references to China's attitude toward the United States. That passage in Mao's work distinguishes between U.S. policy in an earlier phase—when the United States "followed a Munich policy in the Far East"—and its abandonment of this policy by 1940 "in favor of China's resistance." The reader following Red Flag's advice to turn to "On Policy" for current guidance is thus amply rewarded in understanding the differentiations underlying Peking's moves to strengthen its hand against the Soviets. As Red Flag observed, the view that "all enemies are of one cut and are a monolithic bloc does not conform to objective reality." On the contrary, it is of utmost importance to "be good at seizing opportunities" to capitalize on the "rifts and contradictions in the enemy camp and turn them against our present main enemy."

The significance of Peking's rethinking could hardly be lost on its allies, and the Chinese have tried to put developments in perspective. The PLA chief of staff, speaking before a visiting North Korean military delegation— and to the international Communist gallery—on August 18, 1971, revived a significant cue for his audience in observing that the present world situation is one of "great upheaval, great division, and great reorganization." This observation, it will be recalled, was made in the November 11, 1965, policy statement explaining Peking's line at another time of "astonishingly abrupt changes." At that time, the Chinese conceded that there was bound to be "a certain unevenness in the degree of people's understanding" of Peking's position. A comparable "unevenness" had been exhibited by Peking's allies in the wake of the invitation to President Nixon. In particular, the Chinese were of course aware of the blistering lecture intended for them that was delivered by the North Vietnamese army paper, which in a long polemical article earlier in August had denounced the view of a multipolar world. Taking a line remarkably reminiscent of Peking's polemics against Moscow in an earlier era, the article insisted that the United States remains "the main and most dangerous enemy of all the people of the world" and that its offers of détente and negotiation were an invitation to betrayal of the revolution. Other polemical North Vietnamese comment at the time pointedly warned that Washington was seeking to divide the socialist camp.

On one point, however, the Chinese undoubtedly were in agreement with their North Vietnamese comrades. To quote the DRV army paper, "the question of evaluating foe, friend, and oneself has always been one of primary importance" and "the starting point" from which strategy and tactics are devised. Peking had been at this starting point several times since Mao decided to lean to one side more than two decades earlier. It had now returned to the starting point to try, once more, to cope with what might be termed its strategic imperatives: to complete the revolution and establish sovereignty over Taiwan; to secure its borders, now menanced by a massive Soviet military presence; and to act as an independent agent free of superpower control.

In assessing Peking's moves to translate these imperatives into military policy and strategic planning, the observer might be well advised to take Peking's assurances that it never intends to become a superpower with some degree of seriousness. Shorn of its invidious associations, the concept of a superpower can be defined as denoting a country whose vital interests embrace its far-flung global commitments, however distant from its homeland. A superpower, then, seeks to have the military capability—such as overseas bases, a global navy, and so on—to defend these vital interests wherever they are threatened. The emergence of the two superpowers, so defined, can thus be viewed as a development of the bipolar rivalry after World War II in which distant points of tension became tests of the global lines of the two major rivals. Taking the Chinese denial of any aspiration to achieve superpower status as an hypothesis, one would not expect Peking, acting in an increasingly multipolar environment, to follow the pattern set by the superpowers in seeking a projection of military power to match the reach of its political influence. The development of the PRC's strategic planning, its nuclear-weapons program, and its force structure and deployment, among others, will test the validity of this hypothesis in the long term. In the shorter term, the PRC might be expected to continue its highly active effort to enhance its international political assests. Its purpose would be to make hostile moves against itself as politically prohibitive as possible at a time when it cannot exact a sufficiently painful military cost. To that end, one may expect Chinese military leaders to continue to accent deception warfare.

NOTES

1. Ch'en Po-ta, "Yugoslav Revisionism—Product of Imperialist Policy," HC, No. 1, 1958; translated in PR, I, June 17, 1958, pp. 8-12. (Emphases added.)

2. "The Origins and Development of the Differences Between the Leadership of the CPSU and Ourselves," People's Daily and Red Flag, editorials, PR, Vol. VI, September 13, 1963, pp. 6-23.

3. Statement of the Soviet Government, September 21, 1963.

4. M. I. Makarov, I. Ya. Bednyak, et al., Foreign Policy of the PRC (Moscow: Mezhdunarodnyye Otnosheniya Publishing House, 1971; translated in Joint Publications Research Service 53461.

5. Vol. II, October 6, 1959, p. 10.

6. Ibid., VIII, February 12, 1965, pp. 6-7.

7. Ibid., February 19, 1965, pp. 6-7.

8. "Struggle to Safeguard Sino-Soviet Unity," Ibid., pp. 11-13.

9. Ibid., p. 12.

10. "A Comment on the March Moscow Meeting," People's Daily and Red Flag editorials, ibid, VIII, March 26, 1965, pp. 7-13.

11. "Carry the Struggle Against Khrushchev Revisionism Through to the End," PR, VIII, June 18, 1965, pp. 5-10.

12. Lo's article and other pronouncements of that period have been subjected to considerable textual analysis. Interpretations developing links between strategy and alliance relations are found in the articles by Uri Ra'anan and Donald Zagoria in Tang Tsou and Ping-ti Ho, eds., China in Crisis, II (Chicago, Univ. of Chicago Press, 1968).

13. PRC government statement of February 13, 1965, PR, VIII, February 19, 1965, pp. 5-6. The analogy with Korea was prominent in statements associating Vietnam with defense of the socialist camp. Thus a People's Daily editorial on June 27, marking the fifteenth anniversary of the U.S. interdiction of the Taiwan Straits after the outbreak of the Korean War, said American strategy was "directed against China and the entire socialist camp as well as against Vietnam. . . . The Signs are that the United States is very likely to expand its war of aggression against Vietnam into a partial war of the Korea type" (emphases added). The editorial was transmitted by NCNA, June 27, 1965. It is intriguing to note, in light of the contentious issues of that time, that this loaded passage was deleted from the version published in PR, VIII, July 2, 1965, pp. 9-10.

14. Lo Jui-ching, "Commemorate the Victory Over German Fascism! Carry the Struggle Against U.S. Imperialism Through to

the End!," HC, No. 5, 1965; and in PR, VIII, May 14, 1965, pp. 7-15. Note that the title of the June 14 editorial called for carrying the struggle against Khrushchev revisionism through to the end (see note 11).

15. "The Historical Experience of the War Against Fascism," JMJP, May 9, 1965; and in PR, VIII, May 14, 1965, pp. 15-22.

16. NCNA, Peking, May 24, 1965.

17. Ho Lung, "Democratic Tradition of the Chinese People's Liberation Army," PR, VIII, August 6, 1965, pp. 9-30. The policy conflict at this time was recounted a year later on Army Day in a Liberation Army Daily identifying it as the third of three major struggles between the professional military and Maoist lines since the founding of the PRC. According to the editorial, those emphasizing military preparedness as a top priority "opposed absolute leadership by the party over the army" and demanded "bourgeois regularization" of military affairs. The editorial stressed Lin Piao's role in "giving prominence to politics" rather than to military training and praised his program for strengthening political and ideological work in the PLA. This editorial, appearing at an important point in the Chinese Cultural Revolution, showed how the claims of Maoist domestic programs, in which the PLA played a key role, took precedence over the demands for preparedness and commitments in behalf of the Communist camp ("Make Our Army a Great School of Mao Tse-tung's Thought," PR, IX August 5, 1966, pp. 8-10).

18. Lin Piao, "Long Live the Victory of People's War," PR, VIII, September 3, 1965, pp. 9-30.

19. In contrast, Lo Jui-ch'ing used the same occasion as Lin's tract (V-J Day) to reaffirm his position that the existence of "a powerful socialist camp" was of prime significance in the confrontation with the United States. Lo again insisted that "full account" be taken of the danger that the Vietnam War might spread to China. Speech at a Peking rally, September 3, 1965, ibid., pp. 31-39.

20. "Refutation of the New Leaders of the CPSU on 'United Action,' " People's Daily and Red Flag editorials, ibid, November 12, 1965, pp. 10-21.

21. The chief victim of the Cultural Revolution, Liu Shao-ch'i, issued a statement as late as July 22, 1966, that challenged the line that had emerged victorious in the policy conflict of the previous year.

In an unprecedented personal statement on behalf of the government, Liu used the formulation that "U.S. imperialist aggression against Vietnam is aggression against China" and declared that the Chinese were ready to undertake "the greatest national sacrifices" to support their Vietnamese brethern. Liu's statement was particularly intriguing for its condemnation of "national chauvinism and national egoism which betray the interests of the revolutionary people of the world"—the sort of charge that such formerly close allies of Peking as the North Korians leveled at the Chinese. It is worth noting here that a Soviet account of this period says Lo Jui-ch'ing in 1965 urged united action on Vietnam and, "supported by Peking Mayor Peng Chen, and later in 1966 by Liu Shao-chi, feared that the United States might transfer the war to Chinese territory." According to the Soviet account, Lo appealed to Mao "to give active support to the DRV and to join the Soviet Union and the other socialist countries for this purpose." V. Bolshakov, Komsomolskaya Pravda, December 1, 1968.

22. PR, XIII, October 30, 1970, pp. 9-11.

23. A few weeks later, a Chinese Party-government statement on December 13, 1970, contained Peking's first endorsement of the Vietnamese Communists' peace proposals (ibid., December 18, 1970, pp. 3-4).

24. Ibid., XIV, February 19, 1971, p. 6.

25. "Don't Lose Your Head, Nixon," JMJP, "Commentator," February 20, 1971; and in PR, XIV, February 26, 1971, p. 6.

26. PR, XIV, March 12, 1971, pp. 18-21.

27. Ibid., pp. 15-17.

28. "Powerful Weapon for Uniting People and Defeating the Enemy," HC, No. 9, 1971. The article was published in People's Daily on August 17; two weeks later it was disseminated internationally by NCNA. The same issue contained the August 1 Army Day joint editorial, which propounded "Mao's revolutionary diplomatic line"—in effect a line on negotiation as the continuation of revolution by other means.

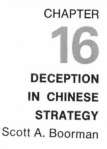

DECEPTION
IN CHINESE
STRATEGY

Scott A. Boorman

INTRODUCTION

Like deception in love, deception in war has a long and venerable history. Probably no competent strategist of any age or nation would definitively deny the usefulness of the artifices of war—ruse, stratagem, camouflage, and the like—in successful execution of the military art. Most writers on war and strategy make some gesture, however token, in the direction of recognizing the importance of strategic deception.[1] In war, as Napoleon took pains to emphasize, the moral is to the material as three is to one;[2] and deception of the opponent is

———————
———————

The author is indebted to the following individuals for critical reading of an earlier version of the present chapter: Captain Clarence O. Fiske, USN; Mr. Frank A. Kierman, Jr.; Mr. Terrence G. Des Pres; and Professors Burton S. Dreben, John C. Harsanyi, Frederick H. Hartmann, Thomas C. Schelling, and Harrison C. White. The author also thanks Professors Everett I. Mendelsohn and Jaakko Hintikka for discussion on the history of the concept of probability and Parris H. Chang, Henry E. Eccles, William R. Harris, Fred C. Iklé, Harry H. Ransom, Amos Perlmutter, Martin Shubik, and William W. Whitson for lively conversations on topics related to cover and deception operations. Several of the philological and semantic points related to Sun Tzu were discussed with Professor William Hung (Hung Yeh), and this chapter has profited greatly from his remarks.

nothing else than one type of manipulation of his human, or moral, qualities to one's own advantage.*

Taking into account these cautionary observations, however, one sees stratagem playing very different roles in warfare and other forms of conflict at different times and places in history. Strategy is like any other form of "combinatorics." The Chinese military theorist Sun Tzu (c. fourth century B.C.) remarks:

> There are not more than five musical notes, yet the combinations of these five give rise to more melodies than can ever be heard. . . . In battle, there are not more than two methods of attack—the direct and the indirect, yet these two in combination give rise to an endless series of manoeuvers.[3]

That particular form of the indirect approach known as stratagem is a manifestation of strategic style that modern Western cultural mythology tends to associate with the Orient.[4] The cannotation is that of psychological subtlety and (to introduce another cultural referent) Machiavellian sophistication. Yet, few students of strategy have cared to go beyond such facile labels and to inquire what role deception has actually played in various strategic traditions, Western and non-Western.[5] The problem is really one of intellectual history. What is needed is comparison of different, historically evolved systems of strategic values along the evidently fundamental dimension of how they incorporate reciprocal expectations and mutual conditioning into the dialectic of conflict.

Current strategic thinking in the United States places comparatively little stress on stratagem or deception practices.[6] Where the theory of deception is most highly developed is significantly in the area of electronic warfare, which is minimally concerned with the long-run influencing of the behavior and intentions of an enemy operational commander.[7] By contrast, American thinking is extremely sophisticated in other areas of military policy, such as logistic planning (well symbolized by the mammoth Annual Department of Defense Bibliography of Logistics Studies). American military planning tends to be overwhelmingly based on evaluation of enemy capabilities—of his physical and logistical situation.[8]

---

*In fact, broadly enough construed, it is the only form of such manipulation in the case where the interests of the parties are diametrically opposed (the pure-competition case in game theory).

Doctrinal pronouncements are, to be sure, only imperfect mirrors of how commanders behave in the field. It is true, for example, that in Vietnam American forces have attempted to use small advance units as bait for enemy ambush forces deployed along the route of advance of a column.[9] Capabilities orientation of American strategy is, however, well symbolized by the following quotation from a basic doctrinal source: "The U.S. Defense Establishment must be fully capable of attaining national objectives regardless of any course of action the enemy can employ."[10] Insofar as the rationale for this position is explicitly formulated, it is usually phrased in terms of a kind of risk aversion: in modern warfare, the argument runs, the risks and the stakes are too high for operational planning to rest on the assumption that enemy intentions can be effectively manipulated. Concealed within this line of reasoning, of course, is an implicit lack of confidence in one's psychological technology and distrust for fighting a war on "subjective" rather than "objective" lines.

Asian strategy embraces too complex and diverse a group of cultures and historical periods to present more than superficial unity.[11] The role of stratagem in classical Chinese strategic theory is, however, unambiguous. In most classics of Chinese military thinking, successful deception is held to be a mark of high strategic merit. Moreover, and even more important, exchanges of strategem and counterstrategem are expected to be the normal currency of conflict interaction.[12] The difference from Western warfare is still to a great extent captured by C. W. C. Oman's classic The Art of War in the Middle Ages: "For centuries war was studied as an art in the east, while in the West it remained largely a matter of hard fighting."[13] A more contemporary rendition would substitute hard bargaining for hard fighting, but the idea remains the same. The great strategists of Chinese history, men such as Chu-ko Liang and Ts'ao Ts'ao (third century A.D.), were explicitly admired by later generation for their skill in stratagem much more than for their courage or organizational ability:

> In his military operations, he [Ts'ao Ts'ao] followed in the main the tactics laid down in the Sun-tzu and the Wu-tzu. In accordance with different situations, he took extra-extraordinary stratagems; by deceiving the enemy, he won victory; he varied his tactics in demonic fashion.[14]

This concept of strategy through stratagem goes beyond attempts merely to outwit the opponent by conveying false intentions; it involves the more sophisticated task of directly manipulating his perception of reality, and in particular his perceptions of the values to him of various outcomes of the conflict. The aim, most particularly, is to manipulate his concept of his own objectives and his own "face,"

to induce him—for whatever reason—to assign great psychological
utility to courses of action favorable to one's own interest.[15] "If we
lose the field," said Shakespeare's Lartius, "we cannot keep the town."[16]
If one can cause the enemy's face to be inextricably bound up with
holding the town first and foremost, one may thereby induce him to
neglect the field. Control of the countryside will lead to encirclement
of the city, and city and countryside will both fall victim to the enemy's
own evaluation of his priorities.

STRATAGEM: CONCEPTS AND DEFINITIONS

Concepts of stratagem and of strategic deception are widely
scattered through the theoretical and historical literatures of many
eras, as well as in the active military parlance of many nations.[17]
Unfortunately, explications of these concepts seem not to be similarly
frequent. One basic problem to an expositor is that military thinkers
seldom differentiate strategic deception proper from other actions
and effects (ambush, surprise, indirect maneuver, and so forth) to
which it is related but not identical, nor from the all-embracing indirect approach of Liddell Hart and his disciple Andre Beaufre.[18]
Especially in the work of this last man, the indirect approach seems
to subsume everything except a brutal and continuing frontal assault.
Existing theoretical work provides, in short, an incredibly tangled
skein of theoretical concepts founded in many languages and embedded
in expositions of widely differing purpose. What is very much lacking
is any systematic attempt to differentiate the pictures of conflict and
strategy underlying these diverse usages and to trace their historical
development and cultural relativity.* Only in this way can the concept of stratagem cease to be a meaningless term, pejorative or
laudatory at the will of the user.

It is scarcely possible within the present brief compass to set
up a complete typology of the varieties of strategic behavior, any
more than such an enumeration would be possible for the immensely
more developed and sophisticated field of ethical conduct. Within the

----

*To introduce a parallel with social ethics and moral philosophy,
one of the main lessons that the study of strategy could derive from
these fields is a realization that there is no unequivocally correct
picture of the way the world is put together and that the most profitable
pursuit may be dissection of the relations among alternative Weltan-
schauungen. The exigencies of unambiguous policy-making, however,
make the pressure toward finding universal strategic truth overwhelming in most contexts where strategy is studied.

age-old military distinction separating capabilities from intentions, however, a finer gradation of nuance may be profitably established.

First, there is a level of strategic behavior targeted on reacting only to the enemy's capabilities. The psychological interaction between the two conflict actors is minimal, though a competent strategy oriented toward capabilities does not exclude applications of mass psychology, both as targeted at one's own forces and at those of the enemy. (What the French theorists of the 1950s would call la guerre psychologique and l'action psychologique.) Contrary to the mythology implicit in some of the European theoretical literature, such a strategy of action need not rely solely on the direct approach. Encirclement, outflanking, infiltration—in fact, most of the apparatus customarily associated with unconventional warfare—may be among its tools; the only defining requirement is that a strategy is capability oriented in so far as it does not try to probe and influence the mind of the enemy commander himself.[19]

Next, there is a level of strategic behavior targeted on attempting to relate one's own actions to the enemy's intentions. One can simply try to learn these intentions (by espionage, reconnaissance, and so forth). The obverse activity is to prevent the enemy from learning one's own intentions, i.e., maintenance of uncertainty.[20] What is more, one can try to control the enemy's intentions as well as to infer them. It is at this last transition point, where pure intelligence (and counterintelligence) is transformed into the manipulation of enemy intentions, that stratagem or strategic deception becomes a valid description of the phenomena. This is the level of bluff: signaling, in the parlance of certain game theorists, now becomes crucial and is the behavioral mechanism by which appropriate information and misinformation may be transmitted.

Looking at stratagem in the reinforcement terms of behaviorist psychology rather than from the information-theoretic perspective of signaling, one sees yet a deeper level of relating one's own actions to the enemy's intentions. Consider a typical zero-sum game-theoretic situation of classical von Neumann-Morgenstern type. The basic invariant aspect of the game is the payoff matrix that defines it (strictly speaking, invariant up to rescaling the utility function); it is from this fixed-payoff matrix that any formal decision theory will take its rise. Suppose, however, one now looks not at the formal model (which, after all, is a very recent theoretical development), but rather at the underlying conflict situation that it is designed to represent. As any military officer who has been exposed to game-theoretic concepts will confirm, there is no truly invariant set of numerical labels that can be used, even in principle, to describe the outcomes of a situation in real life. Military payoffs are notoriously subjective, dependent upon an evaluation of a complex set of future developments and past contingencies.[21]

The value ascribed to possession of a town may strongly depend upon a wide variety of subjective factors, such as the face involved in abdicating its control and the importance of towns in one's over-all strategic concept. When one side explicitly tries to manipulate such factors determining the shape of the subjective utility function of the opponent, a new level of strategic complexity is achieved. Stratagem now becomes the manipulation of the opponent's concept of reality in such a way that his utility function, and a fortiori his course of action, shifts in a direction favorable to one's own best interests. An example would be inducing the opponent to commit himself to defense of a particular strong point far out of proportion to its intrinsic strategic worth.[22]

It is this level of strategy through stratagem that is central to some very important threads of continuity in the Chinese strategic tradition and is very much unemphasized in Western strategic thought, even in the indirect approach synthesized by Liddel Hart.[23] At the second level delineated above, that of interactive signaling and the phenomenology of "He thinks I think . . . ," the strongest proposition that would be valid is that historically the Chinese have developed it more than the West, possibly excepting certain specific historical periods in Europe such as the Italian Renaissance.[24]

It should be stressed that this proposed gap between Western and Chinese thinking in the area of strategic deception is in no sense identical to the failure of Western military doctrine adequately to integrate itself with its political objectives. This latter failure has been stressed in great detail by Schelling and other bargaining theorists, and its remedy is closely connected with the cognitive advance from a zero-sum to a nonzero-sum viewpoint. Sun Tzu and other premodern Chinese military thinkers are just as unpolitical as Jomini and Clausewitz, and an emphasis on stratagem has little connection with political sophistication or lack of it.[25]

STRATAGEM: THE CHINESE VIEW
IN THE SUN TZU

The ancient Chinese strategist Sun Tzu is the only Chinese strategic thinker who has ever gained much cognizance in the West, with the latter-day exception of Mao Tse-tung.[26] This recognition, though not based in most cases on deep historical evaluation, is well merited, since Sun Tzu is also cited among military thinkers with overwhelming frequency in Chinese historical and political literature, as well as being studied by most Chinese statesmen with pretensions toward strategic competence and by most officials confronted with the handling of military situations.[27] When one gets deeper into the historical source material, to be sure, one wonders whether statesmen and soldiers have paid much more than superficial respect to the writings of Sun Tzu (or any other theoretical exponent of strategic matters); but there is no doubt that this brief book (in present form, it is only a few thousand characters) has had a far more controlling influence on Chinese strategic behavior than any comparable work, including that of Clausewitz, has had in the West. The main point, in any case, is the guiding picture of strategy through stratagem. A remark by a Western Sinologist on a classic of Chinese rhetoric was not directly intended for this context, but bears verbatim quotation: "It would not matter whether the Intrigues were one-fifth or four-fifths fictional, this would remain the central political fact of the age."[28]

Although, as previously indicated, the Sun Tzu text is at least tolerably well known in contemporary Western strategic circles, in the Western literature there is no interpretation of its significance that is very helpful to understanding its central themes.[29] To evaluate the picture of the world presented in the Sun Tzu, several concrete aspects of the organization and style of the text should be discussed at the outset. As in most Chinese social-theoretical and philosophical works of the period, the style is terse and epigrammatic and consists of a sequence of maxims strung together, roughly organized by topic, but offering no consistent sequential argument.[30] Metaphors and analogies are frequent; historical examples are lacking, though the standard commentaries fill in many examples from later epics. The commentary interpretations are of great importance, since for the most part they have heavily influenced the interpretations of the text for at least the last millennium.

Following is an excerpt from a standard translation of the first chapter of the text, which follows some introductory remarks stressing the importance of the study of war and the basic aspects of the military art. The relevance to the topic of stratagem needs no comment:

> All warfare is based on deception. Hence, when able to attack, we must seem unable; when using our forces, we must seem inactive; when we are near, we must make the enemy believe we are far away; when far away, we must

make him believe we are near. Hold out baits to entice the
enemy. Feign disorder, and crush him. If he is secure at
all points, be prepared for him. If he is in superior strength,
evade him. If your opponent is of choleric temper, seek to
irritate him. Pretend to be weak, that he may grow arrogant. If he is taking his ease, give him no rest. If his forces
are united, separate them. Attack him where he is unprepared, appear where you are not expected.

These military devices, leading to victory, must not
be divulged beforehand.[31]

It is clear that Sun Tzu is here stressing primarily that level
of stratagem that consists of attempting to induce the enemy to make
a wrong decision because he is misled as to one's own situation and
strategy. The possible devices for implementation of this aim are
numerous, and it is to the credit of the text that it does not bog down
in an attempted catalog of the mechanisms (by contrast to certain
much later Chinese strategic works, which, as Herbert Franke has
pointed out, fairly reek of armchair stratagems).[32] In a later chapter
(Chapter 9), however, there is a very interesting and quite concrete
discussion of counterstratagems: the problem of filtering one's intelligence with the aim of disclosing the enemy's true situation when
he is trying to present it deceptively. For example, "Humble words
and increased preparations are signs that the enemy is about to advance. Violent language and driving forward as if to the attack are
signs that he will retreat."[33]

For a modern Chinese, perhaps the most familiar collection
of stratagems and counterstratagems of this nature is that contained
in the fictionalized San-kuo chih yen-i (Chronicle of the Three Kingdoms).[34] This is a rather romanticized, and hence very popular,
narrative account in the colloquial style of a famous period of factionalism and dynastic decay in the third century A.D., known to
have made a deep impression on the young Mao Tse-tung.[35] Carried
to its romantic limit, this aspect of Chinese warfare leads to the
near-paranoid view of Chinese conflict behavior advocated many
years ago by a former French military attaché stationed in Peking.
He argues,

Leur diplomatie consiste ordinairement à faire croire à
l'ennemi qu'on veut s'entendre avec lui, ou aux rebelles
que grâce leur sera faite, à leur promettre des honneurs
pour les attirer dans son camp et les massacrer à
loisir.[36]

Ruses of this kind are deeply bound up with Western perceptions of Asian strategic subtlety. From a less culturally chauvinistic viewpoint, stratagem of this nature is scarcely profound; in fact, to quote Balzac, "Il n'y a pas de théorie, il n'y a que de partique dans ce métier."

It should be noted, however, that a certain element of the last, and highest, form of stratagem—that which seeks to manipulate the opponent's utility function itself—appears in Sun Tzu's prescriptive list, where he speaks of angering the enemy and encouraging his arrogance.[37] This subtle, but significant, distinction is supported by various standard commentaries on this particular passage. Li Ch'uan (himself an author of a well-known military text of the eight century A.D., the so-called T'ai-po yin-ching [Secret Classic of Venus]) remarks, for example, that the purpose of angering the enemy commander is to cause his spirit to vacillate—i.e., to lose his head.[38] Another commentator, Chang Yu, makes the point even more strongly. By irritating the enemy, he remarks, the commanding general can cause the former to "advance lightly, without stratagem."[39] Even more extensive commentary has been generated by the remark on encouraging the arrogance of the enemy, with many historical examples being cited on instances where wars were lost because a commander was induced by the enemy to be overconfident of his own capabilities and thus to have a distorted view of the over-all situation.

A few isolated quotations, to be sure, prove nothing. But the image of manipulating the enemy's view of the world is pervasive. To quote the much later (eleventh century A.D.) Tzu-chih t'ung-chien [Comprehensive Mirror for Aid in Government]:

> Now, the Way of War is this: attacking the heart is the best, attacking walls is the worst; battle launched at the heart is the best, battle launched at soldiers is the worst. I would wish that Your Excellency subdue their minds only.[40]

Carried to its logical conclusion, manipulation of the mind of the enemy implies perturbation of his utility function to the point where he does not fight at all. The real development of our highest level of stratagem occurs only in the third chapter of the Sun Tzu, entitled "Attack by Stratagem" In this section, the emphasis shifts from merely outwitting the enemy (deception in the limited sense) to attempting to break his will without fighting. This is not a humanitarian concept, any more than is the indirect approach of Liddell Hart, though one can indeed trace a continuum between the type of bloodless victory imagined by the Sun Tzu and (for example) the almost totally ethical and nonstrategic remarks in such texts as the Huai-nan tzu.[41] The objective is to hold one's own intent invariant, while simultaneously maneuvering the enemy into a position where he is willing to grant it.

> Hence to fight and conquer in all your battles is not supreme excellence; supreme excellence consists in breaking the enemy's resistance without fighting. . . . The general, unable to control his irritation, will launch his men to the assault like swarming ants, with the result that one-third of his men are slain, while the town still remains untaken. Such are the disastrous effects of a siege. Therefore the skilful leader subdues the enemy's troops without any fighting; he captures their cities without laying siege to them; he overthrows their kingdom without lengthy operations in the field. With his forces intact he will dispute the mastery of the Empire, and thus, without losing a man, his triumph will be complete. This is the method of attacking by stratagem.[42]

The picture that emerges from this passage is very different from that suggested by a contemporary Western treatise: "The ultimate goal of stratagem is to make the enemy quite certain, very decisive, and wrong."[43] The example of the town and countryside cited at the end of the Introduction provides a modern paradigm case of the kind of stratagem Sun Tzu is talking about in the above passage. In point of fact, large numbers of KMT military units scattered in cities and Schwerpunkte across the North China plain eventually surrendered quite passively without a fight to encircling Chinese Communist forces based in the countryside. Chinese Communist guerrilla warfare effectively played upon the rigidities of thinking always present in the Nationalist command to maneuver the Nationalists into an inflexible strategic policy inimical to their own best interests. This kind of stratagem does not fit naturally into the disjunctive framework provided by Liddell Hart's concept of "alternative objectives."[44]

Having once introduced the Chinese Communist revolutionary movement, it is relevant to suggest a view of the interrelations among the triad formed by the concept of stratagem in the abstract, Sun Tzu, and Maoist strategy. In another work, the present author has argued for a structural analogy between Maoist revolutionary strategy and the game of wei-ch'i (Japanese go). Essentially, the role of wei-ch'i was to provide for Chinese Communist doctrine a concrete, representational model of what have been well-labeled as the geometrical and physical aspects of warfare.[45] There remains, however, a considerable

realm of strategic action in revolutionáry warfare with which no
analogy to a complete-information game can cope. Broadly speaking,
this is the realm of incomplete information and imprecise objectives.[46]
Although various analogies have been drawn between Sun Tzu and
Maoist strategy as a whole, it is this latter, highly psychological,
realm of strategic behavior that furnishes most of the common ground
between Sun Tzu and Mao Tse-tung.

In other words, the main influence of Sun Tzu on Mao has been
in the area of strategy centering around deception and stratagem.[47]
Analogies between Maoist insurgency and the thought of Sun Tzu are
much weaker in the sphere of warfare more geometrico—the realm
of strategy customarily associated in the West with the name of Antoine
Jomini. In no sense does Sun Tzu recommend protracted guerrilla
warfare with widely dispersed base areas of the type essential to
Maoist thinking and—under suitable structural transformations—to
the game of wei-ch'i.[48] Eventually, with more historical and theoretical work, one may hope (in a felicitous phase of Benjamin Schwartz)
to analyze the organic chemistry of the Chinese strategic tradition
in much greater detail; but some of the distinctions here suggested
may provide a crude beginning.

GAME THEORY AS A CONTROL CASE

When the strictly twentieth-century phenomenon of the mathematical theory of games is selected as a Western counterpoint to the
ideas of a most concrete-minded Chinese strategist who lived four
centuries before Christ, an intelligent first reaction should be one
of skepticism. The mathematical model-builders say that one cannot add apples to oranges. How then can one meaningfully compare
formal constructions of Borel and von Neumann with an aphoristic
classic of an ancient agrarian society?

On deeper reflection, however, the comparison is not so implausible as might be thought. For the strongly traditionalistic culture
that was imperial China, there is little or no question that to get a
key to Chinese thought one should go to the sources of tradition.[49]
For a rapidly evolving, essentially antitraditionalistic society, such
as that of the West since the Renaissance, it is only plausible to take
game theory as a syncretistic microcosm of the frequently inconsis-
tent beliefs that make up Western strategic thought. Game theory
furnishes a rather unusually concentrated encapsulization of some
Western strategic values. Being formal, the theory takes beliefs that
are often vaguely and elusively characterized by earlier qualitative

theorists and pushes them to their formal asymptotes, thereby crystallizing their exact implications.

Following are several suggested fundamental values that differentiate game theory as an intellectual tradition of conflict theory from the tradition represented by Sun Tzu and his disciples. In each case, it is quite clear that the divergences are mirrored by differences between other branches of Chinese and Western social philosophy and behavioral theory, though the topic thus broached is far larger than can be effectively handled in this brief chapter. The discussion that follows is explicitly focused on classical zero-sum two-person game theory. This is the case where game theory is usually considered to be most highly developed and its results the least contestable it is also—despite some sophisticated examples of Schelling—probably the most relevant game-theory model for operational military situations in conventional warfare.

To begin with, two-person zero-sum game theory is deliberately psychologically naive; the only information determining strategy formation is assumed to lie in the payoff matrix—in capabilities, that is, rather than in intentions. The mini-max concept of strategy is an attempt to factor out enemy intentions by assuming that one wants as much as one can get <u>regardless</u> of what those intentions may be.[50] This mini-max viewpoint carries over equally to more complex situations that nevertheless preserve the pure conflict character of the classical case. An excellent example is a recent study by Morris Friedell that extracts a clever mini-max solution from a game model incorporating the "He thinks I think . . ." that lies at the core of the interaction when both sides are trying to use deception.[51]

This dominant emphasis is quite consistent with the evolution of Western strategy in recent centuries, emphasizing as it has more and more the economic and organizational bases of military power and national-security policy. In fact, a work such as <u>Makers of Modern Strategy</u> gives the impression that there is a <u>negative</u> relation between predilection to use stratagem and the <u>psychology</u> engendered by a modern military establishment and technology.[52] One elementary fact is that a mini-max strategy is a rich man's strategy; the implicit supposition is that the conservative, mini-max value is worth living with.* Explicitly not taken into account is the possibility

---

*The author is indebted to Commander James A. Barber, USN, for his stimulating discussion on this point in a seminar on game theory at the Naval War College.

that a player may prefer a nonmaximin gamble, preferring death to continued existence should he lose. The formalism does not easily handle the utility to a player of his own death. At a deeper level still is the possibility that one player may in fact be able to psychoanalyze the other, but not vice versa. In this case where symmetry is violated, the maximin concept no longer makes sense.[53]

The capabilities-oriented nature of game theory may be interpreted in another way. A strategy based only on capabilities has the effect of cutting through the potentially infinite regressions connected with the dynamics of mutual outwitting. This is very near to the meaning of social structure in Western culture; the basic idea is very close to that of neoclassical Walrasian general equilibrium theory, which decouples economic actors by the device of a competitive price system.[54] Much of the thrust of the second generation of game theorists, such as Schelling, is how to extend this framework to a more general nonzero-sum context, where, instead of decoupling, the emphasis shifts to the coupling of the interests of the participants through tacit or explicit cooperation. Typically, however, because of the unwillingness of the theorists to impose powerful behavioral constraints upon the players, the analysis constantly skirts indeterminacy in the grey area where conflict and cooperation coexist.[55] The type of strategic thinking that springs from the Sun Tzu, by contrast, thrives on the impossibility of achieving either a clear-cut coupling or decoupling in the interactions between the participants.

On a more fundamental level, the Chinese emphasis upon what has been labeled here as the deepest level of stratagem—that which attempts to structure the opponent's view of the world—strongly clashes with the invariant utility concept presupposed by mathematical game theory. The Western concept is strongly bound up with the concept of the inner man, received directly from Greek (and Hebrew) social theory: the idea of an internal will that controls its physical shell and is inviolate to any external control.[56] In Western strategy, this is reflected by deemphasis on attempts to enter the mind of the enemy by trying to understand his intentions—the construct of the mind itself argues against this possibility. (Western military ethics, centering around a rather inflexible concept of duty and honor, are also deeply connected with the presupposition of an inner man; it is clear from even casual reading in the history of Chinese military art that comparable concepts are deemphasized by that cultural tradition.[57])

In a certain sense, therefore, one might look at strategy in the Sun Tzu as intrinsically closer to the behaviorist tradition of modern Western thought than to its cognitivist and voluntarist rivals. A very simple example illustrates the point, though it does not, of course, prove it. A universal gambit in military tactics may be called the "ruse of the illusory campfires." One example from the Western military literature may be found in the Strategemata of Frontinus.

> Iphicrates, when campaigning in Thrace, having on one occasion pitched his camp on low ground, discovered through scouts that the neighboring hill was held by the enemy, and that from it came down a single road which might be utilized to overwhelm him and his men. Accordingly he left a few men in camp at night, and commanded them to light a number of fires. Then leading forth his troops and ranging them along the sides of the road just mentioned, he suffered the barbarians to pass by. When in this way the disadvantage of terrain from which he himself suffered had been turned against them, with part of his army he overwhelmed their rear, while with another part he captured their camp.58

Not surprisingly, this episode has at least one Chinese counterpart, which is referred to in one of the commentaries on the Sun Tzu text. The anecdote is from the history of Ssu-ma Ch'ien and follows the translation of Giles.

> In 341 B.C., the Ch'i State being at war with Wei, sent T'ien Chi and Sun Pin against the general P'ang Chuan, who happened to be a deadly personal enemy of the latter. Sun Pin said: 'The Ch'i state has a reputation for cowardice, and therefore our adversary despises us. Let us turn this circumstance to account.' Accordingly, when the army had crossed the border into Wei territory, he gave orders to show 100,000 fires on the first night, 50,000 on the next, and the night after only 20,000. P'ang Chüan pursued them hotly, saying to himself: 'I knew these men of Ch'i were cowards: their numbers have already fallen away by more than half.'59

Soon, of course P'ang Chüan is ambushed and killed by Sun Pin, and his whole army is thrown into disarray and completely routed.

Whatever the historicity of either of these incidents, their differences are evident and perhaps significant. The Greek story involves little more than what current jargon would label cover and deception; the Chinese case is a genuine example of conditioning and reinforcement of a desired behavior on the part of the enemy commander. Even the language used by the classical Chinese theorists to describe such stratagems is reminiscent of behaviorist concepts. For example, the above stratagem falls under the general rubric of (chih-ti), literally "regulating (controlling) the enemy."[60] At one point, the Sun Tzu text develops the idea at some length. "Water shapes its course according to the nature of the ground over which it flows; the soldier works out his victory [chih-sheng] in relation to the foe whom he is facing.[61] It is remarkable that here Sun Tzu employs precisely the modern behaviorist metaphor that behavior has a "topography" that may be "shaped" by a programmed environment.[62]

Except in set-piece cases such as the example of the campfires just given, it is very difficult in general to draw a hard-and-fast line between the second level of stratagem, which involves mutual out-witting in a context of alternative choices, and the third, which involves genuine shaping of behavior. The main point is that the two levels of stratagem are practically and psychologically distinct. What is at the core of the distinction, however, is that these two different perspectives not only lead to different practical emphases, but also involve fundamentally different conceptions of man. The different approaches to strategy that they represent can be traced right back to the axiomatics of social philosophy, even as can comparable differences in ethics or politics.

To say that Sun Tzu was a Skinnerian, to be sure, leads either to the unpalatable hypothesis that the social theory of conflict has advanced little in 2,500 years or else to reinforcement of the myth of Asian cultural superiority and precedence. Some cautionary observations are therefore relevant. While superficially somewhat behaviorist in the modern sense, in many ways the strategic framework adduced by Sun Tzu, and omnipresent throughout Chinese history, is very primitive, in a strict cultural evolutionary sense.[63] In fact, there is considerable evidence that a distinguishing feature of the warfare of so-called savages is characterized by predominance of strategy through stratagem.

> In general, it may be said that primitive man in fighting
> relies mainly on striking power, particularly striking
> power at a distance, with bow and arrow, and on mobility,
> utilizing the stratagen of surprise from ambush or dark-
> ness. His war is one of pounce and maneuver.[64]

Of course, within the context of the various approaches to stratagem, the ideas in the Sun Tzu are quite highly developed, as comparison with truly savage warfare immediately makes apparent.[65]

One crucial respect in which the stratagem of Sun Tzu diverges from a modern behaviorist interpretation of interaction phenomena, despite similar emphasis on conditioning and reinforcement, is the absence of a concept of probability calculus. The calculus is as essential a tool of contemporary behaviorist theory as it is of the theory of games. The impression one obtains from reading Sun Tzu is strictly preprobabilistic, and this often leads to paradoxes because he does not know how to formulate his propositions probabilistically.[66] As at least one Chinese Communist philosopher has taken pains to point out, Sun Tzu's emphasis is on <u>certainty</u>: "These five heads should be familiar to every general; he who knows them will be victorious; he who knows them not will fail."[67] This emphasis leads to paradoxes when the text grows more concrete in the later chapters; the fixed interpretations of enemy behaviors given there are likely to make a commander who literally followed them himself vulnerable to stratagem. The similarly preprobabilist language of early Western military thinkers (among the Greeks, for example, Aeneas Tacitus, Asclepiodotus, and Onasander) makes them less susceptible to similar doctrinal difficulties, precisely because they emphasize strategy through stratagem much less.[68]

CONCLUSIONS

It has been the hope of the present chapter to lay out one fruitful area for development of the almost nonexistent field of comparative strategic studies. The study of stratagem will play a role in giving substance—and credibility—to the study of strategic phenomena in general. Such study permits investigation of some very interesting parallels and contrasts between Chinese and Western approaches to conflict, between formal and pre-formal interpretations of strategic behavior, and between strategy and the larger body of social theory and social practice in which strategy is imbedded.

NOTES

1. Thus, Carl von Clausewitz devotes three pages (out of roughly one thousand) to the topic (see his <u>On War</u>, trans. by Colonel J. J. Graham, [London: Routledge and Kegan Paul, 1956], I, 205-7); see also Colonel G. F. R. Henderson, <u>The Science of War</u> (London: Longmans, Green, and Co., 1905), p. 178, for another typical example.

Military theory, however, sometimes approaches incredibly close to the point of total neglect of stratagem, as in the case of

French strategic doctrine before World War I. This seems to be characteristic of the French in this century; see Barton Whaley, "Stratagem: Deception and Surprise in War" (unpublished manuscript, Center for International Studies, M.I.T., 1969), p. 79: "Even the two most prominent early 20th Century French military theoreticians, Foch and DeGaulle, give only passing mention to deception and then only in some of its tactical applications."

2. As Liddell Hart points out in Strategy: The Indirect Approach (Rev. ed.; New York: Praeger, 1955), p. 24, this is a maxim with which most professional soldiers would concur. Unfortunately, since it justifies equally the most circumspect approach and the élan of a bayonet charge, it is effectively void of content as a determining factor in policy.

3. Translation following Lionel Giles, Sun Tzu on the Art of War (London: Luzac and Co., 1910), pp. 36-37. For relevant analysis of translation problems connected with the binary opposition (cheng— direct and ch'i—indirect), see D. C. Lau, "Some Notes on the Sun Tzu," Bulletin of the School of Oriental and African Studies (University of London), Vol. XXVIII, Pt. 2 (1965), pp. 319-35.

4. See Howard L. Boorman and Scott A. Boorman, "Strategy and National Psychology in China," in Don Martindale, ed., "National Character in the Perspective of the Social Sciences," The Annals of the American Academy of Political and Social Science (Philadelphia), Vol. CCCLXX, 1967, pp. 143-55. It is fascinating to note how pervasive is the cultural stereotype of Asian psychological sophistication: a science-fiction essay that the author once read projected some years into the future to foresee a bipolar world engaged in an outer-space war, with the "Eastern" side more sophisticated in biochemistry and neurophysiology, the "Western" more advanced in physical hardware.

5. One notable exception in this regard is Whaley, Deception and Surprise. This work, however, barely touches the interesting theoretical issues of intellectual history and behavioral science that the subject of stratagem raises and restricts itself, moreover, almost entirely to case studies of European and American practices in the present century. For example, the role of stratagem in the history of Islam has, to the author's knowledge, never been adequately studied.

6. The author is indebted to various persons in seminars at the United States Naval War College in Newport, R. I., for discussions

on this topic. As far as the field of war gaming is symbolic of the state of American thinking as a whole, it is relevant to note that such works as William D. Coplin, ed, Simulation in the Study of Politics (Chicago: Markam, 1968), leave the impression of gross psychological naiveté on the part of the field of simulation as a whole.

7. For a survey focusing on deception principles, see James C. Aller, "Electronics Warfare Concept," Naval War College Review, Vol. XXII, 1970, pp 75-79.

8. See Walter Millis, American Military Thought (Indianapolis, Ind.: Bobbs-Merrill, 1966), p. xv. It is fascinating to note how completely even the contemporary American counter-culture has inherited a classical American strategic framework. See, e.g., the issue on "Guerrilla War in the U.S.A.," Scanlan's, I, 8 (January, 1971), which gives little or no emphasis to deception and stratagem.

9. See "New Tactics Used by 101st Airborne," New York Times April 4, 1967.

10. This quotation is taken from a section entitled "Fundamental Army Beliefs," United States Army and National Security, ROTCM 145-45 (Washington D.C.: Department of the Army, October, 1962), p. 148 (emphasis added). For the same quotation, see also Department of the Army Draft Copy, Department of the Army Field Manual, Land Warfare—Basic Army Doctrine (Carlisle Barracks, Pa.: U.S. Army War College, January 4, 1962), pp. 4-6. For a general analysis of American doctrine as it relates to deception, see Whaley, Deception and Surprise, pp. 52-61.

11. It might be pointed out in this regard that the Sun-tzu text (under its Japanese name Sonshi) has played an important role in Japanese military thinking. See, however, Brigadier General Samuel B. Griffith, USMC (Ret.), Sun Tzu. The Art of War (Oxford: Clarendon Press, 1963), App. II, "Sun Tzu's Influence on Japanese Military Thought." The conclusion General Griffith reaches is noteworthy: "Thus it appears that in spite of devoted study the Japanese understanding of Sun Tzu was no better than superficial" (p. 178). The main point is clear: it is as fatuous—and as dangerous—to argue for the existence of a unified Asian approach to strategy as to make the comparable argument for ethics or for politics.

12. See, e.g., Kuan Feng, Ch'un-ch'iu che-hsüeh shih lun-chi [Analyses of the Spring and Autumn Annals] (Peking: Jen-min ch'u-pan she [People's Publishing House], 1963), p. 550ff.

13. C. W. C. Oman, The Art of War in the Middle Ages. A.D. 378-1515, revised and edited by John H. Beeler (Ithaca, N.Y.: Cornell University Press, 1953), p. 33.

14. See Achilles Fang, The Chronicle of the Three Kingdoms (220-265), Chapters 69-78 from the Tzu Chih T'ung Chien of Ssu-ma Kuang (1019-86), Harvard Yenching Institute Studies VI (Cambridge, Mass.: Harvard University Press, 1952), I, 16. Contrast Sarva Daman Singh, Ancient Indian Warfare with Special Reference to the Vedic Period (Leiden: Brill, 1965), p. 148: "The commander's personal bravery is lauded more than his strategic ability."

15. This is closely related to the Chinese concept of face, of which there is unfortunately no adequate discussion in the literature of Asian studies. See, however, the brief discussion in Arthur H. Smith, Chinese Characteristics (2d rev. ed.; New York: F. H. Revell, 1894), which makes interesting reading in conjunction with his parallel discussion of indirection in Chinese interpersonal behavior. See also Hsien Chin-hu, "The Chinese Concepts of 'Face,' " American Anthropologist, New Series, Vol. XXXXVI, 1944, pp. 45-64.

16. See Coriolanus, I.7.

17. See the brief discussion of relevant Western military terminologies in Whaley, Deception and Surprise, p. iv.

18. See Général d' Armée André Beaufre, An Introduction to Strategy, trans. by Major-General R. H. Barry (New York: Praeger, 1965), Ch. 4; and the present author's remarks in his review of the same work (with Howard L. Boorman), Political Science Quarterly, Vol. LXXXI, 1966 pp. 508-10.

19. Thus the concept of ch'i (indirect) methods in Chinese military theory needs in no way to imply stratagem. See Benjamin E. Wallacker, "Two Concepts in Early Chinese Military Thought," Language, Vol. XXXXII, 1966, pp. 295-99.

20. Compare Whaley, Deception and Surprise, p. 131: "The enemy's choice may, of course, be left entirely to chance." Whaley goes on (pp. 131-32) to emphasize the crucial role of the quantum jump that occurs when the enemy has to respond to two distinct possibilities, rather than to one alone.

21. For a relevant analysis, see Captain R. P. Beebe, "Military Decision from the Viewpoint of Game Theory" (Naval War College,

Advanced Study Group, 1957). It is not at all an accident that game theory originated in an economic context, where the problem of utility measurability, though acute, is not a priori insuperable.

22. For related ideas on strong points and the concept of territory in Chinese Communist strategy, see Howard L. Boorman and Scott A. Boorman, "Chinese Communist Insurgent Warfare, 1935-49," Political Science Quarterly, Vol. LXXXI, 1966, p. 181.

23. One noteworthy if obscure exception are the works of the seventeenth-century Jesuit Baltasar Gracian (translated by Martin Fischer as a Truthtelling Manual and the Art of Wordly Wisdom [Springfield Ill.: Charles C. Thomas, 1934]), which are in spirit reminiscent of the Sun Tzu in many ways, though of course not military in focus.

24. A clear appreciation of this emphasis may be found, oddly enough, in J. E. Garvey, Marxist-Leninist China: Military and Social Doctrine (New York: Exposition Press, 1960), pp. 134, 193-95, 273-75, 278.

25. As the Chinese Communists are eager to point out in conjunction with their emphasis on the "primitiveness" of early military thought. See Kuan Feng, Ch'un-ch'iu, p. 547.

26. For a recent translation of Sun Tzu, see Samuel B. Griffith, Sun Tzu, The Art of War (Oxford: Clarendon Press, 1963).

27. See Giles, Art of War, pp. xlii-xliii. See also Herbert Franke, "Siege and Defense of Towns in Medieval China," forthcoming from Harvard University Press in edited volume on Chinese military history from the proceedings of a conference in the summer of 1969, which further corroborates the influence of the Sun Tzu.

28. See J. I. Crump, Jr., Intrigues: Studies of the Chan-kuo Ts'e (Ann Arbor: University of Michigan Press, 1964), p. 91.

29. One can forthwith discount such works in the French tradition of Sun Tzu studies as E. Cholet, L'art militaire dans l'antiquité chinoise. Une doctrine de guerre bimillénaire tiré de la traduction du P. Amiot (Paris: Charles-Lavauzelle, 1922), which essentially turns Sun Tzu into an early humanitarian thinker. See also Roger Caillois, "Lois de la guerre en Chine," Preuves, No. 49, March, 1955, pp. 16-30.

30. In connection with the organization of the text, the theory has been proposed that it is seriously out of order in its present version, the bamboo slips on which it was originally written having been disorganized at an early point of transmission. This does not contravene the stratagematic interpretation of Sun Tzu here proposed. See Kuo Hua-jo, Chin-i hsin-pien Sun-tzu ping-fa [Modern Interpretation and New Arrangement of Sun Tzu's Art of War] (Peking: Jen-min ch'u-pan she [People's Publishing House], 1957), and the entry under Kuo Hua-jo in Howard L. Boorman and Richard C. Howard, eds., Biographical Dictionary of Republican China, Vol. II: Dalai-Ma (New York: Columbia University Press, 1968), pp. 270-71.

31. See Giles, Art of War, pp. 6-7.

32. See Franke, "Seige and Defense," with special reference to the Wu-ching tsung-yao (eleventh century A.D.) and the similar Wu-pei chi-yao (nineteenth century A.D.).

33. Giles, Art of War, pp. 90-91.

34. Translated by C. H. Brewitt-Taylor as San Kuo, or Romance of the Three Kingdoms (Shanghai: Kelly and Walsh, 1925), 2 vol.

35. See Boorman and Howard, Biographical Dictionary, Vol. III: Mao-Wu (1970), p. 2.

36. G. de Cotenson, "L'Art millitaire des Chinois, d' apres leur classiques," La nouvelle revue (Paris), 1900, p. 556.

37. Compare the discussion of the personality of the scholar-hero in Robert Ruhlmann, "Traditional Heroes in Chinese Popular Fiction," in Arthur F. Wright, ed., The Confucian Persuasion (Stanford, Cal.: Stanford University Press, 1960), p. 161ff. From a behaviorist point of view, the scholar-hero is essentially defined to have very low behavioral plasticity, while exploiting the higher behavioral plasticity of others. Ruhlmann illustrates this point in connection with the various classic stratagems of Chu-ko Liang.

38. On Li Ch'uan, see Giles, Art of War, pp. xxxvi-xxxvii. For this particular commentary entry, see Sun-tzu chi-chu [Sun Tzu Collected Commentaries], Chuan 1, t'se 1, folio 23, verso 6 (Cambridge, Mass.: Harvard-Yenching Library). (Ssu-pu Ts'ung-k'an edition.) (SPTK Edition).

39. Sun-tzu chi-chu, chuan 1, ts'e 1, folio 24, recto 3.

40. Fang, Chronicle, I, 182.

41. See the (inadequate) partial translation by Evan Morgan, Tao, the Great Luminant (1933).

42. See Giles, Art of War, pp. 17-20 (emphasis added). Of course, Giles (evidently a strong partisan of strategic universals) is able to uncover a parallel in Western military history (Von Molkte at the Sedan), remarking that "Here again, no modern strategist but will approve of the words of the old Chinese general." In 1910, when these words were published, Verdun and the Somme were yet to come.

43. Whaley, Deception and Surprise p. 135 (emphasis in original). It should be pointed out that there is some ambiguity with the sense of the last sentence in the Sun tzu quotation given. For representative opinions, see the classical commentaries in Sun-tzu chi-chu, chuan 3, ts'e 1, folio 3-5, verso 8; Kuo Hua-jo, Chin-i hsin-pien, p. 57; and Chiang Fang-chen, Sun-tzu ch'ien-shuo [Sun Tzu Made Easy], (Peking: Chün-hsüeh pien-chi chü, 1915), p. 19. But the general remarks in the text still hold.

44. Developed by Whaley, Deception and Surprise, as the basis of his decision-theoretic perspective on stratagem.

45. Ibid., p. 128. Whaley notes the important fact that the physico-geometrical aspects of war relating to mass, maneuver, and strategic points are easily communicated and taught (at least to Western audiences): "Consequently they can be and are successfully taught in all military schools and barracks, presented in organizational charts, vectored maps, tables of equipment, and similar quantitative or representational models." A board game is, of course, a natural model for such aspects of conflict. See Ch. 2 of Scott A. Boorman, The Protracted Game: A Wei-ch'i Model of Maoist Revolutionary Strategy (New York: Oxford University Press, 1969).

46. Of course, one could artificially perturb the rules of wei-ch'i, thereby incorporating an appropriate degree of fuzziness, but this is a somewhat artificial and unpromising possibility. It should be noted that exploitation of bad play on the part of the opponent is considered bad procedure by good players (see The American Go Journal: An Anthology [n.p.: American Go Association, n.d.], p. 24). There is, of course, the sophisticated concept of reconnaissance tactics, i.e., tactics designed to sound out the enemy's intentions.

See Kaku Takagawa, The Vital Points of Go (Tokyo: Japanese Go Association, 1958), p. 118.

47. See Griffith, Art of War, p. 53ff. for related ideas.

48. For a general caveat on the uncensored drawing of parallels between Sun Tzu and Mao Tse-tung, see Scott A. Boorman and Howard L. Boorman, "Mao Tse-tung and the Art of War," The Journal of Asian Studies, Vol. XXIV, 1964, pp. 129-38. See, in particular, the remarks of Sun Tzu on war of quick decision in Giles, Art of War, p. 10. These are hard to reconcile with such essays by Mao as "On Protracted War" (translated in Selected Military Writings [Peking: Foreign Languages Press, 1963]).

49. On the particular case of siege doctrine, see Franke, "Siege and Defense", for confirmation of this opinion in a specialized case. Comparable detailed studies for other areas of Chinese military behavior unfortunately do not exist.

50. This point of view is clearly brought out in Ch. 12 of Anatol Rapoport, Two-Person Game Theory (Ann Arbor: University of Michigan, 1966).

51. Cf. Morris F. Friedell, "On the structure of Shared Awareness," Behavioral Science, XIV, 1969, pp. 28-39.

52. Cf. Edward Mead Earle, Makers of Modern Strategy (Princeton, N.J.: Princeton University Press, 1943), esp. p. viii. There is, to be sure, very little relation between what passes for strategy in this work and the stratagem-filled methods of modern professional football. See Paul Zimmerman, A Thinking Man's Guide to Pro Football (New York: Dutton, 1970).

53. See related ideas in an appendix to Thomas C. Schelling, The Strategy of Conflict (Cambridge, Mass.: Harvard University Press, 1960), entitled "For the Abandonment of Symmetry in Game Theory."

54. See Tjalling C. Koopmans, Three Essays on the State of Economic Science (New York: McGraw-Hill, 1957) for a presentation of economic theory from a decoupling viewpoint. For the more general significance of the decoupling idea, see also Harrison C. White, "Notes on Coupling-Decoupling" (unpublished course notes, Harvard University, 1966).

55. As an example of the difficulties into which the analysts frequently fall, see the rather ambiguous concluding remarks of Thomas C. Schelling, "Assumptions About Enemy Behavior," in E. S. Quade, ed., Analyses for Military Decisions, RAND Corporation Report R-387-PR (November, 1964), p. 216.

56. For a clear exposition of this view, see B. F. Skinner, Beyond Freedom and Dignity (New York: Knopf, 1971). The author is indebted to Prof. Skinner for the opportunity to read this manuscript prior to publication. An initial attempt to consider the problems of utility function modification in a strategic context is Fred Charles Iklé, in collaboration with Nathan Leites, "Political Negotiation as a Process of Modifying Utilities," The Journal of Conflict Resolution, Vol. 6, 1962, pp. 19-28; see also Fred C. Iklé, Every War Must End (New York: Columbia University Press, 1971).

57. Described by Franke, "Seige and Defense," as the Chinese predilection for certain "highly non-Confucian" practices. The whole concept of honor and morality in Chinese warfare is, however, a little-touched subject.

58. See Charles E. Bennett, trans., Frontinus: The Stratagems and the Aqueducts of Rome (Cambridge, Mass.: Harvard University Press, 1925), pp. 49-51.

59. Giles, Art of War, p. 40.

60. For this term see, e.g., the commentary of Mei Yao-ch'en, Sun-tzu chi-chu, chuau 1, ts'e 1, folio 18, recto 5-6. The idea is that of having the enemy "in a bag."

61. Giles, Art of War, p. 53. More literally, the latter part of this quotation might be rendered: "bring about victory by utilizing what he knows [of the circumstances] of the enemy."

62. See, e.g., G. S. Reynolds, A Primer of Operant Conditioning (Glenview, Ill.: Scott, Foresman and Company, 1968), p. 26ff.

63. It might not be irrelevant to note here that deception has been studied in children in Hugh Hartshorne and Mark A. May, Studies in Deceit (New York: Macmillan, 1930). See, in particular, Ch. 1, "Deceit as an Object of Study."

64. See, in particular, Quincy Wright, A Study of War (2 vols.; Chicago: University of Chicago Press, 1942), Ch. 6, "Primitive

Warfare," from which the above quotation is taken (p. 82). Some interesting kinds of stratagem also occur in the predator strategy of nonhuman species. See, in particular, J. Ishay, H. Bytinski-Salz, and A. Shulov, "Contributions to the Bionomics of the Oriental Hornet (Vespa orientalis Fab.)," Israel Journal of Entomology, Vol. II, 1967, p. 65.

65. See Morton H. Fried, The Evolution of Political Society (New York: Random House, 1967), p. 99ff.

66. This is probably at the root of Whaley's complaint (Deception and Surprise, p. 147) that "Exhortations to avoid being deceived are, I suspect, as uselessly homiletic as those to use it." He then proceeds to mention Sun Tzu in this regard.

67. Giles, Art of War, p. 3. See Kuan Feng, Chien-ch'iu, p. 563ff., for semantic analysis of causality in the Sun Tzu.

68. On Greek probability ideas, see S. Sambursky, "On the Possible and the Probable in Ancient Greece," Osiris, Vol. XXII, 1956, pp. 35-48.

**THE PLA
AND CHINESE
POWER ABROAD**
John E. Coon

Only with guns can the whole world be transformed.
Mao Tse-tung

Transformation of the whole world along Maoist lines is hardly
one of Peking's objectives for the 1970s. It is, however, a long-term
goal; and during this decade most of Peking's moves on the international chessboard, regardless of immediate considerations, will be
accommodated in one way or another to the ultimate achievement of
that goal.

In 1961, the secret Kung-tso Tung-hsun informed PLA cadres
at and above the regimental level that "without the participation of
China, none of the important problems of the world can be solved."[1]
Mao's 1956 views on the subject were reprinted ten years later by
Lin Piao for PLA consideration: "China is a [huge and populous land],
and she ought to have made a greater contribution to humanity. Her
contribution over a long period has been too small. For this we are
regretful."[2]

The question under examination here is the manner in which the
PRC is likely to consider the employment of armed forces beyond its
own borders. The PLA is an instrument of the Chinese Communist
Party—"an armed body for carrying out the political tasks of the
revolution."[3] That statement, of course, referred originally to

Views expressed in this chapter are solely those of the author
and do not reflect the official position of any U.S. government agency.

339

revolutionary development within China. Once Peking saw itself
charged with more definite responsibilities for the world revolution,
however, a logical extension of the PLA's role as a CCP instrument
abroad became almost inevitable. This is all the more true in view
of the extent to which the military and its members have played key
roles in the formulation and execution of Party and government policy
at every stage of PRC development. The Cultural Revolution and its
aftermath have merely accentuated such PLA participation.

An abstract analysis made in Peking might show three general
types of potential use of the military as an instrument of foreign
policy. The first would be deterrence or defeat of aggression from
beyond China's borders to assure the survival of the CCP in control
of a nation "building socialism"; the second would be the deployment of
Chinese troop units beyond those borders in furtherance of national
aims; and a third would be the use abroad of PLA members, individually
or in small groups, as military executors of external policy. Each of
these types of PLA employment deserves more detailed consideration
as a possibility for the 1970s in the light of the recent past.

NATIONAL DEFENSE

Military aggression from abroad could assume a variety of
forms ranging from intrusions into Chinese waters or air space,
through localized border clashes, to a major invasion. The two prime
agents of such aggression are seen to be the U.S. "imperialists" and
the Soviet "social-imperialists," though numerous lesser nations,
with or without the backing of these major foes, are capable of acts
short of invasion that Peking would classify as openly aggressive.
The PLA consequently must be capable of counteraction at whatever
level required.

The June, 1961, statement, "The United States after all looks
upon Korea, Indo-China and Taiwan as three battle fronts against our
country," besides pointing to indirect aggression, implies Peking's
views on the areas in which the U.S. might consider direct action
against the People's Republic.[4] Memory of the enemy advance to
the Yalu with the resultant threat to Manchuria is still strong. The
American ground force build-up in South Vietnam and air action in
North Vietnam and Laos were, for a time at least, watched carefully
as a distinct threat to the southern borders. And, of course, the so-
called American occupation of Taiwan is seen as a particularly
galling foreign military presence on Chinese soil with the potential
of leaping the strait onto the mainland.[5]

The Soviet threat, however, apparently is viewed now as the most immediate danger. Sinkiang in the'northwest, Manchuria in the northeast, and even the Peking area—with the substantial USSR military presence in Mongolia—could be subject to Soviet thrusts. The build-up of Soviet forces along the Chinese borders has been accompanied by a redisposition of PLA elements within China. Border talks in Peking have resulted in minor agreements on navigational matters, but have provided no settlement of basic problems. New trade agreements have been drawn up, ambassadors have been exchanged, and apparent caution on both sides has resulted in restraint along the boundaries where clashes had occurred. The threat, however, persists; because of it, a substantial portion of the PLA faces north.*

As a lesser but still sensitive matter, the Indian border remains a focus of concern. Here, too, the PLA faces foreign forces in an armed truce across unsettled borders. The Sinkiang-Tibet road through Ladakh is of vital interest to Peking and an embarrassment to New Delhi. With all its potential for armed clashes, however, it is unlikely that Tibet is considered an area in which any serious threat to Chinese security could develop in the near future.

Against the threats from abroad as Peking sees them, deterrence is the first line of defense. In spite of his subsequent dismissal as chief of the general staff, Lo Jui-ch'ing's 1965 statement is an example of the propaganda use of PRC military capabilities as a deterrent: "The strategy of active defense does not stop with driving the aggressor out of the country but requires strategic pursuit to destroy the enemy at his starting point, to destroy him in his nest." (This is not to imply that the Lo strategy was endorsed by Mao; the significance of the quotation is its propaganda use of military power, not the strategy itself.)

---

*Cf. the joint editorial of the People's Daily, Red Flag, and the Liberation Army Daily of August 1, 1970, which includes these comments: "Social-imperialism greedily eyes Chinese territory. It has not for a single day relaxed its preparations to attack China. It claims that it poses no threat to China. Why then does it mass troops in areas close to China's borders? Why has it dispatched large numbers of troops into another country which neighbors on China? Why does it frenziedly undertake military deployments to direct its spearhead against China? It is clear that social-imperialism, like U.S. imperialism, says that it poses no threat to China only to weaken our vigilance, to fool the people of its own country and the world."

In the field of deterrence, more noteworthy than the maintenance of large, modern, regular armed forces—and the concurrent plan to bog down an invader in a sea of armed people—is the development of the PRC's own independent nuclear capability. This not only reduces the necessity for reliance on a Soviet nuclear umbrella but also places respectable though limited deterrent power in Chinese hands. The PRC was quick to renounce the idea of first-strike employment. The possession of even a modest striking force, however, introduces a new factor into calculations on potential power in the Far East and the world at large. Moreover, as Vincent Taylor has commented, "The validity of people's war [for internal defense] would be greatly enhanced by the Chinese possession of a nuclear capability."[6]

A concomitant use of military power, should deterrence fail, is the defeat of actual foreign aggression. Despite what appears to have been a genuine debate within the Party leadership on the proper strategy to meet aggression, the qualified successes of the Maoist line as a result of the Cultural Revolution have reaffirmed the concept of People's War for the defense of the Chinese mainland.[7] For a People's War, China requires large, modern, regular armed forces; it requires millions of organized, equipped, and trained guerrillas under centralized regular control; and it requires even more millions of local defense forces. The strategy involved would be one of mobile defense in depth with the aim, over a prolonged period, of bogging down any invader in a sea of armed people. The tactics would combine guerrilla action with conventional operations by regular forces.

The PLA, with over 2.5 million men in its ground, sea, and air forces, is well equipped, well supplied, and well trained for its conceivable missions in such a war. Whereas its arms and equipment lag behind the leading world powers, they far surpass those of any potential aggressor except the United States and the Soviet Union. The militia, too, is a significant factor in the defensive power balance. Primarily a basis for economic mobilization of the masses, the militia nevertheless provides a huge organized pool of manpower that, though lightly armed and poorly trained on the whole, could readily supply the nucleus for disciplined guerrillas and for the ubiquitous local defense forces envisaged in Peking's strategy.

On balance, all available evidence indicates both the common sense of this PRC defensive strategy and the effectiveness of the resources at Peking's disposal for carrying it out. Barring the unlikely event of a preemptive strike by the Soviet Union, time will serve only to improve the present capabilities. Balanced modernization of equipment, continued emphasis on training, and unswerving attention to political reliability give every promise of assuring the continued responsiveness of the PLA to Party guidance for the security of the nation.

ARMED FORCES ABROAD

As for the employment of combat units of the PLA beyond China's borders, Korea is the case that leaps most immediately to the American mind. Korea, however, is a distinctly atypical example. Without going into detail on China's decision to cross the Yalu, it should be noted that, at the time, there was an apparently immediate threat to Chinese territory coupled with the imminent defeat of the neighboring Communist regime.[8] Mao's response in sending "People's Volunteers," even conceding Soviet pressures in the matter, could logically be subsumed under the previous portion of this chapter.

Peking's participation in the war in Indochina during the past decade, however, could be considered an intermediate case. Once more, in the eyes of Chinese planners, there was a threat to China's borders and air space; once more a neighboring Communist regime had been challenged. The restraint observable in actual PRC participation was significant. Anti-aircraft and engineer units of the PLA did enter North Vietnam, though they seem to have been largely withdrawn subsequent to the U.S. bombing halt in the north. There appears to have been no other participation by Chinese Communist troop units. Substantial material support continues, of course, presumably with the presence on Vietnamese soil of liaison-type missions associated with such aid. Peking, too, issues periodic statements of solidarity, including carefully qualified affirmations that "the Chinese people will resolutely take all necessary measures, not flinching even from the greatest national sacrifices, to give all-out support and assistance to the Vietnamese people and the other Indo-Chinese peoples. . . ."[9]

There seems to be little prospect of the employment of actual combat elements of the PLA anywhere in Indochina in the near future, particularly with the well-publicized and easily verifiable withdrawal of American armed forces from the area. For the long-term struggle in South Vietnam, Laos, and Cambodia, there is no evident necessity for such employment, and in Hanoi's eyes massive Chinese participation would be undesirable. Laos, however, as shall be seen presents a separate case.

More typical than the two cases just mentioned is the use of the PLA in strategic road-building projects across China's borders. Here,

Laos enters the picture in another context. In the early 1960s, by agreement with the Royal Laotian government, Chinese Communist engineer troops with civil laborers were building roads from Yunnan province into Phong Saly, the northernmost Laotian province. In the late 1960s, construction on another, more significant road began. Running generally southward from the Chinese town of Meng-la, that road passed through Muong Sai in Luang Prabang Province of Laos and, by 1971, reached at least to Muong Houn, north of the Mekong River and some thirty miles from the Thai border. A separate Chinese road, part of the same network, pushes roughly northeast from Muong Sai to link up, eventually, with North Vietnamese construction from the Dien Bien Phu area.[10]

This road complex is all-weather and graveled, with numerous reinforced concrete bridges—a superhighway by regional standards. Its construction and defense against ground or air attack have been and continue to be the responsibility of sizable PLA units augmented with civilian labor to a total strength estimated at 14,000 to 20,000 men. Its primary purposes remain a matter for speculation, though several observations can be made.

The nature and extent of the construction activity suggests strong concern by Peking over northern and northeastern Laos. The area is just across China's southern boundaries, where no effective control has ever been established, much less maintained, by any government. Here, tribal groupings spread a potential for instability across the international boundaries, while both North Vietnam and Western powers have actively demonstrated their interest. The PRC seems determined to assure that its own influence in this uneasy border region outweighs that of any possible challenger.

The road alignment, moreover, points clearly toward opportunities beyond the limited territory of that portion of Laos itself. If pushed to the Mekong, or even beyond to the Thai border, the network becomes a direct threat to Thailand. Even without such an extension, it already imposes psychological pressures since it is obviously not for the promotion of tourism.* Its use as an axis of massive military invasion is unlikely, but no strategist in Bangkok would be apt to ignore that possibility. Its use to channel increased Chinese support

---

*The reader is referred to Chapter 16, on deception warfare, for consideration of alternative Chinese methods for altering Thai and U.S. perceptions of reality in Laos.—Ed.

to insurgents in northern Thailand or Burma, now or in the years to come, is a logical development. And, of course, there remains the capability of opening a new, direct link for commerce between China, Thailand, and the Malay Peninsula should Bangkok swing more toward accommodation with the colossus to its north.

Toward all of these potential goals, the PLA, in its road-building activities and in the defensive dispositions associated with the roads, serves as an instrument of the CCP and the Chinese Communist government. The case is clearly one of the extension of PRC influence abroad by the calculated use of military power, even if that power is primarily aimed at a psychological goal.

There are similar cases involving PLA road-building along the rest of its southern border. The road from Sinkiang to western Tibet through Ladakh played a major part in the Sino-Indian flare-up of 1962. A more recent instance is the route opened through the Pamir Knot from China's extreme west to Pakistan.* Roads through the Himalayan passes to the south have been built and are being maintained by military engineers. Presumably, too, improvement of transportation to the Burmese borders or even across them are PLA responsibilities.

There is a temptation to speculate on the possibility of a future in which numerous land links with South and Southeast Asia will have broken through the natural barriers that have for thousands of years restrained Chinese trade and influence in that part of the world. What psychological and political readjustments would be required in Peking as well as in the capitals to the south? Such speculation, however, is beyond the scope here except insofar as it involves the use of the military in the opening of new doors for tomorrow's international relationships.

The Himalayan barriers, however, were breached at least temporarily in 1962, when China used the PLA in a convincing demonstration of its concern over Tibet and the borders with India. The historical background of claims and counterclaims in that area as well as the diplomatic maneuverings of more recent years are well

---

*Its alignment was reported (Washington Post, April 24, 1968) to be from Kashgar through the Mintaka Pass to Gilgit in Kashmir. As of the date of the report, the Chinese portion was said to be complete, "capable of carrying 3-ton trucks throughout the year."

documented elsewhere.[11] Suffice it to say that New Delhi, miscalcula-
ting Peking's sensitivity, applied a blend of political and localized
military pressures without the ready strength to back them up. The
Chinese reaction was a swift application of force that left India without any effective recourse.

In Ladakh, where one key issue was the Chinese road through
territory India considered its own, the armed clashes were principally
small-unit engagements involving outposts. This is not to imply that
the area was unimportant in the eyes of either contender. On the contrary, anything casting doubt on India's position in the Kashmir question is political dynamite in New Delhi, and communications through
the area remain vital to Chinese civil and military activities in
western Tibet. The isolation of the region and the limited forces
available, however, particularly on the Indian side, make Ladakh a
secondary scene of conflict.

In the Northeast Frontier Agency, battle was joined on a larger
scale. Maneuver and attack by PLA companies and battalions, with
light artillery support, were obviously coordinated at regimental level
or higher. More significant, the planning and execution of such a
major push down to the foothills overlooking the Brahmaputra could
not have taken place without participation by the Tibet Military Region
Headquarters and the blessings of Peking. Similarly, the abrupt un-
ilateral ceasefire and withdrawal of Chinese forces, once the international politico-military objectives had been achieved, were at
specific direction of the central government.

The 1962 operations were an explicit demonstration both of
CPR willingness to employ its military strength for the achievement
of foreign objectives and of Peking's restraint in tailoring the application of force to the results desired. The circumstances were unusual,
the provocation—in Chinese eyes—extreme. The action taken was
prompt, firm, limited, and effective.

Something of a different situation faces the Chinese leadership
on the northern borders. Here, again, the principal issue has been
one of disputed territory and incursions. The USSR, however, can
bring superior forces onto the scene and the PLA cannot reasonably
serve as the major instrument to achieve a solution. A whole gamut
of influence has been brought to bear, and various tactics are being
employed as occasions arise. Public and private Party-to-Party or
government-to-government demands, propaganda, and appeals to
world opinion all have their place. Both of the nations involved have
redisposed their ground and air forces to threaten or to counter

envisaged threats. What actual clashes took place were brought under control as soon as practicable, but the potential for future armed conflict persists. Neither side, apparently, would deliberately put the other in a position where major military action was its only recourse; but neither side will ignore the dangers of escalation. The issues at stake between the USSR and the CPR, of course, go far beyond the question of border clashes or disputed boundaries. The divergence of Chinese and Russian national interests is an enduring matter with a long historical background; it has been intensified by the ideological differences of recent years. Among the instruments of persuasion available to each side, armed strength will continue to play a key role. Once more, Peking is planning and tailoring the application of that strength to meet whatever tests may result from the long-term confrontation with its northern neighbor.

Off the coast to the east, another unsolved problem faces mainland China. The Nationalist government—in Taiwan, on the Pescadores, and on the Chinmen, Matsu, and Pai Ch'uan island complexes close to the mainland—presents tangible evidence that the civil war has yet to be brought to an end. In a twenty-year political, psychological and military confrontation, the PRC has periodically brought armed force to bear against the smaller islands. The only unqualified success, from Peking's point of view, has been its uncontested occupation in 1955 of the Ta Chens and other small islands north of the Taiwan Strait.

The Taiwan situation remains, as Thomas J. Weiss put it, a "thorn in the side of the People's Republic, and stone in the shoes of those American policymakers eager to tread the path toward eventual detente with Peking."[12] The application of military pressures to resolve the problem is only one of the options open to the Communist regime, but it is an option that can be realized against the offshore islands with little or no prior warning. The current pattern of shelling with propaganda materials on alternate days could suddenly become one of all-out bombardment by artillery and air. Nationalist forces are in heavily fortified positions and are well stocked with supplies, but they probably could not withstand such bombardment indefinitely without a sustained major resupply effort. Still, for Peking, political considerations remain the overriding ones.

The international climate, particularly world opinion in connection with UN membership, may well act as a restraint. The PRC, however, has consistently maintained that the Taiwan question is an internal Chinese affair and just as consistently has refused to renounce the use of force in the area. While the United States has definite treaty obligations for the defense of Taiwan proper and the Pescadores, an attack on the offshore islands would fall into an area of imprecision, requiring presidential decision as to whether or not U.S. action was "required or appropriate in assuring the defense of" the territories explicitly covered by treaty.[13] In the light of current trends in American public opinion and of reactions to be expected from other governments, Peking might well judge, in the near future, that circumstances favored another determined strike at Chinmen and Matsu. Prescinding from the casualties and destruction involved, the results could be seriously damaging to the positions of the PRC and the United States.

In any case, the Taiwan Strait has seen the use of force by the PRC in the past and may see it again in the future. The probabilities are that the PLA will be called into action in the area only when political and psychological considerations indicate that such action is necessary and will produce results favorable to Peking; the type and degree of controlled violence employed would be fitted carefully to the requirements of the day.

Further south along the coast, Hong Kong and Macau present unresolved situations of a different type. Here, however, the use of armed force seems unlikely. The Portugese Overseas Province is now, to all effects and purposes, an area over which the PRC exercises a degree of de facto suzerainty. This state of affairs resulted from the intense pressures—including shows of force by land and sea elements of the PLA—that brought about substantial concessions from the Portugese officials in 1967. A modus vivendi appears to have been reached that could last until the matter of Hong Kong comes to a head. The British Crown Colony flourishes under effective British control, serving the present interests both of London and of Peking. The lease on the New Territories, however, expires in 1997. There seems little prospect that the regime in Peking—or any other Chinese regime, for that matter—would renew it. Once this 356 square miles (out of a total of approximately 400) reverts to Chinese sovereignty, the remainder of the Colony will become a nonviable entity unless an unprecedented agreement is reached on some sort of free-port status. Whether circumstances twenty-five years from now would make such an agreement acceptable to Peking is a moot question; but the possibility of military action against Hong Kong appears extremely remote.[14]

In each case, actual or potential, in which PRC use of troop units abroad has been discussed, three points stand out. Basically, the Maoist leadership considers the PLA a valuable and flexible instrument of foreign policy. Furthermore, Peking has no hesitation in employing that instrument when favorable results can be expected without undue risk. Finally, the measures taken and the degree of force applied are accommodated with great care to the mission or missions to be accomplished.

MILITARY MEN ABROAD

Somewhat different considerations pertain in the case of PLA members employed abroad as individuals or in small groups. Here, it becomes important to distinguish various types of Chinese Communist foreign relations. There are the state-to-state relationships that Western tradition has considered normal between the governments of two nations, but which have found a place in Chinese political thought only in this century. There are Party-to-Party relationships developed within the relatively recent framework of international Communism. And there are the complex and often covert relationships between Peking and dissident groups in other nations.

Making such a triple distinction in the abstract does not imply a clear-cut distinction in practice. With other Communist states, for example, Peking deals on both national and Party levels; in the case of non-Communist states it often deals formally with governments and informally with nongovernmental groups from which some advantage may be obtained. Under many circumstances, it becomes difficult to say just where the line should be drawn between specific instances of one type or another. A wide spectrum of potential actions is available to the PRC to further its own interests or those of "world transformation," and in practice the hues fade into one another.

As might be expected, then, the roles of PLA representatives are many and varied. In Peking, assuming that the Cultural Revolution has produced no drastic change in these elements of central organization, the staff office of foreign affairs of the State Council receives support from the Ministry of National Defense when military considerations are involved; and the Ministry of National Defense itself has a foreign affairs bureau responsible for PRC military attaches in the embassies abroad, for dealings with visiting military delegations, and for coordination of military and politico-military training in China for foreign personnel.

On the diplomatic level, as has been suggested, the PRC follows the usual procedure of assigning military attaches to its embassies, sometimes with the formal title, sometimes under a shallow cover. Additionally, it sends military delegations on visits to various nations.

Some of these visits are for such stated purposes as "to participate
in Armed Forces Day celebrations" or, as in the case of Burma and
Algeria, "to participate in the observation of the anniversary of
independence." Others, with no publicly expressed purpose, are for
military liaison and international prestige. A partial listing of such
tours during the past fifteen years follows; it suggests a variety of
interests within and outside the Communist nations, with a significant
gap during the Cultural Revolution's preoccupation with domestic
concerns:[15]

1956-57:	USSR (3); Czechoslovakia-Bulgaria; Burma
1958-59:	India; Poland; Czechoslovakia-Bulgaria-Poland-East Germany-Hungary-Rumania-Albania-Mongolia; Indonesia
1960-61:	Burma; UAR-Albania; North Korea; Mongolia; North Vietnam
1962-63	Iraq; North Vietnam; Cuba; Sweden; Algeria
1964-65:	Algeria (2); Pakistan; USSR; North Korea; North Vietnam
1966-67:*	North Korea
1968-69:	Guinea; Albania; Algeria
1970-71:	North Korea; Congo (Brazzaville); Albania-Rumania; Algeria.

Other trips and contracts have been made on the government-
to-government level in connection with military-assistance programs.
Within the Communist world, one can mention Albania, heavily
dependent on Chinese military aid with the reported presence of 3,000
Chinese advisers, and Rumania, where recent PRC initiatives have
incited Soviet complaints. With Bucharest, Peking has signed a loan
"for the supply of equipment and installations for whole projects."
Significantly, the presence of Ch'iu Hui-tso (chief of the PLA GRSD)
at the signing of that agreement raised the possibility that military
materiel may be involved, particularly in the light of a Rumanian
military delegation's visit to China in October, 1969.

In the world of developing nations, two among several PRC
assistance programs merit special consideration—one with Pakistan
and one with Tanzania. These two are selected as particularly
illustrative of the variety of PLA contributions, not with any intent
to ignore similar initiatives by Peking elsewhere.

---

*There was a twenty-eight-month suspension during the Cultural
Revolution, from May, 1966, to September, 1968.

In the case of Pakistan, public announcements at the end of 1964 indicated that the PRC was to sign an agreement with Pakistan to provide the equivalent of 30 million U.S. dollars in "industrial commodities."[16] By the end of 1970, other press reports affirmed that "with the moderate shipments provided by China in recent years, Pakistan reportedly has equipped three army divisions and put into service, in addition, some Chinese-made MIG-19 fighter planes, light and medium tanks, anti-aircraft guns, radar installations and other equipment."[17]

Much of the period when Chinese military assistance was being sent to Pakistan during the Cultural Revolution. Despite the turmoil at home, including upheavals in the Ministry of Foreign Affairs, the Ministry of National Defense evidently managed to maintain a modest but significant flow of materiel. The apparent aims of challenging Soviet and American influence in South Asia and maintaining a posture of challenge toward India were important enough to prevent disruption of military agreements with Karachi. And PLA personnel, though they maintain a low profile, are present in Pakistan in connection with the materiel being furnished.

The conclusion of the 1971 treaty of friendship between India and the Soviet Union, in the context of Pakistan's civil war and the unresolved conflict over Jammu-Kashmir, makes the Sino-Pakistani relationship a complicating element in the unstable South Asian situation. Informed UN observers have expressed private opinions that war between the two nations of the subcontinent is inevitable. The recent intensification of Sino-Soviet rivalry in the area adds a new dimension to the confrontation, with the PLA remaining in the wings as an instrument of PRC policy. The development of such policy, in view of contingencies that may develop during the 1970s, must necessarily be under close scrutiny in Peking.

In Africa, and specifically in Tanzania, the PRC has been even more active on the government-to-government level. Between 1954 and 1969, Peking pledged 246 million U.S. dollars to African nations south of the Sahara—one quarter of the $949 million extended worldwide as aid credits and grants in those fifteen years. Tanzania received $53 million during the period.*

---

*The author is heavily indebted to Mr. James Curran for facts and opinions on PRC activities in Tanzania. While a State Department student at the U.S. Army War College, he shared, in numerous discussions, the results of his personal experience and research on the matter.

At the end of 1970, in a ceremony outside Dar es Salaam, the most ambitious foreign-aid program in PRC history was formally launched. It was the Tan-Zam Railroad, discussed between China, Tanzania, and Zambia since 1965. Almost 1,200 miles of new rail line is to cross Tanzania and half of Zambia to link up with existing facilities in the latter landlocked country. The cost is estimated at $412 million, to be provided by the PRC as an interest-free loan with repayments not to start until 1983 and then to be stretched over a thirty-year period.[18] The amount involved in this single project is far more than the total aid extended to all of Africa during the past fifteen years. As for PRC motives, James Curran, after examining and rejecting the basic significance of economic aims, goes on to say:

> Except by way of demonstrating that it is now an industrialized country capable of producing a wide range of capital and consumer goods, China's interest in the Tan-Zam project is manifestly not economic or commercial. It is strategic. . . . China, now the largest aid giver to Tanzania and Zambia, and Tanzania's sole external source of military equipment and assistance, is working up to the status of an indispensable friend and protector to the two countries.[19]

China's armed forces, of course, remain an essential tool of this African strategy. PLA involvement in PRC activities in Tanzania takes a multitude of forms. In connection with the Tan-Zam Railroad, there is little doubt that at least the engineers, survey crews, and foremen are members of the PLA's railway engineer corps. Nowhere else in mainland China is there the organized expertise to furnish such specialized personnel. At Dar es Salaam, work on the new naval base begun in 1970 is under PLA supervision; the PLA, too, is training the Tanzanian navy in the maintenance and operation of patrol boats, which the Chinese are supplying. As for air power, late 1970 press reports claimed that the PRC was to supply Tanzania with two squadrons of MIG-17s, presumably giving conversion training in China to Tanzanian pilots already trained by the Canadian air force.[20]

Throughout the country, Chinese military men have supplanted the former Canadian Military Assistant Advisory Group (MAAG) with the regular Tanzanian forces, and in the south they staff training camps for black African guerrilla forces. In that connection, Stanley Meister, in an article from Dar es Salaam, has suggested:

> The Communist Chinese are clearly gambling that a future race war in Africa will make them the main foreign

influence here. That seems to be the logical goal of their heavy economic and military assistance program in Tanzania. . . . They train both the army and black guerrillas trying to wrest control of Southern Africa from its white supremacist governments.[21]

One further area of possible PLA involvement in Tanzania is in connection with its ICBM program. Here, the matter is highly speculative, involving the naval activities in Dar es Salaam, the PRC military mission on Zanzibar, the closed U.S. satellite-tracking station there, and the suitability of the Indian Ocean as an impact area for ICBM's launched from Chinese ranges. One could posit the desirability of a land-based tracking station in addition to instrumentation ships should the Chinese decide to take the political risks of using the Indian Ocean in its missile program.[22] There is, however, little firm evidence on the matter beyond the already heavy investment in men and material that Peking has made in the area.

In government-to-government relations, PRC policy is largely established by the Ministry of Foreign Affairs under Party guidance. Where military training and assistance policies are involved, however, the influence of the PLA undoubtedly is extremely strong both through the MAC of the CC of the CCP and through the Ministry of National Defense in the central government. At the levels of implementation, the PLA role is the dominant one. On the other hand, when one considers Party-to-Party relations, in nations where the Communist Party is in control of the state, the direct PLA role is negligible— and naturally so. The CCP in its dealings with "fraternal parties" would hardly put forward its armed forces as an instrument of policy except as an alternative to or, possibly, a shield against the Soviet armed forces. The existence and increasing effectiveness of the PLA, however, is a background factor enhancing the persuasiveness of Peking's voice in international Party dealings where power plays an implicit part.

The final area for consideration in the use of military individuals or groups as tools of PRC/CCP foreign policy is one in which the PLA role, while significant, is largely covert. It consists of the provision of arms, munitions, and training to insurgent groups throughout the world. Some of these groups are Communist-led, but the majority would appear more aptly labeled "national liberation" organizations.

The subversive effort in Asia, closest to the wellspring of Maoism, is supported by a substantial and sophisticated school system. In Yunnan province alone, strategically near the southern border, there are said to be at least fifteen camps for the politico-military training of native cadres from the countries of South and Southeast Asia. Nagas and other minority groups from the Northeast Frontier Agency of India, Kachins and Shans from the Burmese hill tribes, Thais, Khmer, Lao, Meo, Malays, and Indonesians have all been reported as students in these Chinese schools. In addition, according to the press, there are twenty-five training camps staffed by the PLA in Laos.[23] These efforts are almost certainly under the immediate direction of the Kunming Military Region, with general supervision and policy direction from Peking.

In Burma, under present circumstances, it is the Maoist White Flag Communists who receive most support from the PRC, though non-Communist Kachins and Shans as well are known to receive arms, ammunition, and encouragement from across the border. Formal PRC aid to the Burmese government ended in mid-1967, and the Chinese technical group had been withdrawn by November of that year. In spite of recently renewed overtures by Ne Win to the Peking leadership, what aid is now flowing into Burma—most of it military and under PLA control—is going to antigovernment forces with the obvious aim of keeping a weak and neutralist nation on China's southern borders.

In Thailand, insurgency in the north and northeast is under evident PRC influence, while that in the south is linked to the Malaysian Communist bands dominated by overseas Chinese. The clandestine station "Voice of the People of Thailand" broadcasts from South China. Weapons and explosives of Chinese manufacture are in the hands of the guerrillas, and there is direct access from China to Thailand through the PLA-occupied areas of Laos where road-building is in progress.

Cambodia at present is a special case, with North Vietnam the predominant foreign intruder. PRC influence, largely indirect, remains strong, however. Prior to the change of government in Phnom Penh resulting in Sihanouk's exile, Sihanoukville was the port of entry for the vast majority of food, medicine, and munitions reaching the Viet Cong in the southern parts of South Vietnam and in their border sanctuaries on Cambodian soil. This vital flow of supplies came from China by sea, obviating the necessity of long and arduous shipment over the Ho Chi Minh trail.

Throughout the rest of non-Communist Asia, PLA encouragement to instability continues at a level more or less intense depending on localized circumstances. As the U.S. News and World Report remarked on April 8, 1968: "Cambodia, Thailand, Malaysian Borneo all report Chinese-trained guerrillas turning up with Chinese-made arms in their back country." In the long term, there are three obvious aims: to reduce the Asian presence of "imperialist nations," particularly the United States; to block Soviet approaches to Asian states and Communist parties in the Far East; and to win the maximum practical degree of Chinese influence in a part of the world that should naturally, in Peking's eyes, center on China.

In the Middle East, as Angus Fraser states, the Palestinian Liberation Organization, which professes a debt to the "thought of Mao Tse-tung" and maintains a mission in Peking, received messages of support from the PRC even during the Cultural Revolution.[24] Israel has announced that terrorist leaders captured during raids into Jordan during the same period were trained in mainland China.[25] In 1970, two leaders of the Popular Forces for the Liberation of Palestine on a visit to Peking acknowledged gratitude for several arms shipments, including rifles, machine guns, mortars, rocket launchers, and mines.

The Arabian Peninsula, too, has seen recent Chinese influence. A CPR mission arrived in Yemen in July, 1969, and a technical-economic agreement was signed the following year. Again, according to Angus Fraser, Peking is supporting the Front for the Liberation of the Arabian Gulf; some arms have been provided, and two Chinese military advisers are reported with the some fifteen small guerrilla bands operating in the area. Over thirty of these guerrillas, it is claimed, are graduates of training courses in China.

Sir Kennedy Trevaskis, formerly British high commissioner for Aden and the Protectorate of South Arabia, asserts that South Yemen can be expected to continue paying off its debts to the USSR and the PRC by exporting revolution "to Oman and thence to the Gulf and Saudi Arabia." Based in southern Yemen with an advance base on the Oman frontier, these guerrilla operations "are controlled and sometimes conducted by Chinese advisers."[26]

Across the Red Sea, in Ethopia, further Chinese influence is reported in the Eritrean Liberation Front. A guerrilla leader of that movement who surrendered in late 1967 stated in a press conference that some of his men had received training in the PRC and implied the receipt of munitions from Peking.[27] Informed observers have speculated that one motive for the sudden recognition of Peking by the Ethiopian government may have been the hope of reducing PRC support to the Eritrean insurgency.

Throughout black Africa, Chinese military advice and assistance is directed to the various "liberation movements." At the end of 1968, as an example related to the previous discussion of Peking's influence in Dar es Salaam, radio broadcasts by the Federal Military Government of Nigeria alleged that Chinese arms were being channeled to Biafra through Tanzania and "that Biafrans were being trained by Chinese military instructors in four secret camps in Tanzania before being sent to Nanking for training. . . . that through Tanzania's intercession, China had given Biafra 'an almost blank check to draw on its arsenals.' "28

A partial list of other African states in which forces are alleged to have received PRC arms and training includes Angola, the Cameroon Republic, the Congo (Kinshasa), Kenya, Malawi, Mozambique, Nigeria, Rhodesia, and Ruanda. "Chinese military advisers train police units on the slopes of Mt Kilimanjaro."29 In the Congo (Brazzaville), "a secret school for black guerrillas operates . . . just inland from Pointe-Noire where Chinese Red ships bring arms, equipment and supplies."30 This activity presumably is directed against countries other than the Congo (Brazzaville).

This has not been an attempt to provide an exhaustive survey of PRC aid to worldwide subversion. Rather, it is intended to present examples of the types of movements supported, the general nature of assistance given, and the intimate involvement of the PLA in these aspects of Peking's foreign policy. The expenditure of resources in money, materiel, and manpower is minimal, and the results to be gained for the PRC are potentially of great value—all the more so in the light of the 1961 statement by the PLA GPD: "The general situation is the forced withdrawal of old colonialism from Asia . . . and the changing of the last battlefield to Africa."31

CONCLUSIONS

This chapter's focus on the PLA's role and on military applications of PRC power abroad may have given a lopsided view of Peking's conduct of foreign affairs—even in the context of a book entitled The The Military and Political Power in China in the 1970s. Such is not the intent. The PLA's role, while significant, is only one part of a complex of action and interaction by which the Maoist central government seeks to exert its influence beyond China's borders. Diplomatic maneuvers, psychological ploys, and economic dealings all play their important parts in that complex. The PLA is only one of the tools of Chinese foreign policy; but it is an extremely effective tool.

To return to the beginnings, the question under examination has been the manner in which, at least during the coming decade, the PRC may employ its armed forces as instruments of power in the international arena. The domestic role of the PLA as the "pillar of proletarian dictatorship" has received considerable attention from China-watchers, particularly during and since the Cultural Revolution. The external role has been less studied, and these few pages do not pretend to exhaust the subject. Nonetheless, the PLA has provided a continuity of service—from the 1950s, through the Cultural Revolution, into the 1970s—in the realm of foreign affairs.

What may be expected during the years immediately ahead is a logical development out of the past twenty years, with thirty previous years looming in the background. Evolution in the Workers' and Peasants' Army, the Red Army, the 8th Route Army, and the PLA has brought significant changes, but basic concepts remain firm. The PLA is still, as was the Red Army in 1929, "an armed body for carrying out the political tasks of the revolution"; and the revolution is now explicitly conceived not as confined to China, but as directed toward an eventual victory over imperialism throughout the world.

Within China it is affirmed that "without a people's army, the people have nothing." Externally, Mao proclaims, "The people who have triumphed in their own revolution should help those still struggling for liberation." That statement, of course, was qualified by numerous admonitions on the necessity of self-help. The fact remains, however, that aid will be given wherever there is the prospect of benefit to China or world Communism, without danger to China's economic or political security. When such aid has military aspects, the PLA is at the Party's disposal.

NOTES

1. J. Chester Cheng, ed., PLA Kung-tso Tung-hsun: The Politics of the Chinese Red Army (Stanford, Cal.: Hoover Institution on War, Revolution, and Peace, 1966), p. 480.

2. Quotations from Chairman Mao Tse-tung, (Peking: Foreign Languages Press, 1966), pp. 179-80.

3. Ibid., p. 100.

4. Quote is from Cheng, Kung-tso Tung-hsun, p. 367.

5. A map in the People's Daily of January 29, 1966, entitled "The Military Encirclement of China by American Imperialism," presents graphically Peking's official view of U.S. hostility. It has been reprinted in several recent Western works, among which are Arthur Huck's The Security of China (New York: Columbia University Press, 1970), p. 12, and Michael Oksenberg's "China, the Convulsive Society," Headline Series No. 203, p. 65.

6. Comments on Morton Halperin's "Chinese Attitudes toward Nuclear Weapons" in Tang Tsou, ed., China in Crisis, II (Chicago: University of Chicago Press, 1968), p. 160.

7. Cf. Harry Harding, The Purge of Lo Jui-ch'ing: The Politics of Chinese Strategic Planning, (Santa Monica, Cal.: Rand Corporation, 1971), passim.

8. For the pioneering and authoritative treatment, see Allen Whiting, China Crosses the Yalu; the Decision to Enter the Korean War (Santa Monica, Cal.: Rand Corporation, 1960).

9. Final communiqué (Hanoi Radio) after Chou En-lai's March, 1971, visit to Hanoi.

10. For further detail on PLA road-building in Laos, see U.S., Congress, Senate, Committee on Foreign Relations, Hearings before the Subcommittee on United States Security Agreements and Commitments Abroad, Prts. 2 and 3, 91st Cong., 1st sess., 1969.

11. A recent and controversial treatment is in Neville Maxwell, India's China War (New York: Random House, 1970).

12. Thomas J. Weiss, "Taiwan and U.S. Policy," Orbis, XII, 4, (Winter, 1969).

13. Public Law 4 (H.J. Res. 159), January 28, 1955.

14. See the last 20 pages of Richard Hughes, Hong Kong; Borrowed Place-Borrowed Time (London: Andre Deutsch, 1968).

15. Information derived from newspaper or radio accounts, primarily in the PRC. For additional detail on the earlier trips, see Source Book on Military Affairs in Communist China (Hong Kong: Union Research Institute, 1965). Despite the English title, the text is in Chinese.

16. New York Times, January 29, 1965. Note that a three-man military delegation headed by Liu Ya-lou, then PLA air-force commander, visited Pakistan from August 31 to September 2, 1964.

17. Ibid., November 12, 1970.

18. Cf. James C. Curran, "Communist China in Black Africa: The Tan-Zam Railway, 1965-1970, an individual research report submitted to the U.S. Army War College, April 26, 1971, passim. Note, too, the existence of a $50-million railway agreement between the PRC, Mali, and Guinea, signed in 1968 but in abeyance since the successful coup against the President of Mali.

19. Ibid., pp. 43, 44.

20. Daily Telegraph (London), October 22, 1970.

21. "Red Chinese Gambling on African Race War," Los Angeles Times, June 16, 1970.

22. Newsweek, March 22, 1971, in "Peking's Missile Men Put to Sea," asserts that "a 12,000 ton freighter is being fitted in Shanghai with radar antennas and other tracking gear . . . to be ready for . . . international missile tests late this year or early in 1972."

23. The Washington Post, May 3, 1970.

24. Angus W. Fraser, in a paper presented to the Indian Ocean Conference, Georgetown University, Washington, D.C., March 18-19, 1971.

25. U.S. News and World Report, April 8, 1968.

26. Sir Kennedy Trevaskis, "The Arabian Peninsula and Adjacent Islands," a paper presented to the Indian Ocean Conference, Georgetown University, Washington, D.C., March 18-19, 1971.

27. Graham Taylor, African Report, December, 1969.

28. African Report, February, 1969.

29. Harrisburg Patriot News, November 30, 1969.

30. U.S. News and World Report, April 8, 1968.

31. Cheng, Kung-tso Tung-hsun, p. 484.

18

THE MAKING
OF CHINESE
MILITARY POLICY

Harry Harding, Jr.

An understanding of the making of military policy in the PRC is still far from complete. Although the Cultural Revolution has provided Western scholars with invaluable information about the policy process in China,[1] the analysis of Chinese military policy still combines, in frustrating proportions, intuition, speculation, largely untested assumptions about bureaucratic politics, and fragmentary evidence from public statements, captured documents, and Red Guard materials. Any attempt to describe the formation of military policy must necessarily be highly tentative, but the importance of the subject justifies the effort.

The first section of this chapter presents a framework for the analysis of military policy in China. It attempts to identify the major criteria used by Chinese leaders and interest groups to evaluate alternative strategic options, the preferences of major participants in the policy-making process, and the most important determinants of policy outcomes. In the second section, this framework is employed to provide a brief history of the evolution of Chinese military policy since the Korean War. Finally, the chapter concludes with some speculation concerning the prospects for China's strategic posture.

For their helpful comments on earlier versions of this chapter, the author wishes to thank William Whitson of the Rand Corporation, Alexander L. George and John W. Lewis of Stanford University, and members of the Department of Political Science of the United States Air Force Academy, particularly Captain Donato Strammiello.

361

A FRAMEWORK FOR ANALYSIS

The Evaluation of Alternative Military Policies

Ever since 1949, the makers of Chinese Communist military policy have faced a set of basic questions. What kind of army should they build? What organizational form should it adopt? What strategy, tactics, and weaponry should it employ? And what nonmilitary roles, if any, should it perform? In both China and the West, these issues have frequently been cast as a choice between two fundamental options: to maintain an army organized and equipped to fight a People's War or to develop a military establishment designed to engage in modern conventional and nuclear warfare.

If the first option were adopted, the Chinese army would consist primarily of regular infantry forces, guerrilla units, and a large militia, each armed with simple weapons and skilled in both close fighting and night fighting. In defending China against invasion, it would employ the strategy known as "luring deep": retreating before an enemy advance, falling back to prepared defense positions, encouraging the invaders to disperse their forces and overextend their supply lines, and then surrounding and annihilating isolated enemy units. Because military success would depend as much on the morale and dedication of the troops as on their technical skills, political education in such an army would be as important as military training. To assure active popular support, effective coordination with the local civilian government, and proper political training military commanders would share authority with Party committees within the army. At the same time, military regions and units would be granted a large measure of autonomy and would be coordinated less by specific commands from their superiors than by a shared understanding of the political principles and military aims of People's War.

If the second option were adopted, in contrast, modern air, ground, and naval forces, coordinated at the national level and equipped with sophisticated weapons, would largely supplant lightly armed guerrilla forces and local militia. Rather than lure the enemy deep, and thereby permit him to plunder China's cities and destroy its industrial and agricultural capacity, the Chinese army would be prepared to conduct a linear defense of China's borders, to open a second front outside China, or even to preempt an anticipated enemy attack. Because modern warfare requires less reliance on popular support and greater technical training, the authority of political commissars and Party committees would be restricted and time allocated to political education reduced.

These, then, are the two fundamental options facing Chinese leaders. It would be a misleading oversimplification, however, to see the evolution of Chinese military policy as a continual choice between these two options alone. The problem faced by Chinese decision-makers has been less to choose between the two extremes than to find the most desirable mix of the old and the new,[2] the political and the professional,[3] the red and the expert. Indeed, as will be shown, Chinese military policy has increasingly represented a blend or compromise between the two basic options.

Chinese leaders appear to have used three criteria in their search for this balance. In public, they have most frequently discussed alternative military policies in terms of their relative effectiveness in meeting China's defense requirements, revealing, in turn, underlying disagreements concerning the type of threat that China faces. In general, the proponents of People's War have argued that the most serious threat to China is a ground invasion by modern, well-equipped enemy forces and that China, a poor and underdeveloped nation, would be ill-advised to meet such an enemy on his own terms. The most effective defense against invasion, from their viewpoint, would be to utilize China's superiority in manpower and vast territory, to engage in strategic retreat, and to rely on highly mobile infantry and guerrilla forces waging People's War.

The advocates of a modern specialized army, on the other hand, have argued that People's War is outmoded, particularly now that China must face the threat of conventional and nuclear air attacks as well as a ground invasion. China can effectively meet those threats, they have insisted, only if its army is converted from a semi-guerrilla force to one with sophisticated equipment, nuclear weapons, advanced air-defense capabilities, and contemporary strategic doctrines.

While there are still those in China who seem sincerely to believe in the continued applicability of People's War, particularly as a deterrent, there is increasing doubt that, when evaluated in terms of strategic effectiveness alone, options that approach the People's War ideal would provide the optimal defense posture. Clearly, a modern professional army would cope more effectively with a broader range of threats. But strategic effectiveness is not the only criterion used to evaluate military alternatives. In her major work Communist China's Strategy in the Nuclear Era, Alice Langley Hsieh has developed the proposition that discussions of strategic policy in China concern not only the military effectiveness of competing options but also their effects on the budgets of both military and civilian agencies.[4] Each of the military services takes into account the budgetary implications of the various strategic proposals and tends to favor the option that would mean the greatest increase (or the smallest decrease) in its own budget. Thus, as will be seen below, not all elements of the Chinese army are necessarily supporters of professionalization. Even more important, civilian agencies can be expected to be skeptical of defense proposals that would involve a sacrifice of their own programs.

On this level of debate, the advocates of military modernization are at a great disadvantage, for their proposals are expensive. To build a professional army, particularly on a crash basis, would necessitate major reallocations of economic resources, great disruptions in the civilian economy, and readjustment of the roles and missions of the various military services. To justify all this, the proponents of professionalization have frequently sought to demonstrate the existence of a serious external threat that requires a "quick fix" of China's strategic posture. In turn, opponents of such quick fixes have usually argued that the external threat was not as great as the professionals thought, that a crash program of defense preparations was therefore not warranted, but that a longer-range plan for gradual military modernization would be acceptable.

A third element in military planning, and one that has received insufficient attention in Western analyses,* is the fact that the PLA is not confined to a strategic role, but, following a long tradition of revolutionary warfare, is routinely involved in the political and economic life of Chinese society, providing internal security, manpower for civilian economic projects, training for government and Party cadres, and, particularly since the early 1960s, leadership for ideological reform campaigns. At the same time, as a part of a nation undergoing intensive efforts to remold its political culture, the PLA has been expected to receive political indoctrination and ideological education as well as military training.

To a very large degree, Chinese military leaders appear to accept the necessity and desirability of performing these domestic roles.** Nonetheless, beyond a certain point, the performance of

---

*A noteworthy exception is the work of John Gittings.

**There have been, however, disagreements on how best to perform them. These debates have most frequently involved the proper relations between the military command structure of the PLA, on the one hand, and civilian and military Party committees, on the other.

domestic roles becomes increasingly incompatible with the creation of a professional army. A specialized air-defense unit, for example, probably has neither sufficient time nor appropriate skills to engage in essentially civilian work. To build a professional army requires a concomitant reduction in the soldier's sideline occupations as policeman, cadre, teacher, ideologue, and laborer.

This has provided the proponents of People's War with their most persuasive case. Unlike a professional army, an army designed to wage People's War can readily perform domestic economic and political roles. Its simple weaponry requires that little time be devoted to technical training; its militia are but part-time soldiers; its nonspecialized organization can relatively easily be turned to civilian tasks; indeed, its very strategy requires close ties with the local population. At times when the international environment is not threatening and when there is need for the army to take part in domestic affairs, a strategy of People's War does offer a possible resolution of the contradiction between the domestic and strategic roles of the PLA.

In short, discussions of military policy in China have not involved only the cost-effectiveness of competing strategic doctrines but also the extent to which the PLA should be an active participant in the economic and political life of Chinese society. Each of the two fundamental strategic options—People's War and professionalism—is compatible with a different conception of the military's role. Those who place the greatest emphasis on the military's domestic tasks tend to champion People's War, despite its questionable strategic effectiveness. Those who favor a modern professional army must be willing to sacrifice some of the PLA's domestic roles. For this reason, the assignment of priorities to the PLA's various roles is a major factor in the determination of strategic posture.

Major Participants and Their Preferences

Different Chinese civilian and military agencies appear to have conflicting, and predictable, preferences concerning alternative military policies. This conclusion is, admittedly, based as much on assumptions about bureaucratic politics as it is on evidence concerning specific

---

During the early 1960s, there also appear to have been disagreements over the content of political training programs.

Chinese organizations. And because this is so, these assumptions should be made explicit.

Basically, bureaucratic and organizational models of the policy-making process assume that the policy preferences of each organization are shaped by two fundamental organizational interests: to increase or preserve its prestige and resources and to prevent encroachment by other organizations on its roles and missions.[5] When problems, challenges, or opportunities arise, each organization involved with the issue will tend to advocate solutions in which it would play a major role (provided, of course, that they believe they have a good chance of performing successfully). At the same time, other organizations will oppose proposals that would encroach on their positions and reduce their resources.

These assumptions are persuasive but clearly do not permit infallible predictions of the policy preferences of various organizational participants in the Chinese policy-making process, let alone the preferences of individual decision-makers. First of all, organizational self-interest is not the only motive at work. In China, as elsewhere, organizational representatives are expected to rise above the advocacy of narrow bureaucratic interests, "to proceed," as Mao has said, "from the interests of the people," and to seek the most effective solution for the problem at hand, regardless of its impact on organizational budgets and prestige. Models of bureaucratic politics, in other words, may unfairly impute cynical organizational opportunism to all participants in the policy process. Second, policy proposals are shaped not only by what an organization wants, but also by what it feels it can get. Organizations may well seek the acceptable rather than the optimal. Finally, the views of major decision-makers and organizational spokesmen may be influenced by their own background as well as by the demands of their current roles. Indeed, a frequent tactic of organizational control in China is to place in key positions men whose loyalties, because of their personal relationships or past experiences, are expected to lie outside the organization and who therefore are more likely to resist cooptation by their subordinates.

These considerations reduce the explanatory and predictive value of propositions based solely on assumptions about organizational interests. Indeed, as will be seen below, there have been several cases in the history of Chinese military policy in which organizational spokesmen appear to have espoused positions that ran counter to a strict definition of their organizational interests or refused to support proposals that would have benefited their organizations. The following discussion of organizational interests concerning military policy

reflects, therefore, only one factor in the determination of policy preferences. As a result, it does not represent firm conclusions but
rather tentative, yet reasonable, hypotheses to be refined in future
research.

The study of bureaucratic politics suggests that, in discussions
of military policy, Chinese organizations will support strategic options
that they consider to offer the most effective response to external
threats, that maximize their own political and economic resources,
and that conform with their conception of the proper role of the military
in Chinese society. Based on these propositions, it seems reasonable
to conclude that there are basically four sets of bureaucratic preferences concerning military policy in China.[6]

First, there are several organizations and groups that favor
emphasis on the domestic roles of the PLA and thus advocate strategic
options that approach the People's War Ideal.* These include Party
leaders at all levels who, because of their concern with maintaining
the ideological purity of Chinese society, value the role of the PLA
as organizational model, political work team, and ideological instructor
and who therefore favor a "political" army and a People's War strategy
as being the most consonant with this role. In addition, other, less
doctrinally oriented Party and government leaders in such fields as
agriculture and water conservancy, which require large investments
of semiskilled manpower, will support the People's War doctrine if
it permits participation of the PLA in their economic projects. Finally,
within the PLA itself, those who are charged with the implementation
of domestic roles (particularly the GPD) and units who would be
assigned a major role in waging People's War (especially the local
forces and the interior military regions) could be expected to oppose
the creation of a professional army.

Second, there is an important group that favors a balance between
the strategic and domestic roles of the PLA and a military posture
that combines elements of People's War and professionalism. That
group includes primarily the coastal and border military regions.**

————————

*This is not to say that they advocate a "pure" People's War
strategy. As will be seen below, there is a general consensus that
it is currently desirable to construct and maintain a nuclear deterrent.
The group discussed here advocates military policies that resemble
People's War more than professionalization.

** China is divided into eleven military regions, of which seven

Because they represent China's front line, these military regions are particularly sensitive to the need for effective defense of China's borders and reject People's War as an inadequate strategy. At the same time, however, they also prefer a defense strategy based on regional autonomy rather than on national coordination and thus on ground forces rather than on naval and air forces. And, because of their membership on, or close ties with, Provincial Party Committees, commanders of coastal and border regions are also aware of the need for the army to play certain domestic roles, particularly in the field of public security.

Third, there are probably civilian agencies who agree that military modernization is strategically desirable, but who nonetheless fear that their own budgets would be cut to finance rapid professionalization. These agencies, such as ministries engaged in light industry and also research and development units within the defense establishment, may well seek to moderate the pace of the modernization of the PLA.

Finally, other groups and organizations favor emphasis on the strategic roles of the PLA and advocate military policies that fall along the professional side of the continuum of strategic options. Within the PLA, these include the General Staff Department, the navy, the air force, and elements of the GRSD; their motivation probably stems both from conviction that the defense of China can be effected only through the modernization of the PLA and from the realization that the adoption of a professional strategic doctrine would increase their own budgets. Similarly, the creation of a modern professional army would benefit most sectors of the defense construction industry. Finally, it is likely that civilian managers, technicians, and specialists, particularly in industry and commerce, finance and trade, and culture and education, support the concept of a professional army disengaged from political and managerial activities in civilian sectors.

This tentative prediction of the policy preferences of civilian and military bureaucracies and groups in China should illustrate a major point: the formation of military policy in China is not characterized by a clear and fast polarization between military and civilian interest groups. Disputes over military policy are not Party/army debates. Rather, the participants tend to be complex coalitions, each

---

can be considered coastal or border regions: Canton, Foochow, Kunming, Nanking, Shenyang, Tsinan, and Sinkiang.

of which contains both civilian and military elements. The members
of each coalition seem to support their shared policy preference for
significantly different reasons.

Some evidence for this point is provided by an examination of
the rates of turnover in three major positions: those of Minister of
Defense, Chief of the General Staff, and director of the GPD. If the
major cleavage in the military policy-making process were between
civilians and the military, one would expect that the position of Minister
of Defense, which in a sense is at the border between the military and
civilian sectors, would be characterized by a high rate of turnover.
In fact, this is not the case; there have been but two Ministers of
Defense since 1954—P'eng Teh-huai and Lin Piao. Instead, the high
rates of turnover occur at the two positions that symbolize, respectively,
the "red" and the "expert" in the PLA—the director of the GPD and
the chief of staff. Each position has seen five occupants since 1949.
Since, as has been argued, the major issue in military policy is
whether to build a "political" or a "professional" army, this is not
surprising; for it is in these positions that, as John Gittings has
written, "the conflict between political demands [for a politicized
army] and military demands [for a professional army] is likely to
be most acute."[7]

Conflict, Consensus, and Compromise

The determination of military policy in China is, in essence,
the determination of the proper balance between People's War and
professionalism and between the domestic and strategic roles of the
PLA. The evolution of China's defense posture since 1953 can be
seen as a series of shifts in that balance. Three types of shifts have
occurred over the years. At times, there has been widespread agreement to emphasize one role, and the corresponding strategic option,
over the other. Borrowing a bit of Chinese terminology, this first
situation may be called "leaning to one side." At other times, there
has been a general consensus to pursue a mix of People's War and
professionalism and to pay roughly equal attention to the army's
domestic and strategic roles. This second situation may be termed
"walking on two legs." Finally, at still other times, there has been
disagreement and controversy over both the priorities to be assigned
to the domestic and strategic roles of the PLA and the relative desirability of People's War and professionalism.

The first situation—leaning to one side—has occurred when
there has been agreement among Chinese Communist interest groups

that a serious foreign or domestic problem demanded the attention of the army and that strategic posture should be shaped accordingly. This is not to say, of course, that this diagnosis is unanimous; beyond a certain point, it appears that consensus is obtained when the emerging coalition has such predominant support that it can silence its opponents and force compliance. Between 1952 and 1955, for example, largely as a result of Chinese experience in the Korean War, the perceived hostility of the United States, and, more generally, a tendency to emulate the Soviet Union in most areas, there appears to have been widespread agreement that China should stress the strategic roles of the PLA and move fairly rapidly in the direction of a modern, specialized, professional army. During the Cultural Revolution, on the other hand, there seems to have been general realization that the active participation of the army in domestic affairs was necessary if a total breakdown of the economy and political system were to be prevented.

Conflict over the assignment of priorities to the various roles of the PLA has occurred in two sets of circumstances. Conflict has emerged, first of all, when some participants in the policy-making process, but not others, felt that a previous decision to lean to one side had been carried too far and that a more-balanced approach to military policy was now necessary. In 1959, for example, major elements of the PLA, whose spokesman was Minister of Defense P'eng Teh-huai, argued that the emphasis on the politicization of the PLA and on its active participation in domestic political and economic affairs had been so exaggerated that the PLA's combat effectiveness had been seriously compromised. Whereas, as will be seen, military policy was later altered to take some of P'eng's views into account, his position was initially strongly opposed by those who favored a continued emphasis on the domestic roles of a PLA prepared to wage People's War.

Conflict has also appeared when some interest groups, but again not others, believed that the domestic or international environment had changed so that a reallocation of resources and redefinition of policy was necessary to cope with the new situation. This is likely to occur, as studies of bureaucratic politics show, because organizations scan the environment to find new problems, challenges, or opportunities that can be used to support (or rationalize) their demands for greater resources and responsibilities. Two different organizations, in other words, may react to the same environmental change in different ways, one arguing that it necessitates a change in established policy, the other arguing that it does not. Even more important, two organizations may simultaneously see two different "threats" and struggle vigorously over which threat is the more severe.

In 1955, for example, changes in the international environment led some military leaders to demand the accelerated modernization of the Chinese army, but they were unable to convince other interest groups that the strategic situation was sufficiently threatening to warrant programs that would so drastically reallocate economic resources within Chinese society. In 1965, the chief of staff argued that American escalation in Vietnam posed a severe external threat to China and that more attention should therefore be paid to the strategic role and military preparedness of the PLA. (Here, as predicted above, there is some evidence that he might, because of his own role, have been more sensitive to American actions in Vietnam than other Chinese leaders or, even worse, that he might have exaggerated the external threat in order to enhance or protect his own position). He was, however, unable to convince Mao Tse-tung, among others, that the external threat was significantly great to justify diversion of the PLA from its domestic roles.

Conflict in the military policy-making-process—of which there have been three serious cases—has generally been resolved through the construction of a compromise that would satisfy most of the competing interests. Mao Tse-tung and, since 1960, Lin Piao have played decisive roles in the construction of these compromises. At the same time, in all three cases, resolution of the debate has been accompanied by a purge of some of the participants—either because they espoused extreme positions in the debate or because their performance caused them to lose credibility and support among their own organizational constituents. In cases where purge victims can be seen as representing policy preferences held by a wider interest group or organization, their purge is a means of controlling the wider group without directly coercing it. Limiting the purge to the most prominent or outspoken "deviant" provides other dissenters with a "way out"; they are encouraged to "renounce" their views and to attribute their "mistakes" to the "evil" influence of the purge victim.

Increasingly, Chinese military policy has been characterized by a balance between People's War and professionalism and between domestic and strategic military roles. The greatest priority has been assigned to the maintenance of light infantry forces, whose weaponry and training are considerably less sophisticated than those of a fully professional army, but attention has also been paid to the development of nuclear weapons and to the gradual modernization of the air force and, more recently, the navy. This decision to walk on two legs, which may well have been made by Lin Piao after his appointment as Minister of Defense in 1959, has basically been in effect ever since the Great Leap Forward, despite demands to abandon it in 1965 and the need to modify it during the Cultural Revolution.

It appears to have been adopted for several reasons. First, it provides an effective compromise between two extremes that are largely infeasible. Because of the broad range of military threats facing China and the commitment already made to the modernization of the Chinese armed forces, People's War is neither strategically effective nor politically practical. At the same time, "pure professionalism" and accelerated military modernization are compatible with neither rapid economic development nor the PLA's domestic tasks. Second, the regional military commanders who benefit from a balanced military posture have acquired, particularly since the Cultural Revolution, increasing influence in the policy-making process. A third, and perhaps most important, advantage of the balanced approach is its ability to accommodate fairly wide shifts in military role without requiring concomitant alterations in force structure.

The burden of these shifts appears to affect different military services in different ways, however. The air force and navy, as befits their high degree of professionalization, appear to be relatively immune from demands to perform domestic roles. The ground forces, on the other hand, are greatly affected by changes in over-all military mission, being expected to perform strategic and domestic tasks with equal proficiency. To Chinese leaders who see China's security threatened both internally by revisionism and externally by "imperialism, social-imperialism, and reaction," this balanced military policy provides armed forces able to perform domestic and strategic roles both effectively and flexibly.

THE EVOLUTION OF CHINESE COMMUNIST MILITARY POLICY

The preceding analysis of the major issues and participants in the policy-making process, and of the types of policy outcome, provides a useful framework for a discussion of the evolution of Chinese Communist military policy since 1953 (see Table 8). Of particular interest during this period are the three instances of serious controversy and debate that occurred in 1955-56, 1959, and 1965. It is important to realize that none of these three episodes was concerned exclusively with military policy; each also involved other issues that, in some cases, were even more significant than military matters. The debate of 1955-56, for example, accompanied a broader discussion of the optimal pace of economic growth and the best allocation of resources among various sectors of the economy. The controversy of 1959 represented a relatively minor part of an extensive criticism of the Great Leap Forward. Finally, the strategic debate of 1965 may have

TABLE 8

Chronology of Chinese Military Policy Since 1953

Year	Policy	Situation
1953-55	Leaning to one side	Emphasis on professionalization
1955-56	Conflict	Demands to accelerate modernization clash with demands to reduce military expenditures
1956-57	Walking on two legs	Continued modernization, but at relatively protracted pace; increasing attention to politicization and domestic roles of PLA
1958	Leaning to one side	Emphasis on politicization to accompany Great Leap Forward
1959	Conflict	Objections to excessive politicization
1960-63	Walking on two legs	Under Lin Piao, attention to domestic roles of PLA, but continued protracted modernization and development of nuclear weapons
1964	Leaning to one side	Emphasis on domestic roles under "learn from the PLA" campaign
1965	Conflict	Demands for crash program of defense preparations, including reduction in domestic activities of PLA, to counter American escalation in Vietnam
1966	Walking on two legs	Deeper involvement of PLA in domestic activities as Cultural Revolution begins, but precautions to reinforce defense and deterrence postures
1967-69	Leaning to one side	Preoccupation with maintaining or restoring domestic order
1969-71	Walking on two legs	Attempts to bring domestic and strategic roles into better balance

been connected with resistance to Mao's increasingly powerful attack on the Party and governmental bureaucracies in general and on cultural and educational institutions in particular. As the purpose of this chapter is to describe military policy, the other issue-areas will, for the sake of brevity, be set aside.

Due in part to the difficulties experienced by the Chinese People's Volunteers during the Korean War, Chinese military leaders embarked on a program of military modernization during the first few years following the Korean armistice.[8] This program placed considerable reliance on the Soviet Union as a source of weapons, organizational principles, and strategic doctrine. During this period, the PLA's equipment was largely modernized and standardized, the construction of weapons-production facilities begun, a system of formal ranks and military discipline inaugurated, specialized service branches created, and formal military training emphasized. Conscription was introduced, as a means of obtaining recruits who would be most adept at learning the technical skills associated with a modern military force.

By 1955, however, consensus over the pace of modernization began to break down. The debate of 1955-56 concerned a proposal that the modernization of the PLA be accelerated through significant expansion of weapons production, increases in expenditures for research and development, and the purchase of weapons from the Soviet Union.[9] Those who argued for this quick fix of China's strategic posture—most notably Chief of Staff Su Yu, Director of Military Training Liu P'o-ch'eng, and Inspector-General Yeh Chien-ying— claimed that the development of American nuclear delivery systems, American threats to use nuclear weapons during the Quemoy crisis of 1955, the stalemate in the Sino-American ambassadorial discussions in Geneva, and the signing of the Mutual Defense Treaty between Washington and Taipei, all indicated a hostile American policy toward the PRC and a significant probability that the United States would launch a nuclear attack against China. The international situation, in other words, made the strategic role of the PLA even more salient to China's military professionals. Fearful that existing preparations were inadequate, they proposed that China embark on a crash program for improving its defense and deterrence postures along the lines suggested by recent revisions in Soviet strategic doctrine.

Those arguments were not convincing to a coalition of military and civilian interests desiring acceleration of economic development through reduction of the military budget. Led by Defense Minister P'eng Teh-huai, and probably including Liu Shao-ch'i and Finance Minister Li Hsien-nien, this second group reasoned that the most

likely form of hostile American action would be an invasion, not a
nuclear attack, and that an American invasion could be deterred both
by a cautious Chinese foreign policy and by the invocation of the Soviet
nuclear deterrent. In the unlikely event that deterrence failed, China
could rely on its reserves and on People's War. It was neither necessary nor desirable, they argued, to divert funds from civilian projects
to short-range military preparations; balanced military development
could best be achieved as a part of a long-term program of general
economic growth, not through costly and inefficient quick-fixes.

The debate was resolved in April, 1956, by Mao Tse-tung's
speech "The Ten Great Relationships." Mao agreed that modern armed
forces were necessary, but declared that military expenditures must
be reduced so as to accelerate economic development. Accepting
P'eng's argument that only a program of long-term economic construction could lead to sustained progress in military modernization, Mao
asked, "Do you want atom bombs? Then you ought to reduce defense
expenses proportionately and spend more on economic construction.
If you only pretend to want atom bombs, you will not reduce defense
expenditures proportionately and will spend less on economic construction."[10] But Mao's speech indicated that the way to "resolve" this
contradiction between defense preparations and economic construction
was to find the proper balance between the two goals, not totally to
sacrifice one for the other. Thus, after Mao had clearly indicated
the priorities that he believed to be desirable, the stage was set for a
compromise: the military professionals would be permitted to improve
research and development and increase the production of modern
weapons, but would neither receive as much as they wanted nor as
soon as they wanted it. The modernization of the military would proceed, but it would not be permitted to inflict short-term disruptions
on the Chinese economy.

The domestic functions of the PLA do not appear to have been
a major factor in the debate of 1955-56. Indeed, both sides in the
debate appear to have agreed that the army's domestic functions
were less important than either military economy or China's strategic
posture. Later in 1956, however, increasing priority was assigned
to the domestic roles of the PLA, in particular the political training
of the troops and participation in agricultural production.[11] Initially,
the argument that emphasis on modernization had gone too far and
that a shifting of priorities was necessary appears to have been widely
accepted. The decision to emphasize the domestic roles of the PLA
seems to have been consensual, based on both the fear that the revolutionary spirit of the army was threatened by single-minded modernization on the Soviet model and on the hope that the Great Leap Forward

would indeed produce rapid economic expansion, part of which could be channeled to military development.[12]

By the end of 1958, however, the consensus collapsed and a new debate began.[13] The crisis was occasioned by two factors. First, many professional combat officers believed that the politicization of the PLA had been exaggerated and that there was too much emphasis on the army's domestic roles. The amount of uncompensated time the PLA contributed to production had, for example, increased fifteen-fold from 1956 to 1958. While the average soldier spend 1.5 days in "free labor" in 1956, he spent 8 days in 1957 and 24 in 1958.[14] At the same time, military strategies that relied on the Soviet Union's nuclear umbrella, as China's did in those years, appeared questionable after the Quemoy crisis of 1958.[15] To the Chinese, Soviet support in the crisis came only after the Chinese had borne the greatest risks, while American reaction to the artillery blockade of Quemoy was both firmer and more effective than had been predicted. The Quemoy crisis may have contributed to the increasing conviction of China's professionally oriented officers that the strategic roles of the PLA had been slighted. Predictably, the readoption of People's War and the strengthening of the militia were touted during the Great Leap Forward as means of improving China's defense posture without reducing the army's participation in domestic political and economic projects and without draining funds from the civilian economy. But the professionals saw in the militia an inadequate military force and in People's War a denigration of the role of the regular armed forces.

When viewed from this perspective, the purge of Minister of Defense P'eng Teh-huai, Chief of Staff Huang Ko-cheng, and other military officers in 1959 can be traced to their objections to an in-effective program of national security and overemphasis on the domes-tic economic and political roles of the PLA.* As in 1956, the outcome was a compromise. Although priority continued to be assigned to the domestic role of the PLA, Lin Piao, P'eng's successor as Minister of Defense, redressed significantly the balance between the army's domestic and strategic functions.[16] Lin is, of course, associated with the intensification of political training in the PLA, the rejuvenation of Party branches throughout the military hierarchy, the reinforcement of the authority of the political commissars, and the introduction of

---

*P'eng was also purged because of his criticisms of the economic elements of the Great Leap Forward, but here the concern is only with the military issues involved.

the study of the works of Mao Tse-tung. But he resumed the modernization of the PLA in several significant ways: the militia was gradually
relegated to domestic economic and political, rather than strategic,
functions; considerable effort was devoted to the development of nuclear
weapons; and several new machine-building ministries, charged with
the production of sophisticated military weapons, were established.
The success of Lin's policies was demonstrated as much by the easy
Chinese victory in the Sino-Indian border war of 1962 as by Mao's
increasing reliance on the PLA in the years just preceding the Cultural
Revolution.

By 1964, however, Mao Tse-tung appears to have considered
emphasis on the domestic activities of the PLA to be crucial to the
successful conduct of his intensifying campaign to stop "revisionist"
tendencies in Chinese society and to "mold revolutionary successors
to the cause of the proletariat." During 1964 in particular, the army
was used as an organizational model for the Party and state, and PLA
cadres led ideological campaigns in sectors of civilian society ranging
from economics to the arts. Thereafter, any proposal that the PLA
withdraw from these domestic roles so as to improve its military
preparedness would, predictably, have aroused Mao's opposition.

In March, 1965, however, when the United States launched a
sustained program of air strikes against North Vietnam, Chief of Staff
Lo Jui-ch'ing made just such a proposal. Lo began calling for a
reorientation of China's military posture so as to assign top priority
to the PLA's strategic roles. Even with China's relatively cautious
policy toward Vietnam, Lo argued, the Americans might "lose all
sense of reality" and carry the war to China. In speeches and statements during the summer of 1965, Lo warned that China was not prepared to meet the entire range of threats posed by the United States,
ranging from retaliatory air strikes and large-scale conventional air
assaults to a nuclear attack or a full-scale invasion. To Lo, there
were "a thousand and one things to do" before China would be ready
for war.

In veiled language, Lo seems to have proposed a new strategic
posture—one that resembled the professional option of a nationally
coordinated, technologically sophisticated defense. While he continued
to praise the role of the militia and the strategy of "luring deep," he
also called for greater emphasis on the conventional, standing ground
forces and for prepared defensive positions fairly close to China's
borders. More specifically, he appears to have sought construction
of additional defense installations in South China, redeployment of
existing air-defense capability to the south, increased military training,
and perhaps an increase in the size of the standing army.[17]

The debate occasioned by Lo's proposals was conducted on two levels. Most of the public statements critical of Lo, particularly Lin Piao's "Long Live the Victory of People's War!," dealt with the issue of military strategy, questioning both the estimates of American intentions and the strategic doctrine that Lo used to justify his proposals for intensified defense preparations. Calling for continued reliance on People's War,* Lin rejected Lo's argument that significant changes in China's defense posture were necessary for the PLA to perform its strategic roles effectively. An even more important discussion, however, was conducted privately. Lo's proposals were opposed by a coalition of bureaucratic interests concerned variously with maintaining the army's involvement in domestic activities, preserving the established allocation of resources among military regions, and preventing the diversion of budgetary funds from the civilian economy to military programs. Although a few indications of this aspect of the debate are evident in the Chinese news media that summer, most of the information here has been obtained from Red Guard publications issued during the Cultural Revolution.

In the first place, Lo's proposed defense preparations involved decisions on resource allocations that would have harmed sectoral and national-defense interest groups, particularly cadres associated with the militia and with public-works projects that relied on army cooperation and support, organizations engaged in research and development of advanced weapons, and those regional military leaders whose equipment and personnel would have been redeployed to South China under Lo's plans. The most telling criticism of Lo's proposals, however, was that they would have had a crippling effect on the crucial immediate political functions of the GPO and on the roles Mao planned for the army in the future.[18] If political training were sacrificed for military training, then the political reliability of the PLA would suffer; and if security affairs came to demand more of the army's time, then the army's involvement in domestic political activities would be reduced.

This conjunction of disagreements over strategic estimates and domestic priorities added a significant element to the debate. If Mao and Lin had disagreed with Lo as to the proper defense strategy but had agreed with him that the American threat was imminent, then

_____

*In so doing, Lin seemed to ignore the fact that his own policy since 1960 was one that departed significantly from the People's War ideal.

Lo might simply have been accused of misjudgment. But since they saw no significant American threat to China that would warrant immediate and wide-ranging defense preparations, the Maoists could logically have concluded that Lo had ulterior motives for suggesting major adjustments in domestic priorities. They have accused him of concocting an elaborate rationalization for proposals whose real purpose was to force the disengagement of the PLA from political activity, reduce its political reliability, and thus encourage the spread of revisionism in China.

> Lo Jui-ch'ing dwelt considerably on "war preparations," and it seemed as if he was concerned over our country's security. This is not true. What he called "war preparations" were in fact preparations for usurping the army leadership and opposing the Party.[19]

In short, the Maoists believed—whether correctly or not—that Lo's behavior was, at the minimum, an effort to improve his personal position and, at worst, an attempt to keep the army from supporting Mao's developing campaign against Party revisionism. From the Maoists' viewpoint, Lo was not just mistaken, he was treacherous.

While Lo's position aroused considerable opposition in Peking, it probably attracted substantial support as well. Lo's supporters would have included other "professional" military men who either sincerely believed that Lo's proposals were essential to China's military security or saw in his program an opportunity to further their own bureaucratic positions. They may also have included, as the Maoists charged during the Cultural Revolution, high-ranking Party leaders who saw in Lo's proposals an opportunity to divert the attention of the PLA, and of the nation more generally, from the intensifying search for domestic "revisionists" and toward the external threat to China posed by American participation in the Vietnam War. Although Lo was ultimately purged, it appears that the outcome of the strategic debate was, once again, a compromise attractive (though in different ways) to three main groups of participants—the Maoists, the military professionals, and Lo's opponents within China's defense industry.

The compromise involved the rejection of the elements of Lo's program that were especially objectionable to major interest groups within the defense industry, including Lo's proposals to cut back on research and development in order to permit rapid expansion of production and the completion of defense preparations on a crash basis. On the other hand, paeans to Peoples War notwithstanding, there is evidence that some of Lo's other proposals for the improvement of China's defenses were ultimately accepted. Over-all troop strength was increased, defenses in the south reinforced, and aircraft production expanded. But these measures were implemented more slowly and geographically more widely than Lo had originally proposed, in accordance with both Mao's preference for long-term defense planning and the reluctance of China's regional military leaders to disrupt the established "balance" among China's military regions.

The Maoists, too, gained major benefits from the Lo Jui-ch'ing affair. The purge itself, perhaps conducted with the acquiescence of some of Lo's own colleagues, allowed the Maoists to eliminate a powerful politician apparently opposed to Mao and possibly allied with Mao's opponents in the Party and to warn military professionals not to interfere with the continued involvement of the GPD in the Cultural Revolution.

By early 1967, however, the PLA was called upon to play an even greater domestic role than Mao had anticipated. Its somewhat incompatible tasks were to "support the left," restore order and protect state property, supervise governmental operations, guide the rebuilding of the Party, participate in revolutionary committees, and mediate disputes among revolutionary rebel and Red Guard factions.[20] To do so, it is estimated that the PLA assigned some one million men to political and economic activities.[21]

And yet, the shift in military roles was not as great as might have been expected and was not accompanied by the adoption of a People's War strategy. The expansion of the domestic functions of the PLA was made possible by increasing the strength of the ground forces;* the air force, the navy, and military units concerned with nuclear testing and missile development seem to have been largely insulated from the Cultural Revolution. While People's War was described as the correct "proletarian military line" and while increased attention was paid to the militia—largely because it provided an important instrument of military control below the county level—neither aircraft production nor nuclear testing was substantially affected by the Cultural Resolution, and a decision to modernize China's navy and merchant marine appears to have been made during its later stages.

---

*The estimated strength of the PLA rose from 2.7 million in 1967 to 3.3 million in 1969.

The Cultural Revolution, then, provides striking evidence of the proposition mentioned earlier: that a balanced military policy has evolved since the Great Leap Forward, that considerable shifts in military role can occur within this policy, and that such shifts affect the ground forces and militia more than the more sophisticated branches of the PLA.

Although the first years of the Cultural Revolution required greater emphasis on the PLA's domestic roles, efforts have been made since 1968 to bring the domestic and strategic functions of the army into better balance.[22] While army men still occupy major ministerial and vice-ministerial positions and dominate provincial RCs and Party committees and while the PLA still engages in domestic economic and political work, increased attention has been paid to its strategic roles, particularly in light of the Sino-Soviet border clashes. In sharp contrast to his statements in 1965 justifying the concentration of the army's energies on domestic problems, Lin Piao called in 1970 for "preparations against their [the USSR and the United States] launching a big war and against their launching a conventional war and against their launching a large-scale nuclear war."[23]

The compromise of 1965 appears still to be in effect: a policy of gradual, regionally balanced improvement of defense capabilities that would be acceptable to the central military elite, regional military leaders, and civilian economic managers alike. As in the early 1960s, Lin Piao seems to be the spokesman—if not the draftsman—of this policy.

PROSPECTS

Several factors combine to make the projection of the future of Chinese Communist military policy a hazardous undertaking. First, of course, is the tentativeness of descriptions of the past. But even if current understanding of the evolution of Chinese military policy since 1953 proves to be accurate, the context of military policy has changed so significantly that it may be grossly inaccurate to attempt to predict the future on the basis of the past. For one thing, military leadership increasingly belongs to a new generation of officers, perhaps more oriented than their predecessors to a professional military line,[24] and yet placed by the Cultural Revolutions in powerful civilian positions in unprecedented numbers. For another, the international environment is considerably different from that of the 1950s or even the 1960s: the United States is no longer considered China's major enemy, and China's responses to the actions of Japan and the Soviet

Union may, for reasons of history and doctrine, respectively, differ from its pattern of responses to the United States.

Nonetheless, it is possible to venture a few predictions about the short-term future of Chinese Communist military policy. First, there is every reason to believe that the process of military policy-making will continue to be marked by tension between the "political" and "professional" viewpoints—between those who advocate military modernization and those who advocate reliance on the strategy of People's War. At the same time, however, the Chinese have already taken several decisions that will place significant limits on the range of policy options that can seriously be considered. First, the Chinese have committed themselves to the construction and maintenance of at least a minimum nuclear deterrent force, although the relative emphases to be placed on bombers and on medium, intermediate, and long-range missiles appears to be a possible issue. Second, the question of the degree to which China should depend upon the Soviet Union either for diplomatic support in crisis or for military assistance appears to be permanently moot, although it was significant in the late 1950s and even the early 1960s. Third, and more generally, the Chinese have clearly made a commitment to gradual military moderni-zation that could be reversed only with great difficulty. It is important to realize that, despite his association with polemical defenses of People's War as a strategy, Lin Piao has presided over the long-term modernization of the PLA. And the balanced policy associated with Lin appears to permit the army enough flexibility to play both strategic and domestic roles simultaneously.

It seems likely, therefore, that the compromise constructed by Lin Piao in the early 1960s, and reaffirmed by him since 1969, will continue in effect for the short run. Both the domestic and the strategic functions of the PLA will receive attention, and China's strategic posture will combine long-term modernization, semi-autonomous military regions, emphasis on ground forces, and—with the exception of a continuing missile program—minimal concern with ability to pro-tect China's military power beyond its borders. At the same time, there are several situations that could lead to a resurgence of con-troversy over military policy. One is different reactions by different interest groups to changes in the international environment. Should Japanese rearmament continue at its present high rates or should the Soviet Union continue to reinforce its troops along the Sino-Soviet border, then it is possible that some Chinese interest groups would argue that a quick-fix of China's strategic posture is once again required. If other interest groups refuse to accept the dislocations that such a quick-fix would necessitate, the stage would be set for another debate of the 1955-56 or 1965 varieties.

Another controversial situation involves the pace of the disengagement of the military from its presently commanding presence in civilian affairs. It is probable that, as reconstruction of the Party and state bureaucracies continues, many civilian cadres will increasingly resent continued military dominance over nonmilitary matters. It is also likely that their resentment would be shared by professionally oriented military officers as well. At the same time, their demands for a readjustment of the balance between the two military roles and for emphasis once again on the strategic functions of the PLA might meet active resistance from the politically oriented elements of the PLA, as well as civilian Party leaders who feel that China can escape revisionism only through continued military involvement in domestic affairs.

Perhaps, as in so many issues confronting Chinese leaders, the most crucial factor is Mao Tse-tung. While Mao has clearly not been able to impose his People's War ideal on his colleagues, he nevertheless has been instrumental in constructing, or at least legitimizing, the compromises that have resolved past disputes over military policy. Mao's death would remove both a powerful advocate of People's War and the major force in authoritatively resolving controversies over military policy.

NOTES

1. Michel Oksenberg, "Policy-Making Under Mao, 1949-68: An Overview," in John M. H. Lindbeck, ed., China: Management of a Revolutionary Society (Seattle: University of Washington Press, 1971), pp. 79-115.

2. Ellis Joffe, "The Conflict Between Old and New in the Chinese Army," China Quarterly, No. 18, April-June, 1964, pp. 118-40.

3. William Whitson, "The Concept of Military Generation: The Chinese Communist Case," Asian Survey, VIII, 11 (November, 1968), 921-47.

4. Alice Langley Hsieh, Communist China's Strategy in the Nuclear Era (Englewood Cliffs, N.J.: Prentice-Hall, 1962).

5. For a pioneering discussion of the "organizational process" and "bureaucratic politics" models, see Graham T. Allison, Conceptual Models and the Cuban Missile Crisis: Rational Policy, Organization Process, and Bureaucratic Politics, P-3919 (Santa Monica, Cal.: The Rand Corporation, August, 1968).

6. The following discussion draws in part on William Whitson, "Organizational Perspectives and Decision-Making in the Chinese Communist High Command," in Robert Scalapino, ed., Elites in Communist China, forthcoming.

7. John Gittings, "The Chinese Army's Role in the Cultural Revolution," Pacific Affairs, 39, 3-4 (Fall-Winter, 1966-67), 277.

8. For details, see John Gittings, The Role of the Chinese Army (New York: Oxford University Press, 1967), Chs. 6, 7.

9. Hsieh, Nuclear Era.

10. Mao's speech is available in Jerome Ch'en, ed., Mao (Englewood Cliffs, N.J.: Prentice-Hall, 1969), p. 71 (emphasis added).

11. For details, see Gittings, Chinese Army, Ch. 8.

12. William Whitson, "The Military: Their Role in the Policy Process," in Frank N. Trager and William Henderson, eds., Communist China, 1949-1969 (New York: New York University Press, 1970), p. 106.

13. For analyses, see Philip Bridgham, "Factionalism in the Central Committee," in John Wilson Lewis, ed., Party Leadership and Revolutionary Power in China (Cambridge, G.B.: Cambridge University Press, 1970), pp. 203-35; David A. Charles, "The Dismissal of Marshal P'eng Te-huai," China Quarterly, No. 8, October-December, 1961, pp. 63-76; Gittings, Chinese Army; and The Case of P'eng Te-huai, 1956-1968 (Hong Kong: Union Research Institute, 1968).

14. These figures are calculated from data in Gittings, Chinese Army, pp. 181-82, 305.

15. For discussions of the Soviet role in the Quemoy crisis, see Hsieh, Nuclear Era; Donald S. Zagoria, The Sino-Soviet Conflict, 1956-1961 (New York: Atheneum, 1964), Ch. 7; and John R. Thomas, "Soviet Behavior in the Quemoy Crisis of 1958," Orbis, VI, 1 (Spring, 1962), 38-64. For a contrary interpretation, arguing that Soviet support of China was both timely and firm, see Morton H. Halperin and Tang Tsou, "The 1958 Quemoy Crisis," in Morton H. Halperin, ed., Sino-Soviet Relations and Arms Control (Cambridge, Mass.: M.I.T. Press, 1967), pp. 265-303.

16. See Ellis Joffe, "The Chinese Army Under Lin Piao: Prelude to Political Intervention," in Lindbeck, Management, esp. pp. 368-69.

17. For details, see Harry Harding and Melvin Gurtov, The Purge of Lo Jui-ch'ing: The Politics of Chinese Strategic Planning, R-548-PR (Santa Monica, Cal.: The Rand Corporation, February, 1971).

18. The following pages are drawn, with modifications, from ibid., pp. 55-61.

19. "Big Military Competition is Big Exposure of Lo Jui-ch'ing's Plot," JMJP, August 28, 1967; in SCMP, No. 4022, September 5, 1967, pp. 9-10. Emphasis added.

20. On the role of the army during the Cultural Revolution, see Gittings, "The Chinese Army's Role"; Jürgen Domes, "The Cultural Revolution and the Army," Asian Survey, VIII, 5 (May, 1968), 349-63; and Jürgen Domes, "The Role of the Military in the Formation of Revolutionary Committees, 1967-68," China Quarterly, No. 44, October-December, 1970, pp. 112-45.

21. William Dorrill et al., China in the Wake of the Cultural Revolution, RAC-R-81 (McLean, Va.: Research Analysis Corporation, September, 1969), p. 23.

22. For further discussion, see Harry Harding, "China: Toward Revolutionary Pragmatism," Asian Survey, XI, 1 (January, 1971), 51-67.

23. "Heighten Our Vigilance, Defend the Motherland," PR, August 7, 1970, pp. 6-7, 23.

24. Whitson, "The Concept of Military Generation."

WILLIAM W. WHITSON is Senior Social Scientist on China at the Rand Corporation. He has served on the Policy Planning and the Systems Analysis staffs in the Office of the Secretary of Defense, as a political analyst of Mainland China and Far Eastern Affairs in the American Consulate General in Hong Kong, and has been attached to the American Embassy in Taipei as a political analyst. He has contributed articles to Asian Survey and The China Quarterly, and is the co-author of Chinese Communist High Command, 1928-68.

Dr. Whitson is a graduate of the U. S. Military Academy. He received his M.A. and Ph.D. from the Fletcher School of Law and Diplomacy.

JAMES R. BLAKER is a staff member of the South East Asia Intelligence and Force Effectiveness Division of the Office of the Deputy Assistant Secretary of Defense (Regional Programs). Prior to this he was Operations Research Analyst, United States Army Intelligence Threat Analysis Detachment, Office of the Assistant Chief of Staff. He received his Ph.D. in Political Science from The Ohio State University.

SCOTT A. BOORMAN is a Junior Fellow of the Harvard University Society of Fellows and a member of the Harvard Sociology Department. He is currently doing research in mathematical modeling of social, economic, and ecological processes. He is the author of The Protracted Game: A Wei-ch'i Interpretation of Maoist Revolutionary Strategy and various articles on Chinese military history and comparative strategic theory. Mr. Boorman received his B.A. in Applied Mathematics from Harvard University.

PARRIS H. CHANG teaches in the Department of Political Science, Pennsylvania State University. He has contributed to Elites in Communist China and Taiwan: From Prehistory to Modern Times, and has written articles for such publications as Far Eastern Economic Review, Chinese Law and Government, and The China Quarterly. Dr. Chang received his M.A. from the University of Washington and his Ph.D. from Columbia.

JOHN E. COON is Director of Chinese and East Asian Studies, U. S. Army War College. Colonel Coon was formerly Chief of Current Intelligence at Military Assistance Command, Vietnam, Headquarters, and has served at the American Consulate in Hong Kong, the American Embassy in Taipei, and on the China Desk in the Pentagon. Colonel Coon studied Chinese History for two years in Taiwan after receiving his master's degree from Stanford.

GLENN G. DICK is an analyst for the Defense Intelligence Agency. His areas of interest include Chinese military strategy and doctrine, political aspects of the PLA, and recent Chinese military history. He received his M. A. in Chinese History and Language from the University of Chicago.

EDWARD L. DREYER is Assistant Professor of History, The University of Miami. He has also taught at Harvard and at The University of British Columbia. Portions of his doctoral dissertation, concerning mid-fourteenth century China, will be published in the forthcoming book, Chinese Ways in Warfare. Professor Dreyer received his B. A., M. A., and Ph. D. degrees from Harvard University.

PAUL ELMQUIST is presently employed in the reference service of the Central Intelligence Agency. He has lectured on Chinese and East Asian geography at the Foreign Service Institute and at various colleges. He received his B. A. from Augustana College (Illinois) and did graduate work at Harvard.

RICHARD E. GILLESPIE presently serves in the Office of the Assistant Chief of Staff for Intelligence, Department of the Army. Prior to this assignment, he held the position of Assistant Professor of Asian History at the U. S. Military Academy and, after undergoing the Army's China Foreign Area Specialist Training, he was assigned within the Defense Intelligence Agency. Colonel Gillespie received his M. A. from Yale and his Ph. D. from The American University.

HARRY HARDING, JR., is Acting Assistant Professor of Political Science, Stanford University, and a member of Stanford's Institute of Political Studies and Center for East Asian Studies. He was previously an Instructor of Political Science at Swarthmore College. As a consultant to the Rand Corporation he has written on Chinese Communist theories of policy-making and organization and the politics of Chinese strategy-planning. Professor Harding has studied at Princeton, Columbia, and Stanford Universities.

JOSEPH HEINLEIN is an instructor of Chinese language at the U. S. Military Academy. He served as Deputy Chief of Operations of the North Vietnamese Affairs Division of the Joint U. S. Public Affairs Office, Saigon, and as Strategic Intelligence Analyst in the production of joint and national intelligence estimates dealing with China, Korea, Japan, and Southeast Asia for the U. S. Army General Staff. He received his M. A. in Far Eastern Area Studies from The American University, where he is currently working toward his doctorate.

CHARLES HORNER was, at the time his contribution to this volume was written, affiliated with the Social Sciences Department of the Rand Corporation. He received his M. A. in History from the University of Chicago, and he is presently completing his doctoral dissertation concerning relations between the southwest Chinese provinces and the various Vietnamese nationalist groups from 1900 to 1950.

JAMES D. JORDAN is a lecturer at The American University in Washington, D. C. and a consultant on Far East Affairs. Having lived in China for twenty-three years, he reads, writes, and speaks Chinese, and has an intimate knowledge of the Chinese people and their aspirations. Mr. Jordan received his master's degree in Far East Studies from The American University.

FRANZ J. MOGDIS is Senior Political Scientist, Office of National Security Studies, Bendix Aerospace Systems Division. He received a B. A. from the University of Michigan and studied Mandarin Chinese at The National Defense Language School.

HARVEY NELSEN, during the period of the Cultural Revolution, worked as a civilian analyst for the Department of Defense, studying the leadership of the PLA and the military involvement in Chinese politics. He received his master's degree in Chinese History and Culture from Columbia University and is in the process of completing his doctoral dissertation at George Washington University.

THOMAS W. ROBINSON is a Visiting Fellow at The Council of Foreign Relations in New York, where he is currently writing a book on Chinese foreign policy. He was formerly a member of the research staff in the Social Sciences Department at the Rand Corporation, Santa Monica, California, and has taught at a number of universities in the United States. His books include The Cultural Revolution in China and Lin Piao: A Political Biography, forthcoming. Dr. Robinson received his Ph. D. from Columbia University.

JOHN D. SIMMONDS is a member of the Australian Defence Department. Born in Tientsin, China, he served in the British Army in Hong Kong, and later joined the U. K. Commissioner-General's Office, Singapore. Mr. Simmonds studied Asian History at the Australian National University. He has written numerous works on contemporary Chinese politics, including China's World.

JOHN C. SIMS, JR. , is currently assigned to the Office of the Assistant Chief of Staff for Intelligence, Department of the Army. He previously served as the Assistant Army Liaison Officer at the American Consulate in Hong Kong. Lieutenant Colonel Sims has studied Cantonese at the Defense Language Institute in Monterey, California, and Mandarin and Cantonese at the Foreign Service Institute in Taiwan. He is a graduate of the Army's China Foreign Area Specialist Training Program, and he received his M.A. from Indiana University.

TING WANG is a researcher at the Mass Communications Center of the Chinese University of Hong Kong, head of the research department of Ming Pao, a leading Chinese daily in Hong Kong, and chief editor of its Books Section. He is the author of A Brief Biography of Chiang Ch'ing, Commentaries on the Great Cultural Revolution, Chinese Communist Organization and Personnel During the Cultural Revolution Movement, and A Preliminary Appraisal of the Personnel of the New CCP Central Committee. Mr. Wang graduated from the Wuhan University in China.

RICHARD WICH is a research analyst specializing in Sino-Soviet affairs for the Foreign Broadcast Information Service.